Mountbat

Samurai

EX LIBRIS

Steve Lawrence 18/6/2019

MADE IN USA

Mountbatten's Samurai

Imperial Japanese Army and
Navy Forces under British
Control in Southeast Asia,
1945–1948

Stephen B. Connor

SEVENTH CITADEL

Cover illustrations: Front: Southern Expeditionary Army Group Commander's seal （南方軍総司令官之印）. Image digitally enhanced by Seventh Citadel (National Archives, London). 'The new situation': British and Japanese troops in post-surrender Hong Kong, August 1945 (Author's Collection). *Back:* Imperial Japanese Army 10-yen note. Admiral Lord Louis Mountbatten and General Douglas MacArthur in Manila, July 1945 (MacArthur Memorial Archives, Norfolk, VA). British General Service Medal with clasp for 'South-East Asia 1945-46' (courtesy Neate Medals). (For full credit information for period photographs see 'Illustrations'.)

The author is grateful to SAGE Publishing Ltd for permission to reprint long extracts from his article entitled, 'Side-Stepping Geneva: Japanese Troops under British Control, 1945-47', first published in the *Journal of Contemporary History, Vol. 45* (2) April 2010: 389-405.

The rights-holder to the Java maps drawn by L. Maddocks (Gale & Polden, 1951) is invited to contact the publisher (editorial@seventhcitadel.com).

Editing and proofreading by Victoria Fisher.

Cover by John Amy (promodesign.co.uk) from an idea by S. B. Connor.

Index by Mark Wells.

Seventh Citadel, 10 WA4 2XA, UK.

For Wilf and Monica,

my parents.

CONTENTS

ILLUSTRATIONS

MAPS

'Japanese Forces in SEAC as at December 1945', pp. 74–75. CAB 122/1182. Colour original enhanced for b/w. (National Archives, London.)

'Java', p. 37 and 'Central Java', p. 38 from: A. J. F. Doulton, *The Fighting Cock: The Story of the 23rd Indian Division 1942-1947,* p. 231/p. 269.

TABLE

'JSP requirements in SEAC, December 1945', p. 200. CAB 119/206. (National Archives, London.)

PHOTOGRAPHS

1. Japanese Mitsubishi G4M1 ('Betty') bombers carrying surrender envoys near Ie Jima, Okinawa prefecture on 17 August 1945. The aircraft were painted white with green crosses. (United States Navy/National Archives and Records Administration: NARA)

2. Two IJN I-400 Class submarines intercepted by the US Navy on 23 August 1945. These 122m-long vessels, flying black flags of surrender, were returning from the abandoned attack on Ulithi Atoll. (US Coast Guard/NARA).

3. Lt General Numata Takazo, Chief of Staff, JEFSR and Rear Admiral Chudo Kaigye walk from their plane at Mingladon airfield, Rangoon (Burma), to meet with British commanders on 24 August 1945. [Detail.] (© Imperial War Museum.)

4. Indonesian TKR (People's Security Army) troops in Java in mid 1946. The TKR evolved from the Japanese-founded PETA militia. Note the Japanese-issued uniforms and equipment. (AC)

5. 'The new situation.' British and Japanese troops outside the Peninsula Hotel, Hong Kong, in late August 1945. (AC)

6. (L to R) Major General Nishimura Otoshi, Major General Yamamoto Moichiro and Rear Admiral Maeda Tadashi aboard HMS *Cumberland.* off Batavia, Java, 16 September 1945. (US Signal Corps/NARA)

7.   (Front right) Vice Admiral Shibata Yaichiro, Commander, Second Southern Expeditionary Fleet and (front left) Lt General Nagano Yuichiro, Commander 16 IJA, Java, c. April 1945. (Courtesy Goto Ken'ichi/IJA/IJN)

8.   Major General Mabuchi Itsuo (Commander, 27 Bde, Java). (c.) 1944. (Courtesy of Mabuchi Itsuaki.)

9.   *Kenpeitai* unit, 16 IJA, Semarang, c. 1944. (Mr Aoki is pictured back row, end right.) (Courtesy of Aoki Masafumi/IJA)

10.   Major Kido Shinichiro and Captain J. Tomlinson (RA) in Semarang, Java, in late October 1945. Kido *Butai*, considered by the British to be the most dependable Japanese battalion in Java, was listed in the British Order of Battle. (Scan: Image Bank WW2 NIOD, © D. H. K Soltau/Courtesy of Martin Soltau.)

11.   Troops of Kido *Butai* (behind centre group) during a truce in Semarang, Java on 16 October 1945. (Centre L to R) Dr Soekario (CBZ Hospital), Wongsonegoro (nationalist governor), War Correspondent. (© D. H. K. Soltau. Courtesy of Martin Soltau)

12.   (L to R) Lt C. 'Tam' Wishart (PARA REGT), Sara Paton (British Red Cross), Capt David Soltau (RAMC) and Capt Dennis Broadhead (RAMC) outside the Hotel Bellevue after the 'first battle of Semarang', on 20 October 1945. (Scan: Image Bank WW2 NIOD, © D. H. K Soltau/Courtesy of Martin Soltau.)

13.   Former internees awaiting transfer to Jakarta with armed JSP escort (visible on the truck at the extreme right) at Semarang docks, Java, 25 November 1945. (© D. H. K. Soltau. Courtesy of Martin Soltau.)

14.   Brigadier Richard B. W. Bethell, DSO, in November 1945. Bethell was the senior British officer in Central Java. (Courtesy of Hugh Bethell.)

15.   British, French and Japanese officers plan operations in Saigon against the Viet Minh in late 1945. (2L to R) Lt Yoshiaki Shoji (Japanese Liaison Officer; Lt Col E. D. Murray, OBE, acting Commander Northern Sector Saigon; French Liaison Officer. (By permission and courtesy of the Trustees of the 10th Princess Mary's Own Gurkha Rifles Regimental Trust.)

16.   Lt General Tanabe Moritake, Commander of 25 IJA, c. 1943. General Tanabe wrote the 'underdogs' signal to Japanese command HQs (*see* Chapter 5) that infuriated SEAC commanders. (IJA)

17.   Field Marshal Count Terauchi Hisaichi, Commander, JEFSR, c. 1941. (IJA)

18.   Japanese prisoners in US Navy custody. (Date unknown.) Possible reasons for the men being naked include fuel-oil contaminated and/or wet clothing after rescue, weapons search or standard hygiene procedures (delousing). (TLFU 1/BuAer/USN/AC.)

19.   Admiral Lord Louis Mountbatten and General Douglas MacArthur, in Manila, Philippines, in July 1945. (US Army Signal Corps. MacArthur Memorial Archives Norfolk, VA)

35. JSP arriving from Singapore enter the Ujina Repatriation Centre, Hiroshima prefecture, on 27 June 1946. The signs read (L) 'Let's do our best!' and (R) 'Ujina Repatriation Centre'. (Allan G. Cuthbert/Australian War Memorial)

36. Some of the last British-held JSP to return to Japan eat lunch outside a barracks at (probably) Ujina Repatriation Centre in 1947. (Ian Robertson/ Australian War Memorial).

37. Lt W. A. Weightman (Durham Light Infantry) and [to his left] Major S. Takahara (IGR) and other officers of the IJA Aceh Land Garrison in Malaya in December 1945, after their emergency evacuation from Aceh. (Courtesy Bill Weightman/AC)

38. Two Mitsubisihi A6M ('Zeke') naval fighters taken over by the Allies displaying RAF and other SEAC markings during evaluation tests in Malaya in 1946. The IJN pilots were supervised by RAF pilot officers. [Detail.] (© Imperial War Museum)

KEY TO PHOTOGRAPH SOURCES

AC	Author's Collection
AM	Aoki Masafumi
AWM	Australian War Memorial, Canberra
HB	Hugh Bethell
IJA	Imperial Japanese Army
IJN	Imperial Japanese Navy
IWM	Imperial War Museum, London
MI	Mabuchi Itsuaki
MM	MacArthur Memorial Archive, Norfolk, VA
MS	Martin Soltau
NA	National Archives, London
NARA	National Archives and Records Administration. (Washington, D.C.)
SG	Stuart Guild
T10GKRT	Trustees of the 10th Princess Mary's Own Gurkha Rifle Regimental Trust

ACRONYMS

ACJ	Allied Council for Japan
AFL	American Federation of Labor
AFNEI	Allied Forces Netherlands East Indies
AFP	Allied Forces Pacific
ALFSEA	Allied Land Forces South-East Asia
AMFA	Australian Military Forces Area
APWI	Allied Prisoners of War and Internees
ASDIC	Anti-Submarine Detection Investigation Committee
BAS	British Army Staff
BCOF	British Commonwealth Occupation Force
BDCSEA	British Defence Committee, South-East Asia
BIC	*Banque de l'Indochine* (Bank of Indochina)
BKR	*Badan Keamanan Rakjat* (People's Security Organisation)
BRC	British Red Cross
CCS	Combined Chiefs of Staff
CLO	Central Liaison Office
COS	Chiefs of Staff
COSSEA	Chiefs of Staff [signal to] South-East Asia
CRA	Commander Royal Artillery
CSAB	Combined Shipping Adjustment Boards (CSAB)
DEF	Disarmed Enemy Forces
EAC	European Advisory Commission
EPS	Economic Planning Staff
FARELF	Far East Land Forces
FEC	Far Eastern Commission
FEPOW	Far East Prisoner(s) of War
FIC	French Indo-China
FO	Foreign Office
GHQ SCAP	General Headquarters Supreme Commander Allied Powers
GR	Gurkha Rifles
ICRC	International Committee of the Red Cross
IJA	Imperial Japanese Army
IJGS	Imperial Japanese General Staff

IJN	Imperial Japanese Navy
IMTFE	International Military Tribunal for the Far East
JAPS	Joint Advisory Planning Staff
JEFSR	Japanese Expeditionary Forces Southern Regions
JLO	Japanese Liaison Officer
JPW	Japanese Prisoner(s) of War
JSM	Joint Staff Mission
JSP	Japanese Surrendered Personnel
KNI	*Komite Nasional Indonesia* (Committee for the Independence of Indonesia)
KNIL	*Koninklijk Nederlands Indisch Leger* (Royal Netherlands East Indies Army)
MISLS	Military Intelligence Service Language School (US)
MOD	Ministry of Defence
MOT	Ministry of Transport
MWT	Ministry of War Transport
NEI	Netherlands East Indies
NICA	Netherlands Indies Civil Administration
OSS	Office of Strategic Services
PAOC	Principal Administrative Operating Committee
PARA REGT	Parachute Regiment
PETA	*Pembela Tanah Air* (Defenders of the Fatherland)
PPKI	Committee for the Preparation of Indonesian Independence
PW	Prisoner(s) of War
RA	Royal Artillery
RAMC	Royal Army Medical Corps
RAPWI	Recovery of Allied Prisoners of War and Internees
SACSEA	Supreme Allied Commander South-East Asia
SCAP	Supreme Commander Allied Powers
SCAPIN	Supreme Commander Allied Powers Index
SEAC	South-East Asia Command
SEACOS	South-East Asia [signal to] Chiefs of Staff
SEALF	South-East Asia Land Forces
SEATIC	South-East Asia Translation and Interpretation Corps
SEP	Surrendered Enemy Personnel.
SOE	Special Operations Executive
SWNCC	State-War-Naval-Coordinating Committee
SWPA	South-West Pacific Area
TKR	*Tentara Keaman Rakjat* (People's Security Army)
UKLM	United Kingdom Liaison Mission
UMA	United Maritime Agreement
WPC	Working Pay Credit
WSA	War Shipping Administration

ACKNOWLEDGEMENTS

This book has its origins in a PhD thesis. I would therefore like to express my utmost gratitude to Richard Aldrich, Matthew Jones and Neville Wylie, my post-graduate supervisors, for their expertise, advice and, above all, encouragement throughout the academic process. A host of other people: military veterans, scholars, members of research groups, as well as the staff of numerous archives and libraries were extremely generous with their time and advice, or in helping me obtain photographs. My sincere thanks to the following:

Aoki Masafumi, Hugh Bethell, William J. Frederick, Goto Kenichi, John Hudson, Philip Kaiserman, Jeroen Kemperman, Mabuchi Itsuaki, Maekawa Kaori, William F. Nimmo, Ian Nish, Oba Sadao, John Pike CBE, Remco Raben, Andrew Roadnight, Iwao Peter Sano, Martin Soltau, Takado Eichi, Takahashi Kazuhiro, Tamayama Kazuo, Robin Woolven, James Zobel.

Australian War Memorial, Canberra; The British Library, London; British International History Group; Diplomatic Record Office, Japanese Ministry of Foreign Affairs, Tokyo; Firepower, Royal Artillery Museum, London; Imperial War Museum, London; Liddell Hart Centre for Military Archives, King's College, London; MacArthur Memorial Archive, Norfolk, VA; Manchester Central Library (UK); The National Archives, London; Netherlands Institute for War Documentation (NIOD), Amsterdam; Nationaal Archief, The Hague, The Netherlands; RAF Museum, Hendon, London; Semarang Kai (Kido *Butai* Association) Kyoto; Waseda University Library, Tokyo.

The Burma Star Association
A great many served in those troubled days of peace in Southeast Asia but a special note of thanks and appreciation is due to the many members of the Burma Star Association who responded so enthusiastically and generously with information and suggestions to my advertisement in *Dekho!,* the

Association's newsletter. Their accounts of their experiences with 14 Army and particularly 20 Indian Division and 23 Indian Division in Burma, Malaya, Thailand, Indonesia and Vietnam were of enormous interest and relevance to my research. I am particularly grateful for information from Stanley Angell, 178 Field Rgt, Royal Artillery; Harold Ball, 20 Indian Div; Edward G. Baker, 50 Indian Tank Bde; Major Humphrey G. N. Gore, 1 Royal Ulster Rifles, 15 Indian Corps; Stuart Guild, 114 Field Rgt, Royal Artillery; Sidney G. Higgs, 31 Sqdn, Royal Air Force; Edward Holden, 5 Parachute Bde; Arthur T. Lappage, 164 CRE, Royal Engineers; Iain Mathieson, 1 Bn Seaforth Highlanders; Philip Malins MC OBE, 20 Indian Div; E. J. E Stowers, RN, attached 20 Indian Div; Frank Thake, RN (HMS *Ophir*); Geoff Turner, 684 Sqdn, RAF; William ('Bill') Weightman, 2 Bn Durham Light Infantry; Charles Wicksteed, 114 Field Rgt, Royal Artillery. The rather plain name of the medal issued to them and their comrades in recognition of post-war service in the Far East, the General Service Medal with clasp for 'S. E. Asia, 1945-46' (shown on the back cover), does not do justice to the efforts of those who were there. Indeed, the word 'samurai' derives from a term for 'one who serves'. It is not, therefore, exclusive.

Han Bing Siong

I am indebted to the late Mr Han for correspondence and discussions about Kido *Butai* in Java, for his assistance in contacting the Semarang Kai, and for the information that ultimately led me to the unpublished memoir and photographs of the RAPWI team in Semarang by Dr David Soltau.

Names

Japanese and other non-Western names are presented in family name then given name order. (Macrons over long vowels have been omitted.) Until recently most Indonesians, especially Javanese, did not have 'family' names in the Western sense, and went by only one name.

Copyrights

Considerable effort has been made to identify and contact the relevant rights-holders of copyrighted material. The publisher would be grateful to hear from any rights-holder who is not here acknowledged and will undertake to rectify any errors or omissions in future editions of this book.

Finally the great moment came when the Semarang kenpeitai...stormed the prison and killed the last group of guards, including the leader who was hacked to pieces. We cheered and cheered the incoming Japanese...the most brutal unit in Java, now our liberators. I must say it was an incredible experience.

F. de Rochement
(see Chapter 2)

What I am trying to say is that after six years of war there is no moral high ground left. It's all mud and we're sinking fast.

War reporter in Rory Marron's *Merdeka Rising:*
Part Two of Black Sun, Red Moon: A Novel of Java

INTRODUCTION

The Japanese military forces, after being completely disarmed, shall be permitted to return to their homes with the opportunity to lead peaceful and productive lives.

—The Potsdam Declaration, 26 July 1945, Article 9.[1]

There are a great many books devoted to the dramatic arrival in Southeast Asia of Japanese forces in late 1941 and early 1942, their three-year occupation of the region, and their abrupt surrender in August 1945. In contrast, their far more leisurely departure, in a deliberately delayed, arguably Geneva Convention- and Potsdam Declaration-breaching and ultimately shambolic repatriation programme under British control, has received far less attention. This book aims to redress this balance.

The period after Japan's surrender in 1945 was a time of flux in Asia. Turmoil and disorder gripped the region. Japan, the dominant regional power, had collapsed. Local economies were in ruins. Britain remained, if only by default, one of the Great Powers but had barely re-established a presence in former colonial territory. Revolutions occurred in Indonesia and Vietnam. Civil war was pending in China, and order in Burma was balanced on a knife edge. Within this Asian maelstrom of revolutions, famines, epidemics and millions of refugees, one of many problems awaiting a British solution, was the fate of the huge Japanese diaspora, both civilian and military. Officially, the demilitarisation of Japan and the demobilisation of the Japanese armed forces remained a declared Allied (ie, US, British,

Chinese and Soviet) objective but in Southeast Asia Britain was very much on its own.

During the Second World War, the military campaign against the Japanese received only cursory attention from the British Government and public. It had always come second to the European Theatre in terms of claims on men, equipment and transport resources. Indeed, such was the lack of interest at home that the British 14 Army fighting in Burma dubbed itself the 'Forgotten Army'. Little was to change after the Japanese surrender. More immediate domestic, economic and political problems in Britain and Europe, combined with widespread war weariness, resulted in general disinterest in distant lands. Those forgotten soldiers, whose own and their dependants' priorities were a quick return home, were subsumed into an enlarged but equally forgotten command, fighting what have been described as 'forgotten wars' in the Netherlands East Indies (NEI), now Indonesia, and French Indo-China (FIC), now Vietnam, Cambodia and Laos.[2]

Britain's government could not, of course, turn its back completely on the East, nor did it want to. Imperial wealth was viewed as a lifeline for Britain's shattered economy. Resumption of Asian trade was anticipated with urgency. There were also trade and future security concerns in the wider area 'east of Suez'. The sudden upsurge of nationalism and the uncertainty it created was unwelcome to the Western Allies, despite Britain's public embrace of the right to self-determination in the Atlantic Charter of 1941. It was a widely held belief in London that stable, ie, European-controlled, neighbours would in turn help keep Britain's own colonies and territories stable. Yet this did not mean that nationalism was not tolerated or British Imperial limits remained unacknowledged. By mid-1945, with Germany defeated and a conventional Allied victory over Japan considered only a matter of some (still appreciable) time, Britain, unlike France and the Netherlands, was preparing for a reduction in its formal control of territories in Southeast and South Asia. Yet while Britain had already conceded the idea of independence for India, it anticipated exerting continuing influence there and further East via more subtle means of financial investment, trade and security treaties.[3] Thus in London there was 'no intention' of abandoning valuable colonial possessions in Asia and 'no inclination' among officials or ministers (either Conservative or Labour) to embark on a 'wholesale retreat from empire or to renounce a world-power role after 1945'. Britain, France and the Netherlands were desperate to re-harness the natural resources of their colonies to help rebuild their domestic economies. In plans for Britain's economic recovery, however, it was Malaya, not India, which assumed pride of place. Malayan tin and natural rubber were viewed as key exports to provide the all-important dollar earnings for Britain and so support the vulnerable Sterling area.[4]

Similar considerations were behind the desire of France and the Netherlands for a speedy return to their own colonial possessions. They were dismayed, however, by the reception they received from their former subjects. All the European colonial powers had underestimated just how well the Japanese had fostered an ideology of Asian liberation.[5] That ideology also had foundation in fact, for Oriental forces had dramatically defeated Occidental armies in a swift, spectacular campaign in 1941–42. White colonial power had been shattered in full view of millions of Southeast Asians. They had also seen the white elites handled roughly, imprisoned, humiliated and put to demeaning manual work. In the end, the policies and behaviour of the replacement colonial power, Japan, did not impress and, yet again, few tears were shed when they were forcibly removed. Japan's legacy was nationalism. However selfishly or limitedly encouraged by the Japanese, once unleashed, nationalism was unstoppable. Japan's Imperial Army had also prepared for the future defence of that fledgling ideology. It had trained and armed local militias drawn from larger religious or ethnic majorities, a potent demonstration of trust never fully made by the former colonial masters in Asia (with the exception of the British in India). Only a handful of Indonesians had been trained as Royal Netherlands Indies Army (KNIL) officers in the late 1930s but the KNIL recruited mainly from Christian (and anti-nationalist) Ambonese and Mendanese. Javanese Muslims were considered unreliable. (Even in the panic of December 1941 prior to the Japanese invasion, KNIL emergency conscripts were Dutch or Dutch-Eurasian, not Javanese.)[6] Thus after three years of Japanese military tutelage Burmese, Indonesians and Vietnamese no longer receptive to ideas of white supremacy or even a loosened colonial leash had, for the first time, some capacity to resist those ideas.

In Indonesia and Vietnam that resistance was immediate, with declarations of independence following just days after the announcement of surrender in Tokyo. In Burma and Malaya, however, the British return was unopposed by the militias. In the former, the strength of the nationalist forces—after a last-minute anti-Japanese revolt—was sufficient to demand and receive from the British a recognised political role. In the latter, ethnic and political divisions in the country left the nationalist leadership unprepared for the Japanese collapse. They were disarmed and rounded up.[7] (Within a few years, however, a British-trained but avowedly Communist guerrilla force would present a major challenge for the control of Malaya.) Violent nationalist resistance demanded a response from colonial authorities. South-East Asia Command (SEAC), the wartime Allied command responsible for a region extending from Burma to Vietnam, headed by Admiral Lord Louis Mountbatten, would have to be both policeman and peacekeeper.

In one key area in particular, however, that of military capability, SEAC faced an impending and drastic change and challenge. Indian independence meant the impending loss of the Indian Army to British strategists and planners. In European and the Far East campaigns millions of Indians had bolstered Allied formations. SEAC's dependence on Indian troops on land was almost total. Indeed in Indonesia and Vietnam it was largely Indian Army divisions incorporating some Gurkha battalions that helped restore *ante-bellum* order. (Throughout this book reference to 'British' forces generally assumes British and Indians and/or Gurkhas.) The clock was ticking, for India's leaders-in-waiting were deeply unhappy that their own soldiers were visibly propping up the colonial order in Asia. British commanders were all too aware that SEAC's existence as a functioning, legitimate entity was itself limited. There would be no assistance from the United States. Washington's enthusiasm over participation in SEAC had waned quickly after 1944 to the point where no United States forces remained under Mountbatten's direct orders. A similar attitude was expected from New Delhi. On 1 August 1947, the official date of Indian independence, no matter what the local strategic or security situation(s) facing SEAC (or any successor), it would lose 90 percent of its forces and so be rendered powerless. Britain's aim therefore was to fulfil its Potsdam-derived responsibilities and obligations in Southeast Asia as quickly as possible while at the same time avoiding new, solely British ones. In this it was singularly unsuccessful, as its handling of the Japanese repatriation issue reveals.

Amidst the post-war political uncertainty, economic chaos and myriad problems in Southeast Asia stood the former foe: some 750,000 soldiers, sailors, airmen and military nurses of the *Nanpo gun* (南方軍) or Japan's Southern Expeditionary Army Group and Fleets. (Note: To prevent confusion with 'South-East Asia Command' and 'SEAC', 'Southern Expeditionary Army Group and 'SEAG' are not used in this book. Instead 'JEFSR' standing for 'Japanese Expeditionary Forces Southern Regions'— an English usage found in some Japanese Army documents in the National Archives, London—is used instead.) There were also tens of thousands of Japanese civilian officials, trading-company employees and pre-war immigrants scattered about the short-lived Great East Asia Co-Prosperity Sphere. Japan's political collapse and unconditional surrender had left them stranded in a lost empire that for many was now hostile territory. For some time their situation excited little international concern. Just as there was scant interest among the war-weary British public in distant revolutions, so the fate of the defeated Japanese went largely unreported and unquestioned. Assumptions that all Japanese military personnel had become prisoners of war, as captive Allied troops had been during the war, were widespread but inaccurate. In fact Japan's servicemen and women had been declared 'Japanese Surrendered Personnel' (JSP), a newly created category outside the Convention on Prisoners of War signed in Geneva in 1929.[8] For the already overstretched SEAC, the retention and obligations towards surrendered Japanese became burdensome; for the British Government, however, these issues became vexing, expensive and ultimately embarrassing.

The resumption of Anglo-Japanese relations in Southeast Asia in August 1945 was sudden and unexpected. Fighting in Burma had been prolonged, bloody and merciless. Considerably more of the same had been anticipated for the planned advance across Malaya to Singapore and beyond, all the way to Tokyo. The jarring, atomic halt to the war caught all parties by surprise. For London, victory was welcome but brought with it new responsibilities and fresh uncertainties. British forces had not yet liberated many of their territories and their absence was conspicuous. In the confusion their first urge was to rush to repossess what they had lost in 1941–42, lest it be lost to someone else. For the Japanese, defeat had always meant a fight to the death. Individual surrender had been unthinkable, and Japan's unconditional capitulation unimaginable. As well as confusion there was also a temporary power vacuum in which the Japanese were presented with opportunities and 'choices' that were to have consequences for Western colonial control.

This book focuses mainly on the Japanese political and military choices made in Java and on the 105,000 Japanese detained in Malaya. There are a number of reasons for this. First, JSP (and Japanese Prisoners of War (JPW)) remained in Malaya and Indonesia under British control far longer than they remained in Thailand or Vietnam. Second, military co-operation between Japanese and British forces to re-establish colonial control, although occurring in both Indonesia and Vietnam, lasted considerably longer in Indonesia. (Both had major repercussions for Western interests, particularly, if much later, for the United States with regard to Vietnam.) There is therefore an element of parallel example, and a risk of duplication, in considering Japanese military deployment by the British in the two countries. Third, since JSP in Vietnam were under only nominal British control after January 1946 and repatriated on American ships by the late summer of that year, they were neither the subject of diplomatic exchanges between the HQ of General Douglas MacArthur, Supreme Commander

Allied Powers (SCAP), in Tokyo and SEAC, nor of undue concern to the International Committee for the Red Cross (ICRC). Consequently, with the exception of certain post-surrender financial irregularities common to both Vietnam and Indonesia, Vietnam receives less attention.

Incidents on the Indonesian island of Java reflect a number of 'generic' post-surrender examples common to many other states and territories in Southeast Asia in 1945. Some choices were idealistic and of significant import: the decision to 'assist' with the declaration of Indonesian independence being one (see Chapter 1). Others were purely personal but no less dramatic: whether to commit suicide to atone for the disgrace of surrender, or to join with nationalists and continue the fight for 'Asiatic' liberation, or to sit tight—not as prisoners of war but as 'surrendered personnel'—and await their fate.

Even as the choices became apparent, the time available to make them shrank rapidly. After Emperor Hirohito's noon radio address to his incredulous nation on 15 August 1945, Japanese authority in its overseas Empire dissipated by the hour. Orders from the British filtered slowly down the fractured chain of command from Japanese Southern Expeditionary Force HQ in Saigon. These demanded a return to a pre-war political *status quo*. Japan's temporary influence was to be erased and Asian nationalist ambitions utterly quashed. After some uncertainty, most Japanese commanders accepted the 'new situation', as Japan's surrender was euphemistically coined, and followed the instructions to the letter. A few, however, were determined to bequeath a last-minute legacy of revolution nurtured by political machination, arms handovers and financial duplicity.

Britain returned as Allied 'guardian' to Burma, Malaya, Hong Kong, the NEI, Thailand (Siam) and the southern partition of FIC. Great Power obligations inherited at the Potsdam Conference prevented a quick withdrawal from hostile NEI and FIC. Under-resourced and under-manned, Britain engaged in an unenthusiastic holding campaign on behalf of the Dutch and French. British commanders also required the Japanese to fight. This proved necessary on several occasions, even though this new 'Anglo-Japanese alliance', distasteful as it was to London, was lambasted in the United Nations by representatives of the new Soviet bloc. For several hundred Japanese who chose to obey British orders and retain their arms, oppose nationalists and, ironically, protect Japanese-interned European civilians from mobs, their choice proved fatal. Even as Britain sacrificed Japanese and (largely) Indian troops to prop up the white colonial order it drew upon other detained Japanese to man the docks and airfields to maintain the flow of supplies and equipment. Official acknowledgement of Japanese support for European colonial restoration was given grudgingly and very quietly. Suspicions remained, for not all Japanese fought on Britain's side. In Indonesia the gamut ran from decoration—a recommendation for a *British* Distinguished Service Order for one Japanese officer—to desertion, as hundreds of Japanese joined the independence struggle.

As Southeast Asia gradually quietened, the Japanese were disarmed and shipped out of sight of questioning and impressionable locals. Undertakings made at the Potsdam Conference were set aside as demands for reparations smothered obligations for repatriation. A second emergency, this time economic, resulted in many tens of thousands of Japanese being put to work as coolie labour on civil and military reconstruction tasks, particularly in Malaya and Singapore Colony but also in Java. Retention of these Japanese and the question of payment for their labour would become the subject of inter-Allied friction, legal argument and financial wrangle. Even within the British Government there were doubts over the legality and morality of the ruse to sidestep obligations under the PW convention. But the Potsdam obligation to repatriate had been made in public and it slowly undermined British confidence in its stance. International criticism grew, especially from the United States. In Japan democratic reform was underway. The Americans wanted to move on, and quickly. They also demanded that the detained Japanese be sent home. Only with the return of these 'stragglers' could Japan be declared disarmed and demobilised and the Potsdam obligations met in full. Still, Britain doggedly sought to hold on to its captive labour. To the dismay of the ICRC and even the Vatican, London defended its reinterpretation of the PW Convention and its right to retain the Japanese. Along the way, to the increasing irritation of the Americans, it pleaded varying combinations of necessity, special circumstances, poverty and lack of shipping. American opposition, and control of the purse strings, meant British prevarication could not last. When the about-turn came, more diplomatic damage, most of it self-inflicted, was to embarrass London even further.

NOTES TO INTRODUCTION

1. S. Woodburn Kirby, *The History of the Second World War: The War against Japan: Vol. 5. The Surrender of Japan* (London, 1969), 486.

2. Christopher Bayly and Tim Harper, *Forgotten Wars: Freedom and Revolution in Southeast Asia* (London, 2006), passim. John Keay, *Last Post: The End of Empire in the Far East* (London, 1997), 289, quoting Lucien Bodard, *The Quicksand War: Prelude to Vietnam* (London, 1967).

3. John Darwin, *Britain and Decolonisation: The retreat from Empire in the post-war world* (London, 1988), 58–61.

4. Matthew Jones, *Conflict and Confrontation in South East Asia, 1961–1965: Britain, the United States, Indonesia and the Creation of Malaysia* (Cambridge, 2001), 2–3.

5. See, for example, Christopher Thorne, *The Issue of War: States, Societies and the Far Eastern Conflict of 1941–1945* (London, 1985), 144–72.

6. Joyce C. Lebra, *Japanese-Trained Armies in Southeast Asia* (Hong Kong, 1977), 3. See also 'The Beginning of an Army: An Interview with Lt. Gen. G. P. H. Djatikusumo', in *Born in Fire: The Indonesian Struggle for Independence, an Anthology*, eds, Colin Wild and Peter Carey (Ohio, 1988), 72–74; and Remco Raben, 'Introduction' to *The Collapse of a Colonial Society: The Dutch in Indonesia during the Second World War* by Louis de Jong (Leiden, 2002), 32–33.

7. Lebra, *Japanese-Trained Armies*, 121.

8. *Convention Relative to the Treatment of Prisoners of War*, Geneva, 27 July 1929.

'A GRAND OPPORTUNITY'

JAPAN'S IMPERIAL CODA IN INDONESIA

Seeing that Indonesians are now obliged to miss a grand opportunity of obtaining independence, I cannot but shed floods of tears, and moreover...I am really broken hearted.[1]

—Valedictory address by Lt General Nagano Yuichiro,
Japanese Commander in Java, 17 August 1945

In August 1945 atomic bombs delivered a dramatic victory to the Allies. However, the sudden peace also brought them unanticipated political and military difficulties. Throughout Southeast Asia Japanese-appointed governments remained in power, Japanese armies east of Burma remained unbeaten and nationalist sentiment soared in the former European colonial territories of France and the Netherlands. After the Japanese surrender the British became responsible for security and law and order in large parts of the region but lacked the resources and manpower for the task. This left them with no alternative but to demand that their former enemy should keep the peace, temporarily, on their behalf. It was an unexpected development. It was certainly the case in the Netherlands East Indies (NEI), now Indonesia. This was the setting for Japan's imperial swansong, for it was here (see the next chapter), particularly in Java, Southeast Asia's most populous island, that post-war Anglo-Japanese military co-operation was the longest lasting and had the most far-reaching consequences for British policy.[2]

By mid-August 1945 the United States, by virtue of its monopoly possession of nuclear weapons and the capacity for chemical attacks on the rice crop, held the power of life or extinction over the Japanese islands.[3] Yet paradoxically, it was the unexpected early end of the war that was to present the Western Allies, particularly Britain, with immense logistic and manpower problems in Asia.[4] These problems would necessitate the use of Japanese forces under British direction in Indonesia, Thailand and French Indo-China (FIC). Even before the atomic bombs, daily, practically unopposed firebombing raids on Japan's cities, coupled with a crippling naval blockade, denying imports of food and oil and exports of weapons and munitions, had brought the country almost to its knees.[5]

In the Pacific a relentless 'island-hopping' advance by United States forces that simply bypassed bastions such as Rabaul (on New Guinea) and the island of Mindanao (Philippines) brought the Japanese home islands to within distance for invasion.[6] But Japan, or more accurately the military dictatorship which held power, would not surrender.[7] Instead, its army- and navy- dominated government sought a last glorious stand, drilling schoolchildren with bamboo spears and urging them to prepare dried frogs as food to sustain them through to the final battle where they would 'shatter like a hundred million jewels'.[8] Only when faced with piecemeal atomic destruction did the resolve of the militarists falter sufficiently for moderate elements to act. Even then, there was a desperate, deluded approach to the Soviet Union, which was itself planning to attack Japanese forces in Manchuria, to try and broker a negotiated peace with the Allies.[9] To the last, Japan's elite was ambivalent about the fate of ordinary citizens either in conventional or atomic war. It was not the prospect of more A-bombs that pushed the request for terms but the spectre of revolution and the end of the Imperial line.[10]

On 15 August 1945 the Second World War ended when Emperor Hirohito addressed his people via radio, calling upon them 'to pave the way for a grand peace by enduring the unendurable and suffering the insufferable'.[11] And yet, even as the Allied troops and civilians rejoiced at the news, the outcome was, for a few days, shrouded in doubt. Had the nearly 3.5 million Japanese servicemen stationed throughout Southeast Asia, Korea and China refused to obey Hirohito's instruction to lay down their arms, fighting could have continued, quite possibly for several years in China alone.[12] In this scenario the atomic option would have been unavailable to the Allies. Shortages of fissile material aside, the governments of Britain, France, the Netherlands and Republican China—if wishing to portray themselves as liberators—could never have sanctioned the use of such destructive weapons in their own colonial territories or in China.[13] Instead, they would have faced continuing and costly conventional war in several separate theatres against quite large, isolated but still determined Japanese forces. (By 1944, largely as a consequence of the US Navy's successful submarine war against the Japanese merchant marine, troops and supplies could no longer be transported by ship other than across the Japan

1. Japanese surrender envoys near Ie Jima on 17 Aug. 1945. (NARA) (See 'Illustrations')

Sea to the Asian mainland. Since Japanese troops were in effect 'marooned', many of these well-defended bases were bypassed with impunity.)[14]

Consequently, the Allies' sole but ultimately compelling threat to the senior Japanese commanders outside Japan was that should they continue hostilities, their homeland and all they held dear—including by implication the imperial family—faced atomic annihilation. Indeed, in announcing Japan's acceptance of the terms of the Potsdam Declaration, Hirohito drew specific attention to his loyal listeners, both domestic and overseas, to the fact that:

> ...the enemy has now begun to employ a new and most cruel bomb, the power of which to do damage is indeed incalculable, taking the toll of many innocent lives. Should we continue to fight, it would not only result in an ultimate collapse and obliteration of the Japanese nation but also...the total extinction of human civilization.

There was, however, little by way of consolation for those people still nominally under the Japanese aegis. They were accorded just one sentence: 'We cannot but express the deepest sense of regret to our allied nations of East Asia, who have consistently co-operated with the Empire toward the emancipation of East Asia'.[15] The Emperor had spoken; the Empire was lost. With that abrupt farewell, Japan withdrew from its responsibilities in much of Southeast Asia but there remained considerable uncertainty. Senior commanders of the largely self-sufficient Kwantung Army (in Manchuria) and other Japanese armies in China, Malaya, FIC and Indonesia argued for or against ending the war.[16] A signal intercepted by the Ultra code-breaking project from an 'incredulous' Lieutenant-General Okamura Keiji, head of the China Expeditionary Army, revealed the strength of emotion:

> Such a disgrace as the surrender of several million troops without fighting is not paralleled in the world's military history, and it is impossible to submit to the surrender of a million picked troops, in perfectly healthy shape to the Chunking [Republican capital] forces of defeated China.[17]

Headlines and editorials in *Syonan shinbun*, occupied Singapore's English-language newspaper, illustrate the die-hard attitude. On 15 August the paper urged readers to discount 'foolish rumours' that Tokyo would agree to the Potsdam terms and trumpeted continuing but invented military successes: 'Enemy being battered in Balikpapan'; 'Lone Nippon submarine sinks six enemy warships, transports'; 'Brilliant exploits in Pacific waters'. The race card was also played bluntly: 'The employment of the new super-bomb against Asiatics for the first time as a test moreover will remain as an imperishable memory of the insult to the Asiatic peoples.' Even on 17 August its editorial was a defiant, 'The Show Goes On'.[18] This hostile attitude and the real possibility that many Japanese units would continue to fight became a major concern of South-East Asia Command (SEAC), headed by Admiral Lord Louis Mountbatten.

ANGLO-AMERICAN RIVALRY AND THE ORIGIN OF SOUTH-EAST ASIA COMMAND

Many of Britain's difficulties in Southeast Asia stemmed from the state of relations with the United States. Attempts by London to co-operate with Washington in the war against Japan were rarely successful or even satisfactory. Often there was bad feeling.[19] British and American military and political priorities in Asia differed markedly. The joint Allied China, Burma, India (CBI) theatre of operations was nominally under General Wavell's authority. However, Washington's reluctance to put American troops under British command resulted in those units being under direct control of General Joseph Stilwell. From the start it was an uneasy mixture of limited resources and rivalries. (For many of those involved, CBI stood for 'Confused Bastards in India'.[20]) American suspicion of a British post-war imperial agenda arose early and remained constant, reducing the Command's effectiveness. Stilwell, in charge of Lend-Lease supplies to China, badgered and cajoled the ever-cautious Chinese to mount operations against the Japanese. The British were less enthusiastic and not optimistic about the potential Chinese contribution.[21]

Stilwell frequently clashed with Wavell and other British officers over the viability of a northern route through Burma to supply China against Britain's preference for operations in southern Burma. In addition to differences over strategy, supply difficulties also sparked differences of opinion. All the Lend-Lease equipment for China came via India through Calcutta. Bottlenecks occurred regularly and slowed the release of China-destined supplies. The US Army pressed for and secured exclusive use of the modern King George Docks, so consigning British military supplies to slower unloading in older facilities. Also, the British were 'persuaded' to appoint a port controller at Calcutta and accept an American as a deputy.[22] British concessions did not improve relations, however, and in August 1943 relentless Anglo-American feuding led the Combined Chiefs of Staff to split the CBI into separate Chinese and South East Asian Commands.[23]

SEAC therefore came into existence as a compromised Command with confusing and vague American and British operational boundaries.[24] Officially it remained an Allied theatre under Mountbatten with Stilwell as Deputy Supreme Allied Commander and an American Chief of Staff (General Albert Wedemeyer), but Anglo-American military co-operation was minimal. Where it did occur, such as after the offensive in northern Burma in late 1943 or clandestine operations in Indo-China, relations were fractious.[25] Stilwell became very critical of Mountbatten, concluding that the British were more enthusiastic about protecting their colonial possessions—with SEAC standing for 'Save England's Asian Colonies'—than in seeing a Japanese defeat at Chinese hands.[26] (In fact the prospect of a Chinese army liberating Burma was truly anathema to London.)

Anglo-American relations in SEAC remained difficult up to and beyond Japan's surrender. One immediate consequence was the swift departure of American forces and, crucially, American resources from SEAC. Even before Japan's capitulation the United States was wary of becoming identified with colonial reconquest by Britain, France and the Netherlands. It was made clear to Mountbatten that American forces would not be available for operations outside Burma. A timetable for American withdrawal agreed in April 1945 meant that by September 1945 SEAC was virtually an all-British (with French and Dutch) enterprise.[27]

Additional strains were placed upon SEAC when, also on 15 August, Mountbatten's area of responsibility doubled as the Command's boundaries were expanded to include much of General Douglas MacArthur's South-West Pacific Area (SWPA). As a result, SEAC's remit covered 'the Andamans, the Nicobars, Burma, Thailand (Siam), French Indo-China south of 16 degrees north latitude, Malaya, Borneo, the Netherlands Indies, New Guinea, the Bismarcks and the Solomon Islands'.[28] It was a vast territory. 'Indonesia' alone comprised:

> An archipelago of six main island groups, Sumatra, Java, Borneo, Celebes, the Moluccas, and New Guinea...over 700,000 square miles of territory [that] extends 3,000 miles from west to east and 1,000 miles from north to south. The population numbers seventy millions. Java, with an area of only 54,000 square miles, less than that of England and Wales...holds fifty of these seventy millions, and is the most densely populated area in the world.[29]

Mountbatten, forced to accept the boundary extension immediately, was far from happy. 'This new order was', he commented, '...unexpected; and the circumstances were quite different...now my responsibilities were immediate and urgent, but neither the troops, the shipping, nor the Intelligence I had asked for were available to me.'[30] Proposed changes to boundaries had been raised with Mountbatten in mid-July with the expectation that they would occur several months ahead, and after the recapture of the key naval base of Singapore.[31] On 24 July, Mountbatten had been informed of the existence of the atomic bomb and was told to expect a Japanese surrender around 15 August.[32] Sworn to secrecy, he was only able to advise his staff of the possibility that the war would end far sooner than anticipated.[33]

After the surrender announcement SEAC tried repeatedly to make contact with Field Marshal Count Terauchi Hisaichi, Supreme Commander of Japanese Expeditionary Forces Southern Regions (JEFSR), at his HQ in

Saigon (now Ho Chi Minh City). Only on 20 August was a non-committal acknowledgement received. Terauchi replied that he 'could act only on orders from his Emperor as and when they were received'.[34] The Allies were unaware that in Tokyo opposition and open defiance to the surrender from some army officers had convinced Hirohito to send Prince Kanin to assure Terauchi that he had made his broadcast willingly and to pressure him to obey.[35] (Two other princes made similar visits: one to Korea and Manchuria, and the other to the China Expeditionary Army and China Fleet.[36]) As these 'internal' peace missions did the rounds, Japanese units stationed from Aceh to Timor and from Harbin to Jakarta waited then, not for 'confirmation' of the Emperor's decision, which many of them had heard, but for the decision of their immediate superiors. Only when Terauchi made clear his intention to obey did his regional subordinates order a stand-down and authorise local press and radio stations to report the euphemistically described 'new situation'.[37] In Java even this decision revealed inter-service tensions and truculence. The Japanese Navy HQ made its announcement to suspend hostilities on 19 August for 'implementation' at midnight on 22 August, whereas the Japanese Army HQ delayed until 22 August, for 'implementation' at midnight on 25 August.[38] A meeting to discuss 'surrender preliminaries' between British and Japanese commanders was arranged for 26 August in Rangoon.

Allied commanders held no illusions over the risk of continuing Japanese resistance. In April 1945 Mountbatten had witnessed 'surly and ill-disciplined' Japanese prisoners of war (JPW) in India.[39] When British warships first returned to Hong Kong on 30 August they took no chances. Some approaching Japanese motor-torpedo boats suspected of being a suicide squadron were sunk and their base shelled.[40] Off Japan's coast, Allied pilots reported enemy aircraft plunging into the sea. These were *kamikaze* out of fuel after an unsuccessful search for Allied ships.[41] Even Operation Zipper, the much-delayed SEAC seaborne invasion of Malaya took place on 9 September on the assumption that it might face opposition. This was two weeks after the Rangoon Conference and one week after the official surrender in Tokyo on 2 September. Zipper went ahead for a number of reasons, chiefly because 100,000 men had been mobilised and many ships had been loaded with stores and equipment. It was delayed by General Douglas MacArthur's insistence that no landings be made in Southeast Asia until after the Tokyo ceremony. Consequently the date slipped by 12 days with the invasion force confined on ships in appalling weather.[42] Fortunately, the Malaya landings were not opposed but there were still many deaths. Poor planning, inadequate reconnaissance and logistical mismanagement resulted in unmitigated disaster as over-laden men drowned in a treacherous bay.[43]

THE JAPANESE TAKE STOCK OF THE 'NEW SITUATION'

Among the Japanese public the immediate reaction to the surrender was shock and widespread confusion. Many people had to await a 'translation' of the Emperor's extremely formal court language by a radio announcer.[44] To members of the armed forces, all of whom were expecting to perish in a last stand, the decision was simply astonishing. After all, Japan's mission in Asia had divine sanction, for Hirohito was a living god. The *Dai toa asia senso* (Great East Asia War) was a holy war and was consistently referred to in those terms by Japan's political leaders and propagandists. Unconditional Imperial surrender begged an immense question for the Japanese people. How does one lose a holy war and still keep the faith? (Reference to the 'Great East Asia War' in Japanese newspapers and other publications was banned by the US occupation authorities in December 1945. Instead, 'Pacific War' (*Taiheiyo senso*) was insisted upon, which suited American sensitivities but did not really reflect Japanese perceptions of the conflict.[45])

It is true that for some Japanese the trauma of the surrender proved too much. For these men, and some women, shame, guilt, ideals of personal honour and perhaps fear of Allied retribution left only one option. High-profile suicides, such as those of War Minister General Anami, Korechika, General and Mrs Sugiyama Hajime, Admiral Onishi Takijiro (the father of the *kamikaze* concept), General Honjo Shigeru (Hirohito's former Chief ADC), General Tanaka Shizuichi (Eastern Army Commander), Admiral Ugaki Matome and several other high-ranking officers, as well as the 30 or so citizens who killed themselves in sight of the Emperor's residence have reinforced a misleading image of the capitulation of 'sorrowful Japanese kneeling on the gravel approaches around the moat of the imperial palace'. This enduring image has, however, obscured the actions of influential personnel in the Japanese military who chose not to take their own life, as well as the open and unrestrained relief shown by other members of the public. Thus there was 'no single or singular "Japanese" response to the defeat' but a kaleidoscope of responses—ranging from looting, the overnight disappearance of the mystique of racial and social superiority, expressions of disgust and anger towards their leaders—against a background of a people reappraising how they thought and behaved. Kido Koichi, Lord Keeper of the Privy Seal, and Hirohito's closest confidant, noted in his diary that some people near the palace were cheering. 'It was clear', Kido observed with some ambivalence, 'that they felt a great burden had been lifted'.[46]

As one burden lifted another descended. Allied troops had taken very few JPW during the war. In Burma, the first Japanese, a few handfuls of

2. Two IJN I-400 submarines intercepted by the US Navy on 23 Aug. 1945. (NARA)

deserters, gave themselves up to the British in early May 1944 at Imphal.[47] One account gives a figure of 150,000 Japanese killed in the campaign against 1,700 taken prisoner, a PW-to-dead ratio of 1 to 88. In comparison, estimates of German dead and PW in the Falaise Pocket during the campaign in Normandy in August 1944 are 10,000 and 50,000 respectively, a ratio of 1 to five.[48] Numbers of JPW remained very low, even allowing for the fact that Allied soldiers, accustomed to booby-trapped corpses and suicide-bombers, rarely gave Japanese the benefit of the doubt. In the Pacific Theatre, where ratios were comparable, if slightly lower. It was only when the fighting neared Japan's main islands, particularly with the battle for

Okinawa, from 26 March to 30 June 1945, that Japanese began to surrender *en masse*, finally abandoning the tenets of the military Field Service Code of 1941 or *senjinkun* (戦陣訓).[49] The Code read: 'You shall not undergo the shame of being taken alive. You shall not bequeath a sullied name'.[50] Since the early 1900s it had become a deeply established Japanese societal norm to consider capture, even when due to incapacity from wounds, as an irredeemable loss of personal honour that was an unbearable shame for the soldier, his family and the Japanese nation.[51] For those few JPW in Allied hands prior to August 1945 it was axiomatic that there would be no happy return for them at the end of hostilities. Once home, they could expect either execution or imprisonment, followed by ostracism by family and friends. Consequently for most Japanese faced with capture, suicide had been the only solution to an immense personal moral dilemma. There was, however, frequent third-party intervention as even wounded men (and some nurses) were 'assisted' in this course of action.

The Imperial command to lay down arms meant that nearly 4 million Japanese soldiers would become PW and therefore shamed. It was an uncomfortable development for the already battered national psyche. Japan's policy had been to categorically deny the existence of any Japanese PW. Officially, all missing men had died in combat. ICRC reports on Japanese prisoners sent to Tokyo were not passed on to next of kin. In any case, captive Japanese rarely gave their real name to their captors or even to their fellow prisoners, using instead those of national heroes or film stars.[52]

Unsurprisingly, the Japanese Government was not slow to appreciate the risk of mental distress that the capitulation might bring for so many of the Emperor's subjects. While there are dangers in transposing the civilian catharsis to the military and assuming similar fundamental reappraisals, there is clear evidence of a collapse of military discipline in the home islands as men looted supplies and deserted in droves.[53] Two of the first follow-ups to the cease-fire orders were the *Dairikurei* (Special Army Regulation) No. 385 and *Daikairei* (Special Navy Regulation) No. 50, which declared that those surrendering were not to consider themselves PW at all.[54] Another semantic crutch was the fact that Hirohito had not used the words 'surrender' or 'defeat' in his broadcast. His loyal forces—and their families—could then, while 'enduring the unendurable', cling to the idea that they remained united and undefeated in *real* battle and that Japan had lost only because the Allies had changed the rules of the game. Even as early as 12 August, Admiral Yonai Mitsumasa described the A-bombs and the Soviet entry into the war as 'gifts from the gods [because] we can now control matters without revealing the domestic situation'.[55]

Japanese domestic politics, however, did not concern South-East Asia Command. SEAC's most pressing initial tasks were to recover Allied PW and civilian internees, and then disarm and repatriate the Japanese throughout its assigned area. Once contact had been established with Terauchi's HQ

3. Lt Gen Numata (left) and Adm Chudo arriving at Mingladon airfield, Rangoon (Burma) on 24 Aug. 1945. [Detail.] (© IWM)

and, most importantly, confirmed that JEFSR would not be continuing the fight, surrender preliminaries began. Representatives met at Rangoon (Burma) on 26 August. While the Allied party, led by Lieutenant-General F. A. M. Browning had prepared a list of instructions, the Japanese, headed jointly by Lieutenant-General Numata Takazo (Chief of Staff, JEFSR) and Rear-Admiral Chudo Kaigye (Assistant Chief of Staff), attempted to negotiate over areas of responsibility, separate treatment for Rear-Admiral Fukudome Shigeru (Naval Commander-in-Chief), the disarming and internment of Japanese troops, and also requested food supplies. According to Mountbatten, General Browning called the Japanese bluff and 'allowed no comments on the terms laid down, and allowed only questions on the terms as they stood'.[5] However, the negotiations dragged on as the Japanese attempted to fight their corner. One clue that the meeting did not go quite so smoothly is that the official history records that, Numata and Chudo, after *three days* of talks, 'agreed to the terms laid down... *and at 1 a.m. accepted them on behalf of Terauchi'*.[57] (Interestingly, though the Japanese agenda was ignored at Rangoon, one month later at Jakarta, Japanese 16 Army commanders presented Allied representatives with very similar proposals on internment and disarmament.)

As Japan's Government descended into factional chaos, communication and control functions for overseas forces withered. Fractures developed in the Japanese chain of command. Indeed, longstanding Army and Navy differences exacerbated local tensions. This vacuum and/or uncertainty at the centre presented certain senior officers outside Japan with opportunities to influence regional events, as their 'local initiatives' were neither approved nor countermanded. A number were keen to encourage a scorched earth policy or strike a last blow for the ideal of 'Asia for the Asiatics'. The actions of the individual Japanese commands in China, Siam, Malaya, NEI and FIC in the closing stages of the war and the first weeks of peace are instructive. Just as there was a multifaceted response among Japanese civilians to the surrender, so there was not one single Japanese military response to the order to stand down.

'ALREADY FIGHTING WORLD WAR III'

Events illustrate this variation in response. Some Japanese officers took a proactive role with far-reaching consequences for the Indonesian revolution and subsequent British policy. Most influential among these officers was Rear-Admiral Maeda Tadashi, an officer in Japanese Naval Intelligence. Both passionately loyal to the Emperor yet keenly pro-Indonesian, Maeda personifies those Japanese whose actions in the quite literally early hours of the Indonesian revolution cast disproportionate influence over subsequent events. Some returning Dutch intelligence officers came to view Maeda as the 'evil genius' behind independence.[58] By 16 August he was, as his Dutch interrogators put it, 'already fighting World War III'.[59]

Maeda arrived in Jakarta in August 1942 as head of the *Kaigun bukanfu* (Navy Liaison Office) to co-ordinate food shipments from Java to the Celebes-based Second Expeditionary Fleet commanded by Vice-Admiral Shibata Yaichiro.[60] Already on the *Bukanfu* staff were several Japanese with pro-Indonesian sympathies including Nishijima Shigetada, an ex-army conscript and former communist expatriate who had lived in Indonesia since 1937, and Yoshizumi Tomegoro, a journalist. (Nishijima later became a controversial figure in Japanese-Indonesian studies. Yoshizumi joined the Indonesians and died fighting the Dutch in 1946.) The *Bukanfu* involved itself in nationalist politics well before official Japanese policy towards an independent Indonesia softened following the Statement of 7 September 1944 by Japanese Prime Minister Koiso Kuniaki, which envisaged independence 'in the very near future'. Japan's original plan, however, envisaged autonomy for only Java and Madura. Other islands were to be occupied permanently.[61]

Both Maeda and Shibata were atypical in their behaviour, for until late 1944 the Navy officially opposed Indonesian independence. In October 1944, however, Maeda established the *Asrama Indonesia Merdeka* (School for Independent Indonesia), which sponsored lectures and public seminars that irked the Army administration and particularly the *kenpeitai* (military police corps) who had no authority in Naval premises.[62] Speakers at the seminars included Sukarno (first president of Indonesia), Mohammad Hatta (first vice-president) and Soetan Sjahrir (first prime minister), who addressed audiences on the history of the nationalist movement, the co-operative movement, and nationalism and democracy respectively. Nishijima himself gave talks on agricultural problems, and Yoshizumi on guerrilla warfare.[63] There was thus demonstrable Japanese Navy and nationalist interaction. Sjahrir, it should be noted, perceived an ulterior motive in his invitations to speak, that of an attempt to restrict his movements.[64]

In February 1945 at a meeting of Second Southern Fleet staff officers, Maeda and Nishijima successfully proposed that the Fleet officially adopt a policy of immediate independence for Indonesia. Admiral Shibata approved and the motion was conveyed to Tokyo.[65] Inevitably, the serious military reversals between March and July 1945 forced Tokyo to put regional politics aside. It was not until mid-July, coinciding with the meeting of the Allied leaders at the Potsdam Conference, that the *Saiko senso shido kaigi* (Supreme War Guidance Council) in Tokyo agreed to grant independence to Indonesia 'immediately'.[66] Strings were attached to this puppet independence: the new state was expected to declare war on the US, Britain and the Netherlands but Japan was to maintain authority over foreign affairs.[67] In late July Marshal Terauchi received the go-ahead to start preparations for Indonesian independence as quickly as possible.

On 7 August, the day after the bombing of Hiroshima, Terauchi, expecting the Soviet Union to declare war on Japan at any moment, hurriedly announced the creation of the *Panitia Persiapan Kemerdekaan Indonesia* (Preparatory Committee for Indonesian Independence) or PPKI.[68] Two days later, a group including Sukarno, Hatta and Japanese administrators flew to Singapore, then on to Dalat (a hill station retreat east of Saigon) for talks at Terauchi's villa. A ceremony followed in which Sukarno and Hatta were inaugurated as chairman and vice-chairman of the PPKI. The Committee's was scheduled for 18 August. When the group arrived back in Jakarta on 14 August where they were formally welcomed by a no-doubt-crestfallen Lt General Nagano and Admiral Maeda. Even so, the reality was that 'on the eve of the Japanese surrender, the military [had] laid the groundwork for an orderly transfer of sovereignty…to a group of… politicians with whom they had worked in reasonable harmony throughout the occupation'.[69]

For the nationalist leadership the timing was indeed unfortunate. Already rumours were circulating in Jakarta that Japan had accepted the Potsdam terms. On 15 August, hearing of a broadcast by the Emperor, Sukarno and Hatta tried to see Nagano but he was 'not available'. They then tried *Gunseikan* (Chief of Administrative Staff) Major General Yamamoto Moichiro who was 'in a meeting'. Maeda, however, agreed to see them. The two Indonesians demanded confirmation of the surrender.[70] They were somewhat disappointed. Nishijima describes Maeda's reply—he had heard the radio broadcast—as, 'I cannot answer with certainty…'.[71] Understandably, the Indonesian leaders left feeling frustrated and confused but virtually convinced of the Japanese capitulation. Yet even at this point they still sought official Japanese sanction for independence. Eventually, the Indonesians went ahead with the PPKI meeting. Before this could happen, however, some of the highly politicised militant youth and student groups in Java, known as *pemuda*, intervened. The *pemuda* rejected any role for a defeated Japan in the independence process.[72] They then took matters into their own hands, kidnapping Sukarno and Hatta early on 16 August, hiding them at a *Pembela Tanah Air* (Defenders of the Fatherland) or PETA militia barracks at Rengasendok some 50 miles east of Jakarta. There they demanded an immediate declaration of independence without deferring to the Japanese. In Jakarta, Sukarno and Hatta's absence caused consternation. Initially, Maeda and Nishijima assumed that *kenpei* (military police) had arrested them as part of secret contingency plans to maintain order. Finally, Maeda telephoned Yamamoto's office to be told that *kenpei* were in fact out searching for the two leaders. When a young Javanese working in the *Bukanfu* confessed that his *pemuda* comrades were responsible, Maeda, alarmed by the possibility of clashes between very jumpy *kenpei* and impassioned youths, promised to co-operate in securing a declaration of independence. On his own responsibility he guaranteed immunity to all the Indonesian groups concerned and offered his home as the venue for negotiations.[73]

4. Indonesian TKR (People's Security Army) troops in Java in mid 1946. (AC)

Maeda then asked for a meeting with General Yamamoto in person to discuss the Indonesians' options. By this time, though, Yamamoto's superiors at HQ 7 Area Army in Singapore had informed him that the surrender terms required Japan to maintain the *status quo* in all occupied territories. All political activities were to be halted. Yamamoto stonewalled, refusing to see Maeda, Sukarno or Hatta, and instead referred them to his subordinate, General Nishimura Otoshi. As for Otoshi, he felt that having surrendered, Japan no longer had jurisdiction over the 'Indonesian problem'.[74] Nishimura was pressed repeatedly by the Indonesian leadership for a full statement on the Japanese position and what independent action the nationalists might take. In reply he stressed that since the military authorities now had clear responsibility for maintaining the *status quo*, and would suffer the consequences for any breaches or dereliction of duty, a declaration of independence was unacceptable.

Reportedly Maeda, hardly a reluctant bystander, challenged this owing to his belief that 'Indonesian independence comes from the will of the Emperor based upon the sacred ideal of *Hakko Ichiu*' (literally 'eight-corners of the world under one roof'). Nishimura riposted that the Emperor's will could change and that 'the same Emperor has ordered us to stop fighting'. Outside pressure also was on Nishimura's mind. The Allies, who controlled Japan's future, were apparently permitting the Emperor to remain on the throne. Consequently, it made no sense to antagonise them over Indonesia.[75] In a measured reply that probably reveals more than a suggestion of *Bukanfu* input, Sukarno and Hatta proposed that the Japanese 'should not complain if the activities of *pemuda* rioters…break Japanese controls'. In other words, that the Japanese should take no action against a declaration of independence by groups beyond their control. Nishimura's convoluted reply hinted that such a course of action might be permissible if it were done 'without his knowledge'.[76] This was the 'green light' for the declaration. That night, at Maeda's residence—the pre-war home of the British Consul—Sukarno, Hatta, some *pemuda* representatives, Miyoshi Shunkichiro (vice-consul in Jakarta from 1936 to 1939 and fluent in Indonesian) and Maeda 'worked' on a draft declaration.[77]

Maeda's role has long been disputed by some Indonesian historians who deny that he and other Japanese were involved. Nishijima describes the *pemuda* representatives staying in another room rather than draft the document at the same table as the Japanese. He also says that the Japanese offered 'opinions' but did not attend the reading of the final declaration in Maeda's study.[78] Ironically, the careful wording of the declaration, which avoids provocation towards the Japanese, suggests considerable Japanese influence. In Nishijima's account, part of the draft that read 'existing administrative organs must be seized from the foreigners…' was specifically altered at Maeda's request to 'transfer of power will be carried out' to prevent reaction from the Japanese Administration.[79] (Months later, Maeda denied his involvement to Dutch investigators determined to cast the revolutionary government as Japanese sanctioned. Maeda insisted he 'had gone to bed'.)[80]

Early on 17 August a short proclamation text was finally approved:

'We, the Indonesian people, hereby declare the independence of Indonesia. Matters concerning the transfer of power and so forth should be carried out in a careful manner and as quickly as possible. Djakarta 17-8-'05. [Signed] Representatives of the Indonesian nation'.[81]

Japanese influence is also apparent in the date, written as 17-8-'05, ie, the year 2605 in the Japanese calendar, not 1945. At noon that day, Sukarno made a public declaration, the date now reading 1945, bearing the signatures simply 'Sukarno Hatta'. The *merah puti* ('red white') flag of the new Indonesian republic was raised and the anthem *'Indonesia Raya'* ('Greater Indonesia') sung officially for the first time. Afterwards, Indonesians working at the Japanese-guarded short-wave radio station in Bandung broadcast news of the declaration worldwide. Meanwhile, in Jakarta, as the *Bukanfu* printing press ran off copies of the declaration to hand out to the public, Maeda held a celebratory banquet.[82] Next day Sukarno and Hatta were informed formally by General Yamamoto of Japan's acceptance of the Potsdam Declaration and that consequently Japan could no longer offer any assistance toward independence. Further, the *status quo* and public order would be maintained, and that all authority would be transferred to the Allies. This announcement, however, came after the PPKI had held its first full meeting that morning and had renamed itself the *Komite Nasional Indonesia* (KNI). In Jakarta nationalist momentum, now free of Japanese influence, but not encouragement, was building.[83]

16 ARMY AND PETA DISARMAMENT

While there may have been considerable sympathy for the nationalist Indonesian cause from Japanese Naval quarters, the polarised nature of Japanese reaction is revealed in the Japanese Army's decision to disarm and disband the 66 PETA militia battalions. (In Occupied Southeast Asia the Japanese established *boei giyugun* (Volunteer Defence Forces), *hei-ho* (auxiliary troops), *keibodan* (Civilian Defence Corps) and *tokubetsu keisatsutai* (Special Police Corps). The PETA was the Java *boei giyugun*.[84]) The disarmament took place between 18 and 20 August 1945. Initially the Japanese saw the PETA as the 'marriage of Islam and Japan', designing for it a flag of the rising red sun on a green field with the Islamic white crescent and a star within the sun.[85]

Long before August 1945, however, enthusiasm for Japanese rule, training methods and authority had faded within the PETA. There had also been unrest. In February 1944 in Blitar, East Java, grievances—over food shortages, poor treatment of local *romusha* (civilian conscript) labour, Japanese arrogance reflected in brutality in training, and incidents over Javanese women—led to a revolt in which 25 Japanese died. Japanese influence and control remained steady, however, evidenced by the fact that the Japanese trusted the loyalty of other PETA battalions sufficiently to use them and not Japanese troops in containing the revolt.[86] Japanese fears that further force risked fanning further violence led to a negotiated ceasefire. Afterwards, in breach of the terms of the truce, *kenpei* launched an investigation.[87] At the subsequent court martial, attended by Sukarno, six PETA leaders were executed and others imprisoned.[88]

Blitar certainly unnerved the Japanese.[89] Equally the shock could well have spurred Tokyo into initiating preparations for independence. From the nationalist viewpoint, however, Blitar marks the true start of the Indonesian revolution.[90]

In the chaotic aftermath of the surrender the Japanese would not tolerate Indonesian demands for the transfer of military authority. This, it has been suggested, had nothing to do with worries over possible Allied reaction but more to do with the fact that the 35,000 well-armed PETA on Java had become a potential threat to Japanese lives.[91] Two incidents gave notice of difficulty ahead. Early on 16 August in Rengasendok, the local PETA company commander seized power and disarmed the few Japanese present. Later that same day at Karawang, a PETA unit disarmed the Japanese and called on the local police and civil service to join them in seizing the town. This time the Japanese counter-attacked, arresting the chief of police and the local governor or 'regent'.[92] PETA disarmament in other areas thus became a priority. Japanese action was calculated and swift. Though rumours of surrender and even a republican call to arms were rife, the PETA generally found the idea of a Japanese surrender very difficult to accept. Their segregated, regimented and still Japanese-controlled environment helped prolong their denial.[93] They were easily duped. Significantly, however, their weapons remained in Java. There were also clear regional differences in the extent to which the Japanese pursued PETA disarmament.

Allied intervention altered everything.[94] Japanese willingness to shoot in Karawang, however, probably had less to do with instructions from Mountbatten and more with straightforward self-preservation. As a short, sharp shock it also served to discourage open revolt, which they sought to avoid. It is not necessarily evidence of an intention to co-operate with anticipated Allied policy. From 21 August onwards, 16 Army began to congregate in well-stocked camps—which included prostitutes—storing much heavy weaponry and leaving only small detachments in cities to maintain a semblance of law and order. This was despite the realisation that the Allies might view such action as a breach of the surrender terms.

One researcher, quoting Nishijima, states that it was during this interlude that a communication from 7 Area Army HQ in Singapore informed them of the similar policy there 'but that in addition the remaining guard/police units were only allowed five rounds of ammunition per man'. A similar policy was readily adopted by 16 Army even though it was patently not appropriate for Java. HQ 16 Army also prepared an excuse in case of Allied censure to the effect that the measures were adopted to avoid the possibility of clashes between the Allies and Japanese.[95] Indonesian police and the *kenpeitai* took over responsibility for public order, which began to deteriorate quickly amidst acute food shortages, anti-Japanese sentiment and increasing revolutionary fervour.[96] In fact, it was nearly five weeks before the first Allied personnel arrived, during which time—a crucial breathing space for the revolution—the KNI attempted to hive off a functioning, independent government from the crumbling Japanese administration.[97]

As nationalist confidence grew so too did awareness that the former colonial masters planned to return. The imminent arrival of the Dutch brought home to the nationalists their urgent need for weapons. Japanese armouries had them in abundance and consequently these became a focus for unrest. One of the major Allied criticisms of the Japanese in Indonesia is over post-surrender weapons handovers to nationalists.[98] Arms transfers had certainly occurred throughout Java, PETA units in particular having been issued with mainly captured former Royal Netherlands Indies Army (KNIL) equipment. Such transfers first happened in 1943. Although by 21 August most PETA battalions had been officially disbanded and men ordered home, not all the units had dissolved. A few men had drifted away, taking their spare rifles and a few rounds of ammunition, some with the blessing of their Japanese training officers.

Bandung, a major city some 90 miles from Jakarta, was an exception. Here PETA disarmament was near-total. On the pretext of issuing new weapons, Japanese instructors collected even small arms.[99] Trust in the Japanese was such that even PETA officers who were asked to hide weapons by their more questioning juniors rebuffed the requests. In two days their disarmament was virtually complete (though some weapons were kept by more enterprising officers and units on manoeuvres).[100] This would have significant consequences, not least because it later allowed the British to fortify the city unopposed and so protect Dutch civilians. In contrast, near the East Java port city of Surabaya, local Japanese commanders gave tanks and armoured cars, again mainly captured KNIL vehicles, to their

PETA comrades who began to form and train new independent regional or town-based militias on PETA lines called *Badan Keamanan Rakjat* (BKR) or People's Security Organisation. In these new formations, former PETA non-commissioned officers (NCOs) became officers and other ranks NCOs. In December 1945 the BKR became the *Tentara Keaman Rakjat* (TKR) or People's Security Army, which eventually formed the core of the nationalist forces on Java. Weapons handovers influenced the internal balance of power for decades. (General Nasution, commander of the Silliwangi Division in central Java, was one such beneficiary.)[101] The ranks of many of these militia units were swelled by spear- and sword-carrying *pemuda*. In time, however, the increasing demand for firearms led to attempts to seize arms from Japanese patrols and isolated barracks. In one instance seven *kenpei* who refused to hand over their weapons were seized and killed in Semarang.[102] More often, however, beleaguered Japanese were able to soothe a clamouring and dangerous mob by giving up numbers of spare weapons.

NEW PRIORITIES FOR THE SPECIAL OPERATIONS EXECUTIVE IN SOUTHEAST ASIA

In late August 1945, SEAC could only hazard guesses at the situation east of Singapore. Rumours of widespread disorder on Java disturbed the British. It was as unanticipated as it was unwelcome. Indeed, Java, Sumatra and Indo-China had hardly registered on British strategic radar until July 1945. There was, however, immense confusion and a dearth of information available to SEAC, even from official Dutch sources. Concern for Allied PW was paramount but planning for the Recovery of Allied Prisoners of War and Internees (RAPWI) was 'not seriously considered by SEAC prior to 29 August', when Operation Mastiff, the sending in of observers and medical staff, was authorised.[103] These small, quickly constituted RAPWI and Special Operations Executive (SOE) teams, tried to fill in the blanks.

Post-Japanese-surrender missions undertaken by the SOE, Britain's clandestine operations arm, deserve to be better known. SOE was established well before its American equivalent, the Office of Strategic Services (OSS). Relations between the two groups, however, were never good.[104] In the Far East, SOE units were known as Force 136. Its members ventured behind Japanese lines raising guerrilla forces among the Karen and Naga tribes, liaising with Burmese nationalists and gathering intelligence.[105] After the capture of Rangoon in May 1945 all of SEAC came within range of air operations. This permitted an expansion of Force 136's activities to include obtaining information on PW camp locations and making contact with resistance movements in Malaya and elsewhere.[106] (In contrast, other Force 136 teams (see Chapter 2) were parachuted into Sumatra in July 1945 to reconnoitre Japanese positions prior to an eventual Allied invasion.) Following the Japanese 'preliminary surrender' meeting with the British at Rangoon on 28 August, the priorities changed and RAPWI operations began using SOE personnel in Malaya, Siam, FIC and the NEI as part of Operation Mastiff.[107] This involved the introduction of parachute teams and supplies to make contact with and relay information about numbers and conditions in Allied Prisoners of War and Internees (APWI) camps to SEAC HQ.

For Java, Mastiff comprised four teams in two components: 'Mosquito' (for the Batavia/Jakarta area) and 'Salex' (for the central area around Magelang). The Mosquito team, which included Captain David Soltau (RAMC), was dropped first on 8 September. It had little contact with nationalist authorities and only local dealings with Japanese military.[108] Unfortunately, some of the first analyses from Java by RAPWI teams, who were not attuned to the strength of nationalist feeling, proved overly optimistic. One report, written in the first week of arrival, concluded, 'once transport and security problems are solved; other tasks will become comparatively simple.'[109]

The lack of intelligence available to Mastiff teams led to further problems. Soltau, in his memoir, noted it was strange in view of the problems encountered later that Major Alan Greenhalgh, his commanding officer, was given no briefing whatsoever about possible trouble with or opposition from Indonesian nationalists. (SEAC HQ at Kandy had, after all, received details about the declaration of independence of 6 September but chose not to pass on the information to the Mosquito team.) Greenhalgh was, however, told specifically that the team was not to discuss the political situation with either the Japanese or Indonesians. There were considerable doubts about the success of the mission. To add to SEAC's worries, General Nagano, Japanese commander in Java, had not replied to messages or acknowledged any British signals. Because of this, Greenhalgh took with him a highly confidential letter from Mountbatten to Nagano, in both English and Dutch, demanding immediate answers to his questions.[110]

Some Japanese officers and some of the senior Allied PW in Jakarta: Wing Commander Alexander, Colonel Vooren and Lt Colonel Laurens van der Post, met the Mosquito team at Kemajoram airfield. Soltau describes Alexander as remarkably collected and in control of his feelings. Van der

Post, on the other hand, was 'overcome with emotion, tears streaming down his face'.[111] That night Greenhalgh met with Nagano and asked him why he had not replied to Mountbatten's signals. Nagano's reply, showing little sign of adverse mental health, is instructive:

> My answer is simple. I know that the war is finished, but as I have not been instructed by Tokyo about my attitude towards the Allied Forces I am not prepared to risk severe punishment by replying formally to this kind of Allied approach. I am, however, not a fool. As long as I am not asked to put anything in writing, you and your team can go ahead with your relief work, and I will appoint liaison officers to help you in any way we can.

Nagano then asked Greenhalgh if he wished him to surrender his sword formally. Greenhalgh was unprepared for the question but it seemed obvious to him even then that the Japanese would continue with day-to-day administration and maintenance of law and order for weeks or perhaps longer. Since it was vital that the General should not lose face with his troops he was allowed to keep his sword. Greenhalgh believed that his spur-of-the-moment decision helped keep the Japanese forces and administration functioning as well as they did for some time. Nagano was, apparently, relieved by the decision. He offered a toast to 'the great Allied victory'.[112] It is interesting that one of the Japanese, Major Count Yamaguchi, an English speaker, requested the British 'especially to leave aside all political problems for the time being'. Soltau realised later that this was 'a partly concealed reference to the Indonesian Nationalist movement, about which we had no information at that time...'. Yamaguchi went on to explain the tasks charged to 16 Army by the Allies, including 'the duty to maintain law and order'. He also referred to some 'problems' facing the Army from the activities of the nationalists, but gave an assurance that the army would 'carry out its own plans' which would 'prove effective'. None of the RAPWI team, exhausted after a tense and sleepless night aboard a Liberator bomber, appreciated the significance of Yamaguchi's remarks about possible hostility from the Indonesians. (Chilled lager served by the Japanese probably did not help them remain alert.)[113]

Immediately after the talk with the Japanese the team held a meeting for PW and internee representatives at the Hotel des Indes. Greenhalgh explained RAPWI directives, emphasising the need for Allied prisoners of war and internees (APWI) to be persuaded to remain in camp, and that the

Japanese were still responsible for food and camp maintenance. Camp leaders were authorised to order the Japanese to carry out anything necessary to improve conditions, acting on Mountbatten's authority. With those words of assurance the few RAPWI personnel, the only Allied representatives in Java, set about their business.

Misplaced optimism was quickly replaced by the realisation that Britain had inherited a most complicated and deadly Japanese colonial legacy. For the Japanese, military surrender had been inconceivable. It also placed them in a dilemma, sometimes even danger. There is little doubt that delays by the Allies in establishing a vestige of control increased Japanese unease and uncertainty, just as it encouraged nationalists to commit themselves to protest. As SEAC joined in the scramble for Asia, however, regional and local confusion also allowed Japanese influence to prevail disproportionately in places after their surrender.

NOTES TO CHAPTER I

1.   David Wehl, *The Birth of Indonesia* (London, 1948), 2. Japan's defeat was apparently such a shock to Nagano's mental health that his deputy took command. See Kenichi Goto, *Tensions of Empire: Japan and Southeast Asia in the Colonial and Postcolonial World,* edited by Paul H. Kratoska (Singapore, 2003*)*, 187.

2.   For analysis of Japanese military co-operation in Sumatra and Western oil business interests in Indonesia see Andrew Roadnight, 'Sleeping with the Enemy: Britain, Japanese Troops and the Netherlands East Indies, 1945-46'. *History* 87, no. 286 (2002), 245–268: 256–61.

3.   Richard B. Frank, *Downfall: The End of the Imperial Japanese Empire* (London, 2001), 304.

4.   For British policy see Christopher Thorne, Allies of a Kind: The United States, Britain and the War Against Japan, 1941-45 (London, 1978), passim.

5.   Herbert Feis, *The Atomic Bomb and the End of World War Two* (London, 1966), 119.

6.   R. Lewin, *The Other Ultra: Codes, Ciphers and the Defeat of Japan* (London, 1982), 248.

7.   Ibid., 285.

8.   Takezawa, Shoji, 'What About the Emperor's Lunch?', in *Senso,* ed. Frank Gibney, New York: M. E. Sharpe, 1995, 254–5.

9.   Thorne, *Allies*, 530; and Frank, *Downfall*, 236–8.

10.   Ienaga Saburo, *Japan's Last War: World War Two and the Japanese* (Oxford, 1979), 230. Also Frank, *Downfall*, 310, 343–6.

11.   John Toland, *The Rising Sun: The Decline and Fall of the Japanese Empire, 1936-1945* (New York, 1971), 945.

12.   John W. Dower, *Embracing Defeat: Japan in the Wake of World War II.* (New York: 1999), 48–9.

13.   See Feis, *Atomic Bomb*, 198.

14.   H. P. Willmot, *The Second World War in the Far East* (London, 2002), 204–5.

15.   Toland, *Rising Sun*, 945.

16.   Louis Allen, *Burma: The Longest War 1941-45* (London, 2000), 544. For the strength of the Kwantung Army in 1945 see Frank, *Downfall*, 280.

17.   Frank, *Downfall*, 328–9.

18.   AS 5204. 'Syonan' is short for 'southern island gained in the *Showa* (Hirohito) era'.

19.   Thorne, *Allies, passim.*

20.   Barbara Tuchman, *Stilwell and the American Experience in China, 1911-1945* (New York, 1971), 483.

21.   Thorne, *Allies*, 335.

22.   Joseph Bykofsky and Harold Larson, *The Technical Services: The Transportation Corps: Operations Overseas* (Washington, DC., 1957), 554.

23.   Tuchman, *Stilwell*, 489.

24.   Richard J. Aldrich, *Intelligence and the War against Japan, Britain, America and the Politics of Secret Service* (Cambridge, 2000), 171.

25.   Ibid., 208-210. See also Tuchman, *Stilwell,* 488-492, 550.

26.   Thorne, *Allies*, 336–7.

27.   Ibid., 521, 588−−92.

28.   Earl Mountbatten of Burma, *Post Surrender Tasks Section E of the Report to the Combined Chiefs of Staff by the Supreme Allied Commander South-East Asia, 1943-1945* (London, 1969), para. 313.

29.   F. S. V. Donnison, *British Military Administration in the Far East, 1943-1946* (London, 1956), 413.

30.   Earl Mountbatten of Burma, *Report to the Combined Chiefs of Staff by the Supreme Allied Commander South-East Asia, 1943-1945.* London: HMSO, 1951, para. 636.

31.   Ibid., paras 629–30.

32.   *The Personal Diary of Admiral the Lord Louis Mountbatten, 1943-1946,* ed, Philip Ziegler (London, 1988), 230–31.

33.   Ibid., 231.

34.   Woodburn Kirby, *Surrender of Japan,* 236.

35.   *See* Pacific War Research Society. *Japan's Longest Day* (London, 1968), passim. Also Toland, *Rising Sun,* 934–65.

36.   Toland, *Rising Sun,* 966.

37.   W. G. J. Remmelink, 'The Emergence of the New Situation: The Japanese Army on Java after the Surrender.' *Kabar Sebarang* 4 (1978), 60.

38.   Miyamoto Shizuo, 'Army Problems in Java after the Surrender', in Anthony Reid and Oki Akira, eds, *The Japanese Experience in Indonesia: Selected Memoirs of 1942-45* (Ohio, 1986), 326.

39.   Mountbatten, *Personal Diary,* 201.

40.   Woodburn Kirby, *Surrender of Japan,* 286.

41.   Stephen Harper, *Miracle of Deliverance: The Case for the Bombing of Hiroshima and Nagasaki* (London, 1985), 149, 195. One of these pilots was Vice Admiral Ugaki Matome, see *Fading Victory: The Diary of Admiral Matome Ugaki* (Pittsburgh, 1991).

42.   Ronald Lewin, *Slim: The Standard Bearer* (London, 1976), 252.

43.   Harper, *Miracle of Deliverance,* 164–78. See also Lewin, *Slim,* 252–3.

44.   Edward Behr, *Hirohito–Behind the Myth* (London, 1989), 377.

45.   See Ian Nish, *Japanese Foreign Policy in the Interwar Period* (London, 2002), 2.

46.   Dower, *Embracing Defeat,* 24–5. Quoting Kido Koichi, 38.

47.   W. J. Slim, *Defeat into Victory* (London, 1998), 331.

48.   Allen, *Burma,* 611. Ulrich Strauss, *The Anguish of Surrender: Japanese POWs of World War II* (Seattle, 2003), 49. Chester Wilmot, *The Struggle for Europe* (London, 1952), 472.

49.   Strauss, *Anguish of Surrender,* 48–9.

50.   Hata Ikuo, 'From Consideration to Contempt', *Prisoners of War and their Captors in World War II,* eds, Bob Moore and Kent Fedorowich (Oxford, 1996), 254.

51.   Ibid., 255.

52.   Ibid., 270.

53.   Dower, *Embracing Defeat,* 59.

54.   Hata, 'From Consideration to Contempt', 275. For the regulations, see Woodburn Kirby, *Surrender of Japan,* 218.

55.   Frank, *Downfall,* 310.

56.   Mountbatten, *Report to the Chiefs of Staff,* para. 184.

57.   Woodburn Kirby, *Surrender of Japan,* 237. (Author's italics.)

58.   Remmelink rejects this. See, Remmelink, 'New Situation', 70.

59.   IC 048339. Also quoted in Theodore Friend, *The Blue-Eyed Enemy: Japan Against the West in Java and Luzon, 1942-1945* (New York, 1988), 220.

60.   Benedict R. O. G. Anderson, *Java in a Time of Revolution* (New York, 1972), 427.

61.   George Kahin, *Nationalism and Revolution in Indonesia* (New York, 1952), 115.

62.   Nishijima Shigetada, 'Army problems in Java after the surrender', in *Japanese Experience of Indonesia,* eds, Reid and Oki, 306. *Kenpeitai* is used throughout for 'military police corps', *kenpei* for 'military police' or 'policeman'.

63.   Ibid., 308.

64.   Soetan Sjahrir, *Out of Exile* (New York, 1948), 251.

65.   Nishijima, 'Army Problems in Java', in *Japanese Experience of Indonesia*, eds, Reid and Oki, 270–71.

66.   IC 059679.

67.   Louis Allen, *The End of the War in Asia* (St Albans, 1976), 74.

68.   Anderson, *Java*, 62.

69.   Ibid., 65.

70.   IC 006830-44. 'Statement' by Maeda Tadashi, 20 April 1946.

71.   Nishijima Shigetada, 'The Independence Proclamation in Jakarta', in *Japanese Experience in Indonesia*, eds, Reid and Oki, 314.

72.   Anderson, *Java*, 71.

73.   Ibid., 77–8.

74.   Friend, *Blue-Eyed Enemy*, 219, citing IC 048339. Nishimura was *Sombucho* (Head of the General Affairs Department).

75.   Ibid., n. 23. Friend suspects bias in this account.

76.   Nishijima, quoted in Anderson, *Java*, 80.

77.   Anderson, *Java*, 63 n. 7.

78.   Nishijima, 'Army Problems in Java', in Reid and Oki, *Japanese Experience of Indonesia*, 321.

79.   Ibid., 322.

80.   'Interrogation of RA Maeda Tadashi by A. Audretsch, Struikwijk Prison, 16 Apr. 1947.' AS 5024-11.

81.   For a photograph of this document see Reid and Oki, eds, *Japanese Experience in Indonesia*, 301, as well as sources online.

82.   Anderson, *Java*, 84.

83.   Ibid., 85.

84.   *See* Lebra, *Japanese-Trained Armies*, 91–8.

85.   Louis Fisher, *The Story of Indonesia* (London, 1959), 72.

86.   John R. W. Smail, *Bandung in the Early Revolution: A Study in the Social History of the Indonesian Revolution* (New York, 1964), 54.

87.   NFKVA, *The Kenpeitai in Java and Sumatra,* trans. B. G. Shimer and Guy Hobbs (New York, 1986), 42–3.

88.   Lebra, *Japanese Trained Armies*, 152.

89.   Miyamoto Shizuo, 'An account of the Cessation of Hostilities in Java', in *Japanese Experience of Indonesia*, eds, Reid and Oki, 226–9.

90.   Lebra, *Japanese Trained Armies*, 153.

91.   Smail, *Bandung*, 53.

92.   Robert Cribb, *Gangsters and Revolutionaries: The Jakarta People's Militia and the Indonesian Revolution, 1945-1949* (Honolulu, 1991), 41.

93.   Ibid., 50–51.

94.   Allen, *End of the War,* 82.

95.   Remmelink, 'New Situation', 60.

96.   For Japanese agricultural policy in Java see De Jong, *Collapse of a Colonial Society,* 227–82; and Sato Shigeru, *War, Nationalism and Peasants: Java under the Japanese Occupation, 1942-1945* (New York, 1994), 115–53.

97.   Anderson, *Java*, 87.

98.   Allen, *End of the War,* 94.

99.   Smail, *Bandung,* 71.

100.   Ibid., 71.

101.   See Abu Hanifah, *Tales of a Revolution* (Sydney, 1972), 152 n. 2.

102.   Author's interview with Aoki Masafumi.

103.   Lt. Col. F. H. G. Eggleton, 'A Report on RAPWI in Java', 2. WO 203/5960.

104.   Aldrich, *Intelligence and the War against Japan*, 143–4.

105.   Woodburn Kirby, *Surrender of Japan*, 21 n. 2. *See also* Neville Wylie, *The Politics and Strategy of Clandestine War: Special Operation Executive, 1940-1946* (Oxford: 2006), 1.

106.   Ibid., 243.

107.   Ibid., 246.

108.   Lt. Col. F. H. G. Eggleton, 'A Report on RAPWI in Java', 2. WO 203/5960.

109.   ALFSEA, Maj. A. G. Greenhalgh, 'Java situation report', 14 Sept. 1946. WO 203/5960.

110.   The late Dr D. H. K Soltau's papers (hereafter 'Soltau Memoir') comprising a largely completed memoir, copies of British files and two albums of his own contemporary photographs, have been donated to NIOD. Soltau Memoir, 18-19.

111.   Ibid., 30. Curiously in van der Post's Java memoir he makes no reference to Dr Soltau, only to a 'four-man', not five-man team: Greenhalgh, 'van Till' and 'two signallers'. This omission is odd, considering the poor state of Allied PW health, which was the reason for Soltau's presence, and the fact that Greenhalgh, Soltau, and van der Post all had rooms at the Hotel des Indes. See Laurence van der Post, *The Admiral's Baby* (London, 1996), 21.

112.   Ibid., 33-34.

113.   Ibid., 34.

2

RELUCTANT PEACEKEEPERS
JAPANESE UNDER BRITISH COMMAND

'Respected Sir', the interpreter hissed...,'Captain Yamagishi respectfully asks your permission to fire his mortars'.
—Communication to Captain J. P. Cross, 1/1 Gurkha Rifles,
French Indo-China, November 1945[1]

As the Japanese struggled to maintain a discredited security *status quo* on behalf of the returning colonial powers, nations were born. Declarations of independence, grudging Japanese indifference to Allied aims and rampant, burgeoning nationalism had set the stage for a complex diplomatic and bloody military entanglement for Britain in Southeast Asia.

A visible symbol of British authority appeared off Jakarta on 12 September 1945 in the form of HMS *Cumberland*. On board was Admiral Sir William Patterson, commander of 5 Cruiser Squadron. Only after his arrival did SEAC start to receive reports that suggested Java was on the brink of chaos. Euphoria over Japan's surrender was therefore relatively brief. New obligations, assumptions and some tragic reverses were to create confusion over policy and capability and doubts over the legitimacy of Britain's role in Southeast Asia.

Prompted by the urgency of signals from *Cumberland*, troops were rushed to Java. A small, advance party from 23rd Indian Division flew in on 25 September but it was not until 29 September that the first infantry, 120 soldiers of 1st Battalion Seaforth Highlanders, arrived by sea from Malaya. The scant numbers of troops reveal British difficulties. A solution, however, was to hand. Brigadier R. C. M. King, commander of the Seaforths, carried secret orders stating, 'if it is necessary to use the help of the Japs to preserve law and order, you will do so.'[2]

Reasons for the five-week delay in sending troops to Java—which the Dutch war-time prime minister, Professor P. S. Gerbrandy regarded as a culpable failure on the part of Mountbatten in particular—were several.[3] For months, British reoccupation priorities, themselves causing friction with the United States, had been Malaya, Singapore and, particularly, Hong Kong (which was not in fact within SEAC). A British naval squadron was rushed to Hong Kong to 'fly the flag' to pre-empt nationalist Chinese forces moving into the British territory. Reports of a nationalist revolution in the Netherlands East Indies (now Indonesia) came as a surprise to the British—and to the Dutch—since the minimal intelligence they supplied to SEAC had significantly downplayed nationalist sentiment.[4] Dutch reports on Sukarno (which ignored his pre-war internal exile for sedition) had regularly portrayed Sukarno as an unpopular and unelected Japanese stooge. This line was maintained after the surrender:

> The Netherlands Government desire to stress the fact that the so-called Soekarno-government in Java is by no means the outcome of a spontaneous and widespread popular movement but, as clearly proved... a Japanese puppet-Government of the Quisling type... and outspokenly totalitarian in character.[5]

As diplomacy and domestic politics returned to centre stage with the peace, these priorities clashed. Britain's new Labour Government was immediately under immense pressure from the Dutch to assist a loyal ally regain control of lost territories, just as it was from France over Indo-China. (Independence was declared in both Indonesia and Vietnam just days after the Japanese surrender.) London's instinct was to preserve the colonial order and security in Southeast Asia. Yet this sudden political uncertainty clashed with a public clamour in Britain (and other countries) for servicemen to be brought home quickly (as promised) from the Far East. At the same time, Mountbatten's own liberal, anti-colonial leanings, particularly over his determination to involve Burmese nationalists in the post-war settlement, caused disquiet both at home and to his political advisors in SEAC.[6]

As ministry and interdepartmental arguments over post-war obligations and expectations developed, the situation in Java deteriorated. Anglo-Dutch relations, so close during the campaign in Europe, were already starting to sour following the slow British military build up, and frank British reassessments of political realities in Java. In quick succession Mountbatten vetoed a draft Dutch proclamation declaring the Republic illegal and then countermanded a Dutch order that the Indonesians obeyed neither the Japanese nor their own republicans. Dutch displeasure and disquiet was

5. British and Japanese troops in Hong Kong in late August 1945. (AC)

open.[7] These decisions were strongly influenced by Admiral Patterson's signals from Java and also by a report from Lady Edwina Mountbatten, who had visited APWI in Java and Sumatra, and talked with General Maisey and van der Post. As a result, Mountbatten 'reversed all the intelligence', which until then had been largely supplied by the Dutch.[8]

Even with Mountbatten's belated recognition of the problem, SEAC faced huge logistical difficulties. Men, equipment and ships were in short supply. Security duties in Burma, Malaya and Hong Kong as well as an increasingly restive situation in India required thousands of troops. Ships that had offloaded for Operation Zipper in Malaya had already been assigned new cargoes and destinations. After the Zipper foul-up, SEAC was no doubt reluctant to rush into another risky beach landing, especially one that might be opposed by Indonesians. Beyond SEAC the situation was viewed with even more caution. From London's perspective, Java threatened to become 'another Greece'. (Anglo–American relations and Britain's reputation had suffered following Britain's use of Indian troops against Greek Communists. British commanders in Athens had also reported resistance among their troops to the hard-line approach being taken against Greek civilians, including the destruction of property.)[9] British resources were seriously stretched. The only division available to Mountbatten, unless he were to divert British, ie, UK troops, from the British Commonwealth Occupation Force in Japan, was 23 Indian Division.[10] (Since the Indian Mutiny in 1858, each Indian Army division had always contained one British-raised battalion.) This choice was problematical because India's Congress Party fundamentally objected to the use of Indians to suppress anti-colonial movements, as indeed did the Viceroy, Lord Wavell, who predicted mass protests.[11] A similar reliance on Indian troops also carried risks for SEAC in Rangoon where political tensions over the incorporation of Aung San's Patriotic Burmese Forces into a new Burmese army were causing concern. Highly secret restrictions on the emergency deployment of Indians were, however, so strict that British security policy in Burma was, according to one account, 'founded on bluff'.[12]

Whether the Japanese were fully aware of British difficulties in Java and elsewhere is not clear. No doubt the few visible troops and the extensive demands made for men, equipment, supplies and facilities revealed the paucity of British manpower and stocks of all kinds. A list of requirements presented to the Japanese in Java included 'eight English-speaking staff officers, 17 American cars, 35 lorries, 6 ambulances, two goods trains, fuel, maps, batteries and Japanese-supervised Indonesian labour'.[13]

Operation Python also started to 'squeeze'. This programme, brought forward by the new British Government, allowed men who had served 40 months in SEAC to qualify automatically for immediate repatriation. Python left gaping holes in administrative and operational ranks as the most experienced and acclimatised men left. Replacements, largely inexperienced and without combat experience, often came directly from Britain. In addition, the sudden end of Lend-Lease whereby US military equipment was supplied to Britain free of charge meant that much requested equipment never arrived.[14] With unexpected security commitments in Indonesia and Vietnam, where a nationalist government had also taken control, as well as in Laos and Cambodia, the British were under considerable pressure. It is no exaggeration to state that they were completely unprepared and under-equipped for the tasks ahead.

On 15 September, aboard HMS *Cumberland*, Major General Yamamoto, Major General Nishimura and Admiral Maeda, representing Admiral

Shibata Yaichiro (recently returned to Surabaya after the main surrender ceremony in Singapore), discussed local surrender terms with Admiral Patterson (see photograph). Here some of the proposals first broached by the Japanese at Rangoon but subsequently ignored or rejected were raised

6. (L to R) Maj Gen Nishimura, Maj Gen Yamamoto and RAdm Maeda aboard HMS *Cumberland* off Batavia, Java, on 16 Sept. 1945. (NARA)

once again in a report written in English. The Japanese offered the Allies 'sincere congratulations' on their 'brilliant victory' and pledged to carry out Allied instructions 'in all sincerity and fairness'. They also assured the Allies that they were 'doing our best to instruct our subordinates and the people concerned'. The report included statements such as 'Japan "sanctioned" the desire for independence of the East Indies on Sept. 7 last year', and an acknowledgement that they were 'still responsible for the military administration *until the arrival* of the Allied Forces'. It concluded with an admission that supplies to 'prisoners and internees were somewhat inadequate...[but are] better now and satisfactory...kindly acknowledge'.[15]

Such terminology, even allowing for difficulties in translation, reveals the extent of Japanese uneasiness over their new role and their eagerness to divest themselves of all responsibility at the earliest opportunity. They stressed that, 'Arms, accounting, medical, legal, veterinary... railroad, installations, marine, information and broadcasting, POWs/civilian internees' were all prepared and 'ready for handover'. But the question of weapons and security caused them the most concern:

> Disarmament will be carried out...[before] the entry of Allied forces in order to prevent clashes or incidents... all weapons will be duly collected and surrendered... Only squads necessary for maintaining law and order and necessary personnel...supplied only with rifles or pistols with ammunition limited to five bullets....[16]

Some weeks later, following fighting and disorder in central and east Java, the Japanese were to respond to criticism of their breach of the surrender terms by claiming Allied restrictions on arms and ammunition had limited their room for manoeuvre. (No such order limiting arms and ammunition for Japanese in Java has yet been found.) Other requests were: for 'Japanese bank deposits and savings accounts [to] remain intact' and for assistance in 'sending remittances to Japan'; to allow private mail to Japan, Korea, Formosa and Manchuria 'for those with families there'; for private property owned by Japanese civilians 'be respected, including factories unless previously the property of Allied nations'; for a camp shop; to establish a hospital; to employ native personnel; to maintain the Japanese military court structure; and to produce a Japanese newspaper 'to keep [informed of] world affairs'. (The reference to bank accounts and 'remittances' is somewhat rich as the Japanese had stolen jewellery and precious metal heirlooms from the Javanese through a state-run compulsory pawning system.)[17]

Clearly the Japanese had set considerable store in their assumption that their 'peace and order' obligations would cease upon the arrival of any Allied force. They were keen to not only avoid responsibility for internal security but also remove themselves physically from the cities and towns where disturbances were likely to occur. The haste with which they were preparing for their own internment, for example, in reducing available forces and constructing and provisioning camps, reveals just how little enthusiasm they had for any duties imposed on them by the Allies. Unsurprisingly, the British were unimpressed by the Japanese approaches. After the discussion, Patterson reported to Mountbatten: 'Have just had Yamamoto on board to rub in his responsibilities which he assured us he fully realizes. Japanese control is undoubtedly deteriorating and new Indonesian nationalist flag is appearing in increasing numbers. Extremists continuing old Japanese-created organisations'.[18]

Concerns remained over controls over Japanese weapons. Mountbatten made it plain soon after the surrender that Japanese who surrendered to to British forces without their weapons would forfeit their right to repatriation. British orders (not authorised at Potsdam) over retention of

7. (Front R) VAdm Shibata and (front L) Lt Gen Nagano in Java, in Apr. 1945. (IJA/IJN)

Japanese weapons were circulated throughout Java, Sumatra and elsewhere to all JSP commands.

Among the final orders given to 16 IJA was an instruction not to open fire on civilian/nationalist groups whatever the provocation. This reluctance to antagonise nationalists yet obey orders from the British was to present some JSP with, quite literally, life or death choices. On 19 September came the first major test of Japanese compliance with Allied authority.[19] A rally to be attended by thousands of flag- and spear-carrying nationalists was planned to take place in Jakarta's Gambir Square to hear Sukarno. British orders obliged the Japanese to prohibit political gatherings, prevent display of the republican flag and seize weapons, using force if necessary. (On 16 September, Japanese troops had barely succeeded in dispersing unarmed crowds by firing over their heads.) Initially, the Japanese seemed intent on enforcing these orders, since three infantry companies and one light-armoured car company from west Java had been summoned to reinforce the Jakarta *kenpei* garrison. Suspect Indonesian police had also been relieved from duty. In addition, new orders from 16 Army HQ cancelled the move to new barracks and instructed troops to rearm.[20]

Also present in Gambir Square was Colonel Miyamoto Shizuo. The Colonel feared a bloodbath would result in open war between Japanese and Indonesians. In blatant disregard of British instructions he overruled a 'furious' *kenpei* officer and let the angry crowd through the Japanese-manned barriers.[21] Miyamoto then managed to convince Sukarno not to rouse the throng against the Allies and to keep his speech short.[22] British observers admired Miyamoto's nerve: 'Crisis reached… Miyamoto walked through 8,000 crowd… and spoke to Sukarno'.[23] Next day the British reminded Miyamoto that the Japanese were required to maintain order at all costs, with tear gas if necessary.[24] Following this warning the *kenpei* arrested some *pemuda* leaders.[25] British criticism of Japanese wavering brought an equivocal response from General Yamamoto, who pleaded mitigating circumstances. The Japanese accepted responsibility for 'public peace and order' but intended 'to allow the Indonesians [to demonstrate their abilities] in spheres of civil administration…while the Japanese will assist them from behind giving appropriate advice'.[26]

In Jakarta the British certainly had their hands full but they also faced trouble elsewhere on Java. On 9 October they informed Lt General Nagano that he was in breach of the surrender terms following the capitulation of his forces and numerous reports of handovers of arms, equipment and installations by Japanese to nationalists. Nagano was ordered to regain control over key areas outside Jakarta, by force if necessary.[27] Again the Japanese stalled and British control began to slip. In Jakarta frequent shootings, murders of British soldiers, looting, and anti-Chinese unrest led to the imposition of martial law within the (quite limited) British zone of control on 13 October.[28]

Beyond Jakarta and Bandung, British presence and influence was at best fleeting and negligible. A combination of revolutionary chaos, brigands and mobs made movement dangerous for outsiders, even in large groups. On 19 October, for example, 86 Japanese, heading from Jakarta to internment near Bandung (a city 90 miles south of Jakarta), were taken from a train and massacred at Bekasi.[29] As the British deployment increased, attempts were made to establish bases at three key locations: Bandung, Semarang (a port city on the northern coast of central Java) and Surabaya (a major east coast port). The differing conditions they found in each place were largely attributable to the Japanese, whose behaviour resulted in dramatic regional differences in the development of the revolution on Java. By the end of

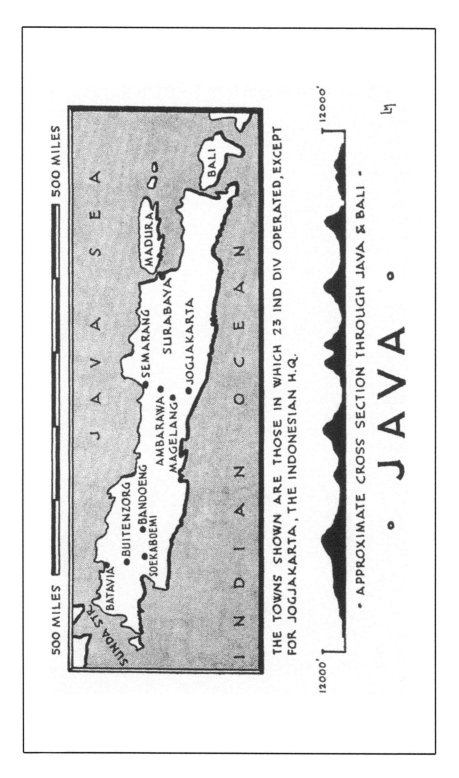

THE TOWNS SHOWN ARE THOSE IN WHICH 23 IND DIV OPERATED, EXCEPT FOR JOGJAKARTA, THE INDONESIAN H.Q.

• APPROXIMATE CROSS SECTION THROUGH JAVA & BALI •

JAVA

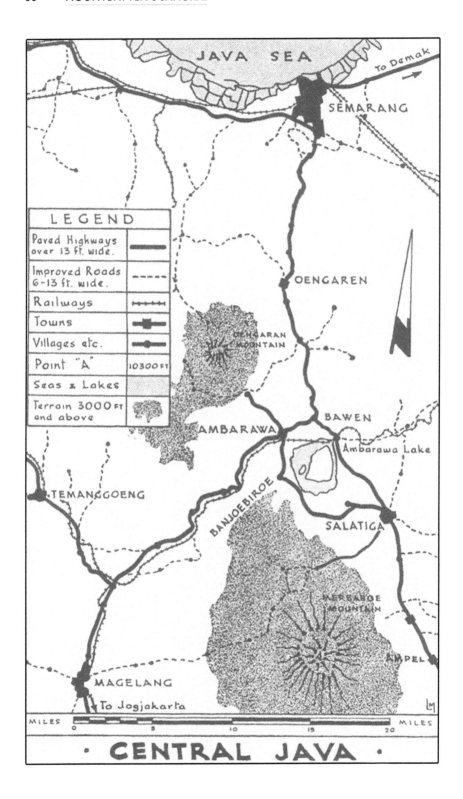

October, 'Bandung was an island of occupied tranquillity, central Java an armed and anxious fortress, and Surabaya a sea of fire'.[30]

JAPANESE VACILLATION IN BANDUNG

In 1945 Bandung was Indonesia's third-largest city with a population of about 440,000. Here, Japanese actions were contradictory. In the early days of the revolution they failed to prevent the seizure of administrative buildings by *pemuda* and *Badan Keamanan Rakjat* (BKR). Looting, robbing of Japanese guards and murder of Japanese civilians was commonplace. In several instances Japanese troops handed over ammunition dumps or proved unwilling to resist takeovers. On the other hand, recently released Dutch internees and former Dutch PW, almost all of whom were hostile to the new republic, were forming vigilante groups and seeking weapons for themselves. In the city itself they restricted the flying of the republican flag to non-governmental buildings until about 15 September.[31] (Perhaps coincidentally this was the day HMS *Cumberland* arrived off Jakarta.) On 18 September, however, Japanese troops forcibly removed flags, perhaps as a result of Mountbatten's instructions to Patterson vis-à-vis recognition of the Republic. In truth, Bandung was a lawless place, the setting for 'a small private war'. After 25 September, when an increasingly bold Sukarno declared all Indonesian civil servants to be servants of the Republic, anti-Japanese feeling among Indonesians mushroomed. Attacks spread to Japanese-owned businesses, plantations and estates, warehouses, private cars, houses and, crucially, military installations. Where Japanese units resisted there was bloodshed, but others just gave in or agreed to negotiated local surrenders.[32]

In early October negotiations between the commander of Japanese 27 Brigade in Bandung, Major General Mabuchi Itsuo, and Puradiredja, the new *Komite Nasional Indonesia* (Central Indonesian National Committee/KNI)-appointed Resident (Governor), led to a secret agreement witnessed by local BKR, KNI and police representatives. This allowed for the flying of the Indonesian flag over armouries and ammunition dumps. Installations were to be protected by joint patrols of 'conspicuous' BKR and 'inconspicuous' Japanese.[33] There is no evidence that physical arms handovers took place..[34] I The arrangement also secured from local leaders some initial co-operation with General Mabuchi, who was probably playing for time until Allied troops arrived. These leaders had their own serious concerns about an armed *pemuda* reign of terror, and thus went along with a KNI-Japanese deal that gave 'visible control' to nationalists.[35] It is doubtful that this was done lightly, for the Japanese were well aware of their unpopularity and vulnerability if they fully disarmed. Such ruses allowed the Japanese to dodge Allied blame for weapons losses that occurred all over Java. There is no record of Mabuchi agreeing to disarm or give up weapons.

Bandung's *pemuda,* however, were not mollified and they forced market traders to boycott Dutch customers. *Pemuda* and well-armed Indonesian Special Police also seized a Japanese-controlled arms factory. The nationalists became increasingly bold. On 9 October Andir airfield was over-run without resistance, and elsewhere three Japanese infantry platoons were disarmed, cowed into surrender by large crowds. (Even Mabuchi's car was 'requisitioned' by revolutionaries.) The next day witnessed a dramatic change. In the morning a hostile crowd attacked the *kenpeitai* HQ. In what seemed a stalemate, the republican leaders were invited in for negotiations. Once inside, however, they were arrested and 'encouraged' to persuade the crowd to disperse, which it did.[36] In the afternoon Japanese troops swept through Bandung, arresting BKR officers, seizing the KNI HQ and key buildings, setting up armed checkpoints and confiscating weapons from the public. Senior BKR officers were then given an armoured 'escort' through the streets while they called on their fellow citizens to halt attacks on the Japanese. The fighting stopped. Within 24 hours the balance of power in Bandung had been reversed by what were relatively small numbers of Japanese troops. Western journalists present reported on operations involving Gurkhas and Japanese tanks, describing the events as 'not the first time our late enemies have proved useful allies'.[37]

Mabuchi's real motives remain unknown. He is on record as saying 'abhorrence of breaching his international loyalty' was behind his actions. (According to the General, he felt as though he were 'balancing on the edge of a sword' for the entire period.)[38] One possibility is that the local British commander, Major Gray, pressed him to act since the boycott directly affected RAPWI security.[39] British authorities were demanding firm action against nationalists and such orders would have eventually reached Mabuchi via the Japanese chain of command.[40] Gray, although with strictly limited legal powers and with no operational military authority, would nonetheless have been able to influence Mabuchi, even exerting 'considerable moral force' over both Japanese and republicans. British orders (possibly from Gray) for firm action against nationalists in order to safeguard civilians are reported to have reached Mabuchi via the Japanese command chain. It is likely that a more simple argument would have been sufficient pressure on the Japanese to act, ie, that as agents of the Allies and therefore bearing responsibility for maintaining order they had to break the boycott.[41] Recent research into Indonesian and Japanese sources suggest that Mabuchi attacked because *pemuda* groups reneged on an agreement reached between the Japanese and the nationalists.[42]

8. Maj Gen Mabuchi Itsuo. (MI)

On 16 October several hundred British, Indian and Gurkha troops under Brigadier General N. MacDonald 'occupied' the northern part of Bandung, reducing pressure on the Japanese. Some British observers were convinced that the ease with which the Japanese had regained control suggested that they need not have lost it in the first place.[43] Bandung was then 'quiet' for some weeks. (So quiet in fact that the Surabaya *pemuda* sent a gift of lipstick as an insult to their Bandung 'sisters'.[44]) It seems the lull was due not to combined British and Japanese military strength but because the shock reassertion of rigid Japanese control had caught the Indonesians off balance.[45] From November onwards north Bandung was effectively besieged, with

Japanese troops manning perimeter lines and observation posts as part of a combined defensive operation until repatriation immediately prior to the British withdrawal from Bandung.

THE BATTLE FOR SEMARANG

In central Java the relationship between nationalists and the Japanese military contrasted sharply with that in Bandung. General Nakamura Junji, commander of the Central Defence Force and based in the large garrison town of Magelang, was openly sympathetic to the nationalist cause, even overruling one local commander who was prepared to fight to keep weapons.[46] Despite personal protests from the commander of 5 RAPWI Contact Team, Wing Commander Thomas S. Tull, Nakamura began to authorise the surrender of quite large amounts of arms and ammunition.[47] In negotiations with the Japanese, nationalists often stressed—the threat of force aside—a combination of 'Asian solidarity', Japan's 'sacred'-yet-broken promise over independence and a 'my enemy's enemy is my friend' argument. Abu Hanifah, a republican commander in west Java, used this last pitch when he convinced a Japanese colonel to abandon a garrison and its entire cache of weapons. He recalls the colonel's cheerful farewell as, 'Give them Hell for me, too'.[48]

First-hand accounts giving a British perspective of the situation in central Java have until fairly recently been largely limited to summaries and official reports by Tull and Tull's own unpublished memoir.[49] Tull, however, was for the most part working out of Magelang and facing problems of his own, so he was out of touch with the two-man RAPWI detachment in Semarang. Two Semarang-specific memoirs, however, have rectified this shortfall. The first, by Major John Hudson, MBE (91 Indian Field Coy, Royal Bombay Sappers and Miners), recounts the bravery and ingenuity of a platoon of Royal Bombay Sappers and Miners in restoring and defending Semarang's power and water supplies.[50] Hudson, who after fighting alongside the Japanese at Semarang, 'beagn to build a new picture of our old enemy', describes Major Kido Shinichiro as a 'fine officer'. He would 'never forget their hordes sweeping over the Imphal heights, nor their atrocities, but...grew to respect them.[51] On a graver note, Hudson had 'no doubts' over the fate of 'would-be assassins' handed over by the British into the custody of the Semarang *kenpei* (see below).[52] The second memoir is the already cited account by David Soltau, which reveals the close co-operation that existed, initially between the RAPWI Semarang team, headed by Captain Crawford ('Tam') Wishart, and later with Brigadier Richard Bethell DSO, the senior British commander in Central Java, and the Kido *Butai* (battalion). Soltau's account reveals that RAPWI Semarang's office was twice ransacked and all its files destroyed by rioters.

9. *Kenpeitai* unit, 16 IJA, Semarang, c. 1944. (AM)

It is therefore an extremely valuable, even unique, additional resource that sheds some light on the friction between Wishart and Tull over command responsibilities and priorities.[53]

In late September 1945 Semarang was largely under *pemuda* or BKR control with most administrative and public works installations in nationalist hands. The local garrisons had surrendered some arms but not without casualties. On one occasion seven *kenpei* patrolling at a tea estate were shot for refusing to give up their weapons.[54] By 6 October, General Nakamura had also 'advised' his junior commanders in Surakata and Yogjakarta to obey Indonesian demands.[55] Wing Commander Tull was not impressed. In his opinion the 1,000 infantry had no need to surrender arms and Nakamura was complicit in the arrangement.[56] In both towns, *kenpeitai* units—under direct orders from Jakarta—resisted. Their HQs were the last to fall to the nationalists. In Yogjakarta, *kenpei*, assisted by the Kido *Butai* from Semarang, fought briefly with BKR forces, killing 18 and wounding over 40. On 7 October, however, the *kenpei* garrison surrendered.[57] In contrast, Kido, who was in direct contact with Wishart at RAPWI Semarang, refused Nakamura's order and returned to his HQ at Djatingaleh in south Semarang.[58]

Major Kido, an artillery officer who had served in China, and his unit have attracted some comment in the years since the fighting in Java. Kido *Butai* was a Special Infantry Battalion and military training school.[59] It did not participate in normal garrison duties on Java and acted as a semi-independent and self-sufficient unit with its own well-stocked own armoury. Some sources have suggested incorrectly that it was an elite unit or armoured corps. (The error may stem from the fact that phonetically *kido butai* also translates as 'strike force'.)

Captain Soltau recalls the Japanese controlling key positions in central Java until early October, then gradually giving way to Indonesian demands. RAPWI Semarang, for example, had secured vital food and medicinal supplies for internee camps from Japanese stocks but as days passed nationalists steadily seized warehouses, without resistance from the Japanese.[60] As news spread of Mabuchi's 'coup' in Bandung and the arrival there of British forces, tension in Semarang increased. Disorder spread and RAPWI work was frequently impeded by numerous *pemuda* roadblocks and inspections. Appeals to the nationalist-appointed governor, Wongsonegoro, proved useless. Soltau describes Kido Butai and the *kenpei* units remaining 'conscious of their duty', guarding camps, hospitals and RAPWI staff. Soltau is critical, however, of the low-profile Japanese approach and infrequent patrols in force.[61]

Nationalist suspicion increased further after Kido Butai began providing armed escorts for convoys of released internees travelling between Magelang and Semarang. On 10 October armed rioters seized 60,000 rounds of machine-gun ammunition from storerooms at the airfield. Two days later Kido Butai's own barracks was surrounded by a mob demanding access to its armoury. Kido refused, then negotiated for four hours at General Nakamura's Magelang HQ with Wongsonegoro and nationalist leaders. During the meeting a signal came from General Nagano stating that no arms or ammunition were to be handed over whatsoever, and that force was to be used if necessary. The meeting ended with Kido feeling 'vindicated'.[62] Several Indonesian-Japanese clashes occurred in and around Semarang on 12 and 13 October.

Following these incidents, *pemuda* gangs retaliated by taking hundreds of Japanese and Dutch hostage, holding many in Bulu (Boeloe) prison.[63]

British officers were not inviolate. Soltau was himself seized with a group of Dutch civilians on 14 October and also taken to Bulu. After hours of arguing that he was the 'personal representative of Lord Mountbatten' in Java and on a purely humanitarian mission he, alone, was released.[64]

10. Maj Kido Shinichiro and Capt. J. Tomlinson in Semarang, Java, in late Oct. 1945. (MS)

Kido was extremely worried about the disorder, imprisonment of RAPWI officers and rumours of violence against civilian Japanese. The internee camps in and around Semarang were also under threat. That night, though considerably outnumbered, Kido Butai swept through Semarang, forcing a retreat, clearing barricades and releasing many captives.

Captain Wishart asserted that Kido 'had taken the only possible course in trying to restore order'. Over the next days Wishart and Soltau had several meetings with Kido, who had lost 20 men, 'to discuss attacks to liberate prisons and restore communications with the camps'. In the immediate aftermath, Soltau and Dutch nurses helped treat Kido Butai's wounded.[65]

On 16 October governor Wongsonegoro proposed a ceasefire. To spread the word the Japanese drove him around the town in an army truck. Fighting continued, however. Kido then learned that hostages at Bulu prison were in grave peril. A *kenpei*-led assault rescued the grateful Dutch but too late to save 130 Japanese civilians who had been murdered in the crammed cells. Soltau describes the scene: 'Some were hung…from the ceiling [and] used for bayonet practice…. Naked bodies [were] lying as they had died, piled high. The floors…were deep in blood, and in several instances the dying men had scrawled their names on the walls in their own blood'.[66] One Dutchman saved by his former captors described the moment of his salvation:

> 'Finally the great moment came when the Semarang *kenpeitai*…stormed the prison and killed the last group of guards, including the *pemuda* [leader] who was hacked to pieces. We cheered and cheered the incoming Japanese…the most brutal unit in Java, now our liberators. I must say it was an incredible experience.[67]

After leaving the prison the *pemuda* mob had continued its murderous rampage. Japanese estimates were that at least 250 of their countrymen and women were dead.[68] (Corpses were found impaled on railings or staked over ant hills in the city's park and ornamental gardens.[69]) Kido Butai reacted with rage, taking no prisoners in the five-day battle that followed.[70] According to Tull (who was not present), 'truckloads' of Indonesians were driven away and not seen again. He estimated Indonesian deaths at 2,000 as well as 500 Japanese dead, 130 of whom were Kido Butai.[71]

By 18 October, Kido reported, 'the enemy's fighting spirit was observed to be weakening'.[72] On the fifth day, completely unaware of any fighting in the city, a Gurkha battalion disembarked at Semarang harbour and headed into the town. Mistaking them at distance for nationalist reinforcements, the Japanese opened fire. In the confusion four Japanese and two Gurkhas were killed before a ceasefire was reached. Kido offered 'profuse apologies'.[73] After handing over the city to the appreciative Gurkhas—they had been saved an inevitably costly street-by-street battle—Kido Butai was disarmed of heavy weapons and armoured cars but not small arms. Soltau did not stint in his praise for Kido:

> Throughout this battle…the Japanese troops were led most efficiently by Major Kido, who co-operated with us in every

possible way to safeguard the thousands of internees in the camps and hospitals. We…owed our safety entirely to [their] efficiency and timely intervention. Major Kido acted entirely on his own initiative, without reference to his superiors who had already handed over all their arms to the Indonesians.[74]

On 25 October General Nakamura and his aide-de-camp were arrested for breaching the terms of the surrender and taken by ship to Jakarta.[75] In the following days *kenpeitai* units and Kido Butai assisted the British in the relief of Magelang and Ambarawa, with a Major Kato receiving a commendation from Wing Commander Tull for the defence of Ambarawa camp.[76] Brigadier Bethell, had no compunction in using Kido Butai to maintain control when necessary. After the British disaster at Surabaya (see below) *pemuda* in Semarang called for a general rising against the British. Bethell, ever short of men, drafted in the Japanese once again: 'I rearmed our Jap prisoners, 100 of them, and sent them out with a troop of mortars, all under a British officer. They went through the locals like a dose of salts. The locals are terrified of them, knowing the form'.[77]

On 3 November 1945 Bethell went with Sukarno, the head of the new Indonesian republic, 'in a formal procession' for a meeting with nationalists at the British HQ at Magelang. The *pemuda* were threatening but Bethell, furious over the murder of Brigadier A. W. S. Mallaby in Surabaya (see below) refused to give way. 'Sukarno told them all to behave', Bethell wrote about it at the time in a letter home, '[and] they agreed like lambs. It really was the most Gilbertian show, sitting in this room with all these thugs and their guards, while tucked away I had about three English soldiers who were going to shoot the lot had they played up'.

As the British 5 Indian Division began its reprisal assault on Surabaya, tension in and around Semarang increased. Bethell remained confident, writing on 5 November:

> I have tanks here and plenty of troops, so if they do start their tricks I shall go through the place and put them all to the sword – and they know it. What they are more terrified of than anything is that I shall use the Japs. In our last little party the Japs got held up at a roadblock, where they proceeded to despatch 50 with the bayonet.[78]

Bethell's appreciation of Japanese assistance is clear. It appears the feeling was mutual. When in mid-December he left Java and his 'fine Japanese',

Kido gave a speech saying they had been proud to serve under him and would do their duty by their next commander. Kido then presented him with a 'lovely, short samurai sword' over 500 years old. Bethell promised that it would hang in an honoured position in his home.[79]

MACHINATIONS AT SURABAYA

Each year on 10 November the citizens of Surabaya, Java's second largest city, celebrate *Hari Phalawan* or 'Day of Heroes'. This festival commemorates the anniversary of the start of the British naval and air assault and the subsequent three-week, street-by-street defence of the port city against the forces of the British 5 Indian Division. This, however, was really the second battle of Surabaya. In the first, which lasted from 28 to 30 October, and which precipitated the second, the ill-prepared and unsuspecting 49 Indian Brigade faced the full fury of the Indonesian revolution. The Brigade suffered almost 430 casualties in three days, including the loss of its commander, Brigadier A. W. S. Mallaby. Dozens of internee women and children travelling in convoys to ships for Jakarta were also murdered. Only an eleventh-hour truce negotiated by Sukarno and Dr Mohammad Hatta saved 49 Brigade from total annihilation.[80] The truce allowed the troops to withdraw unmolested prior to evacuation. It was in fact the first British military defeat since the end of the Second World War.[81] In contrast with events in central Java, Japanese forces took no part in either of the battles. Long before the arrival of the British, local nationalists had disarmed and interned the 10,000-strong East Java Defence Force. Even so, the question of Japanese responsibility for the subsequent deaths and disorder deserves consideration in any evaluation of Japanese actions in post-war Java. These questions include possible charges of negligence, dereliction of duty or even duplicity.

Surabaya was the main colonial administrative centre for east Java, a key port and the main naval base for the Dutch Navy in the Indies. A quick return to and control of the city were therefore priorities for Netherlands Indies Civil Administration (NICA) officials who had arrived in Jakarta. Surabaya's regional and economic importance and the presence within it of a large number of Japanese army and navy personnel who were yet to surrender formally also made it the logical choice for a British landing. These facts were not lost on the nationalist leadership in Surabaya, which was therefore expecting the British. Unlike Jakarta, Surabaya was cosmopolitan, sophisticated and far less class-bound than any other city in Java.[82] In one sense, the old colonial order broke down quicker and more extensively in Surabaya than in Jakarta or Bandung. During the Japanese occupation there had been growing anticipation of significant political change. This was reflected in surging memberships of local nationalist youth organisations

11. Troops of Kido *Butai* (at rear) during a truce in Semarang on 16 Oct. 1945. (MS)

and frequent nationalist rallies. Put simply, the declaration of independence had sent the younger generation of Surabaya into 'ferment'.[83]

As elsewhere in Java, the Japanese forces in and around Surabaya initially took care to maintain law and order. Even before confirmation of their surrender was announced, posters had been distributed declaring that the Japanese were still in authority. Undaunted, nationalists advertised an anti-Dutch *and* anti-Japanese rally for 11 September, which the Japanese tried to prevent by placing press advertisements announcing its cancellation.[84] There was, however, no physical opposition from the Japanese and the rally went ahead. Other unopposed rallies followed, increasing nationalist confidence and expectations. Residents of Surabaya embraced the revolutionary 'red and white' lapel decoration *en masse*. To the large numbers of former Dutch internees moving, on the advice of NICA, to the city from camps in central Java, this simple declaration of allegiance to the republic was provocation enough. In general, colonial Dutch residents were openly hostile to nationalist aspirations. They refused to acknowledge any 'Indonesian' authority whatsoever, preferring instead to approach the Japanese administration in Surabaya to secure food and facilities.

On 16 September the small east Java RAPWI team arrived in Surabaya (by parachute) and set up its HQ in the Yamato (previously Oranje) Hotel in the city centre. They were guarded by Japanese troops. All-Dutch NICA teams then came to work alongside the RAPWI personnel. Consequently the Yamato Hotel became a focus of nationalist suspicion as day-by-day pre-war colonial infrastructure and institutions were resurrected in Surabaya. Dutch ex-internee numbers continued to swell even though Surabaya was not equipped to meet their needs. There were existing shortages of food and shelter in the city and increasing numbers of homeless internees served to amplify anti-Dutch feeling among residents. Fears grew, particularly among the impatient and easily excitable *pemuda*, that the Dutch were to be restored under Allied and Japanese auspices. Resentment brewed easily between the Dutch and nationalists. Violent incidents over flags, slogans or property, sometimes fatal, became frequent. RAPWI staff, and thus the British, quickly came to be seen as Dutch in disguise.

Consequently, General Iwabe Shigeyo and Admiral Shibata, the senior Japanese commanders in Surabaya, were well aware that when the British arrived in any force their own troops would be in a very dangerous position. Their solution was to evacuate about 10,000 army and navy personnel, leaving only 500 guards for the Yamato Hotel and placing small units in internee zones and around port facilities. Announcements and public order instructions were posted about the town but there was no contact between the Japanese and nationalist leaders.[85]

On 23 September another small, all-Dutch team led by reserve naval Captain P. J. G. Huyer, a pre-war resident of the city, arrived to inspect the harbour and docks. News of his short visit increased nationalist unease. Huyer returned again five days later. By 27 September, however, BKR, local militias and *pemuda* bands roving the city were removing Japanese notices. Scuffles occurred and some Japanese soldiers were killed. On 29 September, a car carrying a Japanese officer struck a cart in the market area injuring a Javanese family. A mob beat the officer and his chauffeur nearly to death. Hostility at this stage was directed largely against Japanese. Violence continued to flare up and proved unstoppable. On 1 October *pemuda* invaded the airfield and also attacked *kenpei* guarding internees—but not internees themselves—in the suburbs. Further unrest occurred the next day when the *kenpeitai* HQ was besieged. Elsewhere several Japanese liaison and medical staff were killed when the army and navy HQs were surrounded by mobs armed with machine guns, swords and spears. Clearly Surabaya was chaotic and lawless and increasingly dangerous for any isolated Japanese.[86]

What followed has been the subject of considerable commentary over the years.[87] Certain events remain disputed to this day but it is a fact that on 3 October Captain Huyer, contrary to Admiral Patterson's direct order,

12. (L to R) Lt C. Wishart, Sara Paton (British Red Cross), Capt D. Soltau and Capt D. Broadhead outside the Hotel Bellevue, Semarang, Java, on 20 Oct. 1945. (MS)

received the formal Japanese surrender of Surabaya garrisons on behalf of the Allies.[88] Huyer's message to Patterson was brief: 'Personally accepted surrender Admiral and General on behalf of Supreme Allied Commander [Mountbatten] and put both HQs under command with Indonesian police guard'.[89] According to the terms of the Potsdam Agreement, however, only American, British or Australian commanders could take the official surrender of Japanese forces. Indeed, with this in mind, Patterson had given explicit instructions to Huyer saying he should not issue any orders to the Japanese whatsoever, and that if any were necessary he would issue a directive.[90]

Later Huyer and his Dutch superiors claimed this was a 'fake' surrender in order to convince the nationalists mob that the 'Allies' had officially disarmed the Japanese and that consequently the Japanese weapons were therefore Allied property.[91] In reality, however, Allied 'control', lasted just minutes. Once the Japanese had stood down and Shibata and Iwabe had formally surrendered their swords, Indonesian police allowed BKR forces and *pemuda* free access to the fully stocked armouries. Huyer and his team were arrested on the spot and imprisoned. Shibata's and Iwabe's swords were returned to them and Japanese units in the city were interned (or interned themselves). What was not in doubt was that the citizens of Surabaya were left well armed and capable of defending the revolution in East Java.

Whether the Japanese had lost *de facto* control or the nationalists had taken control of the city by the time of their surrender to Huyer has become an issue for historians. Admiral Shibata's detailed account states the impetus for Japanese disarmament came from Huyer, who chose to believe that formal Allied control of Japanese military stocks and weapons would make them inviolate.[92] In his own report, however, Huyer accuses the Japanese of 'full conspiracy with the Indonesians…to help them in their revolt'. He also states that Iwabe excused his capitulation to the mob on the grounds that 'he could not fight as the Supreme Allied Commander had *only allotted him 5 shots per rifle*'.[93] There were, however, 3,000 armed Japanese troops on the outskirts of Surabaya awaiting orders. Indeed, several commanders of Japanese battalions refused to disarm until as late as 10 October.[94] Iwabe, too, apparently asked for confirmation of Huyer's authority to accept his surrender but was pressured into a decision.[95]

Just days later 49 Indian Infantry Brigade arrived in Surabaya unaware of recent developments and dangers and expecting to undertake what should have been a relatively straightforward internee evacuation. Although initially denied permission to land by the nationalist authorities, Brigadier Mallaby brought his men ashore. Once in the city, he split his forces into multiple, small deployments to the various internee camps. These deployments, with men issued with only patrol-level amounts of ammunition, compounded their vulnerability.

Fate also played a hand. An ill-advised and uncoordinated decision by Major General D. C. Hawthorn's (OC 23 Indian Division) HQ in Jakarta to airdrop leaflets over Surabaya demanding immediate Indonesian disarmament enraged the mobs.[96] Caught by surprise amidst a tinderbox, the split and isolated forces of 49 Brigade stood little chance as some 60,000 *pemuda* rose against them, some 20,000 armed with modern Japanese weapons. Mallaby was killed during negotiations for a ceasefire and his command were picked off piecemeal until the Republican national leaders arrived by air to broker an eleventh-hour truce. The hapless 49th evacuated to Semarang, leaving behind 427 dead.[97]

After an ultimatum to surrender Mallaby's killers was ignored, Royal Navy warships and fighter-bombers attacked Surabaya on 10 November

1945. In this 'second' battle 5 Indian Division fought from the harbour through the streets against quite unexpected and tenacious resistance. The city was finally 'taken' only at the end of November. Such was the strength of Indonesian opposition that the British realised that any campaign in Java

13. Former internees with armed JSP escort at Semarang docks on 25 Nov. 1945. (MS)

would be costly both militarily and politically. It was certainly a turning point in the shaping of policy and forced a wholesale reappraisal of the implications of any commitment to restore the Dutch to power in the Indies. Without weapons the BKR militias and *pemuda* groups in Surabaya might well have been as ineffective as those in Bandung. Arguably, had the Japanese retained control of the armouries for just a few more days, those weapons would have been passed to the nominal control of British troops and thus denied to the Indonesians. Whether the few hundred, scattered and lightly armed men of 49 Brigade could have persuaded or even ordered the Japanese to retain control of their weapons, or by their mere presence could have succeeded in intimidating the nationalists into submission remains a question. Since the arrival of the British force (but one seen as Dutch–British) was itself inflammatory, this is unlikely. British instructions from Jakarta to the Japanese to maintain law and order had been specific. There is no doubt that those Japanese commanders responsible for surrendering the armouries bear some responsibility for the carnage that followed their actions. This, of all the incidents of alleged Japanese 'insubordination' in post-surrender Java, had the severest consequences for Allied troops.

Understandably the Surabaya disaster piled further strain on already delicate Anglo-Dutch co-operation. In the interests of maintaining relations, the British Government decided not to pursue the matter of Huyer's responsibility. (Though the British Army view was that Huyer acted with 'lamentable stupidity'.[98]) No charges were laid against Shibata or Iwabe, no doubt for the same reasons as the Japanese might well have been needed in force at a later date. In 1956 the Dutch held a perfunctory parliamentary enquiry (without British involvement) into the incident, concluding that responsibility lay firstly with the British, due to their 'late arrival' in Java, and secondly with the Japanese for giving up without a fight.[99]

Elated by their success at Surabaya, *pemuda* mobs surged west towards the internee camps at Magelang and Ambarawa, where 11,000 women and children were protected by only two Gurkha companies (about 200 men) and 50 Japanese guards. With the British forces outnumbered and surrounded, air strikes and offshore naval bombardment were again required to repel nationalists. At Semarang, Gurkha and Japanese forces quelled another uprising. A Japanese relief column was then sent to Magelang. Here too, Kido Butai was listed in the British order of battle.[100] A column of British, Indian and some Japanese troops in support then moved east to Ambarawa and forced the nationalists to retreat. The internees were evacuated, with Kido Butai guarding sections of the road to Semarang. Kido's unit performed security duties around the city until January 1946. For his dedicated co-operation in Java Major Kido was recommended for (but subsequently denied) the British Distinguished Service Order.[101] (The denial was hardly surprising in the circumstances. It would have been an admission by Britain that it had absorbed defeated enemy forces into its ranks and exposed them to danger, both prohibited by the 1929 PW Convention.)

ARRESTS OF THE JAPANESE COMMANDERS

Official instructions, drawn up in London, to British forces for dealing with surrendered Japanese in SEAC were detailed and precise. Some were symbolic—Japanese officers were not to wear their swords—others reinforced the new order:

> You will, in the case of senior Japanese officers, use their correct titles. You will not shake hands with them. In no case

will British and Japanese officers feed in the same room, nor will drinks be offered at any meeting. Any Japanese come to receive orders or report should be kept at arms length, e.g., with a table between you and them and they should not be asked, or allowed to sit at the same table.[102]

In contrast, American regulations concerning Japanese were far less rigid. In the Pacific Theatre, for example, Japanese officers were permitted to retain their swords until formal surrender ceremonies. Also there were no restrictions on taking refreshments at the same table. Strict observation of the British protocol was insisted upon in Malaya, Singapore Colony, Rangoon and Hong Kong, not least as a propaganda vehicle to remind locals that Western forces had triumphed over Asian military power. Elsewhere it proved impossible. It was quickly apparent to SOE and RAPWI teams in Vietnam, Siam, Cambodia and Indonesia that if Japanese officers were to retain any vestige of authority over their men, the instruction on swords was best ignored. In many cases these regulations did not reach the Contact Teams until long after military co-operation and/or dependency had made them irrelevant or, as John Cross, an SOE officer in Vietnam described them, 'irksome'.[103] Local realities, inevitably, took precedence. Japanese and British officers toasted 'peace' with chilled lager and hoarded pre-war wine in Jakarta, and with Coca-Cola—the 'last two bottles on the island'—in Sumatra.[104]

Even so, *bonhomie* was in short supply. Allied Contact Teams were often totally reliant for their security upon decisions taken by relatively junior Japanese officers—Major Kido in Semarang for example—who held the local balance of power. Tact was at a premium. Many Japanese officers chose to interpret the absence of orders from their superiors about the end of hostilities as requiring them to maintain a hard-line *status quo*, ie, reflecting the tone of the last order received. Draconian Japanese martial law was not repealed in occupied territories. In Laos, for example, French men, women and children were summarily executed for spying as late as 22 August, a full week after the surrender.[105] In Vietnam, about 100 French parachutists were introduced from mid-August to September. Many were rounded up and arrested, including Colonel Jean Cédile, High Commissioner-designate for Cochinchina. They were not treated well, and Cédile himself very nearly shot.[106]

Peace brought no immediate relief for 'political prisoners'. SOE and RAPWI officers had no authority to order any releases. Sentences passed under Japanese law still remained legal and valid. (In Japan a number of political opponents of the military dictatorship also met with summary execution in the days prior to General MacArthur's arrival in Tokyo.) In Java, prisoners included men and women sentenced to 15 years for listening to forbidden radio sets. At Soekamisking prison most of the 39 priority Dutch male political prisoners had been tortured. One British officer (Captain Soltau), however, 'bluffed' his way through repeated *kenpei* objections and had prisoners 'transferred' from their appalling conditions on medical grounds.[107] Equally, Japanese sensitivity over Allied criticism or perceived loss of face sometimes had dramatic consequences. In Sumatra, one British SOE major's heated complaint to a Japanese colonel ended abruptly when the infuriated officer spun away from him, drew his sword and impaled himself.[108]

For some considerable time after the capitulation, suspicion and expectation of ulterior Japanese motives was, understandably, widespread. Ever alert for manifestations of a 'stay behind' agenda, the British and Dutch response tended towards over-reaction. In Java there were reports of sightings of 'Japanese' among nationalist ranks, of Japanese among enemy dead, of artillery or mortar bombardment far too accurate to be anything other than Japanese directed, and British soldiers involved in skirmishes with nationalists hearing orders shouted in Japanese. This confusion is understandable since PETA militia had been issued with Japanese-style uniforms and drilled by Japanese officers and Indonesian NCOs in Japanese. Indeed, use of Japanese terminology in the Indonesian forces continued during the revolution.[109]

For Dutch colonialists, the mere presence of Japanese was deemed a threat to their interests.[110] They were a constant visible reminder to the Indonesians that their masters had been defeated. At the same time somewhat to the chagrin of the released internees and the new colonial officials it looked as though they were dependent on the Japanese for protection. On the other side, dissatisfaction among Japanese commanders over their post-surrender assistance to the British led, not surprisingly, to complaints and requests for their men to be replaced by Allied troops as provided for under the terms promulgated at Potsdam and in SEAC's own post-surrender announcements. They made no secret of their acute discomfort in being placed between British and Indonesians. In February 1946 General Numata stressed in frank terms to Admiral Mountbatten that it was 'very desirable to move promptly all disarmed Japanese forces to Galang…to avoid any misunderstanding or apprehension on the part of the Indonesians that the Allies might or would rearm Japanese soldiers and use them to fight the Allies' war against the Indonesians'.[111]

On occasion British officers deferred to the Japanese despite SEAC edicts that no Japanese could give orders to an Allied officer. For newly commissioned, inexperienced officers amidst a murderous guerrilla campaign, 'military common sense' argued instead for trusting Japanese

14. Brig R. B. W. Bethell, DSO, in Java in late 1945. (HB)

experience gained in China and elsewhere.[112] British-Japanese relations, from staff officers through to platoon level, were by many accounts good and 'workmanlike'. Expediency rather than legal niceties was the order of the day in FIC as well. Japanese forces proved crucial in the battle for Saigon. With the city's defenders short of weapons, Major Philip Malins (OC 20 Indian Division Mule Transport) led a force of 25 Gurkhas, 25 former Dutch PW and 100 Japanese infantry to bring back 1000 rifles, 100 machine guns and ammunition from a Japanese arms dump 11 miles from the city. On its return journey his convoy was heavily and repeatedly ambushed. The Japanese 'took casualties'. Malins, who received the Military Cross for his command of the convoy, had no doubt about his priorities:

When the first attacks by the Annamites started we had only 300 infantry on the ground and used JSP infantry to help defend Saigon and avoid the massacre of French civilians. This may have been contrary to the Geneva Convention requiring that prisoners must not be exposed to danger, but that was secondary to saving the lives of some 20,000 French and others from being killed.[113]

Early suspicions aside, both sides realised that their mutual dependency against a hostile or certainly unhelpful local population required a degree of trust that three months previously would have been considered absurd. Regular joint British-Japanese patrols and shared security operations against nationalist forces cannot but have forged a degree of mutual respect out of mutual dependence. Reliance on the former enemy for law and order gave rise to tensions in the European colonies. The British presence was itself an irritant to Dutch and French governments seeking to regain sovereignty of their territories and recapture the respect of their former subjects. British use of the Japanese forces was a further demonstration of French and Dutch military impotence. Japanese-Dutch relations in Java and Japanese-French relations in Vietnam remained poor. For the Dutch there was a bitter legacy of embarrassment and resentment over their defeat in 1942. This legacy, coupled with anger over the subsequent treatment of Dutch internees and PW negated any chance of early rapprochement.

In addition, the returning Dutch faced a vocal and determined nationalist opposition. They saw Sukarno as the head of a 'Quisling type' government installed by the Japanese so that the Japanese could continue their attack on colonial territories by proxy.[114] SEAC's inability to secure transport to ship Dutch troops based in Australia to Java led the returning NICA administration to re-arm former PW. It was a disastrous decision since the recently liberated men were mentally and physically unfit for duty of any kind. Unstable and bitter, they often responded violently to any sign of nationalist sentiment (such as the wearing of republican colours) among the Indonesian general public. Baiting of JSP units was also frequent. Even British officers in Jakarta found themselves ordered at gunpoint off pavements or had weapons trained on them from vehicles by bands of 'wild-eyed' Dutchmen. Regular Dutch troops also reacted vigorously to anti-Dutch sentiment. There was also direct rejection of British orders by Dutch commanders, particularly over the occupation of pro-nationalist villages.[115] Their behaviour so appalled General Christison, Commander of Allied Land Forces South-East Asia (ALFSEA), that he ordered the rearmed

Dutch PW and the few Dutch troops in Jakarta confined to quarters. Dutch reinforcements for Java were forbidden to land.[116]

In Vietnam, despite a much shorter Japanese interregnum of just six months, anti-Japanese feeling among the French was high. Anti-Viet Minh

15. British, French and Japanese officers plan operations in Saigon, late 1945. (TI0GKRT)

feeling, however, was rampant. French vigilante killings of Vietnamese civilians disgusted General Gracey, Commander of 20 Indian Division. (Equally the French colonial military's attitudes to Indian and Gurkha troops caused considerable friction between British and French officers and which prompted General Gracey to issue a stern rebuke to the French. British and Japanese troops in Saigon found themselves attempting to police a civil war. Gracey, much criticised later for going far beyond his stated orders to avoid involvement in politics, intervened to win Southern Vietnam, or at least hold it, for the French with considerable Japanese help that certainly reduced British casualties.[117]

British enlisted men's opinion of the (largely Vichy) French forces in Saigon was scathing bordering on disgust. Relations between them were not surprisingly poor. British troops witnessed random killing by released internees or former PW of Vietnamese civilians merely on the suspicion that they held nationalist sympathies. 'Anti-French' crimes often resulted in summary execution.[118]In contrast British-Japanese relations in southern

Vietnam were businesslike, even cordial. There is a great deal of evidence that the British were able to hand over control of much of southern Vietnam to French forces in late January 1946 because of extensive use of the Japanese forces, who also kept French civilians outside Saigon safe. British use of the Japanese was deliberate and frequent, and not simply in a 'defensive' role in and around Saigon. Joint British-Japanese patrols were a regular occurrence throughout parts of southern Vietnam.[119]

Notwithstanding remarkable examples of Japanese co-operation in Bandung, Semarang and Saigon, however, it was never taken for granted but there were limits. One Royal Artillery veteran recalled patrolling Jakarta in charge of a Japanese platoon. He found them reliable troops but 'passed' on looking down their rifle barrels at inspection. [120] Others have been more fulsome with praise. William Weightman, then a second lieutenant commanding a rifle platoon in D Coy 2 Durham Light Infantry (DLI), who had had fought the Japanese 'quite literally face to face' in Burma had 'admiration and respect' for their bravery. In December 1945 he found himself fighting alongside the Japanese in Sumatra following a request from the Aceh Land Garrison (1 Bn 4 Imperial Guard Regiment, 30 *kenpei* and 1,000 Special Landing Force troops), under siege by nationalists, for emergency evacuation. In response, D Coy 2 DLI boarded five Japanese 'troopships' (converted merchantmen) at Singapore and, escorted by HMS *Caprice*, sailed to Uleeheue, on the northern tip of Sumatra. The evacuation was contested from start to finish and *Caprice* was obliged to open fire in support of the operation. Weightman described his former foes' conduct during the evacuation, 'professionals in the same game—war', as 'brilliant' He also viewed the IJA's support of the British in Java as vital.[121]

No doubt SOE and RAPWI officers found their situation uneasy and even intimidating. Deliberately unco-operative individual Japanese could have been arrested, their status changed from Surrendered Personnel to PW, and so be removed from the chain of command. There was, however, a finite number of Japanese officers—even fewer of them English-speaking— to draw on in any locale. Dependency therefore required a certain tolerance and care from the British officers assigned to Japanese command and liaison duties. It was certainly not in British interests for minor contretemps to reduce the available Japanese officer pool. As weeks passed and more territory returned to Allied control, dependency on the Japanese reduced. Once they were no longer required to maintain security they were disarmed and British officers could, if necessary, take a firmer line. Some Japanese military assistance, however, continued well into 1946. At Palembang and Pladjoe (on Sumatra) 10,000 JSP guarded the strategically important oil installations owned by Standard Vacuum and Royal Dutch Shell until 1 August 1946.[122]

By retaining the existing Japanese command structure, SEAC's orders, made directly to HQ JEFSR, were transmitted down the chain of command just as if those orders originated from the Japanese HQ itself. This was to SEAC's great advantage as there was an institutionalised anathema within the Japanese military towards the questioning or any instruction from a superior.[123] Consequently the most predictable Anglo-Japanese 'flashpoints', the risk of argument and insubordination lower down the command chain, was reduced. Evidence suggests, in fact, that friction was far higher at higher, staff officer levels of interaction. At various periods during the Allied interregnum in Indonesia, for example, a number of senior Japanese commanders, including generals Nagano, Tanabe, Iwabe, Yamamoto and Nakamura, and admirals Shibata and Maeda were arrested, suspended or questioned over violations of the surrender terms. It is clear that these senior Japanese officers were by no means pliant, rubber-stamping enforcers of British policy. Political realities in Java and Sumatra rendered a passive role impossible. Indeed the continuing authority of senior Japanese commanders was key to the implementation of British control of Japanese forces. In reality this also gave them a certain influence over British security operations.

In Java, General Nagano's obstructive, openly pro-nationalist behaviour towards British representatives resulted in impasse. He was arrested, declared a PW and sent to detention in Singapore. Yet the reliability of his successor, Lt General Yamamoto Moichiro, 16 Army Chief of Staff, also came to be doubted. British officials believed he, too, harboured strong pro-Indonesian sympathies and was fomenting unrest. Sixteenth Army HQ was at Bandung, and some Japanese there were suspected of aiding Indonesians and of firing on British troops. There were also persistent rumours of 16 Army deserters training TKR (the BKR's successor) units and even fighting with them. As acting commander, Yamamoto was considered responsible, and HQ Allied Forces Netherlands East Indies (AFNEI) wanted him removed.[124] Further reports of arms handovers in central Java resulted in Lt General Yamamoto and Lt General Nakamura (area commander at Magelang) being arrested on the orders of Major Hawthorn, who declared that the two officers had:

> ...wilfully and dishonourably neglected the duties which were assigned to you by the Allies at the time of the surrender. You have failed to keep order in Java as I charged you on my arrival. You have unscrupulously handed over your arms and equipment to the disorderly elements in this country,

thereby making it possible for them to inflict losses on the troops under my command.

Hawthorn held them responsible for the 'treachery' of Japanese garrisons that had handed over arms to nationalists who subsequently attacked Allied personnel and civilians. Yamamoto was replaced by Major General Mabuchi.[125] However, Yamamoto and Nakamura faced courts martial at Singapore within the *Japanese* Army military justice system. There was therefore no Allied involvement in the proceedings. They faced charges of complicity in supplying arms to Indonesians after 15 August *after* receiving Allied instructions to the contrary. Arguments for the defence would have been predictable: the fact that PETA units were issued arms as early as January 1944 under Japanese occupation policy, and that some PETA units retained arms. Another initial Allied assumption, that the regional militias were 'last-ditch' or post-surrender creations was also incorrect and easily proven. Both were found not guilty.[126] Further, the impossibility of quantifying a level of 'acceptable resistance' by Japanese troops when facing large numbers of hostile armed assailants demanding weapons must also have undermined the prosecution cases. SEAC accepted the acquittals, as well as a subsequent request from the JEFSR HQ in Saigon that Yamamoto return to Java in order to advise General Numata, despite his known nationalist sympathies. Indeed, the role of the key Japanese figure in the Surabaya 'surrender', Admiral Shibata, escaped British examination, not least because he was in Indonesian nationalist custody from late October 1945 onwards. That Shibata was not available for questioning reflects the tenuous nature of Allied 'control' of east Java.

GENERAL TANABE'S 'UNDERDOGS'

Anglo-Japanese friction was not limited to day-to-day issues. There was also direct and openly provocative criticism by Japanese senior officers of higher British policy in Asia. The most serious incident occurred in late February 1946, when General Tanabe Moritake, commander of 25 Army in Sumatra, circulated the innocuously titled memorandum, 'Information for Reference' among 7 Area Army Command HQs. He referred specifically to the Indonesian political situation. Though Tanabe's assessment was by no means inaccurate and even echoed Foreign Office concerns that British policy could be viewed as blatantly pro-Dutch, it was nevertheless most unwelcome, not least for its identification of resurgent 'pan-Asianism':

In Java the Japanese Forces are going into action against the Indonesians on orders from the Allied Forces (e.g. operations around Semarang and south of Konbel [Gonbel]) and this is being propagandized among the Indonesians in Sumatra. In spite of the fact that the Allied Forces declared that their duty in landing in the East Indies was to disarm and repatriate the Japanese Forces they are utilising the Japanese troops to suppress the Indonesian Nationalist Movement, furthermore, the Japanese troops are the underdogs of the British-Dutch forces and the feelings of the people are once more rising.

In general the Dutch-Indonesian Conference is looked upon optimistically, however, the Young People of Sumatra have already given up hope and are calling for all out fight and are now preparing for war. Besides close connections between Sumatra and Java recently there seems to be close communications with Burma and Malaya as well. As a result the Indonesian leaders know more about these areas than heretofore thought.[127]

SEAC HQ was indignant and embarrassed. General Itagaki Seishiro, commander of 7 Area Army (in Singapore) and Tanabe's immediate superior, was instructed to issue an immediate 'denouncement' of the message. He was also ordered 'to deprive' Tanabe of his command and recall him under close arrest to face a court of inquiry.[128]

Potentially, this incident also had disturbing implications for Anglo-Japanese co-operation far beyond Sumatra. There was an additional and immediate concern over the possibility that Tanabe might go further and incite open dissent among Japanese units throughout the region. At the time, British planners had been considering ways to break the deadlock over JSP still interned in areas under nationalist control in east Java, and therefore 'hostage'. Britain's Potsdam-derived obligations required the removal of all Japanese from Java and Sumatra. Those troops in east Java, numbering around 20,000, had not yet formally surrendered and were therefore a stumbling block in the creation of even a tentative timetable for British withdrawal. Their situation provided a stark illustration of the extent of Britain's authority in Java. Although in possession of some weapons, the Japanese forces were deemed too scattered and insufficiently armed to attempt a breakout on their own, even if rearmed (by means of airdrops) with British equipment. A combined British-Dutch-Japanese military operation was deemed the only practicable military option. Mountbatten even drafted a proclamation for what would have seen a bloody Japanese 'march to the sea'. In this desperate scenario, Japanese in central and east Java were to regroup with their weapons and equipment under Major General Mabuchi and, supported by British armoured columns and Dutch forces, to fight their way either as far as Allied lines at Batavia or Semarang, or to a coastal rendezvous with Royal Navy transports.

> I Lord Louis Mountbatten…have directed the Japanese High Command to order Japanese forces in the interior of Java to march into the Allied Lines and to surrender themselves… to bring with them their weapons, supplies and sick and that furthermore they are to be ordered to destroy all equipment which they are unable to bring with them. The people of Java are required to refrain from impeding the movement of Japanese troops…and to hand over to the Allied Command all Japanese equipment…The people of Java are likewise required to deliver to the Allied Command all Allied prisoners of war and internees….[129]

Preparations for this planned mass escape attempt were, of course, secret. By its nature it was fraught with difficulties. British officials feared that any proposal to rearm the Japanese would require United Nations approval and strong opposition was expected. It was accepted that intervention in Java would weaken Britain's stance in opposing Russian policy in the Balkans and Persia. In addition, the War Office worried whether the morale of the British and Indian troops was sufficiently high to undertake a rescue of the Japanese. Resistance was expected over any operation that would entail Indians fighting fellow Asians and result in high casualties for the sake of assisting the recent enemy.[130]

In truth, the War Office saw little hope in a contested evacuation from east Java. The plan, which would have required the redeployment of British and Indian troops from Batavia and Semarang, envisaged nothing less than the 'subjugation of east Java by Dutch Forces, if necessary with Japanese assistance', while British/Indian troops held a firm base in Surabaya.[131] General Yamamoto and Admiral Hase were also interviewed. They were asked, without being informed of the purpose of the questioning, about the precise locations of JSP camps, armament levels, estimates of local Indonesian strength, the reliability of junior commanders, whether all JSP could receive broadcasts from Batavia, and whether any abandoned stores could be guaranteed to be destroyed. To this end Lt. Colonel Miyamoto, who had been involved earlier in Indonesian-Japanese negotiations (during the Gambir Square standoff), was sent—oblivious to the 'ultimate reason'—on an unsuccessful reconnaissance mission on behalf of the British.

16. Lt Gen Tanabe, Commander, 25 IJA, c. 1943. (IJA)

Miyamoto did not get far as nationalists prevented him from travelling into the interior.[132]

SEAC had informed London in late 1945 that it was in no position to attempt even a temporary British occupation of east Java without massive reinforcement (of perhaps two full divisions). That position had not changed by March 1946. Realisation of the immense risks inherent in the plan, the inevitable casualties and the increasing stranglehold of nationalists on movement in Java forced SEAC to abandon what was always a last-ditch option and seek a negotiated solution. British ability to influence TKR, local militia or *pemuda* groups in east Java by the threat of military action was evidently, after the disaster in Surabaya, negligible. Any failure of a Japanese operation would have had disastrous consequences for British policy in Java and, indeed, Britain's post-war status as a Great Power and long-term influence at the United Nations.

As the 'Tanabe Incident' developed, less excitable minds took charge. Tanabe had, of course, written his communiqué in Japanese. Other translations were obtained from Japanese HQs, which revealed differing emphasis (though 'underdogs' would appear to be clear enough). These new versions were sufficiently dissimilar for SEAC to take a more cautious approach towards Tanabe. The General did not travel under arrest, nor lose his command. Both he and Itagaki attended the inquiry in mid-March with Mountbatten and General Pyman both present. Tanabe was found innocent of any subversive intent. Itagaki, though, was heavily criticised for allowing his staff to 'submit...an incorrectly translated message'. Mountbatten was, however, thoroughly dissatisfied with Tanabe for 'issuing a signal...which might be interpreted as criticism of Allied policy'. As a consequence of this incident, controls over communications were tightened further and Japanese officers in 7 Area Army were forbidden to address their troops 'by word or by letter' on political or policy matters without prior British approval.[133] Tanabe resumed his command and remained in Sumatra until the British left in 1946. (In a later, separate trial in a Dutch court he was found guilty of war crimes against Allied PW and hanged in 1949.)

This incident provides further evidence to suggest that British 'supervision' of Japanese signals, which would have been numerous, was purely notional. The backlog of day-to-day translations meant it was several days before British officers read Tanabe's message. Japanese-language training programmes in Britain's military were scaled down following the Japanese surrender, unlike the continuing American (actually increasing) Military Intelligence Service Language School (MISLS) programme which was still required for the administration of occupied Japan. This fact, coupled with Operation Python's automatic three-year-four-months' service repatriation criteria meant that Japanese-interpretation and translation capability within SEAC was reducing constantly. From the start, SEAC was therefore heavily dependent upon Japanese resources for JSP administration. Indeed, Japanese HQs, not South-East Asia Translation and Interpretation Corps (SEATIC) linguists, provided the different translations of Tanabe's message submitted for review. SEATIC staff were in any case few in number. War crimes trials in Singapore and elsewhere reduced the pool of specialist linguists available for general duties, and the increasing need to provide Japanese speakers for liaison duties had necessarily distributed them thinly to the 'hotter spots' around the Command. The 'underdogs' incident was, however, resolved surprisingly quickly. Perhaps the possibility of a major operation involving Japanese forces in Java required absolute stability in the Japanese command structure and more than a degree of compromise on SEAC's part.

Tanabe's message reveals something else. 'Gonbel' [Hill] was a main checkpoint on the approach to Semarang assigned by the British to Japanese forces (Kido *Butai*) during the evacuation of internees from Ambarawa. That Tanabe, at his HQ in Sumatra, was able to identify the specific, temporary deployment of one battalion of Japanese troops under 16 Army in central Java, provides further confirmation that the various Japanese HQs were in very close contact and exchanging detailed information on their troop positions and presumably also those of British units. Another interpretation of Tanabe's signal, that it was simply a deliberate swipe at British policy by a resigned and frustrated commander, powerless to serve the interests of his men, also remains a possibility. Either way, it certainly succeeded in getting Mountbatten's attention.

As more British and then Dutch troops arrived in Java, Japanese units were gradually disarmed and interned. After war-guilt screening, those not facing charges could look forward to repatriation. Yet some Japanese would not return home. As order returned to Java, more recent services rendered were forgotten as the Dutch settled older scores—a fact that embittered *kenpeitai* veterans.[134] Convicted war criminals were not the only non-returnees. Deserters, too, missed the boat home. One estimate suggests fewer than 300 Japanese soldiers joined the Indonesian cause.[135] British battalion war diaries in Java list Japanese among enemy dead just as they also record, somewhat incongruously, 'Our casualties, 1 Jap'.[136] There is therefore a possibility that in Indonesia Japanese fought Japanese in open, armed conflict for the first time since the Satsuma Rebellion of 1872. Some of these 'stragglers' returned to Japan in the early 1950s, after the US occupation had ended and by which time Indonesia had gained independence. Until 1991 they were officially classed as deserters. Returnees were not arrested or prosecuted and many settled back into their pre-war jobs with no questions asked. [137]

What then is the verdict on the Japanese contribution to establishing peace and order in Java? From the British point of view, the Japanese record is mixed at best. Many of the instances described above reveal a general disinterest towards British difficulties and others a blatant dereliction of duty. Japanese reluctance to get involved in 'someone else's war', and/or their desire to limit their own casualties arguably led indirectly to the near annihilation of 49 Indian Brigade and to the murder of many innocent internee women and children. Yet elsewhere, acceptance of obligations also led to the deaths of over one thousand Japanese at the hands of the nationalist mob or in action beside the British. One veteran (and scholar) has described this as 'a fair exchange' of guns for lives.[138] Major General Mabuchi and, particularly, Major Kido, however, in helping prevent a potential slaughter of many thousands of innocents in central Java arguably did more than balance the scales. General Christison (who lost his son in the Burma Campaign) would not have contemplated a DSO for a Japanese officer lightly in 1945. Sir Walter Cheshire, Air Officer Commanding AHQ Indo-China in 1945 (later Air Chief Marshal) had a similarly high opinion of the 'Gremlin Task Force'. This was a team of Japanese pilots, navigators and ground crews operating under British control in Vietnam. Cheshire noted that 'the Japs performed their duties with competence and, when necessary, fought with courage and determination' and that 'had they been Indian or British troops they would, without doubt, have earned decorations'.[139] Seven decades on, wider acknowledgement and commemoration of this little-known second 'Anglo-Japanese alliance' is long overdue.

For a period in post-war Java it proved necessary for the victor to treat the vanquished with considerable care. As the need for Japanese military assistance subsided, however, other problems were identified. Throughout Southeast Asia there was a labour shortage and in SEAC the Japanese were quickly identified as an available, dependent and above all cheap resource. A new need was found to side-step the Potsdam Agreement and keep the Japanese at hand. The next chapters will describe the varying success of Britain's attempts to first deflect, then ignore and finally justify its unilateral policy of retention of the Japanese.

NOTES TO CHAPTER 2

1.   J. P. Cross, *First In Last Out: An Unconventional British Officer in Indo-China, 1945-46 and 1972-76* (London, 1992), 14.

2   A. J. F. Doulton, *The Fighting Cock: Being the History of the 23rd Indian Division 1942-1947* (Aldershot, 1951), 229.

3.   Pieter S. Gerbrandy, *Indonesia* (London, 1950), 96–98.

4.   M. Dening (FO Political advisor to Mountbatten), comments on Java. Nov. 1945, WO 203/5567.

5.   'Memorandum on the situation in Java' to the British Foreign Secretary, CAB 121/697.

6.   M. Dening (FO), comments WO 203/5567. For British policy on Burma see Thorne, *Allies*, 606-612.

7.   Clifford W. Squire, 'Britain and the Transfer of Power in Indonesia, 1945-46.' (PhD thesis, University of London, 1979), 33.

8.   Ibid., 73-74. For Lady Mountbatten in Sumatra, see Gideon F. Jacobs, *Prelude to the Monsoon: Assignment in Java* (Philadelphia, 1982), 156–74.

9.   Thanasis D. Sfikas, *The British Labour Government and the Greek Civil War, 1945-49: The Imperialism of Non-Intervention* (Keele, 1994), 35–6. For British policy in Greece, see Thorne, *Allies*, 513–4.

10.   Thorne, *Allies*, 524–5.

11.   Peter Dennis, *Troubled Days of Peace: Mountbatten and South East Asia Command, 1945-46* (New York, 1987), 58, 121–3.

12.   John H. McEnery, *Epilogue in Burma, 1945-48: The Military Dimension of British Withdrawal* (Tunbridge Wells, 1990), 35.

13.   'Group 1. Directive 1.' HMS *Cumberland* at Batavia, 15 Sept. 1945, 'A Report on RAPWI in Java', Appendix E. WO 203/56696.

14.   Thorne, *Allies*, 675.

15.   16 Army Headquarters, 'Report concerning existing matters...', 15 Sept. 1945. AS 5204. Author's italics. [Spelling and grammatical errors in original quoted passages have been corrected.]

16.   AS 5204.

17.   See Anderson, *Java*, 66.

18.   'Meeting on board HMS *Cumberland*, 21/9/4 at Batavia.' IC 059376-11430.

19.   AS 3582.

20.   Han Bing Siong. 'The Indonesian Need of Arms after the Proclamation of Independence', *BKI* 157-4 (2001), 813.

21.   Reid and Oki, *Japanese Experience in Indonesia*, 329; and Allen, *End of the War*, 88.

22.   For Sukarno's speech see Anderson, *Java* 123.

23.   CS5 to SACSEA, 19 Sept. 1945. Quoted in Squire, 'Britain and the Transfer of Power in Indonesia, 1945-46', 71 n. 36.

24.   Miyamoto in Reid and Oki, *Japanese Experience in Indonesia*, 331.

25.   Anderson, *Java*, 123 (n. 32).

26.   Gen Yamamoto to Maj Gen Yamamoto, 3 Oct. 1945. IC 007152.

27.   IC 007207.

28.   Doulton, *Fighting Cock*, 243.

29.   Smail, *Bandung*, 58.

30.   Anderson, *Java*, 139.

31.   Smail, *Bandung*, 77.

32.   Ibid., 77–9, 81–2.

33   'Puradiredja-Mabuchi Agreement.' IC 006626-30.

34.   Smail, *Bandung*, 89.

35.   Anderson, *Java*, 140.

36.   Smail, *Bandung*, 89–91.

37.   Roadnight, 'Sleeping with the Enemy', 254.

38.   Stance Rijpma, 'The Blade's Edge', in *Representing the Japanese Occupation of Indonesia: Personal Testimonies and Public Images in Indonesia, Japan and the Netherlands*, ed, Remco Raben (Amsterdam, 1999), 139-40.

39.   Smail, *Bandung*, 94–5..

40.   Doulton, *Fighting Cock*, 246.

41.   Ibid., 95–6.

42.   Han Bing Siong. 'The Secret of Major Kido: The Battle of Semarang, 15-19 Oct. 1945.' *BKI* 152-3 (1996), 392 n. 34.

43.   Doulton, *Fighting Cock*, 244.

44.   Anderson, *Java*, 142.

45.   Smail, *Bandung*, 97.

46.   IC 07157.

47.   Wing Comdr T. S. Tull, 'Report on Operation Salex Mastiff, Central Java, 10 Sept -15 Dec. 1945'. Tull: 2/12 (27 Dec. 1945).

48.   Hanifah, *Tales of a Revolution*, 172–4.

49.   Thomas Stuart Tull, CBE, DSO, OBE (milit.), 'Mission to Java', memoir, 186 pages, 1982. Tull: 3/1 (1983).

50.   John Hudson, *Sunset in the East: Fighting Against the Japanese through the siege of Imphal and alongside them in Java, 1943-1946* (Barnsley, 2002).

51.   Ibid., 177

52.   Ibid., 137, 149.

53.   Soltau Memoir, 81.

54.   Personal interview with Aoki Masafumi, ex-16 IJA *kenpeitai* (Semarang), Oct. 2005.

55.   IC 007156. Tull stated that the command came from Surabaya.

56.   IC 007156 and Tull: 2/2, 27 Sept.-15 Nov. 1945.

57.   Anderson, *Java*, 145.

58.   For example, Anderson, Java (146); Woodburn Kirby, *Surrender of Japan* (321) and Peter Dennis, 'Netherlands East Indies, 1945-1947: An Unwelcome Commitment', in *The Imperial War Museum Book of Modern Warfare* (London, 2003), 41. Both Han, 'The Secret of Major Kido' (404–5), and Soltau (131–6) refute suggestions of lack or surrender of weapons by Kido *Butai*.

59.   Kido Butai Association, *Taishi II* (Kyoto, 1984).

60.   Soltau Memoir, 84.

61.   Ibid., 123.

62.   Ibid., 122.

63.   Anderson, *Java*, 147; and Roadnight, 'Sleeping with the Enemy', 254.

64.   Soltau Memoir, 124–5.

65.   Ibid., 136.

66.   Ibid., 130–1.

67.   F. de Rochemont. Ibid., 141.

68.   Officer commanding Fifth Guard Unit, Semarang *Keibitai*, 'Report on the Semarang Incident', IC 006762-3.

69.   Hudson, *Sunset in the East...*, 137.

70.   Roadnight, 'Sleeping with the Enemy', 254.

71.   Tull, 'Report on Operation Salex Mastiff'. His source was probably Wishart and Soltau at RAPWI Semarang.

72.   Kido Butai, 'Defence of Semarang: A Short History of Defensive Fighting in the Area of Semarang.' Annexure to Brigadier K. T. Darling, 'Report on activities of 5 Parachute Brigade Group in Semarang, Jan.-May 1946'. WO 203/6011.

73   Richard O. S. McMillan, 'The British Occupation of Indonesia, 1945-46', (PhD diss., University of London, 2002; expanded and published with the same title [London, 2007]), 26.

74.   Soltau Memoir, 137.

75.   Ibid., 158.

76.   Tull, 27 Sept.-15 Nov. 1945. Tull, 2/2 1945.

77.   Brigadier R. W. Bethell, DSO, letter home, 3 Nov. 1945, Quoted in the Soltau Memoir, 163.

78.   Bethell, letter home, 5 Nov. 1945, Soltau Memoir, 165. One 'twitchy' finger in Bethell's HQ and Sukarno's role in Indonesian political history could have been very short.

79.   Bethell, letter home, 15 Dec. 1945, Soltau Memoir, 175. Alas, the sword was lost en route to the UK. Major Kido remained something of a *bête noir* with the Indonesian armed forces. In the 1970s, TNI officers visiting the UK to take British Army Short Courses would sometimes refer to the Kido *Butai* in casual conversation with British instructors. (Author's interview with Lt Col W. A. Weightman.)

80.   'Report on an ambush of a RAPWI convoy in Sourabaya.' WO 203/5960. Also Doulton, *Fighting Cock*, 267.

81.   For accounts of events in Surabaya see J. G. A. Parrott, 'Who Killed Mallaby?' *Indonesia*, No. 20 (1975), 87–111; and McMillan, *British Occupation of Indonesia*, 31–58.

82.   Friend, *Blue-Eyed Enemy*, 225–-7.

83.   William H. Frederick, *Visions and Heat: The Making of the Indonesian Revolution* (Ohio, 1989), 230–-78.

84.   Ibid., 184.

85.   Ibid., 201.

86.   Ibid., 212.

87.   Han Bing Siong, 'Captain Huyer and the massive Japanese arms transfer in East Java in Oct. 1945.' *BKI*, 159.2/3, (2003), 291–-351. Han cites 170 works (in Dutch), over 70 consider the motivation or actions of the Japanese.

88.   The arms surrender at Surabaya has also been discussed by Squire, Anderson, and Dennis.

89.   Huyer to Patterson. AS 3584.

90.   Patterson to Huyer. AS 3584.

91.   Dutch Admiral Helfrich to Gen Christison, 19 Nov. 1945. AS 3584.

92.   Shibata Yaichiro, 'Surabaya after the Surrender', in *Japanese Experience of Indonesia*, eds, Reid and Oki, 341–74.

93.   'Extract from a signed report by P. J. G. Huyer, Capt. RNN.' IC 007177-79.

94.   Han, 'Captain Huyer', 327.

95.   Ibid., 317.

96.   Surabaya reflected badly on Hawthorn, who was castigated by 49 Brigade's survivors for the leaflet drop. See McMillan, *British Occupation of Indonesia*, 38–42.

97.   Ibid., 32.

98.   Doulton, *Fighting Cock*, 252.

99.   Han, 'Captain Huyer', 332.

100.   B. R. Mullaly, *Bugle and Kukri: The Story of 10th Princess Mary's Own Gurkha Rifles* (London, 1957), 391.

101.   Han, 'Secret of Major Kido', 415, and Roadnight, 'Sleeping with the Enemy', 255 (quoting Gen Christison's Cambridge University-held memoir). The Official History also records the assistance from Kido *Butai*, Woodburn Kirby, Surrender of Japan, 321.

102.   HQ Air Command, SEAC. 'Relations with surrendered Japanese forces...', 1 Sept. 1945. AIR 40/1850.

103.   Cross, *First In Last Out*, 11.

104.   Soltau Memoir, 35; Jacobs, *Prelude to the Monsoon*, 86.

105.   Peter Kemp, *Alms for Oblivion* (London, 1961), 33–5.

106.   Peter M. Dunn, *The First Vietnam War* (London, 1985), 37, 45–6.

107.   Soltau Memoir, 55–6.

108.   Jacobs, *Prelude to the Monsoon*, 34–5.

109.   2 Buffs, Battalion Diary, 23 Mar. 1946, WO 172/7108.

110.   CAB 84/77.

111.   Numata to Mountbatten, 27 Feb. 1946. WO 203/2727.

112.   Cross, *First In, Last Out*, 13–14.

113.   Personal Correspondence to the Author, 19 May 2006.

114.   'Memorandum on the situation in Java...'29 Sept. 45. CAB 121/697.

115.   Robert Cribb, *Gangsters and Revolutionaries: The Jakarta People's Militia and the Indonesian Revolution 1945-1949*. Honolulu: 1991, 111.

116.   Gen Christison to Gen Browning, 16 Oct. 45. WO 203/5567.

117.   Dunn, *The First Vietnam War*, p. 130.

118.   In Saigon 'HB', a veteran of the Burma campaign, intervened to stop a young Vietnamese boy being shot by French policemen summoned by a French lawyer. The lawyer had seen the boy with a bicycle belonging to a French girl. HB, who had observed the boy simply pick up the fallen bicycle and stand it against a wall, raised his Bren gun and threatened to shoot all the Frenchmen. The boy was taken away under arrest but the next day HB found him dead in a gutter outside his quarters. For the next few weeks HB often followed the lawyer with his rifle ready, 'But I just couldn't get to him'. Author interview with HB, Burma Star Association Annual Reunion, Blackpool, 16 June 2006.

119.   Nationalists would often ambush patrols by felling a trees across roads and then open fire from houses nearby. One British veteran of Vietnam found the Japanese 'preferable to French troops' in such circumstances. Author interview with (and unpublished memoir by) Charles Wicksteed ex. 114 Regt, Royal Artillery, 7 July 2006.

120.   Charles Ritchie (ex-178 Field Rgt, RA). Author interview, 10 Oct. 2006.

121.   Weightman, who retired as a Lt Col, 'witnessed 14 convicted Japanese war criminals swing at Changi Gaol'. Later he was a member of the Burma Campaign Fellowship Group (along with Maj P. Malins, J. Pike and others), and corresponded with a number of former JSP to foster Anglo-Japanese goodwill. The BCFG 'stood down' in 2003, the reason being, according to Weightman: 'Job done! Reconciliation.' (Correspondence with the Author.)

122.   Personal interview with John Pike, CBE, PNBS, former Financial Secretary of Sarawak, 10 July 2006. In January 1946 Lt. Pike (Intelligence Corps [GSO III]) was one of four Allied officers supervising JSP at Palembang and Pladjoe.

123.   For a description of the extent of obligations to superiors in the IJA see Tasaki Hanama, *Long the Imperial Way* (London, 1951).

124.   AFNEI to ALFSEA. 10 Mar. 1946. WO 203/2727.

125.   Fuller, *Shokan*, 161–2.

126.   Records of these proceedings were not examined for this study.

127.   8 Mar. 1946, WO 203/2727.

128.   Maj Gen Pyman to Gen. Itagaki, 27 Feb. 1946. WO 203/2727.

129.   AFNEI, Top Secret, 19 Mar. 1946. WO 203/2727

130.   Ibid. See also John Keay, *Last Post*, 258.

131.   'Japanese Evacuation', Mar. 1946. W0 203/5662.

132.   Ibid.

133.   16 Mar. 1946. WO 203/2727.

134.   NFKVA, *The Kenpeitai in Java and Sumatra*, 68.

135.   Kenichi Goto, 'Caught in the Middle: Japanese Attitudes toward Indonesian Independence in 1945.' *Journal of Southeast Asian Studies*, Vol. 27 (1996), 44.

136.   War Diary, 49 Indian Infantry Brigade, Dec. 45. WO 172/7108.

137.   Goto, 'Caught in the Middle', 48.

138.   Allen, *End of the War*, 94.

139.   W. G. Cheshire, 'The Gremlin Task Force,' (1965), 3. RAF Museum Library, Hendon. See also L. V. Fraser, 'The Gremlin Task Force: Japanese Aircrews and Aircraft Flying for the RAF in French Indo-China.' *Flight* (6 Dec., 1945), 612.

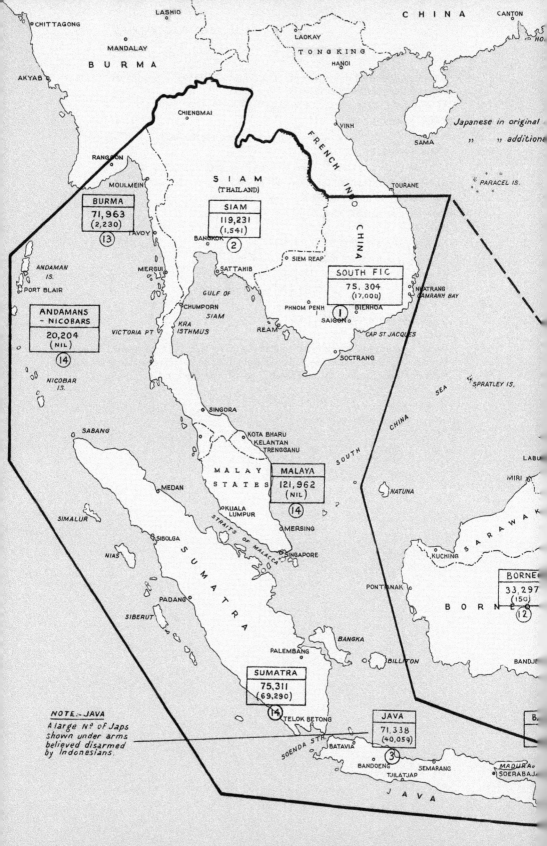

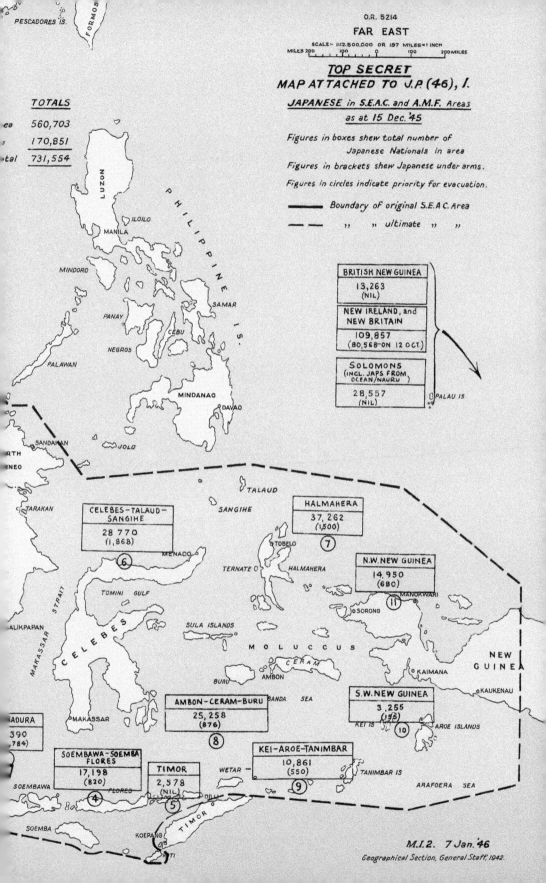

3

SIDE-STEPPING GENEVA

FROM PRISONERS OF WAR TO SURRENDERED PERSONNEL

When belligerents conclude an armistice convention, they shall normally cause to be included therein provisions concerning the repatriation of prisoners of war.... In any case, the repatriation of prisoners shall be effected as soon as possible after the conclusion of peace.

—Convention Relative to the Treatment of Prisoners of War [1]

Britain faced a range of political, humanitarian and economic crises in Southeast Asia in August 1945. In Java, British responses were often spontaneous or instinctive. Similarly, British difficulties were reflected in a remarkably *ad hoc* policy towards the Japanese. On many occasions Japanese assistance was crucial to the success of British security policy. Questions arise, however, as to why the defeated enemy would assist a victor in such uncertain and dangerous circumstances and, indeed, how under the laws of war the victor could demand such co-operation. Answers to these questions are found in the development of Allied policy pertaining to all defeated forces. This subject had taxed the minds of Allied planners long before 1945. It was also a haphazard process and was to culminate in the concept of 'Japanese Surrendered Personnel' (JSP), which allowed Britain to bypass the 1929 Convention Relative to Prisoners of War.

Britain's use of Japanese forces against nationalists in Indonesia and Vietnam was a short-term strategy, yet it was dependent upon the JSP classification. Once the immediate security situation stabilised, however, other Japanese were detained for use as coolie labour, in breach of the Potsdam Declaration and, presumably, the 1929 PW Convention. These deliberate, even extreme, measures underlined Britain's reduced capabilities and starkly limited options in Southeast Asia.

Today, detention of 'captives' taken during 'incursion', open warfare or United Nations-mandated peacekeeping operations generates considerable political and media attention. In late 1945 however, when detained Axis personnel numbered almost 14.6 m (11.1m German PW/SEP and 3.5m JPW/JSP) this was not the case.[2] For the British public, interest in prisoners of war (PW) dwindled with peace and the return of their own. Assumptions that German and Japanese troops also became PW on 8 May and 15 August 1945 respectively remain widely held. This did not happen. In both the European and Asia-Pacific Theatres the Allies found it politic to circumvent the 1929 PW Convention. This was achieved by the simple expedient of calling them something else: Surrendered Enemy Personnel (SEP) in European and the Middle East, and Japanese Surrendered Personnel (JSP) in Asia and the Pacific. Although the origins of each were markedly different—one contrived, the other an eleventh-hour, arguably 'self-inflicted' amendment—the parallels are intriguing. Neither category was recognised under the 1929 PW Convention.[3] As a result, defeated soldiers found themselves without anticipated legal protection or official supervision by a neutral party. From the start there was an uneasy dependency upon the goodwill of the victor rather than established legal protocols. Demands were made of the losers. In the West, these were largely economic in the form of labour. In the East, the primary demand was military. Labour came later. Even as Japan's leaders, generals and admirals marched in public surrender ceremonies, Japanese servicemen were receiving new orders from British commanders.

Peace did not visit Asia in August 1945. Famine, disease and violence swept the continent. Millions were to die from starvation or in cholera and typhoid epidemics that ravaged India, French Indo-China, Manchuria and Java. Widespread conflict claimed more lives as China plunged into civil war, nationalist protests erupted in Burma and Malaya, and Indonesia and Vietnam declared independence. As local civilian interests or emergencies took centre stage, the importance of the repatriation of unpopular or despised enemy soldiers and civilians inevitably slipped down the list of priorities, despite its prominence and significance at Potsdam.[4] In fact, JSP were to play both economic and military roles in immediate post-war Asia. In Java and French Indo-China, it was the latter—as peacekeepers—that materialised first.

In the aftermath of the Japanese surrender, it quickly became apparent to SEAC that the troops available for security and 'stabilisation' duties were insufficient. They were in any case stranded without ships in India and Malaya. Mountbatten's solution, decided upon even before British and Japanese representatives met to discuss the surrender, was to order Field Marshal Count Terauchi Hisaichi, Commander of JEFSR, to instruct his

17. Field Marshal Count Terauchi Hisaichi (IJA)

forces to 'maintain law and order...until such time as the occupation forces arrive'.[5] There was a tense period as SEAC HQ awaited situation reports from their small advance parties parachuted into occupied territory. Mountbatten's frustration and even desperation is clear from a signal to the Chiefs of Staff (COS) informing them that he expected absolute obedience from the Japanese. He felt that 'any policy that places restrictions on the employment of Japanese on labour tasks connected with military necessity is completely unreasonable and is pandering... I therefore propose to issue a directive...that the Japanese may be so employed and that drastic action including shooting should be taken against any who refuse'.[6] Although in their reply the COS cautioned against lethal force, in the event it was the Japanese who did much of the shooting—at Britain's request. During the four months to January 1946 'loyal' Japanese troops helped the British to depose, on behalf of the French, the first popular government of Vietnam; they greatly impeded nationalist aspirations in Indonesia, allowing the British, and then the Dutch, to build up a military presence; they maintained and policed the Burma-Thailand railway; and kept a semblance of order amongst Communist-inspired chaos in large areas of Malaya.[7] Rail transportation links were seen as crucial. IJA railway regiments, formations specialising in the construction and operation of military railways, were kept intact and mobile by SEAC for this purpose.[8]

Initially the Japanese were expected to be a temporary presence, being replaced quickly by Allied forces. But they played their 'supporting' role with an alacrity and efficiency that came as a welcome surprise and relief to the over-burdened British.[9] Indeed, once the scale of nationalist opposition to the return of former colonial masters became apparent, Mountbatten turned increasingly to the Japanese. This 'second Anglo-Japanese Alliance' did not go unnoticed by the press or politicians. In the House of Commons, awkward questions were asked of a socialist, Atlantic Charter-embracing Prime Minister, as to why British and Japanese troops were apparently engaged in joint military operations against independence movements in the colonies of two foreign powers. Attlee rebuffed the suggestion of Anglo-Japanese 'collaboration', replying to his questioner (Mr Sorensen, a Labour MP) that he was of the 'wrong impression'.[10]

Denials aside, the Government was seriously embarrassed over its Southeast Asian predicament. In addition to revealing SEAC's manpower shortage (and perhaps Britain's new interpretation of the Atlantic Charter), publicity over the involvement of the Japanese also highlighted what should have proved a serious charge against Britain: the illegal use of PW for military purposes. International law specified that Japanese forces would become PW once ordered 'to cease the use of armed force and were disarmed'.[11] Mountbatten's policy therefore directly contravened Article 31 of the PW Convention which stated, 'Work done by prisoners of war shall have no direct connection with the operations of the war. In particular, it is forbidden to employ prisoners in the manufacture or transport of arms or munitions of any kind, or on the transport of material destined for combatant units'.

Yet according to the British Government the 1929 PW Convention was not breached because the Japanese were not prisoners of war. A fundamental and key administrative distinction concerning the Japanese armed forces had been agreed during the surrender negotiations which resulted in a new status—Japanese Surrendered Personnel (JSP)—coming into existence on 15 August 1945. Strangely JSP-status was first proposed to the Allies by the Japanese Government which faced a purely domestic but very delicate problem. Japan's military Field Service Code, as well as extremely strong societal mores, forbade servicemen—and by implication, Emperor *and* Commander-in-Chief Hirohito—to allow themselves to be taken prisoner.

18. Japanese prisoners in US Navy custody. (USN/AC) (See 'Illustrations')

(Standard procedure under the 1929 PW Convention would have meant the Emperor being given an identifying number as a PW.) JSP-status was therefore a last-minute fudge by the Japanese to avoid shaming and technically criminalising millions of their citizens as well as the head of state.[12]

JSP-status presented numerous advantages for the Allies and was readily accepted, despite the lack of legal basis. With Allied permission, the Japanese cease-fire order of 18 August specifically stated, 'Japanese military personnel and civilians who are taken by the enemy after the proclamation of the Imperial Rescript will not be considered prisoners-of-war'.[13] Interestingly, the directly comparable status, 'Surrendered Enemy Personnel' (SEP) was imposed by Britain after the German surrender in May 1945. The United States equivalent designation was 'Disarmed Enemy Forces (DEF).[14] In contrast to the situation with the Japanese, however, SEP-status reflected purely Allied self-interest.

In the European Theatre of operations, policies on post-war utilisation of German forces were considered by the European Advisory Commission (EAC) after its creation at the 1943 Moscow Conference. As the Soviet

Union was an EAC member but had not signed (and would not sign) the PW Convention, the status of German prisoners in Russian hands raised fundamental problems in drafting surrender terms which would oblige Soviet commanders to abide by the Convention. (Claims were also made in the British Parliament of secret agreements allowing Russia to detain German SEP for 20 years.)[15] Within the EAC the Allies established that 'they could strip the Germans of all government, including their protection by international law, and be free to punish them without restriction'.[16] By necessity, EAC drafts avoided precise statements on the subject of prisoners to the extent that the intention to evade the terms of the 1929 PW Convention has been described as 'premeditated'.[17] By late 1944 British planners and lawyers were already contemplating the potential economic benefits of mass German military prisoner labour. Key to their overall analysis was the legal assumption that once hostilities had ceased, PW could not be taken and detained.[18] Thus an official German surrender or an armistice would in theory deny the British control over no-longer-hostile forces. A means was sought to bypass the relevant Convention yet still retain viable and flexible post-surrender control of German personnel.[19] In the summer of 1944 the EAC submitted a 'draft instrument of surrender' for consideration by the American Government. This draft required the surrendering German commander to accept that his men 'shall at the discretion of the Commander in Chief of the Armed Forces of the Allied State concerned be declared to be Prisoners of War'.[20]

British proposals had envisaged a limited SEP workforce situated in western Europe specifically for reconstruction-based projects. In the event, however, the crises over food supplies and refugees in the summer of 1945 may well have triggered a far wider assignment of SEP/DEF-status than had previously been expected. Widespread crop failure coupled with mass civilian movement played havoc with Allied estimates for relief supplies. Over 13 million civilians (a mixture of slave labourers and displaced persons) moved westwards from Hungary, Romania and Poland through Germany to the British and American zones beyond the Elbe river to escape Soviet control. Up to 2 million German soldiers also retreated westwards to avoid surrendering to Russian forces. Consequently there were up to 16 million more people in those zones than had been anticipated. Basic 1929 Convention requirements to feed German PW at depot-troop level simply could not be met. In March 1945 General Dwight Eisenhower requested permission from the Combined Chiefs of Staff (CCS) to assign DEF-status to Germans instead of PW because of high numbers and insufficient supplies. This request was granted, the CCS instructing that 'prisoners after Victory in Europe Day should not be declared "Prisoners of War" under the Geneva Convention because of the lack of food'.[21] Soon afterwards, the CCS advised Field Marshal Alexander to take similar steps with the 1.4 million German soldiers coming under British control in Austria. Persistent representations against this classification from the International Committee of the Red Cross (ICRC) resulted in the United States, but not Britain, ending the distinction between PW and DEF from March 1946 onwards.[22]

There were also new strategic concerns for the Western Allies. Winston Churchill had also pondered on a means to exert control over the defeated German armed forces in view of the potential threat from the advancing Red Army. He had concluded that western Europe could not be defended from Soviet attack without rearming the Germans.[23] (In a 1954 constituency speech on West Germany joining NATO, Churchill mentioned his instruction to General Montgomery to postpone the destruction of captured German weapons and 'to stack them so they could be easily issued again to the German soldiers whom we should have to work with if the Soviet advance continued'.[24])

In the Balkan region, Yugoslavian expansionism was also a worry. Near Salzburg the Saint Laszlo Division, an elite Hungarian unit loyal to Hitler, was not disarmed but kept ready to halt Tito's partisan forces should they enter southern Austria. These surrendered Hungarians were given special status and not deported, and some later settled in Britain.[25] Churchill's admission that Britain used captives was not, however, the first. In summer 1945 London newspapers had reported that armed *Wehrmacht* soldiers were assisting the British Army in Germany. The matter was raised in the House of Commons. Reluctantly the War Office admitted to having some 20,000 SEP guarding food and fuel dumps in order to 'relieve British troops'. It emphasised that they 'carry small arms only and a limited amount of ammunition. They have, of course, been submitted to the usual security procedure'.[26]

THE FAR EAST SOLUTION

In the Far East and Pacific Theatres of war, precisely how JSP-status came to be proposed by the Japanese is not clear. It is quite probable that Japanese diplomats in Switzerland, Sweden or the Soviet Union had previously reported to Tokyo on Allied treatment of the surrendered German forces and the 'new' SEP category. A surrendered personnel status of any sort offered the Imperial Japanese General Staff (IJGS) an immediate solution to the huge problem (explained above) of their forces becoming 'shamed' as PW. It is doubtful whether those diplomats were aware of the extent of SEP labour policies or potential military duties. In any case, since the Japanese had not ratified the 1929 PW Convention such details were unlikely to concern the Japanese Government, which by the second week of August 1945 was more concerned with seeking a façade that protected the governing elite domestically rather than safeguarding its personnel outside Japan.[27] Details of the hastily adopted position on PW may well have been carried by the Imperial princes who conveyed secret communications from the Emperor to Field Marshal Terauchi and other Area Army commanders after 15 August.

At Rangoon, where British and Japanese representatives met from 26 August, Lieutenant General Numata Takazo, Terauchi's Chief of Staff, attempted to negotiate over specific areas of responsibility, disarming and internment of Japanese troops with General Browning, Mountbatten's Chief of Staff. Numata, however, also made a separate address on Terauchi's behalf seeking acceptance for the position that 'Japanese soldiers were not to be treated as prisoners of war'.[28] Browning called the Japanese bluff, permitting 'no comments on the terms laid down', and allowing 'only questions on the terms as they stood'.[29] There was no debate over Terauchi's last-minute plea over the status of his men. In fact, there was no need as the surrendered personnel 'precedent' transplanted seamlessly and quickly into Allied policies in the Far East and Pacific.

JSP-status was, however, to prove a double-edged sword for those to whom it was applied. Prisoner of War supervision (including safety), accommodation, rations and entitlements, medical provision, working conditions and pay rates were all regulated by the 1929 Convention. As signatories, Allied governments had to respect and follow those rules. As a consequence of their Government's action, however, although saved from the presumed shame of becoming 'prisoners', JSP discovered that they had been left with no statutory protection or rights whatsoever. Many Japanese officers had assumed that JSP-status would actually bring *superior* conditions and rights over 'normal' PW-status. They saw themselves as undefeated in combat, with command structure intact and still in control of vast territory for which the Allies would not have to suffer casualties to regain. As one former JSP has commented ruefully, 'we thought JSP would be much better than PW but it was worse!'[30]

In effect, a Japanese solution to a purely Japanese-imagined problem allowed the British Government to dodge and deflect formal charges that it was in breach of the PW Convention. There was little in the way of sympathy for the Japanese in Britain. In SEAC and in the War Office there was a widespread and very strong belief that since the Japanese were directly responsible for the parlous state of the region's economies they should make a major contribution to the economic recovery of the region. London informed Washington that 'His Majesty's Government consider it to be only just that the Japanese should contribute at any rate in some small part to the task of repairing the damage they have done'.[31] This was increasingly interpreted to mean that JSP ought to make individual 'contributions' through forced labour.[32]

Mountbatten certainly viewed the Japanese as an asset that could and should be used, though he was aware that he could not impose his own policy towards prisoners unilaterally, even in SEAC, without the assent of the United States. Within days of the Japanese surrender he requested guidance. General MacArthur, Supreme Commander Allied Powers (SCAP) apparently gave him a free hand while explaining United States policy without reference to Geneva:

> The 4 Allied Powers are bound by the Potsdam Ultimatum to permit the return of Japanese Military Forces, after they are completely disarmed, to their homes. Pending such return, which of necessity depends on the availability of transportation, this [sic] personnel may be used for such purposes and subject to such conditions and directives as may be prescribed by the National Commands.... Surrendered Japanese soldiers should be considered as disarmed personnel and not necessarily as prisoners of war.

It seems MacArthur, too, was aware that this was a grey area, for he continued, 'discussion and commitments concerning the treatment of Japanese disarmed forces during the period between their surrender and their return to their homes should be held to essential minimum'.[33]

MacArthur confirmed to Mountbatten that he intended to avoid making Japanese PW 'as far as possible' and that he would leave the question of JSP employment at the discretion of theatre commanders, provided that they had 'sufficient' forces to enforce such policy and that *repatriation was not retarded*.[34] Further clarification came from the British Staff Section at MacArthur's HQ who stressed that 'Disarming of Japanese was entirely at Mountbatten's discretion' but that 'Japanese may NOT be enslaved but may be requisitioned for labour on rehabilitation projects such as remaking roads, repairing ports, building houses *for which work they should be paid*'. Repatriation remained a US priority and was to be 'carried out as shipping becomes available' [in] an 'international phasing-in programme *issued from this HQ*'.[35] Mountbatten was to be highly selective in his interpretation of these instructions, particularly over pay, which would have significant consequences for Anglo-American relations over the next three years.

In London, however, confidence in the British legal position gradually waned. Official records reveal strong doubts over JSP policy. For the Foreign Office the JSP versus PW distinction was an irrelevant and even dangerous semantic distraction. One internal memo is categorical:

> The men concerned are surely Japanese prisoners-of-war and if the War Office, in order to evade compliance with the Geneva Convention, have decided to call them something else, this should not, I think, enable the military authorities to avoid responsibility for decent treatment.... I do not agree that [War Office] subterfuge should throw any responsibility on the Foreign Office.[36]

Meanwhile, from the sidelines, two anxious European powers watched Britain more or less juggle with their colonies, as well as the 1929 PW Convention. Immediately after the surrender, France and the Netherlands had wished, for reasons of prestige, to rid their colonies of Japanese as quickly as possible. The governments of both countries had requested assistance with JSP evacuation—but not ship-hogging repatriation—from their territories to British colonies. According to the Dutch, the defeated Japanese were 'a potential danger [that was] considerably hampering [the] Netherlands Government task of restoring order'.[37] Neither France nor the Netherlands, however, had available sufficient trained and equipped troops, or access to the ever-crucial shipping that remained the trump card in Southeast Asia. Strident Dutch complaints over 'low priorities' granted to their interests bemoaned the fact that while most Dutch merchant vessels were allocated to the Allied Shipping Pool, 'the timely transportation of our troops and civil personnel has been seriously delayed because no sufficient shipping-space... has been allocated to the Netherlands Government'.[38]

Soon, however, the stances of the French and Dutch Governments began to change as between October 1945 to January 1946 JSP deployment in Vietnam and Indonesia gradually tipped the security balance decisively in favour of the returning powers. To the end of February 1946 Japanese fatalities in Vietnam reached 110.[39] In the same period in Java they climbed to 384 dead and 307 wounded.[40] Even so, grateful British commanders later rewarded some units with priority embarkation, extra rations and retention of side arms.[41] In London there was also continuing concern over the number of

'British' or 'Allied' operations in Southeast Asia that were totally dependent on Japanese troops. This led to proposals from appreciative British officers that Japanese assistance be recognised by awards, an idea rejected by Mountbatten.[42] Offensive action using JSP was officially discouraged. Instructions to SEAC

19. Adm Mountbatten and Gen MacArthur in Manila, Philippines, in July 1945. (MMA)

from London over JSP-use in FIC were very specific. They were not to be used 'except in Cambodia [and only] in grave emergency.' The rushed arrival of French troops in FIC in early January signalled orders for disarming and concentration to go ahead 'as fast as possible'. Japanese 'gains' against Vietnamese nationalists, however, were not to be squandered. British orders on this point were also very clear that 'Japanese forces…in North Cochin China and Annam were to remain in position until relieved by [the] French'.[43]

Prestige or at least attempts to regain lost respect also drove British policymaking over the disposal of Japanese materiel. Japanese aircraft, vehicles and weapons stockpiles (often guarded by Japanese troops) were equally stark physical reminders of white colonial set backs. Armouries were a particularly tempting target for nationalist mobs and were frequently the scene of ugly, violent standoffs between JSP and locals demanding weapons. (British suspicions that Japanese were too ready to back down and were handing over weapons to mobs lasted for some considerable time.) JSP-disarming programmes (which included armament destruction programmes) and war-criminal screening processes were inevitably highly politically charged issues. Such policies were of considerable security or political interest to the returning colonial powers and, equally, to would be nationalist governments lobbying for recognition at the United Nations. They were also of significant importance at the regional level. Physical possession and control over Japanese ordnance itself became a cause of great inter-faction unrest among various rural or urban nationalist factions vying for political and/or military status.

French and Dutch authorities were, quite naturally, keen to prevent weapons and other equipment passing to nationalist opposition movements yet their own shortages of ordnance led them to make numerous requests to the British for everything from small arms and ammunition to Japanese Nakajima Ki-43 ('Oscar') fighter aircraft.[44] Requests for access to and use of Japanese equipment delayed its destruction, and subsequently prolonged the security responsibilities of the Japanese. On occasion, nationalist groups were also able to influence British policy by the simple fact that Japanese armouries (still guarded by JSP) were located within nationalist-held territory. By demanding small numbers of weapons for local 'police' forces or 'security duties' in exchange for unopposed Allied access to inspect weapons and ammunition dumps, nationalist groups sought to secure quasi-official recognition from British representatives and/or local supremacy over rivals.

Similarly, the French and Dutch sought with great insistence custody of Japanese accused of war crimes against their captured service personnel and interned civilians. Questions over demarcation and the legitimate transfer of authority over JPW and JSP exercised legal departments in SEAC and Whitehall. Foreign Office concerns over possible American objections to Mountbatten's plan to release southern Vietnam from SEAC and place it under the sole control of the French forced a rethink. There was also a fear that the Japanese who viewed France 'as a defeated nation' would refuse to accept orders from the French military once the British had left. Mountbatten's solution was to identify the difference between 'taking a surrender' which was required by the Potsdam Agreement and 'guarding surrendered troops' about which Potsdam 'said nothing'.[45]

By late 1945 French and Dutch colonial administrators-in-waiting, now well aware of Britain's limited military capability in Asia, came to appreciate the usefulness of the Japanese *in situ* and instead sought assurances that Japanese troops would not be removed prior to the arrival of their own forces.[46] They were also anxious because the sun was setting on Britain's own imperial reach. Mountbatten's authority over Indian Army divisions, who made up the bulk of SEAC forces, was not open-ended. Indian independence loomed and its nationalist leaders, dismayed to see their soldiers aiding the restoration of white colonial rule over their Asian neighbours, were demanding their immediate disengagement and return. In anticipation of the end of Indian co-operation with the British military, further Indian reinforcements for SEAC had already been forbidden by London.[47] For the Japanese, already preparing for repatriation, this unexpected change in role and schedule came as an unwelcome and disappointing surprise.[48]

There is no doubt that for Britain, surrendered personnel status for the Japanese brought with it other immediate, tangible benefits. Under the PW Convention Japanese PW would have required concentrating, accommodating, feeding and guarding (by SEAC personnel) at Britain's expense. They would have also qualified for a weekly allowance in sterling. Providing the food, equipment and considerable number of extra guards would have stretched the Command even further, and the British Treasury, which had already banned the export of sterling to maintain reserves, would have been considerably poorer had it been necessary to find pay for an additional 750,000 men. As JSP, however, the Japanese supervised themselves and drew food from their own stocks, their wages being issued in their own (seized) Japanese currency. With some 'accidental' or at least unintended Japanese assistance therefore, the Allies had neatly side-stepped the demands and expenses automatically incurred by the Detaining Power. Britain argued that since Japan had not ratified the PW Convention (though of course Britain had done so) it was under no legal obligation to treat Japanese surrendering after 15 August as PW. However, it did state that it intended to 'apply parts of the Convention but not quote it as authority', a not dissimilar assertion, in fact, to that of the Japanese who stated in 1941 they would apply the Convention *mutatis mutandis* ('with due alteration of details').[49]

As reconstruction became a priority in SEAC, a second role was identified for the Japanese: their use as coolie labour for both military and civilian construction projects. To this end 105,000 JSP were to be deliberately denied repatriation. This revised policy over retained JSP was to place Britain in a series of complicated and diplomatically embarrassing situations both with its allies and in international civil forums.

THE WIDENING OF BRITISH CONTROLS OVER JSP

Classification of the former enemy as JSP rather than PW, while presenting an administrative 'front' for British policy, did not reduce the immediate burden of post-surrender obligations for SEAC or towards the defeated

Japanese themselves. Circumstances necessitated that much British policy for Southeast Asia was created 'on the go', and the administration of JSP was no exception. Mountbatten's unilateral decision in September 1945 to deny JSP payment for their labour, yet require them to assist in all aspects of operations established basic British policy over captive Japanese. His decision came after a brief exchange with MacArthur, with whom he disagreed:

> View of [MacArthur/SCAP HQ] was that [Japanese] should be paid when employed by me. I replied that I considered no remuneration should be given beyond normal service pay which is a Japanese responsibility. MacArthur has now signalled that nothing done by me is likely to compromise AFPAC Theatre or vice versa. I am therefore issuing orders that no extra remuneration will be paid to Japanese surrendered personnel employed on labour tasks.[50]

It is not clear, for example, whether MacArthur's specific instruction that JSP should be paid for labour, or his equally clear expectation that the repatriation of all Japanese would be co-ordinated from his HQ, were ever considered by the British Chiefs of Staff and/or the Cabinet.[51] If so, it is hard to account for British surprise over subsequent American statements and requests regarding reimbursement and repatriation of JSP.

It should be noted that Mountbatten's actions did not immediately impoverish the retained men. Although the British Government had satisfied itself that payment of surrendered personnel was 'not an Allied responsibility', Japan's Government, through the military chain of command, remained responsible for the maintenance, ie, pay, health, food, accommodation and discipline of all JSP.[52] For some time therefore, most JSP continued to draw upon military stockpiles of food and consumables and to receive their weekly pay in both yen payments credited to paybooks and some cash yen occupation currency, which had been printed in vast amounts.

There were, however, vast regional differences in existing JSP food and supply stocks. (Prior to their surrender, large numbers of Japanese troops in remote areas had pitifully low food reserves. By mid-1945, in places such as New Britain for example, the question of pay had long been subsumed by a daily struggle for self-subsistence survival.) Japanese in outlying areas were not formally abandoned by Britain under the maintenance arrangement, at least once their locations were identified. In fact, the main Japanese HQ at Saigon and even the regional Japanese command HQs had little idea of the precise locations of many of their units or their supply levels. The British, who after the end of Lend-Lease had acute supply problems themselves, undertook to supplement food and medicines to 'the minimum required by humanity and to prevent epidemics'.[53] This undertaking took little account of the poor communications, long journeys and the constant shipping shortage in SEAC.

20. American and Japanese officers on Chichijima in October 1945. (NARA)

After the military stand-down many JSP units began or expanded jungle-clearance projects in order to grow subsistence crops. Those in outlying locations were left very much to themselves with most daylight hours devoted to farming.[54] In late 1945, no proposals existed for the mass utilisation of JSP labour on specific programmes. These would emerge in early 1946 as a consequence of assumptions in SEAC that limited repatriation capacity would strand hundreds of thousands of JSP for at least three years.[55] Mountbatten's strident demand to London that the Japanese obeyed his orders without question was aimed at overcoming immediate logistic, supply, transportation and peacekeeping problems facing his still-scattered forces. Urgent assistance was required, for example, to clear harbours and navigable waterways of mines and other invasion obstacles to enable troop and merchant ships to anchor safely. JSP were also required to maintain and repair airstrips using bitumen-coated hessian ('bit-hess') that kept many airstrips serviceable round-the-clock in Java, and supply hundreds of military vehicles and drivers for SEAC and civilian internee convoys.[56] Entire Japanese stocks of oil and petrol, including 1 million gallons stored at Singapore, were to be made available for Allied use, as were batteries and telegraphic other equipment.[57] SEAC's wholesale requisitions of lorries, ambulances, maps and accumulators reveal the dearth of equipment and mechanised transport. Also JSP were to distribute food from Japanese stores to Allied prisoner of war and internee camps. Since most of this SEAC-related support work was concentrated around the main Allied bases and the major ports such as Rangoon, Singapore, Saigon and Batavia (Jakarta), the labour burden fell on a relatively small number of JSP concentrated in or near those cities.[58]

In the first weeks after their surrender, Japanese commanders were quite willing to accommodate the British. In general, JSP worked conscientiously including, for example, providing aircraft and crews for flights by Allied observers or inspectors, and food drops to APWI.[59] The Japanese Navy, too, undertook limited minesweeping operations. At the Rangoon meeting Admiral Chudo explained that lack of minesweepers and pilots would limit the level of assistance and was concerned lest a proposed 'penalty clause' would be invoked. Yet this early co-operation was given under the expectation that British reinforcements would soon make JSP redundant.[60] In fact, by the spring of 1946, labour requirements for Japanese in docks and farms in Malaya had increased by the thousands.

ANGLO-JAPANESE LIAISON IN MALAYA

In May 1946 HQ JEFSR was first informed by SEAC that certain JSP would be retained for labour. The Japanese requested an explanation and a meeting took place at the end of May at Tanglin Barracks in Singapore. General Numata (still acting in Terauchi's name) sent his own Chief of Staff, Colonel Kushida, as head of the Japanese representatives. The senior British officer present was Colonel W. J. Armstrong who confirmed two bad pieces of news. Payment for labour, which had been raised at a previous meeting as a means of improving morale, had been rejected. JSP, Armstrong stated categorically, were 'not entitled to pay'. He did announce, however, that payment of JPW had been authorised. (JPW-status applied to a tiny percentage of Japanese in Malaya: those captured prior to 15 August 1945 and those charged with 'war guilt' after the official surrender. Only PW could be tried in Allied courts. Pay for PW should have been automatic and not delayed. Armstrong offered no explanation for the delay.) On the subject of the retention, Armstrong said that he had been 'instructed by the COS to inform Gen Numata…that the original figure of 100,000 JSP…was the unquestionable ruling of the Allied authorities'.[61] All British decisions over JSP were always referred to officially as 'Allied', though in this case the opinion of the United States/SCAP had not been sought.

A provisional breakdown of JSP numbers and locations estimated that '35,000 were required for Burma; 9,000 in Thailand; 9,000 in west Java (under British control); and… 47,000 for Malaya and Singapore'. In fact, the final number of retained JSP in SEAC was 105,000. Kushida, no doubt aware of political and security developments in Indonesia following Numata's February 1946 tour of JSP camps in SEAC (discussed in Chapter 6), asked what work was to be assigned to JSP in Java. In reply, Armstrong said that 'British policy was to encourage a Dutch-Indonesian settlement, whereupon Indonesian labour would be available to work in the docks and on railways where JSP were now employed as labour'.[62] This revealing comment demonstrates that the drastic labour 'shortage' was purely political in origin and the result of the Indonesians' refusal to co-operate in any area that might assist resumption of Dutch rule. It also highlights 23 Indian Division's own limited manpower and, equally, attests to the prolonged success of the nationalist boycott.

Numerous Japanese protests over the decision to retain personnel came to nothing, so their concern and disappointment was considerable. Subsequently General Numata informed SEAC of his anxieties. He considered that the risk to morale and the maintenance of discipline warranted that he make a tour of Burma, in order:

> To communicate, on behalf of [Field Marshal Terauchi] to the Japanese Forces in Burma his intentions and policy, in order to help maintain the discipline and elevate the morale of the troops… [And] to give encouragement to them, in view of the new labour condition created by Allied orders.[63]

Numata's request was approved. The state of JSP morale and discipline was obviously a concern for SEAC, not least because British and Indian troop numbers were falling steadily. In locations where the British were already outnumbered by nationalist forces, SEAC had to tread far more carefully.

JSP AS PAWNS IN NEGOTIATIONS

Although the majority of JSP were located in Burma and Malaya, those elsewhere complicated British strategy and relations with Allies. Supply and transportation deficiencies had already created certain inconsistencies in policy towards JSP concentration, movement and labour. Security and political realities on Java had necessitated that within Operation Nip-Off, SEAC's glib name for the Japanese repatriation programme, was the substantive and locally co-ordinated Operation Puff, which dealt specifically with the evacuation from Java. SEAC, however, was by no means in total control of Java, or even of all JSP in Java. Some 25,000 remained in nationalist-controlled areas and, even though they retained some weapons, were de-facto hostages.

Despite local truces, threats continued from various nationalist groups in many parts of Java (and Sumatra) and some notice, or at least lip-service, also had to be paid to local Netherlands Indies Civil Administration (NICA) and wider Dutch interests. As SEAC was an Allied command, Dutch officers were present at all levels of the organisation, from individuals assigned to RAPWI duties in central Java, Sumatra and outer islands, to quite senior staff at SEAC HQ in Singapore. This caused the British serious worries over the confidentiality of their plans. As a consequence, a secret channel for signals headed 'Not for Dutch or French' bypassed non-British officers.

Another difficulty was that political and military problems in Java were considered by different departments in Allied Forces Netherlands East Indies (AFNEI), SEAC HQ and in London. NICA, for example, made several requests for authority over and the use of Japanese labour in Surabaya and Semarang. Even though the Japanese had been informed (at the Tanglin meeting) that all JSP retained in Java would be under British command, in March 1946 Britain had in fact already granted the Dutch permission to retain JSP for labour *after* the British withdrawal. This was, however, conditional upon the Dutch making 'a written undertaking that by so doing they take over full responsibility for the future maintenance and eventual evacuation of the Japanese to Japan'.[64] It was an urgent issue. Plans had been drawn up to evacuate all British and Indian troops—and all British-controlled JSP—from Surabaya and Semarang by 15 April 1946. These plans, which could not have been kept from the Dutch, had in turn prompted their requests for independent control over some JSP. Thus it was stressed early to NICA that repatriation of JSP retained in Java might at some stage become a purely Dutch responsibility. Those same JSP, however, were officially under direct British control.In other parts of Java, SEAC was forced to negotiate with nationalists over the 'release' of Japanese out of reach of British forces. Only then could those JSP move to British zones for final disarmament and evacuation to the holding islands of Rempang or Galang.[65] This release was not without conditions. AFNEI had been forced to agree to a 'settlement'

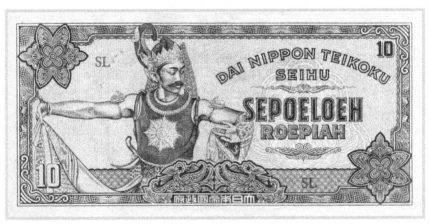

21. Japanese occupation currency 10-roepiah note issued in the NEI. (AC)

with the Indonesians that provided that 'no JSP evacuated from Indonesian-held central or east Java will be re-employed in a military capacity anywhere in the NEI'. A second condition stated: 'existing labour will not be boosted by JSP evacuated under [Operation] Puff'.[66] British officials discussed whether retention of JSP for labour was a breach of faith with the Indonesians. They decided it was not the case. Instead, however, it was concluded that it was a breach of faith with the Dutch, 'in view of their signed undertaking to be responsible for [JSP] maintenance and evacuation'. AFNEI, not SEAC HQ, decided that the documents exchanged with the Dutch (over Surabaya and Semarang) constituted a signed agreement with the Dutch 'by which they are now empowered to retain certain JSP for labour'.[67]

British confidence over the decision to retain JSP for labour throughout SEAC did not, however, remain high for very long. The first doubts arose when United States officials started to enquire about British policy. General MacArthur had by no means acquiesced to the idea of retention, specifically because his own official mission to demobilise the Japanese armed forces and demilitarise Japan required the return to Japan of all Japanese service personnel (except for war criminals). MacArthur therefore risked personal embarrassment as a result of British local, quick-fix policy-making. By September 1946 US State Department officials were lobbying hard for their Government to reject the British request for retention.[68] London, now aware of the considerable support that MacArthur commanded in Washington, began to feel the pressure.

JAPANESE 'FINANCIAL DISARMAMENT' IN SOUTHEAST ASIA, 1945–1946

Shortage of labour was not the only economic issue requiring a solution to a Japanese-created problem. While Britain's Treasury avoided direct, ie, sterling expenditure on pay for surrendered Japanese by bypassing the 1929 PW Convention, a series of sweeping financial measures imposed in quick succession had an immediate impact on all Japanese in Southeast Asia. First, all Japanese occupation currencies (for example, 'rupees' in Burma, 'gulden' and 'roepiah' in Indonesia, 'dollars' in Malaya and 'pounds and shillings' in British Western Pacific territories of the Solomon, Gilbert and Phoenix islands and New Guinea) were declared illegal tender. Second, yen-denominated military currency (gunpyo) was declared worthless. Third, Japanese-owned banks were closed and their assets in Southeast Asia were frozen. Fourth, very strict and effective controls were put in place that made it impossible for any Japanese to exchange yen deposits or notes for local currency or sterling. Currency controls were rigorous. In one example, when French officials tried to finance their own colonial units (stranded in China), they were obliged to change francs into British pounds, then into Indian rupees and finally into Chinese dollars.[69]

As a result of these measures, any direct Japanese influence lingering over finance and regional economies ceased. In fact, British controls went further, with a calculated attempt to prevent financial activity by Japanese even at the individual level. The new policy declared that the Japanese could give normal rates of pay but no payments were to be made in any currency which was legal tender within SEAC.[70] Effectively this measure denied the Japanese the ability to purchase local produce, use shops and services or employ casual labour. In the three years of (combat-free) occupation the Japanese had become major customers for many businesses, shops and farms. They had also—some requisitioned civilian labour programmes aside—become fairly large, direct employers. The new rules were intended to remove all Japanese involvement in local economies at a stroke. This is what happened but there were consequences.

The abrupt removal of the Japanese from the marketplace exacerbated hardship in many areas, as returning colonial administrations could fill neither the employer nor the customer gap—and had no plan to do so. These same administrations were in any case highly cost conscious and operating on limited budgets. British planners took no account of the effect of this blanket policy and its distorting effects on local economies. In London the War Office assumed blithely that since there would be 'little or nothing

22. Japanese military currency 10-yen note issued in Southeast Asia. (AC)

for the Japanese to buy we should have thought few issues of pay [ie, legal tender] would be necessary'.[71] For many JSP barter eventually replaced cash when trading with locals, a situation that would later be criticised pointedly by visiting delegates from ICRC during their camp inspections. Tragically, frustration caused by these rules led to deaths on at least one occasion. In Burma in late 1946 a morale-boosting scheme was introduced that allowed JSP to make and sell arts and crafts to earn pocket money. In December 1946 in Maymyo, Indian Pioneer troops in charge of a Japanese fatigue party confiscated some handicrafts being sold to locals possibly because the sales were outside the 'official' scheme. Furious over the seizure, the JSP attacked their guards with picks and shovels. The guards opened fire 'killing three and wounding nine'.[72]

As ever, unexpected developments meant that one all-embracing currency policy, however desirable, could not be implemented throughout SEAC. Events in Vietnam and Indonesia upset British, French and Dutch financial planning from the start. In anticipation of a smooth return to the East Indies, the Netherlands had prepared tens of millions of new gulden notes and coins to re-finance its colonial economy. This money, printed and minted in 1943 in the United States, had been sent to Australia on Dutch warships, ready for onward despatch to Jakarta with NICA officials. (Anti-Dutch strikes by Australian dockers sympathetic to Indonesian nationalism also delayed movement of currency and NICA troops.[73]) Within Indonesia, however, there was open and widespread opposition to the return of the Dutch. In addition to protest rallies and anti-Dutch violence, there was near-universal hostility to the new currency. Indonesia's revolutionary president Sukarno declared it illegal tender in early October 1945. Shopkeepers and labourers refused to accept the gulden, not least because some extremist nationalist groups promised summary execution of anyone found in possession of Dutch currency, including Allied soldiers.[74] General Sir Philip Christison, head of AFNEI, even issued 60,000 Japanese roepiahs to NICA to enable it to pay local staff and so begin operation.[75]

Fundamental to the opposition to the new Dutch gulden was the fact that all private bank accounts and savings in Java were held in Japanese roepiahs. Tens of millions of people were affected by the currency proposals and not surprisingly they were extremely suspicious of Dutch intentions. As a result, London discovered that Japanese influence over colonial finances could not be neutralised quite as quickly as it had expected.[76] NICA, however, was insistent that occupation currency be banned as a matter of principle. General Christison therefore faced a dilemma. People were being murdered simply for possessing Dutch currency. He was also critical of the low, NICA-proposed exchange rate for the gulden against the roepiah. In a press interview he stated that 'unfortunately some value will probably have to be put on Japanese currency until NEI currency can take its place, and as the bulk of [it] is in the hands of the poorer class I should think it will be a reasonable rate'.[77] Both NICA and the Netherlands Government were furious with Christison's intervention.

In fact, Christison had been disliked by NICA and the colonial Dutch from the beginning. (On arrival in Jakarta, he had pointed to a Dutch flag flying between British and American flags and remarked that it demonstrated that the Allies recognised only Dutch authority in Java. Indonesian press and radio reported him saying it symbolised that Dutch authority could only be maintained with British support. This was just one of numerous early, easily disproved, incidents that sent local Anglo-Dutch relations into freefall over Indonesia. Dutch and NICA officials, however, regularly gave credence to outlandish nationalist press comment and claims.[78])

Mountbatten, besieged by new Dutch protests about Christison's interference, demanded clarification. Christison, equally annoyed by the constant distortions, stood firm, informing Mountbatten that 'currency is the most burning question here and the cause of looting at night'.[79] Since British forces controlled only metropolitan Jakarta they could not hope to enforce use of the Dutch currency beyond the capital. To the immense displeasure of the Dutch, Christison refused to ban the roepiah and pressed the Dutch to suspend importation of their currency. He was not prepared to pauperise a majority of the population, or suffer the certain riots and deaths that would ensue from attempting to impose the gulden. This decision also unintentionally slashed living costs for 23 Indian Division personnel who

23. General Sir Philip Christison, Commander, AFNEI, in Java in late 1945. (AC)

were issued with technically worthless Japanese military scrip for day-to-day purchases in the markets and bazaars of Jakarta. At the same time NICA was invoicing AFNEI for use of local facilities and supplies at the official pre-war exchange rate of NIG7.6 to £1 when the going rate in Jakarta was NIG12.[80] Far from disappearing, therefore, Japanese military currency remained in use in large parts of republican-controlled Java and Sumatra throughout 1946 and well into 1947.[81]

In French Indo-China the Japanese saw no need to replace the piastre after their March 1945 'coup' against the still pro-Vichy FIC government. In addition, military banknotes, denominated in yen, were also in circulation.

This was not demonetised until 17 November 1945. In general, Vietnamese civilians shunned military notes, preferring instead precious metals and other valuable commodities. Old, frequently hoarded, pure silver one-piastre coins had a value and circulation well beyond FIC. (The returning French, for example, bartered with their colonial citizens using pre-war stock piles of silver piastres and opium.[82])

For French colonial officials, however, the biggest financial problem centred on one of their own banknotes. In late August 1945 Japanese authorities in Saigon had ordered the Banque de l'Indochine (BIC) to print new 500-piastre notes for use by the Japanese military. The amount of cash issued was huge and fuelled rampant inflation. By the end of September 1945 most but not all of the new, high-value notes had been seized from Japanese in northern Vietnam by the Chinese military, which was solely responsible for Japanese disarmament north of 16 Parallel.[83] (The BIC main offices and depositories, at Hanoi and Haiphong, lay within Chinese-assigned territory.) In the south of the country, Chinese civilians, particularly businesses, also had large holdings of the 500-piastre notes received in payment for food and other goods supplied to the Japanese military and Japanese trading companies. When in early September 1945 the BIC announced it would no longer honour those particular notes, large-scale riots by Chinese civilians in Saigon, instigated it is thought by Chinese agents, forced the French to reverse their decision.[84]

From late September 1945 onwards, after the arrival in Saigon of HQ SACSEA Control Commission No. 1 and a British Administration in Jakarta, the full extent of Japanese influence over FIC and NEI finances became apparent. Accountants in SEAC expressed serious concerns over the last-gasp currency printing sprees in both colonies. However, even in early December 1945, some 26,000 Japanese were still bearing arms in an unsettled FIC. (French soldiers attempting to come ashore at Hanoi had been fired upon by Chinese troops.) Despite the new rules, therefore, unofficial 'tangible' inducements were necessary to keep JSP in southern Vietnam and Cambodia content, at least for as long as they were providing military assistance.[85] Between September and December 1945 large amounts of piastres were issued to Japanese commanders in Saigon from Japanese accounts to meet their men's pay and other costs. The total amount of negotiable Japanese military assets seized in FIC amounted to an astonishing 77m piastres (about FFr. 1,309,000,000 as at December 1945). This sum included 9.5m piastres in general and canteen funds, a compensation fund for IJA officers and men, and also one for the families of the dead.[86]

Up to January 1946 Japanese units made frequent demands for cash in FIC. To try and control outflows, attempts were made to restrict payments to 50,000 piastres at a time.[87] Little of this money was accounted for once in Japanese possession. Senior British officers in Saigon admitted that the financial responsibilities involved in dealing with Japanese Forces were 'so complicated and involved' that they required specialist help.[88] Later this

24. Japanese occupation currency 10-gulden note issued in the NEI. (AC)

situation prompted a report from Lt. Col. F. H. Sweeny, Force Paymaster, who became extremely concerned about financial malfeasance in parts of SEAC. Sweeny considered it 'probably a good deal more important at present to disarm Japan financially in NEI than physically'.[89] He estimated that the Japanese in FIC and NEI 'put to ground' several hundred million piastres during July, August and September 1945. He saw it as no coincidence that it was in those two countries in which money formerly controlled by the Japanese still had any value.

In the NEI, too, financial manipulations by the Japanese after the capitulation were on a massive scale. Witnesses in Jakarta in late August reported printing presses running 24 hours a day, along with unexplained and unrecorded departures by Japanese aircraft crammed with crates of cash. Notes printed by Nippon Kaihatsu Kinko (NKK) had also been imported. SEAC paymasters were suspicious. When challenged, Japanese officials insisted they had burnt huge amounts of florin and/or gulden banknotes between 21 and 31 August. SEAC's paymasters found evidence to the contrary. At Fort de Koch (Sumatra) there was a discrepancy of fl.734,980,000 and at Palembang (Sumatra) another fl.651,420,000 was missing. The total being estimated at fl.1,479,524,230.[90]

SEAC's manpower shortage and other, more immediate problems meant that investigations into the missing money were cursory at best. Paymaster teams were understaffed and overworked. Little of the missing cash was ever recovered or even seriously pursued. There is more than reasonable suspicion that secret deals were done by senior Japanese military administration officials and nationalists, and that Japanese legacy funding from Jakarta and Saigon helped finance at least two revolutions in Asia and one civil war. For the majority of JSP, however, chaotic financial situations in both Indonesia and Vietnam, the residual value in military script enabled them to continue to purchase, where available, food and medicines locally as and when required for some months after the surrender despite the imposition of draconian currency regulations by the British.

British use of JSP for security purposes in Vietnam ended in late January 1946, shortly before the British withdrawal. By that time, almost all JSP and civilians in the British area of control, ie, south of 16 Parallel, had been concentrated on the southern coast at Cap St Jacques (Vung Tao). Here they awaited repatriation, which still remained a British responsibility. Upon arrival, however, all currency and postal savings books in their possession were confiscated, though receipts were issued.[91]

When General Douglas Gracey, the British commander in southern FIC, left Saigon in mid-January 1946 he bemoaned the fact that his HQ had received no definite instructions about private cash held by Japanese. He signalled General Browning personally that 'it is presumed some arrangement will be come to later whereby on their return to Japan, Japanese personnel will be credited with a similar amount of Imperial Yen in Japan'.[92] Here Gracey was basing his comments on draft demobilisation regulations prepared by the Japanese Government and sent to HQ SACSEA in late 1945 through the Japanese HQ. Articles 12 and 13 of the regulations provided for a gratuity to be paid to servicemen upon demobilisation. General MacArthur, however, had subsequently rejected these regulations but the first the British heard of the change was via the Japanese. Gracey reported that according to HQ JEFSR, both SCAP HQ and the Japanese Government expected returning civilians to arrive with 1,000 yen cash in their physical possession. Similarly, officers were expected to have 500 yen, and NCOs and privates 200 yen. Gracey's HQ had considered this figure 'excessive', since this 'bonus' was estimated as the equivalent of two years' extra pay for a private soldier. (This calculation took no account of massive post-surrender yen devaluation and rampant inflation in occupied Japan, which meant, according to the recollections of former JSP Oba Sadao who finally returned to Japan in 1947, that '800 yen would buy two or three poor lunches'.[93]) Gracey also pointed out that this proposal also involved the 'absurdity' of sending yen from Japan to SEAC then back to Japan with individual JSP.[94]

Fears over possible popular unrest among Japanese over financial uncertainty also concerned Gracey. Many JSP in Vietnam had saved money by under-drawing on their pay entitlement or by remitting money to home through Field Postal Saving Money Orders. JSP were worried about returning home without their Pay Books and Field Postal Savings Books as they would be denied access to their accounts. Gracey saw trouble ahead viewed it as a matter of considerable urgency that the Japanese 'should be given as full information as can be released regarding their future, especially [over financial issues]'. Such uncertainty, he believed, provided 'fertile ground for false propaganda amongst men who are at present quiet and well behaved'.

With British troop numbers being rapidly reduced, Gracey recognised the possibility of 'the French being embarrassed with a large, dissatisfied and restless body of Japanese in their midst'.[95] In acknowledgement of these concerns, SEAC granted permission for Pay and Post Office Savings books to be taken back by JSP to Japan. The question of demobilisation gratuities for JPW and JSP remained unresolved. Browning informed Gracey that a signal was being sent to SCAP requesting confirmation of British arrangements. This signal, however, went unanswered and the wider question of JSP gratuities was subsumed by a new Anglo-American disagreement over working pay certificates for JSP in Malaya (see Chapter 7).[96] In fact, JSP in southern Vietnam avoided a long detention under British control. Repatriation commenced in April 1946 and was largely completed by August that year.[97] Crucially, they travelled direct to Japan using an unexpected surplus in the American-controlled shipping lift, so were not among those evacuated by the British to staging camps in Burma or Malaya prior to (eventual) repatriation. Consequently they were outside the main pool of JSP retained for labour. As a result, the question of gratuities for JSP held in Vietnam was rendered moot.

Within SEAC the concerns raised by Gracey over potential discontent among JSP over their fate, their pay and finances and, more importantly, the confusion existing in British policy over such finances, did not last beyond his own departure from Vietnam in January 1946. Arguably Gracey's concerns were equally relevant to JSP administration outside Vietnam but they were only addressed after much external criticism of British policy.

NEGOTIATIONS BETWEEN THE BRITISH AND JAPANESE HQS, AUGUST 1945–DECEMBER 1946

Although most JSP units had obeyed the first British orders for assistance with the unloading of equipment, supplies and urgent construction projects, HQ JEFSR was concerned that the British had continued to use Japanese personnel after December 1945. No doubt this was an unexpected and unwelcome development for men anticipating 'superior treatment' to PW.[98] As it was, JSP were quickly disabused of any illusions over their status as they were trucked to 'temporary' camps and put to work on repairing roads, railways and bridges, or clearing the drains and sewers of Singapore and larger towns in Malaya.[99]

HQ JEFSR raised the subject of fatigue parties repeatedly with British officers. General Numata sought restrictions on Japanese labour that was, perhaps not surprisingly, 'unpopular' with his officers and men. While he was in no position to refuse SEAC orders, he pressed for assurances that no one would serve in a fatigue party for more than four months or at the longest six months. Instead, Numata proposed sharing the work burden. With tens of thousands of men concentrated on Rempang and Galang islands, he suggested that rotating labour from within this large pool would solve several problems. Men who had worked the longest, he argued, and doing the 'best work' should have priority when it came to repatriation. Numata also raised the question of remuneration. He requested 'fixed scales of compensation' and that 'the sums earned be paid them later…[perhaps even] credited to the Reparation account'.[100]

Numata's fundamental objections to labour and his assertion that his officers and men had 'a tendency…to dislike labour service of all sorts' did not find a sympathetic ear. He emphasised, however, the anxiety his men felt towards labour, which stemmed from their growing fears that their repatriation might well be deferred because they were 'in such service'. Limiting the duration of their labours, Numata argued, and 'granting them definite priority in repatriation', and paying them would not only 'overcome the said tendency' but also make them easier to control, and result in greater productivity since they would have 'definite purpose and direction'.[101]

At this stage (early 1946) the Japanese were pessimistic about their prospects for quick repatriation. Their own most optimistic calculations on the capacity and availability of Japanese shipping had produced an estimate of almost six years.[102] Japanese dependence on Allied assistance was total. (Numata even wrote to Browning to ask if the end of 1947 was a viable date for the completion of repatriation, suggesting that Britain should approach MacArthur directly to secure ships, see Chapter 6.[103])

On paper at least the 700,000 Japanese in SEAC were potentially a vast labour pool. This pool, however, began to shrink considerably once American shipping was secured for the main repatriation programme from mid-1946. JSP units situated closest to British military bases were the ones performing much of the labour. Japanese commanders were aware of this and the growing dissatisfaction it caused. Numata's proposal to spread the work burden found support among British officials, who also saw advantages in using fresh men with the added incentive of speedier repatriation for those doing good work. In reality, the earlier decision to concentrate JSP far away from populated areas created problems for the utilisation of this potential labour as well as organising repatriation. For all practical purposes most JSP remained unavailable for labour not only because of their distant and isolated locations but also due to on-going and unresolved transport difficulties. Shipping shortages in SEAC were so acute that once men had been transported to Rempang or Galang, which lie approximately 30 to 35 miles south of Singapore in (then) Dutch territory, there was insufficient flexibility in schedules even to bring off and return several thousand men every four or six months. Numata's suggestion for labour rotation was, therefore, reluctantly abandoned.[104]

Consequently the men retained for labour beyond April 1946 were generally those same men who had been in working parties since September 1945, a situation that led to considerable resentment. The British solution to growing dissatisfaction among Japanese was at least practical. Colonel Kushida was asked to identify units most likely to 'give trouble if not repatriated'. Rather than rewarding the best workers SEAC, preferring the easier option, was inclined to grant priority repatriation to the more truculent units. One of those identified by Kushida was the 15,000-strong Arima Butai working at Changi. In January 1946 General Numata had also felt it necessary to visit this unit.[105]

Reports of visits to JSP camps in Burma in 1946 filed by ICRC inspectors record 'a certain amount of discontent among the Japanese regarding the [early] repatriation of units from Tenasserim, as most of these had been "Base people", not fighting troops'. British officials explained the earlier repatriation of these men on the grounds that there was no work for them in that part of the country and because there were 'no transport facilities at that time to bring them over to South Burma'.[106]

As new mid- to long-term construction, dockyard and farm labour duties were assigned to JSP in Burma and Malaya, their camps became more permanent settlements. After rebuffing Japanese requests for repatriation, SEAC anticipated a period of stability and consolidation. Robust assertions that surrendered Japanese were outside the scope of 1929 PW Convention had so far proved effective in deflecting criticism. Construction and other projects using Japanese labour began in British-controlled territories. Yet the British position was soon to face challenges from the ICRC and from Tokyo, not from the Japanese Government, but perhaps more unexpectedly from General MacArthur's occupation administration. Charged with the early dissolution and disbandment of the Imperial Japanese Armed forces, MacArthur was not impressed by British arguments that paucity of resources, particularly in shipping, made delayed repatriation unavoidable. Britain would have to find another argument to retain control of its Japanese when faced with the reality of immense American logistic capacity.

NOTES TO CHAPTER 3

1. International Committee for the Red Cross, *Convention Relative to the Treatment of Prisoners of War* (Geneva, 27 July 1929), Article 75.

2. Maschke Commission figures (1956), Takemae's figures for Japanese. See Rüdiger Overmans, 'German Historiography, the War Losses and the Prisoners of War', in Eisenhower and the German POWs: Facts Against Falsehood, eds, Stephen Ambrose and Günter Bischof (Baton Rouge, 1992), 143; and Takemae Eiji, The Allied Occupation of Japan and It's Legacy (London, 2002), 110.

3. Stephen Connor, 'Side-Stepping Geneva: Japanese Troops under British Control, 1945-47'. *Journal of Contemporary History, Vol. 45*, no. 2 (2010), 389. Parts of this article are reproduced here.

4. Nicholas Tarling, 'Rice and Reconciliation: The Anglo-Thai Peace Negotiations of 1945'. *Siam Society Journal, 66*, no. 2 (1978), 59–112.

5. SACSEA to COS, 2 Sept. 1945. CAB 121/697.

6. SEACOS 456, 24 Aug. 1945. AIR 40/1850.

7. See Woodburn Kirby, *Surrender of Japan*, 277, 321; Dunn, *First Vietnam War*, 260, 280, 339-41; Anderson, *Java*, 141–3; Paul H. Kratoska, *The Thailand-Burma Railway, 1942-1946: Documents and Selected Writings* (London, 2005), 327–8; B. K. Cheah, *Red Star Over Malaya: Resistance and Social Conflict during and after the Japanese Occupation, 1941-1946* (Singapore, 2003), 304.

8. Tamayama, Kazuo. *Railwaymen in the War: Tales by Japanese Railway Soldiers in Burma and Thailand, 1941-47* (Basingstoke, 2005), 228-275.

9. Roadnight, 'Sleeping with the Enemy', 255; and McMillan, *British Occupation of Indonesia*, 28-30, 128–30.

10. *House of Commons Debates, Hansard,* 17 Oct. 1945, Vol. 414, c.1151-4.

11. Woodburn Kirby, *Surrender of Japan*, 218.

12. For *senjinkun*, see Strauss, *Anguish of Surrender*, 30-47; and Hata, 'From Consideration to Contempt', in Moore and Fedorowich (eds), *Prisoners of War*, 253–76.

13. Woodburn Kirby, *Surrender of Japan*, 218.

14. Allegations by Bacque of American mistreatment of SEP/DEF in Europe have been comprehensively rebutted. James Bacque, *Other Losses: the Shocking Truth Behind the Mass Deaths of Disarmed German Soldiers and Civilians Under Eisenhower's Command* (New York, 1991); and Ambrose and Bischof, *Facts Against Falsehood*.

15. *Hansard*, 27 Mar. 1946, Vol. 421, 531–40.

16. Brian L. Villa, 'The Diplomatic and Political Context of the POW Camps Tragedy', in Ambrose and Bischof, eds, *Facts Against Falsehood*, 58.

17. Ibid., 62

18. Arthur L. Smith, *Churchill's German Army: Wartime Strategy and Cold War Politics, 1943-1947* (London, 1977), 89. See also Henry Faulk, *Group Captives. The Re-education of German Prisoners of War in Britain 1945-1948* (London, 1977); Matthew B. Sullivan, *Thresholds of Peace: Four Hundred Thousand German Prisoners and the People of Britain, 1944-1948* (London, 1979).

19. 'Policy of Post-War Employment of German Prisoners of War'. War Office Working Paper (1944). WO 32/11131, cited in Smith, *Churchill's German Army*, 70.

20. Villa, 'Diplomatic and Political Context of the POW Camps Tragedy', 60.

21. Ibid., 61.

22. ICRC, *Report of the International Committee of the Red Cross on its activities during the Second World War, Vol. 1* (Geneva, 1948), 540.

23.   Smith, *Churchill's German Army*, 90.

24.   Winston Churchill, Woodford Speech. 23 Nov. 1954. *The Unwritten Alliance: Speeches 1953-1959 by Winston S. Churchill*, ed, R. Churchill (London, 1961), 196–7; and Smith, *Churchill's German Army*, 7–12.

25.   James L. Lucas, *The Last Days of the Reich: The Collapse of Nazi Germany, May 1945* (London, 1986), 232. One of the Hungarians became mayor of a town in Yorkshire.

26.   *Hansard*, 7 June 1945, Vol. 411, 1083-4W.

27.   Pacific War Research Society, *Japan's Longest Day*, 37.

28.   'Second Plenary Meeting with Japanese Delegation', 26 Aug. 1945. FO 371/46459.

29.   Mountbatten, *Report to the Chiefs of Staff*, 184.

30.   Personal interview with Oba Sadao, 20 Oct. 2005.

31.   FO to JSM Washington, 5 Oct. 1946. CAB 122/1183.

32.   It is not suggested that JSP in SEAC experienced widespread ill-treatment comparable to that suffered by Allied PW of the Japanese.

33.   MacArthur to Mountbatten, 22 Aug. 1945. AIR 40/1850.

34.   Mountbatten quoting MacArthur, 25 Aug. 1945. AIR 40/1850. Author's italics.

35.   AIR 40/1850. Capitalisation in original, author's italics.

36.   WO request for ruling on normal deaths among Japanese, 18 Mar. 1946. FO 371/54242.

37.   Netherlands Representative to the CCS, 4 Dec. 1945. CAB 121/511.

38.   Dutch Ambassador to Foreign Secretary, 'Memorandum on the Situation in Java', 29 Sept. 1945. CAB 121/697.

39.   John Springhall, 'Kicking out the Vietminh': How Britain Allowed France to Reoccupy South Indo-China, 1945-46'. *Journal of Contemporary History*, Vol. 40, 1 (2005), 125.

40.   Numata to Mountbatten, 'Report on Inspection Tour', 27 Feb. 1946. WO 203/2727.

41.   Personal interview with Takado Eichi, ex-16 IJA (Kido *Butai*, Java), 25 Oct. 2005.

42.   Mountbatten, *Personal Diary*, 303. Also Roadnight, 'Sleeping with the Enemy', 255.

43.   Handwritten note on policy summary, 1 Dec. 45, WO 203/5963.

44.   HQ Air Cmd. SEA, 'Report on disposal of Japanese Air Force war materials', 28 Dec. 45. WO 203/5963.

45.   SEACOS 596, 'Problem of repatriation of Japanese personnel from within SEAC'. 28 Dec. 45. WO 203 /963.

46.   HQ SACSEA to Air Ministry, 28 Dec. 1945., WO 203/5963.

47.   Roger Buckley, 'Responsibility without Power: Britain and Indonesia, August 1945-February 1946', in *Indonesian Experience: The Role of Japan and Britain, 1943-1948*, Ian Nish (ed), (London, 1979), 43.

48.   Oba Sadao, 'My Recollections of Indonesia, 1944-1947', in Nish, ed, *Indonesian Experience*, 7.

49.   FO to UKLM, Tokyo. 11 Jan. 1947. CAB 537/2493.

50.   Mountbatten to COS, 18 Sept. 1945. AIR 40/1850.

51.   'Views of this HQ [SCAP] on JSP,' 28 Aug. 1945. AIR 40/1850.

52.   HQ SEAC to Commanders in Chief, SEAC, 'Treatment of Japanese, German and Italian Personnel', 11 Oct. 1945. AIR 40/1850.

53.   SACSEA, 'Relations with Surrendered Japanese Forces and with Enemy Civilians.' 24 Aug. 1945. AIR 40/1850.

54.   See Chapter 6, n. 70.

55.   UKNA to SACSEA, 13 Feb. 1946. WO 203/5963.

56.   David Lee, *And we thought the war was over* (Stoke Abbot, 1991), 89.

57.   SACSEA to Cabinet Offices, 'Summary of recent operations', 16 Sept. 1945. FO 371/46459.

58.   'Report on RAPWI in Java. Chapter 2, Appendix E', 14 Sept. 1945. WO 203/5960.

59.   See Chapter 3.

60.   26 Aug. 1945. FO 371/46459.

61.   'Minutes of meeting at Tanglin Barracks...between Col. W. J. Armstrong...and Col. Kushida', 30 May 1946. WO 203/6339.

62.   Ibid.

63.   Numata to Browning, 'Proposed tour [of] Burma', 9 June 1946. WO 203/6339.

64.   C-in-C AFNEI to Lt Gov-Gen of NEI. 'Japanese labour – hand over to Dutch', 30 Mar. 1946. WO 203/6339.

65.   'Minutes of a Meeting Held in Jogjakarta 1-2 April, 1946' in *Republican Forces Fulfilled Two Tasks of Allied Forces in Indonesia.* Ministry of Information of the Republic of Indonesia (Jakarta, 1949), 5.

66.   Christison to Dempsey, 18 Jan. 1946. WO 203/2727.

67.   AFNEI, 'Retention of JSP for Labour by Dutch', 20 May 1946. WO 203/6339.

68.   FO to WO, 1 Oct. 1946. FO 371/554306.

69.   David G. Marr, *Vietnam 1945: The Quest for Power* (London, 1995), 338.

70.   HQ SEAC to Commanders in Chief, SEAC, 'Treatment of Japanese, German and Italian Personnel', Oct. 1945. AIR 40/1850.

71.   WO to SACSEA, 29 Sept. 1945. AIR 40/1850.

72.   McEnery, *Epilogue in Burma*, 95.

73.   Rupert Lockwood, *Black Armada: Australia and the Struggle for Indonesian Independence, 1942-49.* (Sydney, 1982), 109.

74.   Arthur La Bern, 'I was in Surabaya when the shooting began!' *The War Illustrated*, No. 221, (December 7, 1945), 505.

75.   Doulton, *Fighting Cock,* 280.

76.   Robert Cribb, "Political Dimensions of the Currency Question 1945-1947" *Indonesia* 31 (1982), 113-136; 117-9.

77.   SEACOS 505, 3 Oct. 1945, WO 203/5567.

78.   FO to SACSEA, COSSEA 367, 2 Oct. 1945, WO 203/5567.

79.   SEACOS 505, 3 Oct. 1945, WO 203/5567.

80.   Doulton, *Fighting Cock*, 234. See, Donnison, *British Military Administration*, 225.

81.   Kazuya Fujita, 'Japanese Military Currency (1937-1945): Quantities Printed and Issued.' *International Bank Note Society Journal, Vol. 42,* no. 3 (2003), 22.

82.   Marr, *Vietnam 1945*, 327 n. 145.

83.   Ibid., 543.

84.   Ellen J. Hammer, *The Struggle for Indochina 1940-1955: Viet Nam and the French Experience* (Stanford, 1966), 137.

85.   Mountbatten to COS, 2 Dec. 1945, WO 203/4432.

86.   Control Commission No. 1[Saigon] to HQ SEAC, 6 Nov. 1945, WO 203/4583.

87.   'Rate of Pay and Type of Currency for Issue to Jap Forces taking part in Operations in SEAC.' 23 Oct. 1945, WO 203/4583.

88.   Control Commission [Saigon] to HQ SEAC, Jan. 1946. WO 203/4432.

89.   Lt Col F. H. Sweeny, 'Report from Officer Force Paymaster', Control Commission No. 1, Saigon, 29 Jan. 1946. NA 5204.
90.   Ibid.
91.   Gracey to Browning, 16 Jan. 1945, WO 203/4432.
92.   Ibid.
93.   Oba Sadao. Personal correspondence with author, July 2008.
94.   Gracey to Browning, 16 Jan. 1945. WO 203/4432.
95.   Ibid.
96.   SEAC to Gracey, 'Gratuities on discharge'. 20 Jan. 1946. WO 203/4432. Follow-up, 'Working Pay for JSP in South East Asia', 6 Feb. 1947. CO 537/2493.
97.   Marr, *Vietnam 1945*, 543.
98.   Personal interview with Oba Sadao, 20 Oct. 2005.
99.   Genatro Shikimachi, 'In Singapore', in Frank Gibney, ed., *Senso: The Japanese Remember the Pacific War* (New York, 1995), 226-227.
100.   Numata to Browning, 'Fatigue Parties for Allies in Malaya and elsewhere'. 25 Jan. 1946. WO 203/4432.
101.   Ibid.
102.   Numata to Browning, 'Expediting the Repatriation of Japanese Personnel'. 23 Jan. 1946. WO 203/4432.
103.   HQ SACSEA, 'Minutes of meeting held by the Chief of Staff with Lt Gen Numata…', 25 Feb. 1946. AIR 40/1852.
104.   HQ ALFSEA to HQ JEFSR, 'Relief of Work Parties'. 23 May 1946. WO 203/6339.
105.   'Minutes of meeting between Col SD, ALFSEA and Col Kushida', 30 May 1946. WO 203/6339.
106.   ICRC to FO. 'Burma: Japanese Surrendered Personnel and Prisoners of War Visited between November 30 and December 9, 1946 by Mr H. Frei, delegate of the ICRC in India', 2. FO 369/3816B.

4

'SQUEEZING THE AMERICAN GOOSE'
SHIPPING RATES AND DOLLAR SHORTAGE

One of the main tasks of the Allied Forces...is the ultimate evacuation of all Japanese surrendered personnel to Japan. This task cannot be completed until shipping is available and until Japan is in a position to accept the very large numbers of personnel involved. Certain interim measures....

—HQ Allied Forces Netherlands East Indies, 14 November 1945[1]

Shipping remained just as crucial an issue for the British Government in September 1945 as it had been throughout the war. Ships were vital for the feeding of the nation. Policy initiatives played second fiddle to the decrees of the logistics lords in the Ministry of Transport (MOT), whose shipping schedules, arranged months in advance, might have been chiselled in stone. Food shortages in Britain were so severe that requests for ships from distant theatres of, now, 'peaceful' operations such as SEAC had little chance of success. Yet Britain had made 'Great Power promises' and undertakings at Potsdam, however unwise. These could not be shrugged off with the coming of an earlier than expected peace. Mounting problems at home, in Europe and in the Empire forced Britain to juggle priorities. Repatriation of Japanese forces was one.

By the autumn of 1945 sections of the British Government, particularly the Foreign Office and the Treasury, were under no illusions as to the financial and economic crisis facing the country. Reports by Lord Keynes had carried stark conclusions. Britain had lost a quarter of its national wealth (as at 1939). Sterling balances were precarious and there was a pressing need to increase exports by 50-to-70 percent over the pre-war level to compensate for the loss.[2] Inevitably the availability of shipping featured as a fundamental requirement in every blueprint for economic revival. There were, however, a host of claims on the war-reduced British merchant fleet and, with the end of Lend-Lease, the soon-to-be-returned American Liberty Ships. These claims included demands for the prompt repatriation of British service personnel; the Recovery of Allied prisoners-of-war and internees (RAPWI); a requirement to send fresh troops and administrators to reoccupy the colonies; an urgent need to relieve famine in parts of India, Malaya, Netherlands East Indies (NEI) and French Indo-China (FIC); and the repatriation of hundreds of thousands of Southeast Asian labourers who had been transported by the Japanese. Also on this list, ostensibly at the top, was the formal Potsdam undertaking that: 'The Japanese military forces, after being completely disarmed, shall be permitted to return to their homes with the opportunity to lead peaceful and productive lives'.[3]

It is difficult to overestimate the importance of the lack of British or British-flagged merchant shipping in both Britain's wartime and post-war policy and planning in Southeast Asia. Primacy of supply and first claim on shipping had always been given or come from the western European theatre. In a secondary theatre such as SEAC the problems associated with lack of shipping for supply and troop movements were constant and acute.[4] SEAC incorporated a massive land and sea area, as well as myriad islands, and thus extensive coastlines. Burma alone, for example (excluding the narrow Tenasserim 'panhandle' that extends southwards) is in area almost the size of France, the Low Countries and part of central Germany.[5] Ships were therefore the arteries of SEAC. Just as shipping shortages had hampered and even dictated British strategy during the war, those same shortages continued to pose difficulties in peacetime, compounding manpower and logistical deficiencies. In fact, nothing demonstrates the totality of SEAC's dependence on shipping as the problem of Japanese repatriation.

For Britain's Government in 1945 there were no easy options in any area of policy. Anticipated and immediate benefits of peace proved illusory. Multiple, competing claims on shipping required careful deliberation, often at Cabinet level, over allocation of very limited resources. Britain's economic situation was dire. Food was still strictly rationed. Disparate parts of the British Empire had also faced severe food shortages or famine, such as in Bengal, where millions perished in 1943–44. In addition to the question of the surrendered Japanese, millions of British and Commonwealth soldiers were clamouring for repatriation to Canada, India, South Africa, Australia or New Zealand. Indeed, prompt repatriation of all British personnel serving in the Far East had been an election promise by the eventually victorious Labour party. The dangled carrot no doubt had its effect. General Slim had advised a highly displeased Churchill that 14 Army would vote Labour 'to a man' (in fact servicemen under 21 were ineligible to vote).[6]

Britain's struggling economy was dependent upon raw materials and fuels necessary for reconstruction being imported and trade goods exported to earn vital foreign exchange to keep the economy moving. Very often goods and people were seeking to move in different and therefore doubly costly directions. A harbour berth given to a repatriation ship meant one less for those bringing food or raw materials or one waiting to take on an export cargo. Perhaps it was inevitable that Japanese repatriation, despite the Potsdam pledge, could not remain a British priority. Understandably, preference was given to the relatively small numbers of Allied Far East Prisoners of War (FEPOW) who were shipped home in late 1945 and early 1946. As public knowledge of the privations suffered by FEPOW increased—the first of the 'Death Railway' memoirs being published in July 1946—animosity grew towards Japanese in general.[7] Thus one advantage for Britain's Government was that there was little interest in Britain or elsewhere (except for Japan) in the fate of the Japanese armed forces. For a while the pressed British authorities were able to relax under the assumption that the retention-issue had become a regional, mid to long-term problem to be addressed at SEAC's convenience and discretion. Lack of money, however, would keep Britain both a shipping supplicant and debtor.

Overconfidence in the MOT about the speed with which the British merchant shipping industry would revive was another key factor. Once General MacArthur focussed upon the numbers of Japanese in SEAC—as part of his official commitments—British policy was exposed to wider and ever more critical scrutiny.

In the first weeks following the Japanese surrender when the sheer scale of the required shipping lift had been identified, Britain had not hesitated to request and attempt to justify American assistance. By doing so, Britain's own lack of shipping capacity was revealed to the Americans. Another consequence was that this request for help also gave unintended notice to the Americans that a primary American and Potsdam-enshrined policy objective—the demobilisation of the Japanese military—was at risk of delay. Further, in attempting to manipulate and extend a very generous American subsidy to meet that objective, Britain risked jeopardising, at great expense and embarrassment, not only the entire repatriation programme but considerable American goodwill.

As has been described, shortage of shipping was not a new experience for SEAC or for Britain. In the context of Anglo-American negotiations over Japanese repatriation it is important to appreciate that difficulties and disputes over shipping allocation and resources were by no means new to the Alliance.[8] During the war, Britain became dependent on American-built ships and American logistical support. Despite this very obvious dependence British strategists attempted not only to influence Allied strategy but also to dominate that policy. This resulted in the creation of a 'gap between strategic ambition and logistical reality', that resulted in bitter controversy over the Second Front in Europe.[9] Similar unrealistic British assumptions would dog the Far East campaign as well.

ANGLO-AMERICAN FRICTION OVER SHIPPING

Even in early 1945 Britain's lack of merchant shipping capacity was still glaring despite the reduction in U-boat attacks on convoys and bombing of yards and ports. Victory in Europe had eased the pressures on naval shipbuilding but put immediate pressure on inefficient merchant yards, many of which were affected by industrial disputes no longer prohibited by wartime legislation. These yards could not meet the demand from within Britain and the Empire. Dependency on American vessels therefore remained high and not just in Europe. Requests to General MacArthur in Tokyo for more ships to complete JSP repatriation emphasised this dependency. Consequently availability of merchant shipping became key to Anglo-American JSP-repatriation diplomacy. To the dismay of the Foreign Office disagreements over numbers, schedules and ships began to echo the divisive Second Front arguments of 1941–43, with potentially lasting consequences for post-war relations.

In 1939 Britain had still possessed, by a very big margin, the world's largest maritime fleet.[10] How had a once-great maritime nation been so humbled? In the mid-1930s British naval planners had viewed a wartime shortage of shipping as inconceivable. From 1918 onwards, the British-flagged merchant fleet had suffered from marked overcapacity. In the event of a European war it was assumed that British ships would discontinue distant overseas routes and return to home waters. It was also anticipated that ship owners in neutral countries would accede to any British naval blockade or, even more likely, accept contracts going to British ports. In addition, it was widely believed that new ships from British yards would replace any losses inflicted by U-boats. Curiously, the U-boat threat itself was discounted because of technological developments by the Anti-Submarine Detection Investigation Committee (ASDIC). Any risk of the repetition of the threat of famine that had faced Britain in 1917 was therefore discounted. Confidence in the ability to maintain ship numbers was so high that those same planners ventured the opinion that the 'enlarged fleet would compensate for shipping capacity shifted to military service…'.[11]

Alas, when war came, Britain did face both shipping and food shortages, and they were almost immediate. ASDIC failed to prevent U-boat attacks on ships in vulnerable, often-delayed convoys. Yet the need for American ships did not stem from losses due solely to German submarines. While on the outbreak of war some British ships had returned from working distant routes, many neutral ships 'defected' or were seized in ports by the sheer speed of the German advance. Equally unexpectedly a large number of neutral owners proved unwilling to risk their vessels in British waters and moved their ships to safer markets such as routes around South America.

As sinkings increased, so did the need for repairs. Shipping lane blackouts caused frequent collisions and the more northerly courses taken to avoid enemy attacks took vessels into more severe weather and, inevitably, greater damage and wear and tear. Work for British repair yards started to back up, compounded by poor administration and organisation in the yards themselves. Building output did not keep pace with the mounting losses. Britain built 'too few ships, sent them on too lengthy voyages, protected them poorly, and unloaded them slowly'. Britain's Government had been reluctant to insist that the labour unions accept a wartime national plan for docks and yards. The public paid a heavy price. Other planning weaknesses were also revealed, such as the shift to the bigger but fewer western ports such as Liverpool and Swansea. Both were served by limited rail routes. Problems related to antiquated port and transport infrastructure hampered efforts to unload ships and prepare them quickly. The response from the Government was slow and ineffective. The result, inevitably, was that Britain became 'logistically dependent on American allocations'.[12]

Eventually these allocations became available at a considerable and growing cost through the Lend-Lease programme. Weak sterling made all US gold-dollar purchases very expensive for the Treasury. As a consequence, imports from the Sterling Area, ie, the dominions (except Canada), Ireland, Iceland, the Sudan, Egypt, Iraq and Portugal were preferred.[13] Attempts to protect gold reserves and foreign exchange forced ships to undertake longer, more dangerous voyages.[14] By December 1941 American shipping was providing both Lend-Lease cargoes and commercial services for eastern Commonwealth nations of some 1.5m deadweight tons. Some respite for

Britain's economy and citizens was envisaged in American plans for new ships, scheduled for purely British use, which would increase that figure to 7m deadweight tons.[15] This was a very significant increase and there was widespread expectation that this extra capacity would meet Britain's civilian and military needs. However, this belief was founded on another cherished Whitehall assumption: that United States entry into the war against Germany would make ships available in ever-greater numbers and perhaps reduce the crippling Lend-Lease terms that some Cabinet members viewed as sounding the death knell of the Commonwealth.[16] There was even the hope of an arrangement developing into a true 'financial pooling' of resources with consideration for Lend-Lease written off. Expectations of ever greater and cheaper American logistic bounty, however, were unfulfilled.[17] Although the Japanese attack on Pearl Harbor brought the United States into the war in Europe it also opened a new and distant theatre of war that was slow and expensive to supply. In this sense Pearl Harbor was a 'disaster' for Britain's civilians.[18] Competition for shipping resources became intense. Unlike Britain, in the United States the US Army had direct control of its own supplies and troop transports. As a result, the US civil authorities carried much less influence with their Service chiefs. Any prospective advantages for Britain were thus jeopardised because simultaneously 'the needs of the British armies began rapidly to increase and the British-controlled fleet to diminish'.[19]

Britain's official history of the role of merchant shipping during the war is measured and restrained in its analysis of the pressures put on Anglo-American relations by this state of affairs, typically describing it as 'as severe as can be imagined'. Since the Americans built more dry-cargo ships than they lost, but the British lost many more ships than they built, 'American net gains…did not suffice to meet [Britain's] expanding needs'. Since sea-borne imports represented only a tiny percentage of United States' economic activity, food and consumable supplies for American civilians were never put in jeopardy by the shipping shortage. On the other hand the needs of the American armed forces 'appeared to be in constant jeopardy throughout the greater part of the war'.[20]

American military planners were quick to criticise British 'flexibility'. In 1943 for example, British planners identified a short-term shipping glut on Atlantic routes and tried to arrange the transfer of American ships to the Mediterranean. The Americans assumed automatically that Britain was giving priority to post-war Imperial interests over immediate Allied objectives.[21] One noteworthy legacy of this controversy, directly relevant to the situation facing SEAC in 1945–7, was the considerable, almost obsessive, suspicion of British motives among the senior US commanders in the Pacific theatre. British demands for shipping and resources that American commanders considered vital for their Pacific campaigns resulted in considerable animosity. Significantly, two key American commanders in the Pacific remained in powerful and influential roles after the Japanese surrender. One was Admiral Chester Nimitz, who became Chief of United States Naval Operations in Washington. The other was General Douglas MacArthur, appointed SCAP, in Tokyo. Neither was sympathetic to British interests.

In an attempt to resolve continuing and competing Allied demands for resources, 'combined' committees were created in 1942. Two of these supervised shipping. Military needs came under the remit of the Combined Chiefs of Staff (CCS) consisting of the British Chiefs of Staff (COS) and the United States Joint Chiefs of Staff (USJCS). Their civilian counterparts were the Combined Shipping Adjustment Boards (CSAB), which met in London and Washington, and included representatives from Britain's Ministry of War Transport (MWT) and the American War Shipping Authority (WSA). It was an unhappy and not particularly successful association as, Americans and Britons each contributed to and compounded 'strategic delusions and administrative errors'.[22] American interdepartmental warfare meant that the CSAB never functioned effectively. General Brehon Somervell, head of the US Army Services of Supply, suspected the WSA was 'too friendly' towards the British and withheld co-operation at every turn. Somervell recommended severe restrictions on Lend-Lease after the defeat of Germany, and even for Lend-Lease items in British possession not specifically needed for the fight against Japan to be returned immediately.[23] Even within the WSA some officials resented the 'supposed British presumption that the CSAB's task constituted funnelling more American aid to Britain'.[24]

Victory in the Battle of the Atlantic meant the German threat to Britain's supply routes disappeared. Ironically this victory marginalised British influence over Allied strategy, particularly over the scheduling of the Second Front. With Britain's food supplies no longer in danger, the island could serve as a secure staging post for the invasion of France. Its logistical dependence on the United States remained.[25] British interests became further marginalised as the United States focussed on D-Day. As a consequence of European priorities, SEAC either lost or never received the shipping and landing craft essential for a major seaborne landing. (Operation Zipper, the invasion of Malaya, went ahead in September 1945 but with much reduced resources.) Britain also had to consider the dependence and demands of the Dutch and French colonial operations, particularly as some of their merchant shipping was within the British-controlled shipping pool. (The sheer lack of merchant shipping in the Asia-Pacific theatre contrasted with, for example, the situation in the Mediterranean where a great many Italian merchant ships had been captured by the Allies. In contrast, two-thirds of Japanese merchant shipping tonnage had been sunk by August 1945, and little of what remained was seaworthy.[26])

Yet another major British concern was the type of ship the Americans would build to meet civilian needs for the remainder of the war. The American decision to replace Liberty ships with fewer but bigger and much faster Victory ships meant a reduction in overall Allied carrying capacity. These new ships, however, were built to commercial specifications and so were therefore potentially capable of competing with British sea-freight companies after the war. British policy sought to see this decision reversed and pushed for more Liberty ships instead. Operational control of these ships was also of major importance to Britain's planners and, as always, the Treasury. By seeking flag transfers of part of the American allocations, British administrators hoped to gain operational efficiency, convenience and financial savings. American ships were expensive to buy (assuming American shipping 'champions' in Congress would have allowed purchases). Instead, Britain preferred 'bareboat' charters, by which overall wartime control was secured as well as incurring all costs and liabilities. Since crewing, provisioning and fuelling such ships was then a British obligation, all charges remained in sterling. Bareboat charters later became the mainstay of the repatriation programme from SEAC, though the loss of wartime 'discounts' was to be a major disappointment for the Treasury. Subsequent Admiralty parsimony over the supply of fuel oil or coal, the provision of food and even crews for repatriation vessels leaving SEAC would conjure up the familiar spectre of bitter intra-Allied shipping disputes.

REPATRIATION AS A 'PROBLEM' RATHER THAN AN OBLIGATION

Britain did not merely go through the motions in assessing repatriation requirements. Initial estimates for the completion of the repatriation of the 738,000 Japanese illustrate SEAC's serious transportation difficulties. In late December 1945, Mountbatten first brought 'the problem of repatriation' to the attention of the COS, pointing out that the total personnel shipping lift stood at 23,000 but of that only 14,000 was suitable for a voyage to Japan. Admiralty calculations predicted the task would take Britain nearly five years to complete. Mountbatten, who intended to seek extra shipping from

MacArthur, foresaw that 'the probable political, economic and military repercussions' from keeping large numbers of Japanese for such a length of time were 'considerable'. While searching for other transport options, British planners were even forced to consider repatriation via the Burma-Thailand Railway but this was dismissed because of safety concerns over using the crumbling structure.[27]

The British Staff Mission in Tokyo, headed by Lt-General Sir Charles Gairdner (Prime Minister Clement Attlee's personal representative in Japan) was also quick to see the implications of Mountbatten's report. MacArthur's SCAP HQ had recently announced plans to repatriate all JSP from US-controlled territories by mid-1946. Gairdner informed London that he foresaw difficulty developing over the disparity in rates of return and suggested 'closer co-ordination' between SEAC and SCAP.[28] Foremost in Gairdner's mind was the fear that *anti-British* feeling as opposed to anti-Allied feeling might develop in Japan, for both SCAP and the Japanese Government were keeping accurate tallies of repatriation numbers. One early and derisory SCAP report, copied to London, described total repatriation from SEAC up to 3 February 1946 as 'less than one per cent' of those repatriated under SCAP.[29]

MacArthur then offered SEAC 9,000 spare capacity in reconditioned Japanese merchant shipping, this was over a quarter of the long-range passenger spaces available at that time.[30] Even this was less than Mountbatten had hoped for. It shortened the completion estimate to three years but only if the return to owners of Japanese-seized ships was postponed.[31] Unsurprisingly even the revised estimate was poorly received in London. When the United Kingdom Liaison Mission in Tokyo (UKLM) relayed that there were US Government restrictions on the use of Japanese shipping outside the Australian Military Forces Area (AMFA) in the western Pacific, and reported that some repatriation shipping was crewed and paid for by Japan, it fostered a feeling in London's Whitehall that Britain was being hard done by.[32]

In early January 1946 the British chiefs informed Mountbatten that the manpower and financial commitment involved in guarding and feeding JSP for so long and the disparity between the US and British schedules was 'unacceptable'. Further, the unequal allocation of shipping resources was deemed 'unjust'. Repatriation was seen—in London if nowhere else—as 'an Allied commitment', and that as a result Britain had 'a strong case' with which to approach MacArthur, for more free Liberty-Ships, or if that were to fail, the US Chiefs of Staff'.[33] In fact, since much of SCAP's extra shipping had been allocated to speed up repatriation from US-controlled areas, MacArthur could not unilaterally authorise their use in a British Command. Instead, he suggested increased shipping be supplied by the British Government to allow SEAC to complete Japanese repatriation by the end of 1946. This merely highlighted the British problem. With the end of the United Maritime Agreement (UMA), the large passenger ships had been withdrawn from the British-controlled trooping fleet. In truth, reduced British resources rendered this option out of the question. Only the United States had spare shipping capacity to meet MacArthur's preferred date.

By early spring 1946, SEAC had a tolerable and less-embarrassed grip on the wide-ranging problems facing it in Southeast Asia. British troops had left Vietnam in January 1946. This had extricated the British Government from one awkward political problem and dramatically eased the immediate manpower shortage by freeing 20 Indian Division for other duties. Relations with Thailand (Siam) were also improving. JSP were under Thai guard, so allowing British troops to leave. Also Thai rice was being exported to areas in need. Concerns over sabotage and attacks by Japanese 'stay behind groups' had also largely disappeared, as had concerns over revolt or mass breakouts among confined and disgruntled JSP. If anything, the former foe had gained considerable kudos both for their strong work ethic and their assistance with peacekeeping duties (still ongoing in Indonesia). In fact the Japanese were genuinely appreciated, their behaviour being described by the British Foreign Office as 'exemplary so far'.[34]

As immediate political and security problems eased, SEAC was able to start looking towards mid-term rather than short-term solutions. These solutions necessarily included JSP, particularly as British interpretations of repatriation obligations gradually merged with those of 'reparations' in the form of Japanese labour. An early March 1946 report by Major General H. E. Pyman, Chief of the General Staff, ALFSEA, suggested that the large numbers of Japanese presented 'a temporary opportunity to employ Japanese labour on a large scale for constructive and rehabilitation work in Malaya and Burma...'. It was considered unlikely that the work would involve 'any large financial commitment' since it was 'only coolie work of an unattractive kind in unhealthy surroundings'. Interestingly, even at this early date there was an assumption that JSP labour would probably be available 'for the first six months of 1947' despite official targets of December 1946.

Military projects identified as 'ripe for development...[to be] completed with cost-free labour' and which might otherwise have been 'delayed or never begun' included clearing artillery ranges and firing areas, drainage and repair of coastal defences, construction and maintenance of military roads, and a strategic lateral road in Northern Malaya. Potential public programmes included road construction and new railways, and anti-malarial spraying. Private enterprises were also to benefit, though they were to be charged 'market rates for JSP employed'. Pyman considered only hand tools

25. (L to R) Lt Gen Gairdner, Gen MacArthur, Lt Gen Eichelberger and the Rt Hon. A Gascoigne in Tokyo. June 1947. (MMA)

would be needed, there being 'an added attraction that hard manual labour in unattractive areas is the soundest form of indoctrination for a defeated army'.[35]

In March 1946 came unexpected news of an offer from MacArthur to clear all JSP from SEAC within the year (see below).[36] Most awkwardly for SEAC, the Americans were now expecting repatriation to be completed some 18 months earlier than anticipated.[37] Mountbatten, concerned over the loss of this manpower, requested the COS for permission to retain approximately 100,000 JSP in SEAC on the grounds that their labour was 'absolutely essential to the production of food'. He supported his request by saying Lord Killearn, Special Representative of the British Government in Southeast Asia, and the governors of Burma and Malaya had argued for extra labour at a conference on food provision at Singapore. These 105,000 Japanese, one-seventh of the total in SEAC, were to become a huge embarrassment to the British Government and the source of considerable friction between the British and American governments.

Even at this early stage, however, Mountbatten was aware of potential problems over their repatriation, requesting that the COS 'earmark the necessary British ships' in due course as the Americans '*will be unable to do so*'.[38] Two weeks later Mountbatten sent a signal correcting his assertion that Lord Killearn had requested retention and admitting that the JSP were not to be employed on the production of food at all. They were, however, to be employed on key 'related' tasks such as dockyard labour.[39] The COS agreed and so major programmes in construction, agriculture and transport throughout SEAC were given the go ahead. All of these programmes were underwritten by an assumption that—at this stage quite productive—JSP labour would remain available. Yet even as London's approval to retain Japanese in SEAC was granted, concerns were being expressed by the United States over the slow rate of repatriation. Focussed as they were on intra-Command problems, Mountbatten's staff were oblivious to wider issues and were unaware of a rival claimant to JSP in SEAC. That claimant was General Douglas MacArthur.

MACARTHUR'S PRIMARY MISSION AT RISK

General MacArthur's command had settled quickly into an unexpectedly compliant and docile Japan. His occupation administration, General Headquarters Supreme Commander for the Allied Powers (GHQ SCAP), made swift progress in the disarmament and subsequent demobilisation of the Japanese military. These two programmes were key, prescribed components of the United States Initial Post Surrender Policy for Japan, which defined MacArthur's primary mission to Japan.[40] In order to demobilise the Imperial Japanese forces and so complete that mission, however, all Japanese military personnel had to return. While the United States military attended to the repatriation of JPW and JSP from the Pacific islands, the Philippines, Korea and Formosa (Taiwan); SEAC was given a free hand over JSP within its boundaries. Once US-controlled areas were cleared, MacArthur's attention turned, as his remit clearly required, to Japanese in Southeast Asia.

Mountbatten's request to retain 105,000 JSP was being considered by the British COS when MacArthur first made enquiries about JSP, and made known his intention to provide shipping to complete repatriation before the end of 1946. MacArthur's proposal generated a considerable correspondence between Singapore and London. From the start, Foreign Office preference was to meet the American schedule but the War Office and Mountbatten objected, citing that the circumstances behind the request to retain JSP had not changed and that in any case the COS had already approved retention. British dissatisfaction with American proposals had already arisen over both the suggestion to share Japanese repatriation shipping with the United States and to allocate more British shipping to SEAC. Sharing ships was criticised by the COS on the grounds that it 'would not be fully equitable having regard to the longer turnaround from SEAC', which meant that the British fuel and supply bills would be higher than those met by the United States.[41] As for increasing the shipping available to SEAC, with the termination of the UMA the number of passenger ships in the British-controlled trooping fleet was steadily reducing, making it impossible for Britain to assign any 'extra' shipping as suggested by SCAP. (Much of the shipping that was available to Britain was not reliable. The high-capacity passenger liners SS Queen Elizabeth and SS Queen Mary, for example, were limited to Atlantic runs because of frequent maintenance requirements.)

Britain's shortage of merchant shipping in 1946 was acute. According to the MWT, a plethora of tasks and priorities precluded assistance with Japanese repatriation, a situation exacerbated by a post-UMA monthly troop-lift capacity of just 15,000. These included a programme to clear tens of thousands of British soldiers from SEAC and North Africa, repatriation of Canadian soldiers, and new troop movements to British colonial territories. Another factor was the critical food situation in Europe, particularly in the UK, which forced the reassignment of ships with refrigeration space from trooping to meat transport. Air transport, which had provided tremendous operational flexibility during the Burma campaign was similarly affected. Operation Python (the automatic discharge after three years' service in SEAC) forced the cancellation of all air trooping from India because the RAF could no longer supply adequate maintenance crews.[42]

One solution seized upon by the COS was an allocation of 65 'laid up' US Liberty Ships for use in the British and Australian command areas, including New Guinea and New Britain. The idea of paying for these ships post-Lend Lease was, however, 'most undesirable'. Instead, it was proposed that the charge should be raised against Japan, which was the case for some repatriation voyages from United States-controlled areas; a fact not lost on the COS. Crews were another problem but the COS concluded that Dutch, French or Japanese crews might be found since the Dutch—increasingly dissatisfied with British efforts—had already made a separate request to the United States for 20 Liberty Ships to evacuate JSP from Java.[43] One British suggestion was to assign the ships to MacArthur, so bypassing restrictions on their use within SEAC. In fact the Americans decided that since the British proposal affected jurisdiction, the request would have to be reconsidered at a higher level. Foreign Office records describe the Dutch as being 'in despair' at the delay, though the Admiralty Delegation in Washington consoled them by suggesting that they were 'putting the heat on' the Americans.[44]

In reality the British position was very weak. The United States' response depended solely on whether it was concerned over political repercussions that might manifest themselves in largely anti-British sentiment in Japan. There was concern in London on the need to tread carefully while lobbying 'without irritating Admiral Nimitz', the influential Chief of Naval Operations, who was seen as a 'friend' to Britain. The Foreign Office was worried that lawyers would become involved and so prevent a 'practical solution to a very difficult problem'.[45] Rather than being obstructive as the COS suspected, the Americans were simply hampered by administrative procedures and facing legal barriers. Surplus American shipping was controlled by the War Shipping Administration. It was without powers to charter ships other than on gross terms of approximately $3,000 per day. An inventive British solution, that the ships be hired to the US War Department and then to the British but charged to Japan as reparations, was rejected as it still would have left the WSA facing a loss.[46]

American concern and frustration over delays were also rising, leading eventually to the suggestion from Washington that SCAP assume all responsibility for repatriation from SEAC in order to complete the task by December 1946.[47] Charter rates in this case were to be an almost token $200 per day, with fuel supplied by the British but all costs were to be reclaimed from the Japanese. Unexpectedly the British chiefs then decided to 'resist' the fee on the grounds that, first, the Americans were not charging the Chinese for 'precisely similar ships' for repatriation from China; second, that most of the Japanese were 'American captures' and; third, that the entire operation should be seen as 'a combined one in which we are already [contributing] all available British-controlled shipping'.[48]

In late March 1946 the British Joint Staff Mission in Tokyo, presumably also now 'in despair' that the COS could not see the wood for the trees, reminded the Foreign Office that the total cost of the charter was estimated only at US$1.8 million, and free up to 1 July 1946. Clearly concerned at the risk of losing the ships on offer and having to pay gross charter terms, they urged the War Office to 'persuade' the COS to accept this most generous American offer.[49] The possibility of forfeiting the bargain rate led the Foreign Office to seek 'executive' support. Sir Orme Sargent, the Permanent Under Secretary at the Foreign Office, wrote to the COS advising them that Prime Minister Attlee was 'very impressed with the vital need of securing the earliest possible evacuation of the Japanese…with a view to the release of the British troops guarding these prisoners'. He also suggested that the $200 per day charge was 'presumably a very small' one compared with daily JSP maintenance costs.[50] Yet the quest for ever cheaper alternatives continued, and the COS hit on the idea of the shipping still within British control under the UMA. Upon Mountbatten's prompting they suggested a delay in returning non-Japanese ships to former owners and a rethink of the release policy to consider a ship's 'usefulness for other purposes'. Unsurprisingly this signal to the joint Allied Command was marked—and not for the first time—'Not for Dutch or French'.[51]

By early April 1946, however, a consensus had emerged in Whitehall towards accepting the charter rates. A formal memorandum on repatriation to 'invite the assistance' of the American Joint Chiefs of Staff had been drafted. This document concluded that British policy should be to repatriate all the Japanese from SEAC, including the AMFA, by the end of 1946.[52] It came somewhat late for American frustration with Britain over this issue was finally revealed in mid-April 1946. A succinct memorandum to the Combined Chiefs from the USJCS stressed the need to complete Japanese repatriation by the end of 1946. Although the Americans accepted that the Japanese should bear all expenses, they found that for practical purposes 'a satisfactory rate of repatriation could only be achieved by providing certain material assistance to the Japanese Government…principally the ships [and] operating supplies [it] could not provide'. In yet another attempt to help the British, the Americans offered to divert some of their spare capacity and make 'immediately available a very considerable number of Japanese-manned Liberty Ships'. War Department expenses, however, were to be reimbursed by Britain. It was pointed out to London that since the ships were manned, maintained, repaired and partially provisioned by the Japanese the 'remaining costs payable by the War Department'—fuel oil, food and other stores—were 'considerably less than…usual'. Britain merely had to assure SCAP that these costs would be met for the Americans to release the ships. Notice was also given that this arrangement could last only until 30 June 1946, after which the War Department would inherit direct and much higher charter hire fees.

In other words, no assistance with repatriation which involved expending US military appropriations was available, though the USJCS were aware of the British desire 'to avoid further dollar obligations'. In their conclusion, the Americans emphasised that the hire charge, 'even in dollars, represented a relatively small portion of the total operating costs of the vessels' but invited the British to pursue this at Government level. In conclusion, and as a 'minor point', they sought clarification of the assertion that many Japanese in SEAC were 'American captures' and reminded the British that all responsibilities related to the Japanese in SEAC and the AMFA lay 'exclusively' with SACSEA and the Australian Commander.[53]

A pointless British bluff had been called. British diplomats knew that any appeal to higher authority carried risks. Congress, having jumped to end Lend-Lease, was certain to look unfavourably on another cheap deal for Britain. It was well within its power to challenge the American decision and insist on the full rate of $2,200 per ship per day.[54] (Lord Keynes was at this time facing the very firm American negotiating position over the massive loan needed to support the British economy. He had expected to obtain no less than US$5 billion interest free; instead he was shocked and dismayed that the best deal he could secure was US$3bn at 2 percent over 50 years.)

Mountbatten, perhaps caught by surprise by the sudden American interest and rethink over the schedule, again reminded London of his request to retain over 100,000 JSP in Burma and Malaya.[55] On 8 May 1946 the War Office informed the COS of ministerial agreement to the proposed retention noting rather smugly that 'as 600,000 Japanese will have been repatriated by the end of July at no cost to His Majesty's Government, we consider we would be well advised to accept this reduced rate of charter'. It also concluded, with obvious implications for Anglo–American relations, that no British shipping would be available either at the end of 1946 and/or early 1947. Instead, it envisaged approaching the US to provide shipping 'at the same favourable rates when we require them for this delayed repatriation'.[56] There was immediate concern in the Joint Staff Mission (JSM) in Washington. Colonel C. J. G. Fisher, Deputy Director of Movements, wrote privately to a War Office colleague describing the problem created by the COS stance:

> No doubt the request will have a rough passage...[we are] taking advantage of a virtually gratuitous lift...till 30 June and then, as soon...as we have to pay an increase... we conveniently find we have no more Japs to move until the beginning of next year. The Americans would be well within their rights to ask hard questions...each time we squeeze the American goose and get a golden egg the bird shows a greater disinclination to go into production.[57]

Fisher's worries were compounded when Mountbatten, quoting an Admiralty ruling, suddenly reneged on the supply arrangement previously guaranteed by the JSM. He declared SEAC was only willing to furnish fuel for the return journey to Japan from SEAC ports. Thus half the fuel would have to come from American sources which, as the USJCS were quick to point out, clearly ran counter to the terms. Letting some of his frustration show, Fisher informed London that there was a grave danger of the USJCS 'calling off the deal...' and requested advice from London.[58] He again wrote privately to his colleague, pointing out that Britain risked losing 'extraordinarily advantageous' terms and that if they were to refuse to supply fuel there was 'no point' in asking for ships again either at the end of 1946 or even in early 1947.[59]

American patience, however, had been tested too long. On 28 May 1946 the USJCS announced that since the British had not discussed payment for hire of ships after 30 June they were not to sail unless they could return to Japan before that date.[60] Prompt, high-level pressure was brought to bear upon Mountbatten by the Cabinet to accept round-voyage fuelling. It was 'essential', the Cabinet stressed, that 'we should not give cause for any criticism that we are not fulfilling our part of the bargain'.[61] Mountbatten gave way and in Washington the JSM representatives scrambled to confirm and 'acknowledge with gratitude' American assistance and British acceptance of War Department rates. Following Fisher's arguments it was thought prudent to delay the extra shipping request, ie, that for the end of 1946/early 1947, until 'misunderstandings' had been smoothed over.[62]

In August 1946 Britain finally informed the United States of its intention to retain over 100,000 JSP into 1947. General Sir Montagu Stopford, who became Acting SACSEA on 1 June 1946 after Mountbatten left SEAC, received a brief message from MacArthur. It summarised American plans to complete repatriation by 31 December 1946, and then return any Liberty Ships that were 'excess to requirements' to the United States. MacArthur increased the pressure by adding that plans for the 'disposition of Japanese ships being used in the repatriation programme were near completion', and reception centres in Japan for repatriates were being 'progressively closed'. He noted that 'repatriation...is being deferred but without arrangements made for their return except that British shipping will not be available'. 'It was', MacArthur stressed, 'most desirable that SEAC areas be cleared by 31 December 1946 while shipping and reception facilities are still available'. He signed off with a terse, 'Request plan for evacuation of 120,000 Japanese nationals be furnished earliest'.[63] Stopford replied several days later explaining that MacArthur's 'considerations' had been 'appreciated' but that it was considered 'essential that 104,500 JSP' be retained to assist in 'repairing ravages of war'. He also reminded SCAP that 'permission had been given by the COS 'for retention to end 1946' after which the JSP will be repatriated in 'ships of British charter'.[64]

Relations cooled further when the USJCS formally advised the Combined Chiefs of Staff that the British deferral of repatriation from Southeast Asia 'for reasons other than availability of shipping had certain undesirable features from the United States viewpoint'. Repeating MacArthur's observations, the American chiefs reminded the British that he would be able to complete all repatriation from Southeast Asia by the end of December 1946 'provided the Japanese personnel are released'. Any delay would prolong MacArthur's task. A clarification of the original shipping offer, explaining that surplus vessels had left MacArthur 'advantageously positioned' to assist the COS, restated that at the end of 1946 all US repatriation shipping would be withdrawn, that no extension was possible and that in view of this 'the British may wish to reconsider'.[65] American dissatisfaction over British policy was clear. While Britain stalled over JSP in Malaya, however, a contradictory British position developed in Thailand.

COMPLICATIONS IN THAILAND

As the British and American positions over retention in Malaya and Indonesia hardened, another difficulty, this time exclusively British, arose in Thailand. Before the war Thailand had been the only independent state in Southeast Asia. It had also been an ally of Japan and had been rewarded by the Japanese with some contested border provinces that had previously been part of the Malay States.[66] Britain had declared war on Thailand but the United States had chosen not to follow suit. After the war, the US was not inclined to punish the Thais, which in fact strengthened the Thai position in negotiations with Britain over the disputed provinces and terms for exports, and even relations over Japanese within their borders. Reluctantly Britain, now in desperate need of access to Thailand's bumper rice crop to alleviate famine in the region and in India, adopted a softer line than anticipated by British planners in early 1945.[67]

In Thailand the question of the Japanese was, however, also the cause of a dispute among the War Office, SEAC and the Foreign Office. By mid-1946 the Foreign Office was at an advanced stage in negotiations with the Thai Government over the sale of the notorious Burma-Thailand Railway, built by Allied PW and Southeast Asian forced labour. Britain had claimed ownership the railway as war reparations but it was in fact of little use owing to its poor condition and it quickly became a financial burden. Britain desired to sell the railway to Thailand as a going concern. Some 7,600 JSP were involved in maintaining and operating the railway 'internationally' between Burma and Siam with minimal supervision by British forces. They also ran regular security sweeps against bandits and to deter looters. (Another 200 JSP were working in Bangkok docks.) Since SEAC was incurring expenses in Thailand guarding and maintaining the Japanese, Mountbatten (and then Stopford) had pushed for their early repatriation. In contrast, the Foreign Office preferred to delay until 1 October 1946 to increase the prospect of securing the sale of the railway to the Thais. This date had been acceptable to the War Office as long as cheap American shipping was available for repatriation. With the offer of free shipping being withdrawn after June 1946, the War Office faced further supervision and maintenance expenditure as well as much higher repatriation costs. The railway was suddenly a far less valuable asset. This problem was unlikely to garner much sympathy in Washington, and it threatened to undermine the British position on retained Japanese throughout Southeast Asia. Any use of American shipping risked prejudicing the major issue of keeping and retaining 87,000 JSP in Malaya during 1947. In London the War Office feared it would nullify any justification 'on grounds that no transportation was available for their repatriation, for the retention of JSP in SEAC as a whole'.[68]

In the end, the Foreign Office won the day and repatriation of JSP in Thailand from October 1946 was confirmed. In this case, Britain was willing to incur costs for the maintenance of 7,800 JSP for almost 12 months and risk American ire in order to secure the sale of the railway. These short-term needs carried long-term risks. Once again, overconfident assumptions on the future availability of British shipping would come to haunt the Foreign Office, the War Office and SEAC.

'LONG-TERM EMPLOYMENT OF PRISONERS OF WAR IS INDEFENSIBLE...'

American displeasure over delayed repatriation naturally caused concern in Whitehall. Stopford was quickly informed that the whole question of retention was being 're-examined' by the Foreign and Cabinet Offices. He was also asked if SEAC had sufficient shipping to transport JSP from Thailand without American assistance, which was the most immediate requirement, were the offer of free ships to be withdrawn.[69] SEAC was most reluctant to lose its Japanese. Stopford replied, '[J]SP are still being employed...there is an acute shortage of civil labour and both services and civil rehabilitation and new construction programmes will become extremely difficult if [they] are withdrawn before the end of 1947...it would also seriously affect the operation of the Singapore base'.[70]

For SEAC, the chief argument justifying continued retention was the difficulty in obtaining and keeping labour. Civil authorities and the services could not compete with private employers. Southeast Asian economies were starting to recover and the British colonial authorities actually anticipated a need for an overall increase in JSP labour even as pressures to return them were growing. In the Malay States, JSP were repairing railways, quarrying, clearing rivers, operating emergency river-craft, and constructing and repairing civil buildings. In Singapore two types of military employment were identified: 'military construction and maintenance' (specifically airfields), and 'port operation and accommodation construction'. This was also the first acknowledgement from SEAC that detained Japanese were being used for military projects and not solely for food production or civilian relief. Stopford contended that it was 'impossible in Burma, Singapore and the Malayan Union for the Services and Civil Government to obtain civil labour in the numbers required...[and the] position was likely to deteriorate as more civilian undertakings...are opened up'.[71] This highlights the fundamental economic rationale behind JSP retention. Unpaid Japanese were considerably 'cheaper' than local labour, which had begun to drift to higher-paying, labour-intensive mining and rubber plantations. (There is no mention in the report of nationalist intimidation of workers that might have made recruitment for British military projects difficult.) Poor diet was another issue. JSP were also better fed, stronger and more productive than locals, and therefore preferable to civil labour, which 'although available', was 'suffering from malnutrition and its output [was] indifferent'.[72] SEAC was also willing to risk an inevitable but acceptable decline in JSP productivity and morale if retention were extended. It would, however, have to be 'carefully watched'.[73]

In London a rushed but major reassessment of options followed in the form of a report by Lord Tedder (Air Chief of Staff) presented to the Cabinet Office, Minister of Defence and the COS. Tedder had consulted SEAC, the Foreign Office, the MOT, the Governments of India and Burma, and the Colonial Office.[74] The COS were also advised of the 'serious political objections' to retaining JSP when transportation facilities for repatriation were available.[75] For the Foreign Office, however, it was clear-cut: a policy of post-war 'long-term employment of POWs...[was] 'indefensible'.[76] Here once again the Foreign Office was clearly unimpressed by the War Office's distinctions between JSP and PW. What mattered was that retention was upsetting the United States and not just jeopardising the offer of cheap shipping but arousing suspicions over post-war British colonial policy in Asia. The Foreign Office saw only one argument in favour of retention, namely that, 'the Japanese, having devastated and disorganised territories in South East Asia, should themselves contribute in the initial stages to their reconstruction'.[77]

Tedder also reconsidered arguments favouring retention. In Burma the JSP were performing 'essential public services...[and making] repairs to railways and roads'. Another reason was Stopford's opinion that Burmese did 'not make good labour, their output per man being very low'. Political objections had also arisen over suggestions to import casual labour from India, with its implications for potential ethnic rivalries and violence.

Dominating all other considerations in the pro-retention case was the 'extensive essential Service building programme which relied to a large extent on JSP labour'. In Burma this included the construction of 'temporary accommodation...for Headquarters Burma Command, garrison troops, hospitals, married quarters, training establishments, work-shops, reception camps, depots...general recreational amenities...[and] airfield'.[78] (Concerns over new accommodation in Burma for British forces seem odd when negotiations over Burmese independence were already underway and a British departure was only a matter of time.) Similar priorities were listed for Malaya where army building programmes were dependent on JSP who were also 'required for rehabilitation work of public services, including roads and railways, distribution of food and in the economic recovery of the country'. In Singapore, too, the focus was also on JSP use for military construction. There were plans 'to develop Singapore as the administrative base for all three Services in SEAC', which put great pressure on civilian accommodation.[79]

Japanese in Thailand were of little interest to Tedder, other than noting a previous recommendation to repatriate them directly during October 1946. A need of US shipping for this task was now acknowledged. JSP working in Bangkok were described as 'directly assisting the export of foodstuffs', ie, as full-time dockyard labour (in preference to unemployed Thais). Tedder summed up:

> [I]t is clear that JSP labour...will...directly further rehabilitation [of countries] and in part indirectly assist to create the conditions necessary for that rehabilitation... [It is] impossible to recruit sufficient local labour to cover both

Civil and Service projects…The only solution is therefore the employment of JSP… SACSEA's request is fully justified even though their employment is not entirely confined to the production and distribution of food.

Thus the main premise behind the initial requests to keep back some JSP, that is, the need to meet the food emergency, was abandoned.[80] Retention, although prolonging the guarding and administrative commitments of British forces in SEAC and even 'presenting obstacles' was more than offset by the working capacity and productivity of the Japanese. All too aware of accusations that SEAC was feathering its colonial nest, London looked for allies. With this in mind, the COS approved an approach to the Dutch with a view to making 'a parallel request' for the retention of JSP in Indonesia (see below).[81]

For the COS the lack of British-flagged shipping was a secondary problem. The only figures available were estimates. American impatience and disfavour over repatriation was evident, however, and growing. One method of deflecting criticism was to negate the offer of immediate, free shipping, even though this approach limited Britain's options. Reasons were sought to justify retention until the end of 1946 and throughout 1947 that were 'arguable on grounds other than the availability of shipping'.[82] Consequently this decision forced the complete reversal of the British policy on JSP in Thailand. Previously the British had been anxious that the repatriation from Thailand should not use American ships.[83] Now it was found that they could be used for Thailand but not elsewhere. Stopford was encouraged to set up a 'smoke-screen' by using five small Japanese ships under his control for repatriation although their tiny capacity would make hardly any impact on overall numbers. Appearances mattered, as the Chiefs admitted: 'it is unlikely that your present 5 Japanese ships could carry more than a trickle, but it is politically desirable that you should continue to use them throughout 1947…and we assume that it will be possible to marry up the number of [Japanese] you are able to release with the availability of shipping.' Unsurprisingly, the Chiefs made no mention of new military construction programmes to the Americans. They found that in view of the 'urgent needs of rehabilitation, food production and its distribution' in Southeast Asia, SEAC was 'unable to dispense with these JSP in time to take advantage of [the American] offer' of shipping.[84] Britain had therefore chosen to risk further American objections to retaining the Japanese while yet another generous American of transport was on offer.

THE DUTCH REQUEST FOR JSP LABOUR

As Britain defended retention, a further intra-SEAC agreement was to create more complication. Almost immediately upon securing London's approval for retention of 104,500 JSP to the end of 1946, SEAC presented proposals to prolong it up to 31 December 1947.[85] Included in this figure were 13,500 Japanese requested for labour by the Netherlands Indies Colonial Administration (NICA). In June 1946 Allied Forces Netherlands East Indies (AFNEI) approved the transfer to Dutch control without reference to SEAC HQ. By October 1946, however, Britain, faced a diplomatic and security dilemma. Although the Dutch were re-establishing their authority (with British transport and logistic help, and Japanese security 'assistance', ie, securing airfields) on the outer and smaller islands of the Indies such as Bali and Lombok, they were struggling to re-impose control in Java and Sumatra against growing nationalist opposition.[86] British forces were steadily being drawn down but Britain continued to supply the Dutch and provide logistic support for their military operations. While keen to keep Japanese in Burma, Malaya and Singapore, the continued presence of JSP and European internees in Java, particularly those still detained by nationalists, was one factor delaying Britain's withdrawal from Indonesia. London was determined that British and Indian troops should leave Java and Sumatra by the end of November 1946 'whether Dutch troops had arrived or not'. A formal withdrawal programme had been confirmed, 'even if genuine Allied prisoners of war and internees remained' after that date. In short, they were to be abandoned.[87] In addition to the 13,500 Japanese earmarked for labour purposes there were, until 1 August 1946, 11,000 JSP in Sumatra guarding Western-owned oil installations around Palembang.[88] In handing over JSP to the Dutch, London was looking for a way to withdraw from Indonesia and avoid all further obligations to those men as the Dutch had agreed to repatriate them in their shipping.

Britain's difficulty was two-fold. Withdrawal from Indonesia meant that responsibility for the Japanese would also be transferred to the Dutch. As a Potsdam-derived SEAC duty this required Allied, ie, American approval. Also, since under Potsdam terms the Netherlands was not authorised to accept Japanese surrenders, by extension it lacked the authority to exercise direct control over JSP. (As in Vietnam, Mountbatten's distinction between a requirement to 'guard' JSP and to take their surrender was to be extended to allow the Dutch actual day-to-day control.) MacArthur had, of course, to be informed of this new arrangement but once the State Department's strong opposition to retention had become apparent, this was seen as problematic. Official responsibility for all JSP in Indonesia would remain with the British whether British troops were present or not. Were repatriation to be prolonged, for example as a result of Dutch military action against nationalists delaying movement of nationalist-held Japanese to evacuation areas, or—and of far more serious concern to London—Dutch use of Japanese forces in an offensive capacity against nationalists, further American displeasure was assured. Either scenario would have showcased London's failure to meet its Potsdam obligations. Britain felt honour-bound to keep to the signed AFNEI-NICA agreement even though it had originated in chaotic circumstances. (At the time, British and Dutch troops had been jointly deployed and there had been an assumption that British Administration would continue.) Consequently the British COS confirmed the handover of 13,500 JSP to the Dutch but hesitated over the manner of informing MacArthur. British uncertainty was such that SEAC was instructed to 'say nothing' to the Dutch until agreement had been obtained from Washington.[89]

For its part the United States was determined to maintain the primacy of the Potsdam Proclamation over Japanese prisoners. Retention in Indonesia and Thailand had increasingly wider diplomatic ramifications. MacArthur was anxious to press the Russians and Chinese to repatriate 800,000 Japanese servicemen and 200,000 Japanese civilians seized in southern China, Manchuria, Sakhalin (Karafuto) and Northern Korea. On the other hand, in London at least, the British case was seen as reasonable and just: JSP were helping to reconstruct territories they had overrun during the war. As far as the COS were concerned, smoothing any difficulties with the United States was the responsibility of the Foreign Office. The Chiefs still had to reply to their American counterparts, however. Lord Tedder considered that the argument for retention would be strengthened if the USJCS were informed that Britain understood that it would cause the American organisations in Japan some inconvenience and delay the closure of facilities. They were less forthright about admitting the arrangement with the Dutch. Their solution was simply to list them:

> The balance of 104,500...is made up by administrative staffs... non-effective sick and 13,500 handed over to Dutch in NEI. The former also includes 9,000 whose withdrawal from Siam [to Malaya] during October, 1946 has been approved... In view of the urgent need for these JSP in 1947...we earnestly hope [the USJCS] will be able to agree to their retention'.[90]

This wait and see 'strategy' was left to unfold, even though considerable American opposition was anticipated over retention of [sic] 'Japanese POWs'.[91] There was no immediate American reaction. What did occur, however, was far worse for London. Unexpectedly 'news' reports from the Kyodo-AP agency and broadcasts on Radio Tokyo announced that almost all Japanese under British control would be home before the end of 1946:

> An Anglo-American decision to speed the return home from South-East Asia of more than 100,000 Japanese reportedly is in the making. [An] official familiar with discussions now going on told reporters…'the shipping situation was now improving [it was this and the] corralling of scattered Japanese which was responsible for the delays…' They expect the task to be completed by the end of the year. All Japanese in the American occupied zones will come back within the year except for special people. Details will be notified as soon as known. [92]

British planning for the use of Japanese labour came to an abrupt halt. It was an odd reflection of British unease that such a short public comment forced a wholesale review of the retention policy. All announcements, even those relating to improvements in JSP conditions, were postponed as the position was reassessed. Yet again, however, the same conclusion, however, was reached. American displeasure and now Japanese expectations notwithstanding, London decided it could still not do without JSP. Citing continuing food and labour shortages, Washington was informed that the UK Government 'trusted' that in the circumstances the United States might 'feel disposed to waive objections to the retention of a limited number [of JSP] in SEA'.[93]

Once more London waited, during which time Japanese in Java were passed to Dutch control. Responsibility for their ultimate repatriation, it was now considered, rested with the Dutch. Since they were now in a similar situation as the British, they were also a potential ally in future negotiations or, worse, any open dispute with MacArthur. When two months had passed without American comment the Foreign Office began to relax. It advised the War Office that 'we can feel free to make plans on the assumption that no serious obstacles will be placed in our way by the US Government…'.[94] In the light of previous experience over JSP such blanket optimism was perhaps ill-advised. Unsurprisingly it proved short lived. To London's dismay detained Japanese would no longer remain solely a SEAC–SCAP issue. They were to attract further public attention, this time as pawns in growing Western–Soviet antagonism at the Far Eastern Commission and United Nations Security Council, where the Soviet Union raised the issues of Indonesian and Vietnamese independence, and the status of Japanese Surrendered Personnel.[95] In Japan, too, the plight of countrymen overseas began to have mounting political implications far beyond SEAC.

NOTES TO CHAPTER 4

1.   'Statement on Initial Policy', HQ AFNEI, 14 Nov. 1945. WO 203/5963.
2.   Thorne, *Allies,* 504. Also, B. R. Tomlinson, 'Indo-British Relations in the Post-Colonial Era: The Sterling Balances Negotiations, 1947-1949', in *Journal of Imperial and Commonwealth History. Vol. XIII* no. 3 (May 1985), 145.
3.   Ibid., 599.
4.   S. W. Roskill, *The War at Sea, Vol. III, Pt. 1* (London, 1960), 344.
5.   Michael Hickey, *The Unforgettable Army: Slim's XIV*th*Army in Burma* (Tunbridge Wells, 1992), 11 (map).
6.   Ibid., 235.
7.   John Coast, *Railroad of Death* (London, 1946).
8.   Woodburn Kirby, *Surrender of Japan,* 239–40, 505.
9.   Kevin Smith, *Conflict over Convoys: Anglo-American logistics diplomacy in the Second World War* (Cambridge, 1996), xiii.
10.   C. B. A. Behrens, *Merchant Shipping and the Demands of War* (London, 1955). (Tonnage tables.)
11.   Smith, *Conflict over Convoys,* 11.
12.   Ibid., 2.
13.   Allister Hinds, *Britain's Sterling Colonial Policy and Decolonization, 1939-1958* (Westport, CT., 2001), 4 n. 1.
14.   Smith, *Conflict over Convoys,* 6.
15.   Behrens, *Merchant Shipping,* 284.
16.   See R. N. Gardner, *Sterling-Dollar Diplomacy in Current Perspective* (New York, 1980), 61.
17.   R. S. Sayers, *Financial Policy, 1939-45* (London, 1956), 375.
18.   Smith, *Conflict over Convoys,* 72.
19.   Behrens, *Merchant Shipping,* 284.
20.   Ibid.
21.   Smith, *Conflict over Convoys,* 3.
22.   Ibid., 72.
23.   Thorne, *Allies,* 390.
24.   Smith, *Conflict over Convoys,* 81.
25.   Ibid., 3, 177.
26.   John Weste, 'Shipping and Shipbuilding', in *Britain and Japan in the Twentieth Century: One Hundred Years of Trade and Prejudice,* eds, Philip Towle and Nobuko Margaret Kosuge (London, 2007), 107.
27.   SEACOS 596, 28 Dec. 1945. CAB 122/1182.
28.   BSM Tokyo to Cabinet Offices, 5 Jan. 1946. CAB 122/1182.
29.   COS Committee Joint Planning Staff report JP (46) 3 (Revised Final), 'Shipping Availability for Repatriation of JSP', 28 Feb. 1946. CAB 122/1182.
30.   Allocations were based on US estimates of Japanese under SEAC control as at 15 Aug. 1945, ie, 502,000. SEAC's 14,000 lift plus 9,000 SCAP spaces equalled '27% of long-range shipping allocated to SEAC for repatriation of 17% of total [2,894,000] Japanese service personnel'. SCAP to SACSEA, 13 Feb. 1946. WO 203/5963.
31.   SEACOS 650, 1 Mar. 1946. WO 203/5963.
32.   UKLM to Cabinet Offices, 30 Jan. 1946. CAB 122/1182.
33.   COS Committee Joint Planning Staff report JP (46) 1, 'Repatriation of Japanese Personnel from SEAC', 10 Jan. 1946. CAB 122/1182. The COS made their case

to the CCS on 28 Jan. 1946. (Ibid.).

34.   FO to Dutch Ambassador, London, 4 Feb. 1946. CAB 121/511.

35.   'Employment for JSP', 8 Mar. 1946. WO 203/5965.

36.   Draft signal, Mar. 1946. WO 203/5965.

37.   BSM Washington to British Army Staff (Washington), 21 Mar. 1946. CAB 122/1182.

38.   SEACOS 684, 18 Apr. 1946. AIR 40/1852. Author's italics.

39.   SEACOS 692, 4 May 1946. AIR 40/1852.

40.   GHQ General Staff, *Reports of General MacArthur, Volume I, Supplement. MacArthur in Japan: The Occupation, Military Phase.* (Washington, DC; 1966), 32–4.

41.   JPS for COS. 28 Feb. 1946. CAB 122/1182.

42.   JSM Washington to FO, 8 Mar. 1946. CAB 122/1182.

43.   JPS to COS, 28 Feb. 1946. CAB 122/1182.

44.   British Admiralty Delegation, Washington, to FO, 12 Mar. 1946. CAB 122/1182.

45.   FO to British Military Mission, Washington, 14 Mar. 1946. CAB 122/1182. *See* Thorne, *Allies*, 702.

46.   JSM to British Joint Staff Mission [BJSM], Washington, 16 Mar. 1946. CAB 122/1182.

47.   BJSM to Lt-Gen. Sir Gordon Mcready, BA Staff, 21 Mar. 1946. CAB 122/1182.

48.   BJSM to Cabinet Offices, 21 Mar. 1946. CAB 122/1182.

49.   BJSM to WO/FO, 27 Mar. 1946. CAB 122/1182.

50.   FO to COS, 26 Mar. 1946. CAB 122/1182.

51.   COSSEA 505, 28 Mar. 1946. CAB 122/1182.

52.   WO to BAS Washington, 2 Apr. 1946. CAB 122/1182.

53.   'Repatriation of Japanese Personnel from Southeast Asia and Australian Commands.' Memorandum by the JCS. 17 Apr. 1946. CAB 122/1182.

54.   JSM to COS, 18 Apr. 1946. CAB 122/1182.

55.   SEACOS 692, 4 May 1946. CAB 122/1182.

56.   COS (46) 125, 8 May 1946, CAB 122/1182.

57.   JSM (Fisher) to WO (Brig. C. B. G. Greaves), 13 May 1946. CAB 122/1182.

58.   JSM (Fisher) to WO (Greaves), 17 May 1946. CAB 122/1182.

59.   Telegram JSM (Fisher) to WO (Greaves), 17 May 1946. CAB 122/1182.

60.   JCS (K. J. MacFarland) to G. C. Wilson, CiCAFP, 28 May 1946. CAB 122/1182.

61.   Cabinet Offices to SACSEA, 29 May 1946. CAB 122/1182.

62.   JSM to COS, 31 May 1946. CAB 122/1182.

63.   GHQ SCAP to SACSEA, 6 Aug. 1946. CAB 122/1182. The correct figure is 104,500: Malaya and Singapore, 87,000; NEI 13,500; and 4,000 facing 'war guilt' trials.

64.   SACSEA to SCAP, 12 Aug 1946. CAB 122/1182.

65.   JCS to CCS. 26 Aug. 1946. CAB 122/1182.

66.   Thorne, *Allies*, 679–80.

67.   Ibid.

68.   COS 'Retention of JSP in SEAC During 1947', 10 Sept. 1946. CAB 122/1182.

69.   Cabinet Offices to SACSEA, 4 Sept. 1946. CAB 122/1182.

70.   SEAC to Cabinet Offices, 6 Sept. 1946. CAB 122/1182.

71.   Ibid.

72.   Ibid.

73.   SEAC to COS. 'Retention of JSP during 1947'. 20 July 1946. CAB 119/206.

74. PAOC to COS, 10 Sept. 1946. CAB 122/1182.
75. Report to COS, 'Retention of JSP during 1947', 10 Sept. 1946. CAB 122/1182.
76. PAOC to COS, 10 Sept. 1946. CAB 122/1182.
77. Ibid.
78. Ibid.
79. Ibid.
80. Report to COS, 'Retention of JSP during 1947', 10 Sept. 1946. CAB 122/1182.
81. Ibid.
82. Report to COS, 10 Sept. 1946. CAB 122/1182.
83. Ibid.
84. Ibid.
85. SACSEA to Cabinet Offices, 'Retention of JSP during 1947', 20 July 1946. CAB 119/206.
86. H. B. Spencer (ex-Royal Navy), memoir filed online, 29 July 2005: http://www.bbc.co.uk/ww2peopleswar/stories/98/a4607598.shtml.
87. COS to SACSEA, 'Programme of Withdrawal', 4 Sept. 1946. CAB 119/206.
88. See Chapter 3, n. 111; also Woodburn Kirby, *Surrender of Japan*, 359-361.
89. COS to SACSEA, 'Programme of Withdrawal', 4 Sept. 1946. CAB 119/206.
90. PAOC to COS, 10 Sept. 1946. CAB 122/1182.
91. COS (46) 142, 19 Sept. 1946. CAB 122/1182.
92. Telegram, Kyodo-AP News, Radio Tokyo, 21 Sept. 1946. CAB 122/1182.
93. COS to JSM Washington, 5 Oct. 1946. CAB 122/1183.
94. Report to COS, 19 Dec. 1946. CAB 122/1183.
95. Ibid. See Alastair Taylor, *Indonesian Independence and the United Nations* (London, 1960), 384.

5

CONFUSION AFTER COLLAPSE
JAPANESE RESPONSES TO DELAYED REPATRIATION

After the surrender the former Japanese Expeditionary forces… called themselves 'Surrendered Personnel'. This in no way means, however, that they intended to waive the protection and privileges of prisoners of war guaranteed by International Law and practice…

—Japanese Government to SCAP, 26 April 1947[1]

I n the first weeks following Japan's surrender accurate details of the situation facing most of the nearly 7m Japanese nationals scattered through the Asian mainland and the islands of the western Pacific were unavailable to the Japanese Government. Apart from signals received from a very few Imperial Japanese naval vessels still operating in international waters, most radio telegraph links were quickly severed as troops and their communications facilities came under American, Chinese, British or Russian control.[2] There was little that Japan's Government could do for its citizens overseas at an official level other than submit requests or protests to SCAP headquarters in Tokyo. All Japanese political influence ceased and diplomatic activity was severely curtailed as the Allies forbade Japanese consulates in neutral and occupied countries the right to use diplomatic bags. In addition, the American occupation authorities in Japan monitored all consular and Foreign Ministry communications very strictly.[3] General overseas news reached Japan via broadcasts from foreign radio stations or (several days old) foreign-language newspapers, few of which saw any news value in the conditions affecting the Japanese diaspora. Japanese nationals abroad were also denied news from Japan. Radio Tokyo was prevented from broadcasting overseas after 10 September 1945. Japan's Government protested on the grounds that the 'large number of Japanese nationals stranded abroad' (the vast majority of them monoglot) depended on Radio Tokyo's broadcasts for news and instructions.[4] (Japanese Navy estimates were in fact 860,000. This figure either includes units outside SEAC or nominal rolls that exclude casualties.)

Despite Allied impositions and restrictions the Japanese Government made a number of early attempts to preserve some form of diplomatic independence. On 15 August, Japan rejected demands to open all its diplomatic missions in neutral countries to Allied representatives on the grounds that it considered the instruction ran 'counter to the terms of the Potsdam Declaration'.[5] There had been no response from the Americans until 25 October when General MacArthur/SCAP issued a Supreme Commander Allied Powers Index or SCAPIN. This formal directive ordered all Japanese embassies closed, all diplomatic property and archives surrendered and all consular representatives recalled.[6] (Prime Minister Shidehara Kijuro's Cabinet held out for a week before submitting to this demand on 31 October 1945.) In mid-September 1945 the Japanese Foreign Ministry had proposed to SCAP that its staff visit Allied Occupied Areas outside Japan 'to assist' in administration. This request was quickly rejected on the grounds that the various theatre Commanders 'did not concur in such visits'.[7] Also, a late-September attempt by the Foreign Ministry to promote Japanese civil servants based in southern Korea irked SCAP sufficiently for it to issue a curt reprimand, which stated clearly that the Japanese Government 'will not attempt to exercise any administrative authority in Korea'.[8]

While direct and confidential communication was no longer possible via diplomatic channels for Japan's Government, Western Allied controls over the Japanese military remained patchy. This was particularly the case in areas that had not been combat zones, where the Imperial Japanese Army (IJA) and Navy (IJN) communications networks remained intact and fully functioning. At least two Japanese-controlled radio telegraph links to major—and still influential—overseas command headquarters appear to have remained open for some months: that from Saigon, HQ JEFSR to Tokyo, and one from Tokyo to 16 IJA at Bandung (Java) and 25 IJA at Bukittinggi (Sumatra). Oddly, the latter circuit was only closed (again by a SCAPIN) in early December 1945. This perhaps reflects the chaotic security situation in Indonesia. In Java the relatively small British military presence was largely limited to the area around Jakarta.[9] Elsewhere, the Japanese were playing a key role in maintaining order and, on Sumatra, guarding and maintaining the Western-owned oil-refining infrastructure. (British forces were themselves heavily dependent on local Japanese-operated radio in Java for day-to-day communications across the island's circuits.) Regional IJA HQs were all linked to the Singapore circuit for some time. (The Saigon link closed at the end of February 1946 when a new (Japanese) link between Singapore and Tokyo was authorised.) One consequence of these continuing communication routes is that the Japanese Government was quite possibly far better informed about the general political and security situation in Indonesia, Indo-China and elsewhere in Southeast Asia than has previously been assumed. Intriguingly, it also raises the possibility that some post-surrender Japanese actions in Java followed specific instructions or advice from Tokyo. (The stance taken by the Japanese at Jakarta during the first meetings aboard HMS *Cumberland* is one example.[10])

Mountbatten may have ordered the Japanese to maintain law and order to gain time while Allied troops were deployed in Southeast Asia but Britain could not, however, avoid its primary Potsdam obligations indefinitely. General Order No. 1 charged Britain—alone among the European, Indian, Australian and New Zealand Allies—with disarming and repatriating the Japanese military in SEAC. These twin responsibilities could not be delegated. Additionally, it was a tenet of Western Allied policy to screen all JSP and PW in an attempt to identify those accused of 'higher profile' abuses. This undertaking was immense, complicated and time-consuming and required detailed inspection and copious documentation. Consequently it placed enormous demands on the by then rapidly reducing numbers of Allied investigative and legal personnel as well as secretarial and administration staff and other scarce resources such as transport, storage and office space. A reflection of the scale of the task was that SEAC's minimum threshold for war guilt prosecution was triggered only if a comparable civil conviction would result in a prison sentence of at least seven years.[11] (This little-publicised threshold automatically negated the bulk of 'common assault' or 'assault with intent' charges against Japanese, Korean and Taiwanese serving as PW camp guards.)

SEAC's solution for easing the JSP logistical and administrative burden was to group the Japanese in concentrations that were to be 'as large as possible'.[12] Also, much of the day-to-day organisation for the Japanese was left in their own hands. A September 1945 communiqué set out that 'until such time as it is possible for the occupying forces to take over the administration of the surrendered Japanese Forces their maintenance will remain the responsibility of the Japanese'.[13] By the November, the original intent to oversee JSP administration had been abandoned. 'Jap forces will have to be maintained...

although it is the intention that as far as possible the Japs should maintain themselves by growing local produce, and build their own accommodation.'[14]

Other more mundane reasons, however, were also behind the relocations, which had an additional, even symbolic purpose. International and domestic criticism of the military use of Japanese considerably embarrassed British officials. Widespread local law and order problems in Southeast Asia also suggested a less-than-dominant British security presence. With armed Japanese units on regular patrols, manning checkpoints or in garrisons they were a constant and very visible public reminder of the Western powers' retreats and defeats in 1942. Consequently, once the early security threats and public-order issues linked to regional and local political opposition to returning colonial administrations in Indonesia, Malaya and Vietnam had either been countered or at least contained, JSP were removed from flashpoints and, more importantly, out of the view of locals.

As part of this strategy Japanese were ordered to relocate to new camps. Uninhabited or sparsely populated islands were preferred as natural containment areas since they required fewer guards. As a result, JSP were moved far away from metropolitan areas or major transport hubs and ports, which was to have an unanticipated detrimental effect on future repatriation plans. Established Japanese command hierarchies and basic but functioning supply systems also broke down in the inevitable disruption. On occasion, particularly in the early weeks after the surrender, Japanese and British worked at cross-purposes. HQ JEFSR saw its own attempts to formulate an independent repatriation plan using Japanese vessels in the 'South Sea Area' stymied by the hardly surprising requirement to seek British permission before each sailing. Proposals and suggested schedules from 'Marshal Terauchi' (almost certainly General Numata) about evacuation priorities from hazardous locations—that took no account of the practicalities of control of surrendered weapons or screening for suspected war criminals—came to nothing despite a referral to SCAP.[15] In mid-December 1945 Admiral Shibata Yaichiro, Commander of the Second Southern Expeditionary Fleet Naval Forces and the most senior IJN officer in Indonesia, struggled to see the logic behind the planned mass concentrations at Rempang and Galang, two adjoining islands in the Riouw (Riau) Archipelago.

> Japanese in Java have been ordered to Galang Island. It will take nine months with shipping capacity of 8,000 persons. [T]his shifting will not help the repatriation program. Kindly send a request to [SCAP] to postpone the proposed shifting of the Japanese from Java to Galang, and instead remove

those now in east and central Java to Lombok by small vessels and then repatriate those in west Java and south west part of New Guinea using medium size vessels.[16]

Japanese estimates, produced in late 1945, of shipping-lift capacity of only 23,000 per year (and thus equating to more than six years to complete repatriation), bear a strong similarity to later figures for a 'SEAC lift capacity' of 23,000 per year and a programme lasting five-and-a-half-years.[17] Even at this stage it is clear that British assumptions over repatriation schedules were dependent on utilisation of captured or surviving Japanese shipping.

Allied controls over Japanese inter-command and international communications did increase in the months after the surrender but intra-command links were left largely unaffected. As late as June 1946 radio traffic between Singapore and the main Japanese HQs in Burma, Malaya, Siam, Vietnam, Celebes, Java and Sumatra was still being sent over Japanese radio circuits operated by Japanese signallers. South East Asia Translation and Interrogation Corps (SEATIC) staff usually checked messages from the main HQs that were marked for wider circulation prior to transmission. Smaller stations were, however, left unsupervised.[18] General Tanabe's 'subversive' March 1946 message describing JSP fighting Indonesian nationalists as British 'underdogs' (see Chapter 3) suggests that checking of Japanese signals was hit and miss at best. It also confirms that the main Japanese HQs were extremely well informed about the deployments of their forces in British operations.

Other factors served to compound organisational disruption for the Japanese and create needless shortages of basic items. British insistence on sudden, mass movements, despite a chronic shortage of vehicles and ships, resulted in the forced abandonment of much equipment and specially gathered (or hoarded) fresh-food stores, particularly rice. (SEAC also confiscated rice from Japanese inventories for issue to civilians.) Acute food shortages occurred in many new camps in the short- to mid-term and were compounded by this widespread uprooting. These movements, which increased in pace from February 1946 onwards, also physically decoupled lower-tier signal sections from the main Japanese communications network. (Much equipment was dismantled and stored or simply dumped.)

Most of the locations chosen for internment camps had of necessity been the subjects of fairly brief and/or rushed surveys. Rempang and Galang, which both became major JSP staging areas, were only 30 miles south of Singapore but were in the NEI/Indonesia. They were therefore unfamiliar to the new (fresh from the UK) and generally inexperienced British civil-affairs officials, who in addition to limited local knowledge had few maps and almost no topographical data on the Riouw islands. (Old colonial hands liberated from internment camps who 'carried with them the stench of the failure of 1942' were not made welcome by the returning British administration.[19]) Though thick jungle covered all of Rempang and Galang, and all food stores and medical supplies had to be brought in, sweeping assumptions were made about the terrain, the availability of fresh water and JSP productivity. The first JSP fatigue parties sent to clear jungle survived on British military 'compo' (composite) tinned rations. One SEAC report estimated that self-sufficiency on Rempang was unlikely to be achieved in under nine months, 'mainly owing to lack of open space...afterwards they expect to produce two-thirds'. Although agriculture and fishing had commenced, seeds and tools were required. Sickness also spread in the camps due, according to critical British officials, to poor administration and planning among the Japanese, along with 'low standards of hygiene and medical care'. British observers admitted SEAC lacked 'a suitable organisation for supervision and co-ordination' of these camps. There was, however, awareness of basic needs and ration scales were raised to 2,000 calories per-man per-day while four months of heavy clearing work was undertaken.[20] It was not just JSP, however, who had less to eat. Hunger was widespread throughout civilian populations in SEAC in 1945-46. The British also confiscated a considerable amount of Japanese food stocks on the grounds that the Japanese had seized the food from the civilian population in the first place. As a consequence of Japanese seizures civilians had been left with very low food stocks and were on a 'very reduced ration scale'. General Itagaki, Commander of 7th Area Army, was informed directly by HQ Malaya Command that this 'was the fault of the Japanese'. JSP rations were monitored and controlled so as not to exceed the locally available civilian ration at any time. Further, JSP on Rempang were to be encouraged to 'help themselves' and to procure additional food by vegetable planting, starting a local fishing industry (though SEAC admitted suitable fishing equipment had 'not yet been imported and is in short supply') and the issuing (from British stocks) of store tents to protect perishable stores. Assertions from the British that shelter provision would be increased once Japanese sawmill equipment 'now in Johore was moved to Riouw' and by 'each man [moving to Rempang] carrying with him a bundle of thatching grass' cannot have sounded very encouraging to the JSP.[21] Increasing Japanese concern over the health of men in camps in Malaya, particularly over the spread of TB however, was indirectly acknowledged and an inspection by a British doctor was confirmed.[22]

Despite the early reservations of surveyors over potable water resources, Rempang and Galang were eventually to hold more than 100,000 JSP (including some Japanese military nurses). For the Japanese interned there, however, the two islands became synonymous with deprivation, dysentery and death.[23] (An inscription on a monument erected on Rempang in 1981 by former JSP members of the Rempang Friendship Association records 112,708

26. Beachhead of the JSP camp on Rempang Island in November 1945. (© IWM)

repatriated and 128 dead.) Many JSP non-combat-related deaths after 15 August 1945 were the result of combinations of long-term malnutrition, untreated infections and diseases such as malaria, beriberi and amoebic dysentery caused by the Japanese Army's widespread lack of medical supplies and its inability to re-supply combat zones in 1943–5. Disruption and forced relocation, followed by isolation, however, cannot have eased demands on the already basic Japanese military medical infrastructure.

INDEPENDENT REPORTS FROM 'SOUTHERN AREA'

While communication with most JSP camps in southeast Asia was difficult or at least prone to delay, the Japanese Government was able to contact and receive real-time reports from Japanese naval vessels still operating, under SCAP orders, in 'Southern Area' waters. Shore parties often observed the situations of their fellow JSP first-hand. Uncensored descriptions of living conditions, supply levels and health assessments were sent to Japan directly via ships' radio channels. The task of translating and presenting this quite often critical information to SCAP fell to the Central Liaison Office (CLO), an external bureau of the Japanese Foreign Ministry, which acted as the official communication channel with MacArthur's HQ. Its main role was to translate and then turn SCAP policies into action but it also influenced the implementation of Allied policy. SCAP was not unresponsive to CLO submissions. CLO staff were all Foreign Ministry officials and quite often they resisted or championed specific causes.[24]

One SCAP message to the Australian command in Melbourne and forwarded to SEAC repeated Japanese information that JSP in the Australian Military Forces Area (AMFA), a substantive Command in eastern SEAC, had been ordered to form two concentrations of approximately 14,000 and 23,000 JSP respectively on two islands in the Moluccas (Maluku) archipelago, both of which had insufficient rice stocks. This rather critical message was forwarded by the CLO to SCAP as part of a regular submission of routinely gathered reports entitled 'Overseas Information'.[25] SEAC duly instructed Allied Land Forces South East Asia (ALFSEA) to note the Japanese rice needs 'as they will have to be met by you when area concerned is taken over from Australian Forces'.[26] Some reports were more troubling for Tokyo. In December 1945, while on a SCAP-authorised repatriation voyage off New Guinea, the Japanese light cruiser *Kashima* observed 10,700 army JSP under Australian Army control on Nushu (Muschu) Island. *Kashima*'s captain signalled that the soldiers' radio equipment had been confiscated, that they had 'been robbed of money and valuables and left with only one blanket', and that they were being issued with provisions amounting to just 1,400 calories a day. Disturbingly, the report also stated that between ten and 15 men were dying every day from increasing exhaustion and disease. *Kashima* had attempted to unload extra provisions but these had been refused by the Australian commander and *Kashima* ordered to leave. SCAP no doubt passed this information on to SEAC (and thus on to the Australian military through normal channels). It was probably not coincidental that direct communication from JSP in the AMFA to Japan was forbidden from 1 January 1946. This same ban in itself generated numerous 'last chance' messages from isolated JSP concentrations to the major Japanese HQs. One from Seram Island (Lesser Sundas) reporting on general conditions in early January 1946 is typical. It informed Tokyo that communication was to be 'restrained', and that with 24,000 men on the island, 'self-sufficiency is poor, provisions scanty so prospects…are hardly encouraging'.[27] Japanese naval ships' freedom to send independent (ie, unfavourable) messages did not last long. By the end of March 1946 the Royal Navy had assumed entire control of Japanese naval communications in SEAC with the exception of dedicated repatriation vessels, which importantly, remained under SCAP control.[28]

While reports of violent or vindictive behaviour towards Japanese in SEAC occur occasionally in the CLO submissions to SCAP, breaches of the PW Convention no doubt occurred in Southeast Asia or the Southwest Pacific as former enemies came face to face. This was perhaps inevitable. Details of such incidents are beyond the scope of this book but some mention ought to be made in this context of the difficulties that suddenly imposed custodial responsibilities brought to ordinary soldiers, particularly combat veterans. During the war summary execution of Japanese captives had been a common occurrence. Indeed, a 'no-prisoners' policy had been considered perfectly normal practice among Allied combat troops. Some histories and also memoirs by former Allied soldiers have recounted British atrocities. Japanese soldiers, too, rarely took prisoners (post-1943) nor gave succour to a wounded enemy.[29] Individual hostility and hatred continued long after the ink was dry on surrender documents signed in Tokyo and Singapore. In many cases there was an extenuating circumstance: the shooting did not stop. In August and September 1945 numerous, isolated groups of Japanese servicemen without radios simply did not credit reports of Japan's surrender and continued to fight to the end. Attempting to inform Japanese holdouts that the war was over carried grave risks for Allied soldiers and they preferred, understandably, not to take them. Where possible, Japanese captive-volunteers were sent on these very dangerous missions.[30]

Bad feeling was not confined to Allied and Japanese servicemen. An unknown number of Japanese was killed in revenge attacks by 'clandestines' (guerrillas) armed by and fighting for the Allies, as well as by civilians. Many of these deaths are ascribed to the chaos of revolutionary wars, rather than the equally plausible reason of calculated revenge for the death of relatives or friends. As military occupiers the Japanese had alienated very large numbers of people. Its *kenpeitai* was feared and loathed for its swift recourse to brutality, torture and frequent summary execution. Economic policies instituted under the unilaterally imposed Great East Asia Co-Prosperity Sphere had caused widespread agricultural failure and subsequent famine and death. In Indonesia, *romusha* (forced) labour policies had sent hundreds of thousands of labourers to Siam, Burma and elsewhere to suffer abuse, neglect and death through malnutrition and disease. As a result, in the aftermath of the surrender little goodwill was shown towards the Japanese in much of Southeast Asia.[31] There is no question that Japanese lost their lives at the hands of nationalist mobs in Sumatra, Java, Bali and Vietnam. In one example, in October 1945 a Javanese mob killed 86 Japanese marines travelling by train between Jakarta and Bandung.[32] Records of post-surrender deaths elsewhere in SEAC are understandably vague. Japanese brutality towards the hill peoples of Burma is well documented. To the mounting concern of the British, their allies among the various hill peoples of Burma continued to prey upon Japanese in 'dacoit' manner.[33] Allied troops have also been accused of complicity in a mass post-surrender killing of JSP when 'a large number' of Japanese surrendering to an Australian army unit in British North Borneo was 'marched into the jungle and massacred by tribesmen while the Australians looked on'.[34] Although animosity towards the Japanese in Southeast Asia was considerable, efforts were made to prevent brutality towards JSP. This did not extend to JPW suspected of war crimes or some others in Allied hands. JPW were often mistreated or chastised in public by their captors. In Saigon, a British serviceman witnessed the torture and beating to death of Japanese prisoners in French custody from a hospital window overlooking a prison courtyard.[35] One JPW also witnessed fatal beatings by Dutch soldiers in Java.[36] Australian diplomat William Macmahon Ball observed a Japanese internee-camp commander handcuffed and chained, 'unable to make the smallest movement' and 'given neither food nor drink', during a nine-hour journey from Jakarta to Singapore.[37] It was, as George MacDonald Fraser put it, 'the atmosphere of the time'.[38]

In general, the British thought that hard and unpleasant physical labour (such as repairing roads and sewers) was sufficiently demeaning 'punishment' for JSP. Abuses did occur but British provost personnel were in general aware of the risks of extra-legal punishment. Ronnie Noble, a former British Army news cameraman serving in Singapore recalls a visit to a prison to film Japanese commanders. A British captain showed him to a bare, stone courtyard where four shaven-headed and visibly bruised Japanese senior officers were stripped to their loincloths. At the captain's command the Japanese bent over while he walked past them smacking their raised backsides with his riding crop. The formal beating was interrupted by the arrival of a furious and embarrassed superior officer who ordered an immediate inquiry. (The fate of Noble's film is unknown.)[39]

Aida Yuji, a JSP in Rangoon, experienced more subtle and, for him, more lasting demonstrations of the victors' contempt. He was scrubbing the floor of a barracks when a British soldier stubbed out a cigarette on his forehead. On another occasion he was made to kneel and serve as a footstool for an hour. He remembers JSP cleaners at a dormitory for British women auxiliaries were 'totally ignored as human beings' as the women undressed or washed in front of them. Aida remained bitter over his treatment. Another JPW, Ooka Shohei, later a celebrated novelist, was captured in the Philippines in 1944. Though he was well-treated, he incorporated his experiences of alienation

27. JSP clear a roadblock near Saigon under British supervision in Nov. 1945. (© CW)

into his heavily autobiographical novels.[40] Ooka also refers to the 'everlasting disgrace' feared by many Japanese PW on becoming captives.[41]

Animosity and incidents reduced dramatically when long-serving Allied veterans of the Burma and New Guinea campaigns were repatriated or relieved of custodial duties. This happened apace in late 1945 with the commencement of Operation Python's demobbing programme (see Chapter 4). Replacements coming to Malaya and Singapore were usually newly conscripted troops from the United Kingdom or Australia who had not seen action against the Japanese and who by and large bore no personal grudges against the former enemy.[42]

Elsewhere in Southeast Asia, however, Allied dominance was less visible. Former European colonies were in the grip of nationalist fervour, with armed Japanese in an uneasy and generally unwilling peacekeeping role. The men of 23 and 20 Indian Divisions and accompanying detachments from the Royal Navy and Royal Air Force enjoyed just one month of 'peace' before being sent from a relaxed, if ambivalent, Malaya to tense and decidedly unfriendly Indonesia and Vietnam. Manpower shortages in SEAC (further compounded by Operation Python) limited the effectiveness of these rushed, interventionist deployments. Nationalist suspicions over British support for the return of ousted Dutch and French colonial regimes very quickly gave way to open hostility. Allied troops therefore had once again to raise their guard. Their small deployments made them vulnerable almost everywhere. Only the Japanese had the numbers and capability to assist them. Thus within weeks of the surrender some British but mainly Gurkha and Indian soldiers, many of them veterans of the Burma campaign, were co-operating with Japanese forces in trying to maintain law and order.

THE ROLE OF JEFSR HQ IN JSP ADMINISTRATION

With long delays in repatriation for JSP from Southeast Asia seemingly unavoidable, the attention of regional Japanese commanders turned to the living conditions, food stocks, health and morale of their men. Japan's Government reported differences in the facilities and treatment afforded JSP in American-controlled and British- or Australian-controlled areas to SCAP. Among the many dozens of JSP camps in SEAC, however, there were wide-ranging variations in conditions, re-supply frequency, stocks of food, levels of self-sufficiency, incidence of disease and fatalities. (HQ was also well aware of these differences and made an early request for periodic reports on JSP concentrations, health and wellbeing to be sent to Saigon.[43] This was approved, as was an early January 1946 request by Lt General Numata Takazo to inspect JSP camps throughout the Command. SEAC, however, agreed to the tour only once it was clarified that any reports produced would not be sent to 'Japan' (ie, neither to the Japanese Government nor SCAP).[44] This reluctance to allow third-party involvement suggests at best a lack of confidence in camp standards. (Poor conditions in Allied-run camps for political prisoners in Germany were the subject of scathing criticism in the British press at this time, so perhaps a general hesitancy was inevitable.[45])

Britain could not, however, easily bar inspections of camps by representatives of the International Committee of the Red Cross (ICRC). The first of these, of a number of camps in Java, occurred in April 1946.[46] ICRC reports on the camps visited (those in Malaya were visited in July 1946) were forwarded as a matter of course to the British Government, the British Red Cross, the Dutch Government, SCAP and, separately, to the Japanese Government.[47] Since the Japanese were largely responsible for their own administration even after relocation and concentration, the state of supplies and the frequency of adequate re-supply became—after the ever-present dissatisfaction over the rate of repatriation—the second most frequent issue of contention in SEAC-JSP relations. The Japanese were persistent in identifying and reporting reductions or shortfalls as 'shortages' to SEAC. JEFSR HQ was to contend that JSP lost an average of three percent of average bodyweight as a result of Allied supply failures and that 2,000 calories a day was insufficient for men engaged in heavy labour. (The average weight of JSP in Java in 1946 was 56.1kg against a pre-war average of 57.5kg.)[48] Indirect reports of shortages in British- and Australian-controlled areas, for example of food at Rempang, and anti-malarial drugs at Rabaul, continued to reach Tokyo. Shortages were 'revealed' to SCAP by polite requests for 'permission' to send, for example, aid vessels carrying seeds or stockpiled anti-malarial Acrinamine tablets to JSP camps in British-controlled areas 'to help alleviate shortages of food'.[49] (Since Japanese supply efforts had been almost non-existent for 18 months, such criticism must have sounded rich indeed to SEAC.[50])

As a consequence of the decision to maintain the Japanese military command structure, senior Japanese officers continued to play a major role in the supervision, organisation and, where necessary, the disciplining of their junior officers and other ranks. Japan's military code and army and navy regulations continued to have legal force, as did Japanese Army and Navy courts martial. There was, however, an Allied-imposed moratorium on capital punishment verdicts.[51] Allied instructions and information to JSP were issued through Japanese command HQs. Consequently the attitude and co-operation of senior Japanese staff officers at HQ JEFSR in Saigon was considerably important if Allied–Japanese relations were to remain stable. None more so in fact than Lt General Numata. Appointed Terauchi's Chief of Staff in late December 1944, he became extremely influential after Terauchi's stroke in April 1945, news of which Terauchi and Numata withheld from Imperial Headquarters in Tokyo. It was Numata, accompanied by Admiral Chudo Kaigye, who met General Browning, SEAC Chief of Staff, at Rangoon in late August 1945 to discuss the surrender terms (see Chapter 2).

Numata also attended the surrender ceremony in Singapore on 12 September 1945, accompanying General Itagaki, who signed on behalf of the incapacitated Terauchi. After the ceremony Numata returned to Saigon where he resumed overall control of the day-to-day administration of JEFSR, and organised care and strict privacy for the rapidly failing Field Marshal. The repatriation and the welfare of the men under his command became Numata's chief priority. In reality Terauchi was in charge in name only. Numata oversaw JEFSR using Terauchi's seal.[52] Mountbatten met Terauchi in late November 1945 in Saigon where the 67-year-old Field Marshal surrendered two swords to him. In his diary Mountbatten described the semi-paralysed

Terauchi as 'practically ga-ga'. SEAC doctors had also found Terauchi unfit for trial.[53] (Terauchi died on 12 June 1946 at Johor Baru, Malaya. He was buried in Singapore.)

In early February 1946 Mountbatten decided to appoint General Itagaki as Deputy Commander. Whether there was specific dissatisfaction with Numata is not clear. Mountbatten obviously knew of Terauchi's infirmity and was aware that communications signed 'Terauchi' were drafted by Numata. With the planned move of the Japanese HQ from Saigon to Johore Bahru after the departure of British forces from Vietnam in January 1946, army protocol probably required that the more senior Itagaki, who was in Malaya, be appointed formal deputy. In the event, Itagaki's appointment was short lived. In late March he was arrested at the request of the Americans and sent to Tokyo to face war crimes charges for incidents in Manchuria and ill-treatment of Allied PW in Southeast Asia.[54] (He was hanged in December 1948.) Lt General Kinoshita Satoshi (7 Area Army) was appointed Japanese deputy commander in his stead. (In reality the titular appointments of Itagaki and Kinoshita had little bearing on day-to-day JSP administration.) Upon the death of Terauchi Kinoshita became the Japanese Commander in Southeast Asia.[55] He held this title for only a few days before reductions by SCAP to the status, size and remits of the Army and Navy Demobilization Ministries in Tokyo—they became civilian bureaus under a Demobilization Board—led in effect to the official disbandment of JEFSR.[56] Numata remained Chief of Staff until then, when the responsibilities of the now much smaller Japanese Command HQ in SEAC were taken over by a newly created Japanese Liaison Office (JLO).

GENERAL NUMATA'S TOUR OF JSP CAMPS IN SEAC

General Numata communicated frequently with senior Allied commanders. All requests, suggestions and numerous petitions from Japanese command centres in the JEFSR Area were all channelled through the JLO to SEAC HQ. Numata also travelled frequently. His tour from 24 January to 23 February 1946 of the main JSP camps is noteworthy. The General was given unrestricted access to all JSP and JPW in SEAC. (The tour party included a Japanese-speaking British officer from SEATIC.) Numata's 24-page report, submitted to Mountbatten, remains perhaps the only first-hand overview (in English) of JSP conditions in Southeast Asia by a senior Japanese officer. Travelling independently and unescorted in a Mitsubishi Ki-21 heavy bomber with a Japanese aircrew, the aim of the tour was to 'inspect the conditions of the concentrated JSP [and their] discipline, morale, maintenance and health'.[57]

Before leaving southern Vietnam, Numata had inspected JPW prison conditions (see photograph) and Japanese civilian internee camps in Saigon and the large concentrations of JSP awaiting repatriation at Cape St Jacques (Vung Tao). Despite British and Japanese apprehension over possible difficulties arising over of French-Japanese co-operation, direct evacuations of JSP to Japan had begun under French control.[58] Numata's tour itinerary covered several thousand miles within SEAC. He was given considerable freedom of movement, although on average his schedule involved many hours of flying each day. A brief summary of the main stops gives an idea of the distances covered and, equally, the logistic problems facing SEAC. From Saigon Numata's party flew first to Kuala Lumpur to visit General Itagaki at HQ Southern Malaya Forces (at Klang). From there he moved to Singapore where he spent several days. In addition to visits to the local Japanese Liaison Office and Changi Prison (where the Japanese work details reported much improved conditions), he inspected a Japanese civilian internment camp at Jurong. Also he had separate talks with General Browning, and General Pyman (Chief of Staff, ALFSEA) discussing repatriation priorities and schedules.

Opportunities for Numata to have face-to-face meetings with senior SEAC officers were rare. Prior to the trip 'Terauchi' had written to both Mountbatten and Browning listing points that Numata would raise (including fatigue party arrangements, 'low' ration levels and repatriation schedules). Browning's answers were prepared in advance. There was little sympathy for Japanese complaints and briefing notes were typically dismissive: 'It is suggested that the Japanese be reminded that the present shortage of rice is entirely due to their own actions and that their surrendered personnel are infinitely better fed than were Allied PW in their hands'.[59]

Despite SEAC's inflexible stance—ration scales remained an area of contention—Numata pursued a number of formal requests related to JSP fatigue parties. Among them that no person working for the Allies in Malaya and elsewhere should do so for more than four months, or at the longest for six months. He also wanted to see priority repatriation for those who had worked for the longest time, and for fixed scales of compensation to be paid to them later. Browning informed him that there was 'no intention of retarding the repatriation of Japanese surrendered personnel in order to employ them in fatigue parties'. Mountbatten's priority, he stressed, was to return the Japanese 'at the earliest possible moment' and that 'no problem of labour or anything else would be allowed to affect that plan'.[60] Browning's comments were truthful, as no proposals then existed for retention of JSP for labour. Indeed, both the SEAC and JEFSR HQs were working with estimates of between three and five years to complete repatriation. When Browning explained that SEAC hoped to ship the JSP home much sooner, Numata himself had asked if the end of 1947 was a viable date for completion.[61] Numata also requested that SEAC approach the United States for the use of American shipping in order to speed up repatriation. He knew, clearly, that SEAC was stretched and, somewhat tongue in cheek, expressed concern that his request 'might be offensive and injurious to the pride of the British nation'. Browning replied merely that 'Allied shipping was allocated on a worldwide basis' and would remain so for some time.[62]

While at Singapore Numata made side trips to Rempang and Galang islands, and HQ 10 Zone Fleet at Seletar (north Singapore Island). From Singapore he visited HQ 37 Army on Labuan island (off North Borneo), and then to the former Japanese Naval Civil Administration Centre or *Minseifu* for eastern Indonesia at Makassar (Sulawesi). Conveniently, HQ 2 Army was near to Makassar at Pinrang. From Makassar the tour party continued via Ambon to HQ 32 Division at Wasile on Halmahera (Jilolo) island in the Moluccas (Moluku). From there the group moved on to Java. At Surabaya, Numata met representatives from Japanese Army and Navy units, as well as British officers, including General Sir Robert Mansergh, Commander, 5 Indian Division. At Bandung, HQ 16 IJA, Numata consulted General Yamamoto who had returned to Java after his court martial acquittal in Singapore (see Chapter 3) and Major General Mabuchi. While in Batavia (Jakarta) Numata inspected JSP work parties and naval transport operations at the Tandjung Priok docks and flew on to Semarang. The final part of the tour was a visit to Sumatra. Stops here included Palembang, 9 Air Division's base, where several thousand JSP were deployed to guard oil installations. At Fort de Kock (Bukittinggi), HQ 25 IJA, Numata met with General Tanabe. From there the itinerary included Medan and Brastagi, base of 2 Guards Division (also guarding oil industry infrastructure), before returning to Singapore.

At each stop Numata addressed his men on behalf of Terauchi. (Terauchi's failing health meant that he probably had little involvement in composing the speech.) The content of the address had also required SEAC's advance approval. The text reflects British priorities and, quite clearly, lingering Allied suspicions of Japanese collusion with nationalists. In its first draft, after praising his men for having 'borne what was unbearable…despite hardships and privations suffered', it called upon 'Forces in the Southern Regions to demonstrate their iron discipline and the strictest obedience to orders'. It specifically warned against desertion to 'irresponsible extremist elements,

Indonesians and others....' Such action, Terauchi cautioned, would not only reflect gravely on the discipline of the Japanese forces 'in the eyes of the world but would also be in direct opposition to the august Will of His Majesty'.[63] Terauchi's (ie, Numata's) emphasis, however, was too ambiguous for the British. In the final, SEAC-censored version 'extremist' was replaced with 'terrorist', and the entire reference to 'Indonesians and others' was deleted.[64]

With the benefit of hindsight, British anxiety over Japanese co-operation was overly dramatic. At the time, British worries over the existence of Japanese 'stay behind' units in Indonesia and Vietnam were real, however unlikely. In northern Vietnam, for example, one British observer's main concern was over Chinese support for clandestine groups of *Communist* Japanese.[65] By February 1946 the daunting scale of the military and diplomatic problems in Indonesia were becoming increasingly manifest. Deployments of British (ie, mainly Indian) troops in three of Java's port cities had little impact on nationalist activity inland. Large numbers of JSP remained fully armed but in semi-self-internment deep in nationalist-held territory. These 'no-go' areas were a huge embarrassment to Britain. Their very existence raised the serious possibility of Britain failing to fulfil its Potsdam undertaking. In much of Java the personal sympathies of Japanese commanders lay openly with nationalists. Had they so wished, 16 Army units in eastern Java could very well have swung the balance of power in favour of the republican movement with alarming long-term implications for British policy in Southeast Asia as a whole. Certainly such a development would have shattered attempts by Britain to re-establish Great Power status in the region. Nationalists in Burma, Malaya and beyond might well have been encouraged to attempt more militant action. That the Japanese did not do so despite the confusion, increasing dissatisfaction and frustration over delays in securing their extraction from Java, attests to their discipline and Numata's strong influence.

In his report Numata pulls very few punches. Polite and measured in the extreme, he nevertheless states for the record details of food shortages, including 'low calorific minimums', labour projects in difficult conditions, high incidence of disease, lack of hospital provision and continuing deaths of men under his command. In commenting on Rempang, he expresses concern over the numbers concentrated there (68,101 at the time of his visit) and the 'failure of food supplies to arrive as planned'. According to Numata, there had been near disaster in the November when food supplies had been at a 'critically low level'. Heavy labour projects such as clearing over 780 acres of thick jungle had been undertaken with men receiving an allowance of around 1,700 calories a day. Tapioca was being planted as a replacement staple to rice but JSP health remained a concern. Malaria, beriberi and amoebic dysentery were rife on Rempang. To Numata's disquiet, 56 men had died, 26 of them from malaria from the camp's establishment in November 1945 to the end of January 1946.

Australian administration of the 10,825 JSP and civilians (457 women and 612 children) at Jesselton (Kota Kinbalu) in then North Borneo (Sabah) also comes in for criticism. Numata did not visit Jesselton himself but incorporated a separate report from Lieutenant General Baba Masao, Commander of 37 IJA. According to Baba, the Japanese at Jesselton had been 'ill-treated by the Australians en-route' and an unsuitable and unhealthy 'semi-marshland' site had been chosen. Rations had been 1,520 calories per man per day. When the British 32 Indian Brigade took over responsibility for Jesselton the calorific count had improved but some 30 percent of camp inmates remained chronically sick. Morale was low, compounded by the effects of disease, which was rife. There was an average of ten deaths per day. Numata requested priority evacuation from places such as Rempang and Jesselton. SEAC reacted quickly to the complaint from Numata and Baba. Jesselton's JSP were assigned priority repatriation in February 1946. Numata also complained about the remoteness, conditions and low food levels on outer islands, many of which lacked an airstrip. Australian-administered Balikpapan and Seram, where out of a promised 1,600 tons of food only 160 tons had been received, particularly concerned him.[66]

Politically, perhaps the most difficult part of the tour for Numata was his visit to Java. Information on Japanese held in the east of the island was scant, even by early 1946. What information there was came from isolated JSP groups themselves via 16 Army's radio network. Allied aerial reconnaissance patrols were still attempting to locate and estimate JSP concentrations in nationalist-controlled territory. The stakes were high. Terauchi's caution in his message was specifically tailored to 16 Army in Java and, to a lesser extent, 25 Army in Sumatra, especially those out of reach except by limited-range radio. Not surprisingly, and obviously aware of British concern, Numata addressed the question of defections to the nationalist cause in his report to SEAC. He identified '114 army deserters plus a few deserters from the Imperial Japanese Navy'.[67] Even though this figure is inaccurate by perhaps a factor of ten (see note 63), since there were some 68,000 JSP on Java, as well as Japanese civilians, it supports the argument that British fear over widespread Japanese desertions was misplaced.

Other means of potential 'assistance' to nationalists, particularly in the form of weapons handovers were, however, almost of equal concern to the British. JSP units generally retained Japanese ordnance but not Dutch or British weapons captured in 1942. (In Indonesia much captured weaponry had in any case been issued to PETA militia and Special Police long before the surrender. It is arguable that Japanese failures to 'retrieve' these weapons were not strictly breaches of the surrender terms.) Terauchi's address did not mention weapons specifically, but in the context this might have been

28. JSP demonstrate bayonet fighting to Australian troops. Borneo, Nov. 1945. (AWM)

unnecessary given the strict and widely followed requirement in the Japanese Military Code for the soldier to retain possession of his rifle. (Japanese weapons were stamped with the Imperial chrysanthemum crest, symbolically making them the property of the Emperor. Crests on weapons surrendered after 15 August 1945 were usually defaced.)

Numata also visited a tense Surabaya, still no more than a bridgehead for British forces, for talks with JSP commanders. Also visited were Bandung and Semarang, two cities where Japanese had engaged with nationalists in 'no uncertain manner'. Semarang was the base of Kido Butai, perhaps in British opinion the most 'dependable' Japanese unit in Java. While there he met the British officer in charge, Brigadier Richard. B. W. Bethell, MC, who had deployed Kido *Butai* on numerous occasions. Numata commented that at Semarang he received reports from the local Japanese commanders and inspected 'Japanese-built fortifications'. This is the only specific reference he makes in his report to an active military role by JSP, though he added that he thought it 'very desirable to move promptly all the disarmed Japanese forces to Galang [and so] avoid any misunderstanding or apprehension on the part of the Indonesians that the Allies might or would rearm Japanese soldiers and use them to fight the Allies' war against the Indonesians'.[68] This possibility was of far more concern and importance to Numata than a few deserters. Mounting Japanese casualty figures in western and central Java incurred in performing security duties required by the British are given considerably prominence in his report. As at 20 February 1946 these stood at 507 dead and 330 wounded, including armed Japanese civilians newly enrolled in the Japanese forces. Clearly HQ JEFSR was exasperated over continuing Japanese military and civilian exposure to attacks in Java, Sumatra, Vietnam and parts of Thailand. Numata expressed his dissatisfaction in person to General Browning in Singapore and later to General Hedley, Commander of 26 Indian Division in Sumatra. He urged that JSP 'be disarmed' and evacuated 'as soon as possible'. While Hedley agreed 'in principle' to the move, he repeated the British concerns over weapons falling into Indonesian hands. It was in fact many months before JSP ceased their duties on the Burma–Thailand Railway or at the oil installations at Palembang and Pladjoe.[69]

To be fair, it ought to be mentioned that Numata found much to praise during his trip. At Wasile on Halmahera Island, the HQ of 32 IJA Division with over 38,000 personnel, discipline and morale were described as 'very high'. Japanese forces were given the 'full trust' of the Australian forces and accorded 'very liberal treatment'. In contrast with other units, 32 Division was not moved to new camps, so established farming plots and irrigation systems continued to be used. Ration levels were maintained at an average of 1500 calories a day. In fact, 32 Division had 'virtual self-rule'. Even so, Halmahera was no paradise. Sickness had claimed 401 lives in the previous five months and there had been over 23,000 malaria or beriberi cases.[70] Somewhat surprisingly, Numata concluded that post-surrender arrangements were working 'far better than he had been led to believe'. A key reason for this was, he thought, the continuance of the Japanese chain of command. He was also grateful for the generally good treatment received by his men. During his trip Numata must, however, have noticed the paucity of British military manpower and resources. His comments remained courteous. He concluded his report, with no hint of sarcasm, by saying he was impressed by the 'zeal' of British repatriation efforts.

Interestingly the attitude of the Japanese regarding their comrades held 'hostage' in eastern Java was vague and non-committal. Numata describes his forces in western and central Java as being 'unable, though very anxious, to effect their rescue'. Yet again, the reluctance of senior Japanese commanders to sanction force against Indonesians, even in aid of fellow Japanese, is clear. This contrasts sharply with Kido's single-minded determination to liberate Japanese held in Semarang, irrespective of casualties incurred (though he had heard rumours of torture and murders that proved true). It is significant, though, that within a few days of Numata submitting his report, SEAC planners began discussing the viability of ordering the Japanese in eastern Java to fight their way to Allied lines or rendezvous with Royal Navy ships.[71] Quite how Numata would have felt about such a proposal can only remain conjecture. At the same time, however, in quieter parts of SEAC, administrators were already beginning to view JSP as a potential solution to the labour shortage.

GENERAL IMAMURA'S INITIATIVES ON NEW BRITAIN

Widespread food shortages prompted JSP to attempt self-sufficiency farming in numerous locations in SEAC. Complaints from Japanese commanders over insufficient food and medicines, or farming efforts being thwarted by the sheer numbers to feed and the small areas of land available for cultivation, were frequent.[72] (That the British were encouraging self-sufficiency measures so early was in itself another clear indication of limited repatriation capacity.) Indirect attempts by the Japanese to draw MacArthur's attention to shortages in the British and Australian areas had been made via requests to send supplies (see note 46). JSP were, if not quite abandoned, at least left to their own devices and had to overcome local difficulties by themselves with some small groups of Japanese left marooned for years.[73] Results varied. General Numata identified camps that were barely subsistent and failing. Others adapted well. One of the largest and also one of the longest-established concentrations was commanded by General Imamura Hitoshi (8 Area Army) on the island of New Britain (off New Guinea). Imamura had led the invasion of Java in 1942. (In 1948, in Jakarta, he was tried on war crimes charges by the Dutch but was acquitted.)

The JSP 'settlement' on New Britain is also the best documented.[74] Imamura's headquarters at Rabaul had been a major Japanese base during the early years of the war. Like others in the Southeast Pacific the garrison had prepared itself for a last stand but had been bypassed during the rapid American advance and thereafter ignored. Imamura's forces had been effectively marooned and played no further part in the war. After Japan's capitulation, New Britain became part of the AMFA. Pre-surrender Australian estimates of Japanese strength on New Britain were 30,000 men. In fact there were

100,000 at Rabaul and another 40,000 scattered among neighbouring small islands. Australian military supply capability simply could not meet this demand from the start. Yet Imamura's men did not go severely short of food. Since August 1943 they had been by necessity self-sufficient. Military defeats for Japan in the Solomons and the loss of New Georgia had left Imamura's command isolated, even from New Guinea. By drawing on the skills of the farmers, engineers and craftsmen within their ranks they had managed to maintain themselves.

In September 1945 the Australians, under Lieutenant General Sturdee, ordered JSP to produce food for themselves, ie, to remain self-sufficient. Sturdee also ordered their concentration in 13 new camps on the same island on the grounds that this would simplify supervision. Consequently established farm plots and irrigation systems were abandoned. Between October and November 1945 the 140,000 men moved themselves, drawing heavily on their food stocks while they built new buildings and cleared land afresh. Unfortunately, as in other areas of SEAC, the locations of the new camps had not been selected with a view to agricultural potential. Also, Australian forces used a number of the fittest JSP for labour on projects of their own (even removing some to Australia for this purpose).[75] Malaria outbreaks were common and further reduced the number of able-bodied men. This combination of poorer soil, illness and fewer hands overall led to a fall in harvests of 60 percent for a short period.[76]

General Imamura did not brood over defeat but rather over peace, or more precisely, over the periods of inactivity that peace brought his men. He was concerned about them having too much leisure lest it affect the discipline and the stability of his command. A number of his morale-boosting addresses survive. In one message answering general questions about repatriation delays, Imamura stressed the benefits of staying in Rabaul and what he proposed for his men while they were there. He argued that too early a repatriation would make them a burden on war-stricken Japan, and that by staying in Rabaul they would help their country if only indirectly. He also urged his men to make the most of their time by undertaking vocational training that would enable them to contribute to Japan's economic recovery once they reached home. To this end, farmers, builders, plumbers, mechanics and others among the rank and file with skills were encouraged to teach others in organised programmes.[77] Academic courses were also established.

Imamura set out his ideas in two memoranda: 'Frame of mind for life in the Rabaul camps' and 'Guidelines for education in the camps' (both October 1945). Daily (two-hour), timetabled courses included civil education, vocational training, natural sciences, basic English and college preparatory sessions. Creation of the various curricula, textbook compilation and lectures were the responsibility of the officer corps, particularly the military surgeons. Examples of some of the textbooks and JSP camp ephemera survive at the Australian War Memorial (file AWA82).[78] Imamura's ideas were embraced

29. Gen Imamura in Rabaul, 1946. (AWM)

wholeheartedly in what was perhaps the first-ever large-scale adult-education programme for Japanese. At first JSP returning from Rabaul were forbidden to board repatriation ships with their camp-forged tools. Later the rules were relaxed and each ship carried thousands of farm implements, large amounts of clothing, several tons of food and, not least, several hundred highly motivated, semi-skilled labourers keen to aid their families and so contribute to Japan's ruined economy.[79]

THE JSP QUESTION IN JAPANESE DOMESTIC POLITICS

In late August 1945 the fate of Japan's overseas servicemen was not an immediate priority for the new civilian Japanese Government. More immediate domestic concerns were demanding its full attention. Three-and-a-half-years of total war had brought utter disaster to the country. Social cohesion in Japan was virtually shattered. Although the nation had surrendered and the bombing had stopped, Japan's suffering had not ended. The US naval blockade had brought the country's economy to a standstill. All major cities and transport hubs had suffered extensive bomb damage. Most internal rail links were severed. Inflation was rampant. Agriculture had collapsed, and near-famine conditions existed in many cities and towns throughout the country. Diseases swept through the malnourished population. High civilian casualties prior to the surrender had led to a massive shortage of even basic medicines.

There was also widespread public anxiety over the imminent arrival of the occupying American forces. Domestic criticism of those in authority deemed responsible for the country's plight was vocal and increasing. National and local politicians and even the civil service bureaucrats, the lynchpins of Japan's village and town communities, were met with abuse, as were demobilised soldiers too. What is more, anti-imperial sentiment was open and increasing, as were public demonstrations of left-wing sympathies in labour, farming and educational organisations. Japan's social fabric was tearing itself apart and the Establishment feared a communist revolution.[80] Those worries over potential threats to imperial, political and social institutions and practices left the authorities little time to ponder the situation of Japanese outside the country.

Of course the families of those abroad did not forget their relatives but the exhausting daily struggle to obtain food, shelter and medicines in late 1945 and throughout 1946 meant their concerns, if voiced at all, were more often made in private or in their prayers. Little was known about servicemen's precise locations or even if individuals were still alive. Imperial Army and Navy policy had been to classify all information on unit deployment, other than very general 'Southern Area' or 'China' descriptions, as secret. Families and friends addressed letters to soldiers and sailors via military postal sorting offices in Japan for forwarding. In turn, servicemen were forbidden to mention locations in correspondence. Those letters that did were censored. In reality, Allied sea and air blockades had meant few letters had either reached or left Japan's servicemen in the Pacific or Southeast Asia Theatres since late 1943.

In the chaotic days following the surrender, large numbers of troops stationed in Japan ready to meet the expected Allied invasion simply left their garrisons and returned home, taking with them what they could in the way of food.[81] Time was in any case running out for the Imperial Japanese Army and Navy. MacArthur's instructions, set out in General Order No. 1, sounded the death knell for Japan's military order. Preparations for the rapid abolition of the armed forces began almost with his arrival in Japan. By 10 September over 80 percent of naval strength in Japan's home waters had been demobilised. Japanese Imperial General Headquarters was itself abolished on 13 September 1945 and its responsibilities transferred to the Japanese Army and Navy Ministries.[82] By the October some 83 percent of the Army's strength had been demobilised and 95 percent of the Japanese Air Force discharged. By the end of November, all Japanese service personnel under SCAP jurisdiction had been released.[83] Before the end of 1945, JSP were repatriated from Korea and Taiwan. Demobilised, and mostly unemployed, former soldiers were therefore a common sight in Japan's towns and cities.

Approximately 1.2 million non-Japanese nationals were stranded in Japan. Many had been transported as forced labour. With the collapse of military authority within the country, large numbers of them headed towards ports seeking to return home. To cope with this sudden and huge demand on port capacity and an associated threat to public order, SCAP instituted a four-phase, 'two-way', mass repatriation programme. The first phase, which ran from 14 September 1945 to 28 February 1946, repatriated approximately 1.5 million JSP and JPW from the western Pacific and 800,000 of those wishing to leave Japan. Some 650,000 JSP in SEAC and 1.5 million in China were repatriated in the second phase which ran from 1 March to 15 July 1946. The third phase consisted of the last JSP held at American camps in the Pacific and the remnants of troops, civil servants and civilian colonists in Manchuria. An unanticipated fourth phase proved necessary for JSP retained in the USSR and SEAC. This phase ran from December 1946 to mid-1950 when the USSR announced repatriation was 'complete', though the Soviet assertion was furiously disputed by Japan (see below).[84] Overall this was an astonishing operation, as well as a largely unrecognised but almost certainly record-breaking transportation feat. It further emphasises the unrivalled capacity, efficiency and flexibility of the US military from 1945 to 1950.

Japan's own ability to contribute to the international repatriation effort was limited. Apart from what little remained of her naval fleet, only six passenger and 15 cargo vessels were immediately available.[85] Within Japan, however, more resources were at hand. In mid-October 1945 SCAP ordered the setting-up of processing centres for returning service personnel and civilians.[86] (The strict timetable required several to be ready by mid-November.) Plans were submitted to SCAP for the organisation, construction and basic operational guidelines for Repatriation Relief Bureaux at Uraga, Maizuru, Kure, Shimonoseki, Hakata, Yokohama, Senzaki, Hakodate, Moji, Sasebo and Kagoshima. These provided inspection, quarantine and medical services as well as overnight accommodation and telegram facilities for returnees.[87]

Gradually, public curiosity in Japan was aroused over the slower return or fate of kin held further afield. While obtaining information on JSP in SEAC was difficult for the Japanese Government, in other areas it proved impossible. Japanese officials were aware that hundreds of thousands of Japanese prisoners who had surrendered to Russian forces in Manchuria had been transported west to the Soviet Union. Later it would emerge that some 1.3 million of them were working in hazardous conditions, compounded by ferocious cold or heat and malnourishment in mines and farms in Siberia. Perhaps 400,000 were worked to death.[88] This was one extreme. Arguably JSP in the American zone in the Pacific islands were at the other. Records reveal no requests at all from the CLO to SCAP to improve the wellbeing of JSP under American authority. In the Pacific there were 'shortages' of Japanese magazines and newspapers and these the Japanese Government offered to supply. In fact, the Americans were regularly praised for their prompt repatriation of JSP in preambles to numerous pleas for their assistance over delayed (or denied) repatriation from the USSR, a subject on which the Japanese Government was 'most seriously concerned'.[89]

In comparison with the plight of those transported to the uncertain conditions in Siberia, delays in repatriation for 650,000 JSP in SEAC and subsequent retention of 105,000 others was consequently a lesser priority for Tokyo. Repatriation of Japanese PW captured in SEAC (ie, pre-15 August 1945), if only small scale and not JSP, had at least commenced by mid-1946, whereas there would be no large-scale return from the USSR before 1948. The terms of the 1929 PW Convention required repatriation as soon as possible after cessation of hostilities. Since most British-held JPW were in fact in camps in Australia or India, however, the task of repatriating them was not a SEAC responsibility. Australia and SCAP negotiated directly to use spare SCAP shipping.[90] In comparison with United States efforts, however, British arrangements were extremely slow. Only 34,300 Japanese had been repatriated from SEAC by 21 April 1946.[91] Also among the British-held Japanese were some 2,481 JPW captured in Burma who had been transferred from SEAC and who were under India Command. According to the PW Convention and the Potsdam Agreement these men should have been among the first repatriated by Britain. Although SEAC was aware of their location, it was not until May 1946 that provision was finally made for their return. The Indian Government, which was bearing the cost of their maintenance in Rajasthan, insisted that SEAC made special arrangements to repatriate them. These men also travelled via Rempang Island and reached Japan in May 1946.[92]

If there were differences in SEAC's processing of JPW over JSP they were not understood by the Japanese Government. At reception centres in Japan no distinction was made whatsoever between—the relatively few—JPW and the very large numbers of JSP. All were called 'repatriates' or, in Japanese, *hikiagesha* (引揚者). PW is either *horyo* (捕虜) or, more formally, *furyo* (俘虜) or 'captive'. JSP is *kofuku nippon gunjin* (降伏日本軍人), whereas retained civilians are *kofuku nipponjin* (降伏日本人).[93] In the end, the anxiety felt by many JPW that they would face sanction or ostracism upon return to Japan proved utterly groundless. Evidence from former JPW about their reception on their return confirms that Japanese administrators made no attempt to record details of when or where they had come under Allied control, and that they were 'not interested' in whether they were JSP or JPW.[94] Thus the fear of the great 'national shaming' that had so concerned the wartime Government of Japan proved a chimera.

Lack of direct communication between British and Japanese authorities prolonged ignorance of repatriation delays within Japan. Information that up to one-sixth of JSP in SEAC would be retained for labour was never communicated directly to the Japanese Government by Britain. Indeed, MacArthur was first informed of British plans to retain JSP in April 1946, and only then because Whitehall realised that American extra shipping capacity would have removed all JSP from SEAC by the end of that year (see Chapter 5). It fell to SCAP to inform the Japanese Government of the retention. From 1946, however, SEAC was the only Allied Command from which the Japanese Government might, via SCAP, receive any information or at least an acknowledgement of general enquiries about JSP. For unlike the USSR, and to a lesser extent Nationalist and Communist authorities in China, Britain was embarrassed by any suggestion that it was not fulfilling its obligations to detained Japanese and sought to avoid or reduce criticism from the United Nations, the ICRC, the international press and, above all, General MacArthur himself.

SEAC UNDER THE SPOTLIGHT: JAPANESE PROTESTS OVER RETENTION

Understandably, the Japanese public were grateful for the prompt and publicised American repatriation of their compatriots. It was not long, however, before disparities in rates of return from American and British areas of control became apparent. Realisation spread among the Japanese public that the fate of men overseas depended very much on where and to whom they had surrendered. Local support groups mushroomed throughout the country to lobby for prompt repatriation of men detained for labour and information on JPW awaiting trial overseas. Repatriation of JSP was not the only area where Allied administration was slow and capacity limited. Many Japanese waited in vain for news of next of kin facing trial. There were prolonged delays in legal proceedings against Japanese accused of war crimes. Trial of many of them, particularly those on charges in the Australian judicial system, had not commenced almost five years after the surrender, though individuals were imprisoned in Japan pending prosecution. Vice Admiral Shibata, champion of Indonesian independence, was one. In late February 1950, he was one of 90 suspects returned to Manus Island to stand trial for murder and other serious war crimes against Australians that carried the death penalty. Robert Menzies, the Australian Prime Minister, admitted that his Government was concerned to find that there were 'many Japanese suspects who have been imprisoned without trial for more than two years'. Japanese held for lesser offences that if proven would have resulted in a prison sentence were released. Menzies also admitted that the 'extraordinary delays violate the fundamental concepts of British justice'.[95] (Shibata was acquitted of all charges by the Australia War Crimes Court in March 1951.)

American occupation policy now encouraged the Japanese public to embrace pluralist methods and, certainly, their adoption of the democratic process was enthusiastic. Japan's repatriation lobbies were no exception. These groups, which emerged initially at village level, evolved into prefectural-wide associations that sent frequent petitions typically calling for 'acceleration of repatriation' to SCAP. Submitted via the Foreign Ministry, they sought SCAP's 'sympathetic consideration' in securing the return of servicemen.[96] Increasingly petitions were publicised, copied and then circulated to American and—as dissatisfaction increased over tardy return from SEAC— non-American representatives on international bodies such as the Allied Council for Japan (ACJ). William Macmahon Ball, an Australian, is probably the best known of the non-American officials.[97] Japan was, however, still under American military occupation and the Japanese public knew their place. There were no anti-British riots over SEAC's repatriation policy or occupation policy on repatriation. (Since many petitions were jointly addressed to the British Commonwealth ACJ representative, the Foreign Office was certainly aware of their existence.)

Public and press comment or official announcements from Japanese Government officials and political representatives concerning JSP, initially those detained in the USSR, were frequent but predictably formulaic. Most often these took the form of unanimous votes in the national Diet to petition MacArthur to bring his influence to bear on the Soviet authorities. Even so, Japan's Foreign Ministry could only hope for SCAP's 'consideration' and 'good offices' in relaying a particular request. Against the background of the problems facing Japanese in the USSR, the situation of those under SEAC control was at first lost in the assumption that all Western-Allied-held Japanese would be returning fairly quickly, and within at most a few months of each other. Once the Japanese public became aware of 'delays' from SEAC, and then retention, public criticism of SEAC rose to a par with that aimed at the USSR. From mid-1946 onwards public petitions drew specific attention to the 105,000 men kept back for labour.[98] Britain was cast as the villain but occupation regulations forbade criticism of Allied or an individual Allied Government's policies in the Japanese press or on radio.[99] Those same rules banned reporting of the repatriation petitions or photographing anti-retention rallies.[100] This situation caused the SCAP administration some discomfort. First, criticism of a Western ally reflected badly on SCAP and directly upon the British Commonwealth Occupation Force in Japan. Second, it highlighted another area where, after the USSR, MacArthur's authority over Japanese citizens was not absolute and where Allied opinion diverged. Third, it severely limited Allied room for manoeuvre in criticising Russian retention of Japanese at the Far Eastern Commission and ACJ. From the end of October 1947 onwards, however, once Britain had put the last of its JSP on boats for Japan, SCAP relaxed this rule selectively, particularly where a report criticised Russian repatriation policy. Indeed, MacArthur's first mention before the Japanese press of the delayed repatriation from Russia occurred only in late October 1947, ie, after the last JSP were en route home, so sparing British blushes.[101]

Retention remained a sensitive topic in Japan's domestic politics. In January 1950, Emperor Hirohito chose JSP still held (or 'missing') in the USSR as the subject of his traditional New Year Imperial poem. The text, which probably suffers in translation, reads, 'With the nation I wait, my heart in pain; For those for whom we wait in vain.' Since SCAP was promoting the Emperor as the non-political 'symbol of the people', it was rather bold of Hirohito to choose such overtly political subject matter. It is most unlikely he did so without SCAP approval.[102]

Both in SCAP and the Japanese Government, expectations had been that all JSP, excluding those in the USSR (and those held as PW facing war crimes charges), would be home by the end of 1946. SCAP had in fact informed the Japanese authorities in mid-1946 that several repatriate reception centres staffed by Japanese had been put on notice for closure in early 1947 as they would be superfluous.[103] As has been related in the previous chapter, the necessity of keeping some of those centres open as a direct consequence of JSP retention by Britain formed part of the United States Chiefs of Staff strong complaint to London in mid-1946.

Official complaints from the Japanese over retention by the British and the Dutch took, as usual, the form of submissions and enquiries to SCAP via the CLO. In October and December 1946 respectively there had been requests for faster repatriation and improved treatment for Japanese under British and Dutch control. These two memoranda were, however, unusually critical in that they accused Britain of a number of specific—and therefore answerable— breaches of international obligations. They asserted that the Japanese under British control are referred to as 'Surrendered Enemy Personnel' (this was the European Theatre designation) and as such are 'not receiving treatment and protection due to prisoners of war as recognised in treaties and International Law'.[104] According to the submissions, all cash and possessions of the men had been confiscated without receipts; no 'notice of capture' had been served; canteens had not been established by the Allies in the Japanese camps; wages for labour had not been paid; Japanese military ranks had not been recognised (so forcing commissioned officers to perform labour duties); no compensation was available for death or disability caused by accidents during labour for Allied commands; and that regular postal services were not in operation.

In April 1947 a further, far more contentious, memorandum was submitted, entitled, 'Status of Members of Japanese Labor Corps in Southern Areas under Control of British and Netherlands Forces'. It is of importance because it confirms that the proposal to classify Japanese troops as JSP originated from within the Japanese Government in August 1945:

> After the surrender the former Japanese Expeditionary forces in the South called themselves 'Surrendered Personnel'. This in no way means, however, that they intended to waive the protection and privileges of prisoners of war guaranteed by International Law and practice... On the contrary, it was motivated by the wish of the Japanese troops to see that they are treated more honourably than ordinary prisoners of war...Yet in fact they are treated as organized labor units and ordered to work for nothing.[105]

This memorandum also draws attention, perhaps for SCAP's benefit, to the contrasting situation of JSP under American control in the Philippines. Here Japanese servicemen were, according to Tokyo, 'treated as prisoners of war and granted due protection and privileges'. Yet again, however, the hesitancy and real impotence of the Japanese Government is revealed in the weak closing, almost beseeching, request that it would be 'appreciated if SCAP be good enough to give due consideration and use its good offices to see that the situation be rectified by the British and Netherlands authorities'.[106] When news reached Tokyo that the British were keeping 105,000 JSP for labour, there was sufficient concern for Prime Minister Yoshida to write directly to MacArthur seeking his intervention and to request far superior treatment for the retained men. (By then, Japan's Government had received ICRC reports of inspections of JSP camps in Java, Singapore and Malaya.) MacArthur replied personally to Yoshida explaining that conditions for these men were 'improving'.[107]

Requests from the Japanese authorities to SEAC for information and public petitions signed by private Japanese citizens did not only refer to repatriation. In Tokyo the CLO described itself as 'beset' by enquiries from people seeking information about relatives in custody. SEAC sent no notification to next of kin about individual JSP or even JPW facing the death sentence. As late as August 1947 the Japanese Government had received no information from the Dutch authorities as to the identities and locations of JPW charged with war crimes and facing trial and possible execution in, for example, Indonesia.[108] The identities of JSP in SEAC remained largely unknown to the Japanese Government and their next of kin. By December 1946 only the names of those in central and southern Malaya and Singapore had been submitted to Tokyo. Repatriation vessels sailed with a nominal roll compiled only on boarding. Passengers would disembark in Japan and only then complete name and address forms.[109] Names of Japanese detained in northern Malaya, Burma, Sumatra and Java were never forwarded to Japan (if they were ever collected at all). Although investigators working for SEATIC sought individuals in connection with alleged war crimes and graded JSP 'black', 'grey' or 'white'—with those declared 'black' becoming officially JPW—little information was relayed to Japan.

Confusion and multiple players in the international repatriation 'game' prevented the first major and public post-war dispute between Japan and Britain. One reason of course, was Japan's diplomatic isolation since all international issues were directed by SCAP. Japan's press was in any case censored and was not permitted to criticise the Allied Powers. Japan's Government was also a supplicant to SCAP over myriad domestic issues.

Yet at times, even with these advantages British officials in Tokyo became uncomfortable as SCAP's policy-makers increasingly sympathised with the Japanese position and pressured Britain to end retention. Fortunately, for the sake of Anglo-American and Anglo-Japanese relations the situation was relatively short-lived. With the departure of the last JSP ship from Singapore in late 1947, Britain was out of the repatriation spotlight, which then shone solely on the USSR.

NOTES TO CHAPTER 5

1.   See n. 98.

2.   Tanaka, Sayu, 'The Kwantung Army's Final Broadcast', in Frank Gibney, ed., *Senso: The Japanese Remember the Pacific War* (New York, 1995)237–8.

3.   Takemae, Eiji, ed., *Catalogue of Japanese Government Responses to GHQ, Vols 1-24.* (Tokyo, 1993-94). [For Japanese title see Bibliography.] (Hereafter *CJGR*), *1*, 0175, 0179 and 0228, 4 Oct. 1945.

4.   Ibid., 0280, 11 Sept. 1945.

5.   Ibid., 0179, 25 Oct. 1945.

6.   Takemae, Eiji, ed., GHQ Supreme Commander Allied Powers: Directives to the Japanese Government, SCAPIN, Vols 1-15 (Tokyo, 1993). (Hereafter, 'SCAPIN'.) [For Japanese title see Bibliography.] SCAPIN 193, 25 Oct. 1945.

7.   SCAPIN 88, 2 Oct. 1945.

8.   SCAPIN 54, 23 Sept. 1945.

9.   SCAPIN 263. ALFSEA to Malaya Comd., 29 Jan. 1945. AIR 40/1852.

10.   See Chapter 2.

11.   Earl Mountbatten in his foreword to *Trial of Gozawa Sadaichi and Nine Others,* ed. Colin Sleeman (London, 1948), xiii–xiv.

12.   HQ AFNEI, 'Disposal of Japanese Surrendered Personnel', 14 Nov. 1945. WO 203/5963.

13.   SEAC Administration Instruction 34, 7 Sept. 1945. WO 203/4432.

14.   HQ AFNEI, 'Disposal of Japanese Surrendered Personnel', 14 Nov. 1945. WO 203/5963.

15.   ALFSEA to AFNEI, 'Comments on FM Terauchi's proposed "Regulations for Repatriation Transport of JEFSR",' 16 Dec. 1945. WO 203/5963.

16.   *CJGR, 1,* 0507, 14 Dec. 1945.

17.   *Ibid,* 0506, 14 Dec. 1945.

18.   'Communications for the control of Japanese.' PSO Conference Minute, 23 Mar. 1946. WO 203/2727.

19.   Bayly and Harper, *Forgotten Wars,* 55.

20.   'General Report on Rempang and Galang.' Chief Engineer's Office, ALFSEA, 18 Dec. 1945. WO 203/5963.

21.   'Orders to General S. Itagaki, Commander, 7th Area Army given personally by General Officer Commanding in Chief, Malaya Command.' WO 203/5963, 24 Nov. 45.

22.   *Malaya TB infections. HQ Malaya Command to ALFSEA, 22 Dec. 45. WO 203/5963*

23.   *Ibid.*

24.   Takemae, *Allied Occupation of Japan,* 113–4.

25.   *CJGR, 1,* 0504, 14 Dec. 1945.

26.   SACSEA to ALFSEA, 22 Dec. 1945. WO 203/5963.

27.   *CJGR, 1,* 0187, 5 Jan. 1946.

28.   'Communications for the control of Japanese.' PSO Conference Minute, 23 Mar. 1946. WO 203/2727.

29.   See John W. Dower, *War Without Mercy: Race and Power in the Pacific War* (New York, 1966), 52–3; Allen, *Burma,* 540–3, 588 n. 2; George MacDonald Fraser, *Quartered Safe Out Here: A Recollection of the War in Burma* (London,1992).

30.   Louis Allen, *Sittang: The Last Battle, The End of the Japanese in Burma, July-August 1945* (London, 1973), 230–31. Don Jones, *Oba, the Last Samurai* (New York, 1986), 231.

31. Anderson, *Java,* xi, Shigeru Sato, *War, Rice and Peasants,* 133; Marr, *Vietnam 1945,* 96–107, 207–10, Nguyen The Anh, 'Japanese Food Policies and the 1945 Great Famine in Indochina', in Paul Kratoska, ed, *Food Supplies and the Japanese Occupation in Southeast Asia* (New York, 1998), 208–26. See also Paul Kratoska, ed, *Asian Labor in the Wartime Japanese Empire: Unknown Histories* (New York, 2005).

32. See Shibata, 'Surabaya after the Surrender', in Reid and Oki, eds, *Japanese Experience of Indonesia,* 369.

33. Meirion and Susie Harries, *Soldiers of the Sun: the Rise and Fall of the Japanese Imperial Army 1868-1945* (London, 1991), 389. See also Allen, *Burma,* 577.

34. Harries, *Soldiers of the Sun,* 389. No source cited. The depth of their research on other matters is doubtful. When considering 'allegations' that the British used Japanese troops in Indonesia, they state, '[T]here is little evidence, or indeed likelihood, that this was true' (390).

35. Personal interview with Philip Kaiserman, 3 Oct. 2005.

36. Personal interview with Aoki Masafumi, 5 Nov. 2005.

37. Diary entry, 30 Nov. 1945, in Richard Aldrich, ed., *The Faraway War* (London, 2005), 637.

38. Fraser, *Quartered Safe Out Here,* 192.

39. Ronnie Noble, *Shoot First!* (London, 1957), 92–3.

40. Aida Yuji, *Prisoner of the British: A Japanese Soldier's Experiences in Burma* (London, 1966), 49–55. Ooka Shohei, *Taken Captive: A Japanese POW's Story.* New York, 1996. (Ooka's best-known works in English include *Taken Captive* and *Fires on the Plain.*)

41. Frank B. Gibney, Foreward to *Taken Captive* by Ooka Shohei, ix-x

42. Bayly and Harper, *Forgotten Wars,* 53.

43. JEFSR to SEAC, 5 Dec. 1945, WO 203/4432,

44. JEFSR to SEAC, 12 Jan. 1945, WO 203/4432.

45. 'Civil Internment Camps in the British Zone of Germany', 12 July 1946. CAB 134/596.

46. 'Japanese Surrendered Enemy Personnel in Java – (Batavia Area).' Comité international de la Croix-Rouge, 31 May 1946. FO 371/53796.

47. WO 208/4740.

48. Gen. Numata to Adm. Mountbatten. 'Report of inspection of the conditions of Japanese personnel in Southern Regions', 27 Feb. 1946, (Hereafter 'Numata Report'), 10. WO 203/2727.

49. *CJGR, 3,* 0114, 0860, 12 Feb. 1946; *CJGR , 4,* 0114, 27 Mar. 1946.

50. The author is not suggesting that JSP suffered severe shortages comparable to those experienced by APWI and civilian labourers under Japanese control.

51. WO to FO Legal Dept, 26 Jan. 1946. FO 371/54306.

52. SACSEA to JSM Washington, 2 Dec. 1945. WO 203/4432.

53   Mountbatten, Earl. *Personal Diary,* 265.

54. 2 Feb. 1946, AIR 40/1852. See Richard Fuller, *Shokan – Hirohito's Samurai: Leaders of the Japanese Armed Forces, 1926-1945* (London, 1992), 119.

55. SACSEA to ACSEA, 12 June 1946, WO 203/5968.

56. *Reports of General MacArthur, Vol. 1 Supplement,* 126.

57. Numata Report, WO 203/2727.

58. Personal correspondence with Lt Stuart Guild (ex-114 FR, RA) Prison Quartermaster, Maison Centrale, Saigon, Sept. 1945 to Mar. 1946. Feb. 2008.

59. 'Memorandum on JSP, Ref. letter from Marshal Terauchi.' 26 Jan. 1946. WO 203/4432.

60.   HQ SACSEA. 'Minutes of meeting held by the Chief of Staff with Lt Gen. Numata', 25 Feb '46. AIR 40/1852.

61.   Ibid.

62.   Ibid.

63.   Control Commission No. 1, Saigon to SACSEA, 16 Jan 1946. WO 203/4432.

64.   SACSEA to Control Commission No. 1, Saigon, 19 Jan. 1946. WO 203/4432

65.   'Report No. 1 British Military Mission, Hanoi. 25 Nov.-23 Dec. 1945'. WO 203 /4432.

66.   Numata Report, 11. 1946 (WO 203/2727).

67.   A recent estimate is 1,057, including civilians. See Goto, *Tensions of Empire*, 194, 196.

68.   Numata Report, 3, 17.

69.   Roadnight, 'Sleeping with the Enemy', 261.

70.   Numata Report, 10.

71.   See Chapter 3, n. 117.

72.   *CJGR, 1*, 0187, 5 Jan. 1946.

73.   See Teiji Fukami and Wilbur Cross, *The Lost Men of Anatahan* (New York, 1969).

74.   Tanaka Hiromi, 'Japanese forces in post-surrender Rabaul', in Steven Bullard and Tamura Keiko, eds, *From a Hostile Shore: Australia and Japan at War in New Guinea* (Canberra, 2004), 138–52.

75.   AWM (photographs) www.awm.gov.au/collection/NWA1054; and NWA1057.

76.   Tanaka, 'Japanese forces in post-surrender Rabaul', 146.

77.   Tanida Isamu, 'The Army's been a good life', in Haruko and Theodore Cook, *Japan at War: An Oral History* (London, 2002), 416–9.

78.   Tanaka, 'Japanese forces in post-surrender Rabaul', 151.

79.   While detained in Java, Imamura wrote a memoir entitled 'A Tapir in Prison'. NIOD: IC 002457. For a photograph of JSP-made tools, *see* https://www.awm. gov.au/collection/099865/.

80.   Ienaga, *Japan's Last War*, 230.

81.   Dower, *Embracing Defeat*, 59.

82.   SCAPIN 17 and 25.

83.   *Reports of General MacArthur, Vol. 1, Supplement*, 122–3.

84.   Ibid., 149–93.

85.   'Japanese capacity for repatriation'. *CJGR, 1*, 0262, 6 Oct. 1945.

86.   SCAPIN-A G 370.05, 15 Oct. 1945.

87.   'Reception Centers for Processing Repatriates', *CJGR, 1*, 0374, 0375, 6 Nov. 1945.

88.   William F. Nimmo, *Behind a Curtain of Silence: Japanese in Soviet Custody, 1945-1956* (New York, 1988, 115. Memoirs of JSP in Soviet custody include Yamamoto Tomomi, *Four Years in Hell* (Tokyo, 1952) and Iwao Peter Sano, *One Thousand Days in Siberia: The Odyssey of a Japanese-American POW*, (Lincoln, NE., 1997). Sano, an American *nisei* (second-generation Japanese-American), who had been sent to complete high school in Japan in early 1941 was conscripted into Japan's Kwantung Army. He was taken prisoner in Manchuria in August 1945 and eventually repatriated to Japan in 1949.

89.   *CJGR, 4*, 0229. 27 May 1946; *5*, 0137, 0138, 3 July 1946.

90.   *Reports of General MacArthur, Vol.1 Supplement*, 152–7.

91.   Ibid., 176.

92.   T. R. Sareen, *Japanese Prisoners of War in India, 1942-46: Bushido and Barbed Wire* (Folkstone, 2006), 238–9.

93.   Personal correspondence with Oba Sadao, November 2008.

94.   Sareen, *Japanese Prisoners of War in India*, 240.

95.   'Jap admirals will stand trial', *The Argus* (Melbourne), 25 Feb. 1950. Other senior officers sent to Manus included RAdm Tanaka, commander of 21 Special Naval Base (at Surabaya) and RAdm Shinzaburo, commander of 25 Special Naval Base (on New Guinea).

96.   Examples include 'Kokura Women's Association to SCAP. Petition for Early Repatriation of Japanese Nationals Abroad.' *CJGR, 12,* 0666, 16 Dec. 1946.

97.   Chiba Prefecture Repatriation Acceleration League. 'Petition addressed to Ambassador Atcheson…and Hon. W. Macmahon Ball, Member for the British Commonwealth…for [the] Early Repatriation of Japanese Nationals Abroad'. *CJGR, 12,* 0743, 27 Aug. 1947.

98.   'Family Association of Members of Japanese Labor Corps in Burma Area, Petition for Acceleration of Repatriation of Members of Japanese Labor Corps in Southern Area under Control of British Forces.' *CJGR, 9,* 0801, 2 Apr. 1947.

99.   SCAPIN 33 (Press Code) and 44 (Radio Code).

100.   Takemae, *Allied Occupation of Japan,* 101; and Dower, *Embracing Defeat,* 410.

101.   Ibid., 103.

102.   Richard L-G. Deverall, *Stalin's Prize: Japanese Prisoners-of-War* (Baltimore, 1951), 13.

103.   *CJGR, 8.* 0810. 5 Mar. 1947.

104.   *CJGR, 7,* 5711, 29 Oct. 1946; *CJGR, 8,* 6627, 13 Dec. 1946.

105.   *CJGR, 8,* 0779, 26 Apr. 1947.

106.   *CJGR, 10,* 0779, 26 Apr. 1947.

107.   *CJGR, 7,* 0098, 13 Dec. 1946.

108.   *CJGR, 12,* 0536, 20 Aug. 1947; See, for example, Yamaguchi Hideo, 'The reason I don't sing the national anthem', in *Senso,* ed, Gibney, 273–4.

109.   Iwao Peter Sano, *One Thousand Days in Siberia: The Odyssey of a Japanese-American POW,* (Lincoln, NE., 1997), 198; and Sareen, *Japanese Prisoners of War in India,* 240.

6

'STRONG ETHICAL OBJECTIONS'
DIPLOMACY OVER JSP RETENTION TO MID-1947

*We feel that, although strong ethical objections can
be advanced against retaining JSP in SEAC as slave
labour, these do not arise if the JSP are repatriated as
soon as transportation facilities are available.*
—Joint Planning Staff report to Chiefs of Staff, 27 August 1946[1]

During the spring and summer of 1946 Britain's stance over retained
Japanese Surrendered Personnel (JSP) in South-East Asia Command
(SEAC) underwent important changes in response to various international
pressures. As American opposition to retention of any JSP became clear,
enquiries to SEAC about repatriation from both Washington and General
MacArthur in Tokyo became specific and persistent. Britain, seeking
a justification for Japanese labour, vacillated over a response. As a result,
the retention issue became entangled in the wider questions of war
reparations to be paid by Japan, JSP repatriation from the Soviet Union,
and East–West friction over post-war Japanese governance. Consequently,
to growing British discomfort, the JSP question was raised increasingly
outside the confines of SEAC. Britain was thus forced to tread a careful
path balancing specific, short-term interests in Southeast Asia with the vital
need to maintain good relations with the United States and avoid criticism
in international forums.

For several months after the Japanese surrender SEAC was largely
independent in its handling of Japanese under its control. In approving
construction and other projects utilising JSP labour, the Command

anticipated no external influences that might influence its policies. This situation changed quite rapidly, however, after three separate but related developments increased British sensitivity over its retention of JSP. The first was the March 1946 announcement by the United States that it would reclassify Surrendered Enemy Personnel (SEP) in its custody in Europe as Prisoners of War (PW). This move followed intensive lobbying by the International Committee of the Red Cross (ICRC).[2] At this time some 260,000 German PW and Italian SEP were employed as agricultural labourers in Britain. Pointedly Britain undertook no reclassification nor made any official comment on the American decision. Quite clearly, however, the American about-turn meant that any Allied consensus over post-war policies on Axis and Japanese servicemen had shattered. Henceforth, criticism of SEP and JSP designations and their living and working conditions in British-controlled areas in Europe and Asia respectively was directed solely at London. Without the comfortable shield of a unified Allied front, Britain's diplomats had to deal independently with enquiries from German civilian authorities, the ICRC, the Vatican, the Japanese Government through GHQ SCAP in Tokyo, and an increasingly impatient General MacArthur. Within SEAC, however, opposition to any repatriation during 1946 remained determined, particularly from the British Army.[3] Projects using Japanese labour in Singapore and Malaya had even been increased, and their provisional construction schedules expanded, to run well into 1947.

The second key development affecting British policy was the belated admission by Mountbatten to MacArthur in April 1946 that 105,000 JSP were being retained 'indefinitely for labour' and not simply because of shortage of British shipping. In the same communication Mountbatten stated, somewhat fatefully, that he expected 'their ultimate repatriation to be a British responsibility'.[4] This official notification from SEAC about retention marked the start of a particularly awkward period in SEAC-SCAP relations.

While the decision to retain JSP might indeed have affected or delayed American planning and generated a certain amount of friction in Anglo-American relations, the Foreign Office had a third and far more serious concern. This was the inevitable charge that in holding on to these men, Britain was directly repudiating undertakings made in the Potsdam Declaration. Article 9 of the Declaration specifically stated that 'Japanese military forces, after being completely disarmed, shall be permitted to return to their homes...'.[5] The precise, unambiguous text of the Declaration provided for no delay. Perhaps most importantly and inconveniently for

London, the Declaration was neither qualified by any reference to 'prisoners of war' nor dependent upon the prerequisite of 'extant treaties between legally constituted governments' prior to the implementation of its terms. Britain had employed both of these administrative ruses, for example, to retain Italian PW in Britain for farm labour (by November 1945 63,000 Italians were working on farms) and to justify delayed repatriation of both PW and SEP.[6] Potsdam, however, referred simply to 'Japanese military forces', ie, it covered both PW and the recent JSP designation equally. Arguably this wording immediately negated any Allied post-surrender distinctions between the two 'categories'. Interestingly, neither the ICRC nor the Japanese Government pursued this argument with London or the United Nations.

British authorities made no official announcement to the Japanese Government that its citizens were being retained. Had the charge of repudiating Potsdam been made publicly by, for example, the ICRC or the Japanese Government, it would have certainly been difficult to rebut and somewhat embarrassing for Mountbatten who had requested retention, as well as for the COS and the Cabinet who had given formal approval. It would hardly, however, have been a contentious issue with the British public. Thus Britain's Government was probably prepared to disregard accusations from 'minor players' such as the ICRC and the still-cowed Japanese authorities. On the other hand, any charge from Washington, or especially from the publicity-savvy MacArthur, that Britain had repudiated one of the most significant international declarations of the century would have been little short of catastrophic for Britain's post-war diplomatic prestige. Since such potentially damaging criticism was predictable, or at least a possibility, it would have been logical for the War Office and Foreign Office to have prepared a detailed and extensive defence of Britain's position. There was none. The best argument Prime Minister Attlee could offer to the British Ambassador (Lord Inverchapel) in Washington in support of Britain's case to the State Department was little more than the plaintive excuse that: 'While HMG are fully aware of the commitments under Article 9 of this Potsdam Declaration...[it] was drawn up at a time when the true situation in the areas occupied by Japanese Forces had not yet come to light'.[7] This plea reveals the underlying lack of confidence over the issue in London just as developments were making it clear that Britain could no longer treat the JSP question in isolation.

IRRITATIONS WITHIN THE ANGLO-AMERICAN RELATIONSHIP

A number of other diplomatic issues impinged indirectly on the issue of retained Japanese in 1946 and 1947. Throughout the early post-war period Anglo-American relations were becoming further strained. In fact, the last 18 months of the war against Japan had seen increasing friction over potential post-war economic opportunities—and competition—in the Far East and Pacific. For example, American trading companies' expectations of free access to Chinese ports, and the future use of certain Commonwealth territories by American civil airlines had led to considerable jockeying for position long before the Japanese surrender. There were already British and Australian disputes with the United States over Pacific territories, such as Guadalcanal and Manus (Admiralty Islands), still 'occupied' by American forces.[8]

Retention of JSP was yet one more issue to generate ill-feeling between Washington and London. Britain's economic and strategic weakness meant that its main and immediate foreign-policy objectives—including securing massive financial aid, obtaining a United States commitment to the defence of western Europe, the maintenance of trading privileges with China, and aid for nationalist forces against the Communists in China (to protect Hong Kong)—required immense American goodwill and a considerable outlay of American cash. American primacy in Asia was obvious and resented in London. Equally obvious was Britain's total dependency on American largesse. Given this fact, it is perplexing that Britain continued to engage in or even escalate potentially damaging disputes with the Truman Administration, particularly at a time when Congress was quick to object to American subsidy of British interests.[9]

Britain's desperate financial condition meant that a reduction in its influence in certain countries or regions was unavoidable. Indian independence, despite objections from Winston Churchill and the Conservative Party, had all but been agreed. Preparations for colonial withdrawal elsewhere, such as in Burma and other territories and mandates were also in train. It was not quite, however, a wholesale retreat from the international stage. Britain assumed Great Power-status by virtue of being a founder Allied Power and fully exploited the advantages that status provided at the United Nations and the Quadripartite talks on the future of Germany.

Yet at least one early post-war attempt to project Great Power status in Asia failed publicly, as British (and also French, Australian and Russian) expectations of some involvement in the governance of Occupied Japan were comprehensively denied. Prior to the Japanese surrender Britain and other Commonwealth governments had considered participation in any occupation as essential if they were to exert any influence on Japan's post-war economic and military development. Indeed Britain and Australia had hoped to see their military contributions in the Asia-Pacific Theatre rewarded with direct economic benefits. Oddly, in working to that end, and 'to MacArthur's consternation', both would work 'tirelessly' to have Japan placed in the sterling block.[10]

British expectations of an equal voice in deciding post-surrender policy for Japan, however, were promptly dashed. No Four-Power Commission-style administration was created. MacArthur, the United States War Department and the Navy Department were steadfastly opposed to any arrangement that gave the USSR any influence or significant presence in Japan, as had happened with power-sharing in Germany and eastern Europe.[11] Truman, too, was determined not to have divided control or separate zones.[12] By the time the small British Commonwealth Occupation Force (BCOF)—composed largely of Australians and Indians—arrived in southern Japan in February 1946, American control over all military and political aspects of the occupation was complete. At best the BCOF, which at its peak numbered 36,000, played a supporting role far from Tokyo with no military government duties or any other official involvement with the Japanese public.[13] Britain and the other Allies remained unhappy over the American monopoly on key policy decisions ranging from the future of the Emperor system to universal suffrage and post-war industrial capacity to reparations. British Foreign Secretary Ernest Bevin voiced his frustration over this exclusion in late 1946, declaring:

> [I]t is quite proper, having regard to the contribution made by...the British Commonwealth, that we should be closely associated with this present task, both by the employment of our Forces in the occupation and control of Japan, and by our counsel in international deliberations.[14]

Bevin's objection fell on stony ground. Britain, the Commonwealth and the other Allies were shut out.[15]

Elsewhere, Britain trod a less than diplomatic path. When, also in 1946, the reluctant decision was taken to discontinue aid to both Greece and Turkey, Prime Minister Attlee expected the United States would step in and replace Britain as the main Balkans benefactor. Yet this was not an obvious foreign policy avenue for the United States. Congress, facing severe economic tightening at home, was wary of new, unfamiliar and potentially open-ended, not to say risky, commitments abroad. Equally Britain needed a sympathetic, friendly and trusting Administration in Washington. British interests in the Middle East, however, risked not just continuing Western influence in the Balkans but major damage to London's relationship with Washington. Throughout 1946 Arab and Jewish terror attacks in British-controlled Palestine and the Royal Navy blockade against ships carrying illegal Jewish immigrants were causing Britain great diplomatic difficulty. Immigrants were detained in camps on Cyprus or forcibly repatriated. American-Jewish leaders in particular were fiercely critical of British policy. (In 1947 Britain passed the problem to the UN.) As Congressional elections loomed in the United States, Truman announced his support for a proposal calling for the immediate admittance of 100,000 Jews in to Palestine. This announcement was hardly supportive of British authority. A resentful Bevin went public again, bemoaning the fact that his problem had become a topic for 'local elections'. When pressed, he blamed the influence of the Jewish lobby and Truman's desire for votes, describing it as a way for the President to divert Jewish immigration from the United States to Palestine. Truman was furious.[16] Later, he wrote of the 'almost hostile' attack that 'cast a dark shadow over our relations with Britain'.[17]

Britain could not afford an ill-disposed trinity of President, State Department and Congress. If nothing else, Britain's JSP policy rocked the boat in relations with Washington. Within the Foreign Office there was also awareness that the policy risked long-term negative consequences, not just with Truman but with a potentially unfriendly future president. General Douglas MacArthur was a hugely popular figure with the American public and in 1946 was widely viewed as a serious presidential candidate. There were real fears in London that a MacArthur Administration might be unsympathetic to British interests, especially if Whitehall's machinations over JSP retention caused him any personal embarrassment in not fulfilling his primary mission to Japan.[18]

JSP HUMILIATION AND THE RESTORATION
OF WHITE COLONIAL PRESTIGE

Once repatriation of Japanese from SEAC commenced neither the Command nor indeed SCAP in Tokyo could have expected to keep news of JSP retention from reaching the Japanese Government or public. While over 600,000 JSP were waiting for berths on one of the few British ships assigned to repatriation transport, the fact that one-sixth of them were to be retained was not readily apparent. Once the American-organised shipping programme got underway however, the repatriation rate surged. Among Japanese destined to remain behind, however, frustration grew. This was

30. Lt Gen Morimoto (far left) inspecting the Maison Centrale, Saigon. Mar. 1946. (© SG)

to be expected since those retained as dock workers, for example, watched others depart daily and even readied the vessels carrying them home.

British officials were aware of increasing dissatisfaction in the form of a visible fall in morale and quality in the work performed. Regional commands in SEAC first reported the signs—described as a 'lower standard of saluting and incorrect behaviour towards local population'—to the main Japanese HQ in April 1946. Other allegations were that 'Japanese staff officers and others driving on essential duty often stop en route for private business'.[19] It was not the first instance. General Numata's report to Mountbatten following his January-February 1946 inspection tour raised a wide range of labour, rations, health and other concerns, including worries over growing indiscipline.[20]

Whether Numata's concerns had any impact on British policy prior to July 1946 other than suggestions for closer monitoring and identifying troublesome units is not documented. Certain British senior officers, for example the commander in Burma, reported their own concerns over JSP conditions (see below). Burma and Thailand were in any case excluded from Numata's itinerary at SEAC's insistence, and he did not visit Burma until July 1946.[21] Copies of Numata's reports were not, however, forwarded to Japan, so would not have reached either SCAP representatives or the Japanese Government officially.[22]

Once beyond the Command's borders SEAC could not expect to exercise any control over individual Japanese. Although the US Navy supervised the repatriation programme, the ships employed were crewed entirely by former Imperial Japanese Navy and merchant marine personnel. Evacuations from SEAC territory progressed from east to west, with the intention being that the larger concentrations of JSP closer to Japan were the ones dealt with first. This order, insisted upon by SCAP, allowed for more frequent return journeys and so more efficient use of oil and coal prior to the 1 July 1946 cut-off date of the shipping charter arranged in January 1946 (see Chapter 5). SEAC, on the other hand, had pressed for the priority evacuation of chronically sick JSP in remote areas of Burma. These men, who could not work, were seen as a growing financial burden, and not just requiring disproportionate and onerous supervisory duties for British troops. Demands for the return of hospitals and Japanese-occupied buildings from Burmese authorities meant that new facilities would have to be built unless the Japanese were evacuated. There were also concerns that once 'meagre' Japanese medical stores were exhausted they would have to be replenished from British stocks at Britain's cost. With only one Japanese hospital ship for 12,400 chronic sick in Burma, repatriation was estimated at 8 years.[23] Medical evacuation assistance, however, had been refused by SCAP on the grounds that the lift-to-numbers ratio was uneconomic.[24] Thus the first JSP units to be repatriated from SEAC were those in the mass concentration areas, generally on the more remote Indonesian islands, New Guinea and New Britain. (JSP in Vietnam and JPW in Australia and New Zealand returned in separate shipping lifts arranged directly between SCAP and the respective governments.)

Generally JSP holding areas in these outer islands were locations some distance from any settlement. Options for or even the need to assign labour to these men, other than for self-sufficiency farming, had been limited. Evacuations were total, so with the departure of the Japanese, most of these camps were abandoned. Early summer 1946, however, saw the first arrivals in Japan of men from camps in central Malaya. Many of them passed through Singapore where JSP fatigue parties were frequently seen. Indeed labouring Japanese were sometimes kept quite deliberately visible in public parks and squares, near markets or major buildings such as the Raffles Hotel as part of propaganda campaigns aimed at restoring white colonial prestige. Displays of JSP performing unsavoury or heavy tasks had the additional benefit (mentioned in Chapter 5) of reinforcing the message of Japan's defeat among local populations and among the JSP themselves.

Inevitably, JSP assigned to port labour units also found themselves helping with the embarkation of their comrades on vessels heading either for the camps on Rempang and Galang islands or, from mid-1946 onwards, direct to Japan on American ships. Therefore, at least among JSP repatriated from larger metropolitan areas, it became known that a fair number of their comrades were being retained. When these repatriates returned home, their first-hand accounts of camp conditions and the information that others were being kept back spread to the retained men's families (perhaps via hand-carried letters) as well as the Japanese authorities. Before long, therefore, retention became widely known and, in turn, a domestic political issue in Japan (see Chapter 5).[25]

EARLY JAPANESE OBJECTIONS OVER CONDITIONS

Despite the early concerns raised by General Numata and signs of rising insubordination there was little change in JSPs' circumstances. Maintenance of JSP discipline was taken very seriously by SEAC. Periodically it issued stern reminders to Japanese officers that discipline was their specific responsibility. SEAC, however, did not authorise any direct attempt to improve morale until mid-1946. In fact, such 'authorisation' was not strictly within SEAC's power or capability. The Command's resources were extremely limited, as details of the very basic field rations issued to JSP and Indian troops in Burma and Malaya confirm.[26] Even tiny, incremental increases of supplies to JSP resulted in additional expenditure and so required formal approval from the War Office in London via a tortuous bureaucratic chain. This did not mean that individuals in Allied Land Forces South East Asia (ALFSEA), had not sought to improve conditions.

By May 1946, General Harold Briggs, Head of Burma Command, was sufficiently concerned about prospects for unrest and unfavourable comment about British responsibilities to question delays in approvals for certain JSP matters.[27] Briggs considered that the Japanese in Burma were already far from being an asset and fast becoming a burden. Deficiencies in precautionary hygiene and lack of 'necessaries', which would be obvious to the ICRC delegate touring JPW and JSP camps, also concerned him. He informed General Stopford, then head of ALFSEA:

> [I]ndications unrest already apparent and [I] am beginning to doubt the advisability [to] retain any for labour despite acute labour shortage unless action can be taken to improve their general living conditions. Delegate [ICRC] inspecting camps both POW and JSP has already expressed surprise at lack of facilities and is likely to submit report which may not read well.[28]

Worried about the ramifications of any criticism of British control or neglect of JSP, Briggs called for 'urgent steps' to improve conditions. He identified inadequacies and failings, including shortage of amenities, such as soap, toothpowder, matches and cigarettes, absence of pay and no mail. Briggs also pointed out that 'not one single letter has been received or sent by any JSP or POW since [the] end of hostilities'. He considered it vital that an immediate arrangement was made for fast, two-way mail to replace the very occasional shipping between Burma and Singapore.'[29]

For Briggs, pay, regular or working, was one solution. (His signal unwittingly admits a British breach of the PW Convention since he confirms that no pay had been issued to JPW.) Lack of cash and its effect on Japanese morale disturbed him. JSP were 'not able to purchase even the meanest amenities [including] cigarettes...'. His mounting frustration against the bureaucracy is apparent for he had reported in a similar manner in late March 1946 but had received no response. Briggs had described JSP 'working an 8-hour day, possessing only one suit of clothing, half of them in rags'. Authorisation for clothing issues had 'excluded waterproofs for a monsoon country'. His medical staff had also reported that the soap ration was 'completely inadequate to combat skin diseases'.[30]

Stopford replied to Briggs, repeating that while payment to PW was in the pipeline, JSP were not to receive pay. Additional soap could be issued to retained JSP but not to others awaiting ships. As for Briggs's other points, these were dependent on War Office approval and this was being sought 'urgently'. SEAC's cupboard, however, was bare. Stopford refused to allow disbursement from British stores for the simple reason that even the Emergency Field Issue stocks were inadequate.[31]

In mid-July 1946 SEAC sought War Office approval to increase JSP clothing allowances and amenities, particularly cigarettes.[32] Demand for tobacco in Southeast Asia was enormous. As in the Allied forces, in the Japanese military smoking was near universal and had been heavily subsidised. Cigarette supplies for British troops had been deemed similarly vital during the war and given priority over domestic supply.[33] Government intervention had resulted in the bulk of domestic cigarette production being diverted to the services with consequently frequent shortages for civilians. (British officers in SEAC received a drum of 50 cigarettes monthly.)[34] Supply and distribution of cigarettes in Southeast Asia (on both sides) had always been sporadic and had barely kept up with demand. Tobacco yields from plantations had also fallen drastically as a result of economic policy enforced during the Japanese occupation. Millions of Southeast Asian smokers were left craving, including Japanese forces, who had received no issue since the surrender. Widespread shortages of cigarettes resulted in their value rising to a premium where they served as barter currency even within British forces. (The photograph of JSP clearing a roadblock in Vietnam exists because the photographer traded cigarettes for film from RAF technicians.)[35] With no legal tender or desirable goods with which to trade for cigarettes, JSP often went without.

SEAC's struggle to obtain and distribute non-perishable, lightweight, and uniformly packaged items such as cigarettes serves as a good indicator of its serious supply and transportation difficulties. While cigarettes had been promised to JSP in camps in Malaya the Japanese complained that they had not materialised, neither had toilet paper, toothbrushes nor toothpaste.[36] Little of anything had been issued since the surrender. In August 1946 the ICRC reported to the Foreign Office that JSP in Malaya had received only two cigarettes each since April. SEAC's official ration scale, the ICRC noted, was '1 cigarette every fortnight'. (In Burma no cigarettes were issued before November 1946.)[37] A subsequent announcement that the supply of cigarettes would be 'rationed' from January 1947 to five per man per week and one box of 30 matches per 20 men bemused the Japanese HQ in Malaya since none had been issued at all.[38] In September 1946, however, the discovery of 20 million 'low-grade' cigarettes among redundant Indian Army stocks resulted in a proposal to increase the ration to twenty cigarettes per man and one box of 30 matches per two men per week.[39]

Revealingly, SEAC's July request to increase amenities was approved only in late September 1946 as one of a flurry of general proposals related to the improvement of JSP living and working conditions. These included an outline working pay scheme and the supply of surplus used army sports equipment from India (though the War Office raised concerns over whether payment for an 'indefinite quantity of equipment' could ever be recovered from the Japanese).[40] The timing of this approval and changes to several other JSP allowances are unlikely to have been coincidental. Of primary significance, however, is a War Office signal to ALFSEA dated 20 September explaining that confirmation was being sought from the Japanese Government of its agreement over working pay credits. This scheme would see 'working pay at the rate of one penny halfpenny an hour for skilled and three farthings an hour for unskilled work...' credited to men on their return to Japan.[41] This proposal is almost certainly a reworking of the one suggested in late 1945 by General Gracey for JSP in Vietnam. General MacArthur had not responded to that particular proposal and so the War Office had let it drop.[42] Evidence would suggest that this hurried resurrection of War Office interest in a working credit proposal is almost certainly attributable to MacArthur's enquiries over British intentions and, equally, growing British unease over State Department opposition, in consort with MacArthur, to the fundamental idea of retention of JSP.

THE INFLUENCE OF REPARATIONS CLAIMS ON BRITISH POLICY

Remuneration for working JSP was not, however, a SEAC-only issue. Broader international interests complicated the question and effectively placed it outside the Command's control. Although SEAC was acting as an 'employer'—albeit one unwilling or unable to pay market rates for labour—Japan remained nominally responsible for JSP maintenance, which also included the crediting of normal monthly armed service pay rates in Japan. JSP in SEAC received no exchangeable credit or legal tender. In Japan, SCAP had in any case forbidden the export of yen. Britain, too, had already established extremely strict foreign exchange requirements in Southeast Asia as part of attempts to maintain the gold reserves backing sterling at the highest possible levels. In feeding and repatriating the Japanese, Britain was facing daily costs through SEAC's expenditure.

For the British Treasury the issue of remuneration also embraced the question of how expenditure incurred by Britain was categorised, particularly distinctions between specific costs for the occupation of Japan and more general claims. Costs for JSP maintenance were a case in point and of major importance to the Treasury as it attempted to establish reparations claims against Japan's vastly depleted assets. In April 1946 Britain's Economic Planning Staff (EPS) had examined the reparation question and advised that the UK should aim to obtain '10 percent of all deliveries [ie, reparation exports] from Japan'.[43] There were serious doubts within the EPS over prospects for Japan's economic recovery, at least in the short- to mid-term.

Deficits were envisaged for many years to come, and the EPS estimated it would be '1952–55 before Japan generated any considerable surplus'. It also acknowledged the fact that Japan could not be expected to go on making payments indefinitely and that there would inevitably be a 'cut-off date'.[44] Since the Allies had already agreed that any Japanese surplus would first be allocated to pay for occupation costs and not reparations, the available 'pot' was already shrinking rapidly. In addition, Britain's claim for ongoing expenses was not the strongest. Both the USSR and China had far larger numbers of JSP to maintain than Britain. Consequently any application for reimbursement of maintenance costs from the reparations account would have triggered equally strong claims from Moscow and Kuching. Britain's priority, given its own financial position was, to seek hard cash in the very short term. Thus the EPS concluded that Britain faced limited prospects of actually receiving full reparations payments. It estimated British costs in maintaining JSP at 'not less than £30 million and total Allied costs… about £100 million', or a larger amount than the 10 percent of reparations deliveries allotted to the UK. EPS calculations demonstrated it was to Britain's advantage that maintenance expenditure was merged with occupation costs, so becoming 'a first charge' on the Japanese Government and so having priority over reparation deliveries.[45]

Such a proposal, the EPS stressed, would certainly need American approval and it recommended 'sounding out' the State Department.[46] This guarded reference to the quite different viewpoints of Washington/ SCAP and London, and indeed other Allied governments, over ideas for the reconstruction and economic direction of Japan was something of an understatement. Whereas Article 11 of the Potsdam Declaration had sanctioned 'just reparations in kind' for countries with claims against Japan, General MacArthur increasingly pushed for Japan-first policies aimed at revitalising the Japanese economy as speedily as possible.[47] Here he was at odds with his own Government's representative, Edwin W. Pauley, the Reparations Commissioner for Japan. In April 1946 Pauley recommended to Truman that Japan be stripped of almost all its steel production capacity, along with power-generation capacity and machine tool plants.[48] MacArthur, however, viewed reparations as 'war booty', and was unreceptive to the Pauley Mission's conclusions.[49] Only a few months later, in March 1947, MacArthur would take Allied governments by surprise and declare conditions right for the negotiation of a peace treaty with Japan. His views on reparations, based perhaps on a combination of a desire to reduce the immense American bill for relief aid to Japan and concerns over emerging threats to American security in the Pacific, eventually carried the day in Washington.[50] Occupation policy later underwent its famous 'Reverse Course' in order to establish Japan as a bulwark against Communist expansion in Asia, and MacArthur halted Japan's reparations payments unilaterally in May 1949.[51] The EPS's warning over a cut-off date had indeed been justified but London must have been surprised by how quickly it arrived. Britain, however, remained wary of any measures that might have allowed Japan to return to anything close to its pre-war economic strength. It continued to see Japan as a great threat to its traditional Empire export markets in Asia.[52] MacArthur's determination to defend nascent Japanese economic interests meant that prospects for American agreement over merging JSP maintenance and occupation costs were limited. A prompt but ominously neutral reply from the State Department described Britain's working pay proposal merely as 'deserving of careful consideration'. Washington preferred 'not to take a position until the whole question of compensation for such costs' came up for examination in the Far Eastern Commission (FEC).[53] Negotiations stalled.

ALLEGATIONS AGAINST BRITAIN

In early September 1946 the issue of JSP retention suddenly returned to centre stage when General MacArthur presented a list of alarming allegations, almost certainly compiled by the Japanese Government, referring to the circumstances of JSP in SEAC.[54] Coming so soon after the British rebuff of requests to complete repatriation before the end of 1946, the impression is that MacArthur was deliberately making retention as awkward as possible for London. First, it was alleged that living conditions for the detained Japanese were sub-standard. Camps were described as having inadequate shelter and water supplies, and lacking recreation facilities. Second, that the men's health was poor, due to inadequate medical facilities and shortage of medicines. Third, that rations were not sufficient for men undertaking heavy labour. Fourth, that JSP were also overworked with no rest periods during their shifts. An 'observation' questioned the fundamental use of Japanese for labour. Other allegations claimed that the JSP were not permitted to write home or receive mail; that clothing issued was unsuitable or unavailable; and finally that no soap, towels, disinfectant or matches had ever been issued to JSP by the British.[55]

MacArthur may have done little more than relay hearsay from embittered Japanese servicemen but the sensitivity felt by both SEAC and London over this issue, already primed after developments in Europe (over the change of status of SEP to PW) and the refusal of American shipping, was acute. There was an initial rush to answer SCAP and hurried attempts to improve JSP conditions overall. Stopford replied promptly to London, point by point, stating the allegations were 'unfounded' and that they could 'reassure' MacArthur that JSP in SEAC were 'well cared for', their health and well being 'constantly under review'.[56] All JSP were, Stopford insisted, housed in hutted camps or *bashas* with adequate water supply. A veiled admission of shortages, however, referred to conditions varying 'naturally' between different countries, those in Singapore being 'better' than in Burma. In an attempt to justify differences it was asserted— in a further indictment of SEAC's lack of resources—that the variations were common to all personnel, including British and Indians, 'not merely to JSP'. Health issues were dealt with by a denial of poor facilities and a declaration that 'very adequate arrangements' were in place. Stopford even felt it necessary to quote from Numata's (February 1946) report lauding the regular supply of mepacrine, an anti-malarial drug, and 'absolutely effective' results in preventing infectious diseases thanks to 'the British way of latrine construction'. Rations, it was stated, were 'fully adequate' for manual workers.

Again, however, shortages of basics were admitted, particularly rice. This problem was Command-wide and consequently the JSP rice ration had been reduced to 'three and a half ounces daily'. This amount was 'a quarter ounce below the civil ration in Singapore [but] higher than the civil ration in Malaya'. Work hours for JSP were eight daily, six days a week. Those doing heavy labour were permitted 10 minutes rest each hour. 'Marching time' was deducted from hours of work. On the basic question of employment, Stopford repeated that all JSP remaining in SEAC were 'employed on essential rehabilitation and maintenance tasks' in areas where civil labour was 'critically short'. Lack of mail from Japan was explained by 'irregular' service. JSP themselves were allowed to send one postcard per month. The standard JSP clothing issue was two pairs of *mazri* (cheap cotton yarn) shirts and trousers, one cap and one pair of *chaplis* (sandals). Soap and disinfectant were regularly issued.[57] Although Stopford's reply was confident, he felt it necessary to allude to certain forthcoming improvements. SEAC was 'seeking approval from the War Office' to issue cigarettes and 'pay' for working parties. Also, the Red Cross had been requested to provide newspapers from Japan. Another proposal, for payment of compensation to PW injured while at work, had also been sent to the War Office. This measure would 'probably' be extended to JSP. New scales of amenities, such as matches, toothpaste and toothbrushes, were already agreed and awaited final War Office approval. Stopford concluded by suggesting that additional material for rebuttal of the allegations could be extracted from the regular reports by 'satisfied ICRC representatives who were constantly touring camps...'.[58]

London knew that MacArthur's concerns needed to be allayed quickly to prevent wider circulation of the allegations. The War Office was keen to send a brisk statement based upon Stopford's information and passed a draft reply to the Foreign Office for comment. Yet in reviewing the reply and the options available, the Foreign Office became hesitant and raised doubts. General Briggs had already identified areas of concern over JSP in Burma. In the light of the comments by Briggs, Stopford's draft is revealing both in what it denies but also in what it avoids mentioning. For example, he was rather disingenuous, quoting ICRC reports about Singapore camps when less favourable reports from Malaya and Burma also existed.

Both the War Office and the Foreign Office admitted being 'anxious' to improve JSP conditions 'as quickly as possible'. Lack of confidence in London stemmed partly from the fact that sudden changes to JSP living and working conditions were in themselves problematical. For at that time (late September 1946) London was also wrestling with a reply to the memorandum from the State Department in Washington objecting to the retention of JSP in the first place. Since the final decision on retention was officially pending, the Foreign Office saw potential disadvantages in approaching MacArthur on the subject at 'a critical moment'.[59]

A further complication for the Foreign Office was the fact that it was unsure of the primary reason why MacArthur was putting the UK under pressure over JSP. It had to consider perhaps three possibilities: first, that the Japanese Government was influencing SCAP policy; second, that MacArthur was concerned over the possibility of personal embarrassment should he fail to meet his demobilisation targets; or third, that there was widespread irritation within GHQ SCAP over retention by Britain and MacArthur simply wanted the Japanese back. Domestic reform in Japan was proceeding at a swift pace. No doubt the unresolved JSP issue hampered and frustrated those in the occupation administration charged with demilitarisation and ex-service programmes.

For its part, the Foreign Office reasoned that if the decision by COS were to go against retention and all JSP were to be repatriated by the end of 1946, there was little point in issuing the proposed working pay in the first place. What was actually under consideration in Stopford's draft was a deferred working pay credit, payable in yen against the Japanese Government upon repatriation. No local issue of cash or immediately redeemable credit was envisaged, so JSP purchasing ability would have remained virtually non-existent, a state of affairs specifically criticised by Briggs and, indeed, the ICRC. As the Foreign Office saw it, if the proposal were put to him, MacArthur was 'almost sure to infer that we have decided to retain JSP for a considerable time to come'. On the other hand, the War Office saw little harm in making it clear to the Americans that such a scheme was intended. Perhaps by doing so it hoped to soften their objections to retention since the War Office, at least, foresaw that negotiations with Washington over JSP retention in 1947 would be 'somewhat protracted'.[60] Here the War Office was anticipating the Cabinet decision going in its favour. It was always most unlikely that the Cabinet would countermand the COS, who had formally approved Mountbatten's retention request. In the event, the Foreign Office prevailed on the War Office to delay its response to MacArthur until the reply, unsurprisingly justifying retention, had been sent to the State Department.

ADMINISTRATIVE FAILURES IN SEAC

On 19 August 1946 the War Office asked the Treasury if there were any objections to 'the provision of inducements in excess of the minimum standard which has hitherto been considered necessary' for JSP.[61] For the War Office the argument was a simple one: a happier labourer would do more and better-quality work, which was clearly to Britain's advantage. This was, however, the first proposal since the Japanese surrender twelve months earlier to suggest a change in basic JSP conditions. Working pay credits were to be a 'key component' of the new inducements. In seeking a policy position the Treasury looked for a precedent and confirmed that it was prepared to approve payment and credit amounts on the 'same basis as SEP [Surrendered Enemy Personnel] in Italy'.[62] Continuing exchange rate pressures on Sterling remained of paramount concern. An 'acceptable comparison' for the Treasury was the arrangement made for German SEP who 'take the receipts with them to Germany and get what they can from their own government'. A similar procedure for the Japanese would, the Treasury suggested, be satisfactory but with one caveat. MacArthur's own financial agenda was well known and so, determined to avoid foreign exchange losses, the Treasury insisted:

> [W]e would not...agree to any arrangement by which HMG
> had to put up sterling to buy yen for these remittances...

[This] scheme will have to be agreed with SCAP and it may
be that he will raise difficulties…since he is anxious to earn
foreign exchange in any way for Japan. We must, however,
maintain our position on the exchange question since so
long as we have to convert Japan's surplus earnings of sterling
into dollars, the earnings of the SEP might marginally cost
us dollars.

Perhaps unwittingly, the Treasury viewed JSP as a Far East variant
of SEP. This was in one sense accurate since this contrived 'status' also
avoided Detaining Power obligations under the PW Convention. Treasury
officials, however, also chose to refer to JSP and 'SEP in South-East Asia'
interchangeably and sometimes even as 'POWs'.[63] This lack of administrative
precision would prove problematical. In Europe SEP status was already
under fire from the ICRC, and in time the United States would give way
on the issue. By referring frequently to the European SEP precedent, the
Treasury effectively undermined the combined War Office, Foreign Office
and SEAC arguments that depended upon JSP remaining a substantive
group among surrendered Axis forces.

At the end of 1946, though, Britain still considered its position on
retention as defendable, particularly since open American opposition to
retention appeared to have dissipated. Indeed, London was confident enough
to move ahead with a Working Pay Credits (WPC) scheme. Calculations
for WPC, however, required precise documentation. On the Treasury's
behalf the War Office requested copies of records from SEAC's component
army Commands, Allied Land Forces South East Asia (ALFSEA), showing
details of hours worked by JSP. Simultaneously the United Kingdom
Liaison Mission (UKLM) in Japan was also requested to seek confirmation
from the Japanese Government, via SCAP, that payments of 'one penny
halfpenny an hour for skilled and three farthings an hour for unskilled'
labour would be credited to individual JSP in yen on their return to Japan.[64]
This looked to be a workable solution but London's hopes were dashed
by a fundamental administrative failure. HQ South-East Asia Land Forces
(SEALF), part of the British inter-service Command established in January
1947 after the abolition of SEAC, informed the War Office that in Allied
Forces Netherlands East Indies (AFNEI), Burma Command and Malaya
Command 'no records are at present being kept…from which working pay
can be assessed'. (SEALF was superseded by Far East Land Forces (FARELF)
in August 1947.[65]) JSP labour assignment and supervision had been casual in
the extreme. No means existed even to attempt rough calculations of work

performed. The rationale behind the WPC proposal was fundamentally compromised and preparations for the scheme were halted. By early 1947 the Foreign Office was forced to conclude that without the documentation a detailed calculation of working pay was not possible.[66] Thus Mountbatten's emphatic assertion of absolute control over JSP and his 'emotional', explicit rejection of MacArthur's early instruction that JSP were to be paid for work returned to haunt the Command.

In a further embarrassment, information about the lack of records did not reach the Foreign Office before SCAP's failure to reply about the WPC proposal had prompted informal enquiries to the Americans from UKLM in Tokyo. SCAP replied informally to the further enquires by suggesting that agreement would be forthcoming, 'provided HMG undertake to reimburse the Japanese Government in sterling for retention of all certificates issued in respect of working pay'.[67] There was a further disconcerting complication: SCAP's argument was that 'under the Geneva Convention the Japanese Government is entitled to credit or reimbursement from the detaining Power for amounts of yen paid out in redemption of such certificates as represents wages earned by prisoners of war for compensable work done for the Detaining Power'. A counter-argument put by UKLM that this did not apply because of a lack of existence of 'any treaty of obligation on the part of the Allies over JPW'—and by inference JSP—had been rejected. SCAP's viewpoint was that 'a moral obligation rests upon the detaining Power' not only to make actual payment but also to permit retention of these payments by individuals regardless of currency restrictions'.[68] Treasury caution over the financing of work credits had proved more than justified. Financial embarrassment also loomed over British plans for payments to JPW. Despite the known British ban on the export of sterling, SCAP rejected the proposed part-cash, part-reimbursed credit payable by the Japanese Government as part of general reparations as 'unacceptable'.[69]

American inclusion of JSP within the remit of the PW Convention dispirited London. The Foreign Office found itself rehashing familiar arguments over distinctions between JPW and JSP. 'Legal liabilities', the Foreign Office argued, 'would not apply' to JSP. On ethical grounds, however, Britain sought to 'accord surrendered personnel treatment as far as possible equivalent to that laid down in the Geneva Convention without, however, quoting [it] as the authority'. Yet Article 34 of the Convention appeared to grant working PW the right to receive pay from the Detaining Power. If Britain were to follow the Convention as far as possible then, one Foreign Office official concluded, 'HMG should be prepared to foot the bill' for working pay for JSP. Another argued that 'humanitarian spirit' and 'equivalent treatment' were not the same thing and that no such undertaking had been given for SEP and so Britain could, absence of European precedent permitting, 'decide by unilateral act whether or not to pay them, either with the Geneva Convention as a guide or otherwise'. There was 'no question', however, of payment in sterling. Britain was in any case preparing to calculate an 'undoubtedly enormous' claim against Japan for the forced labour undertaken by Allied PW in Burma, Malaya, Thailand and Japan during the war.[70] For the Foreign Office it was therefore important to clarify, before again approaching MacArthur, whether Britain was expecting Japan to bear JSP pay costs directly or whether the payments were to be offset against the huge amount the Japanese 'owed Britain'. The offset option was accepted by the Foreign Office as a consequence of Britain's 'moral responsibility'.[71]

Foreign Office disquiet and sensitivity over the question of retention and the obvious clash with Potsdam obligations was such that American opinion was sought directly. UKLM was charged with presenting the British argument. UKLM's head, General Gairdner, was instructed to seek a private and confidential meeting with MacArthur. Gairdner specifically but unofficially asked MacArthur whether he considered 'the retention of POWs until the end of 1947 was a repudiation of the Potsdam Declaration', and also if the British proposal would 'embarrass him' in his dealings with the Russians. To considerable British relief MacArthur replied 'No'—'emphatically', according to Gairdner—to both questions. Potsdam, MacArthur commented, set 'no time limit on the return of POWs'. It is noteworthy that neither Gairdner nor MacArthur referred at any time to JSP. MacArthur was perhaps following the State Department's March 1946 decision to cease using the term SEP in Europe. On the question of relations with Russia, MacArthur stated that since the Russians would be unlikely to maintain a monthly repatriation target of 50,000, the last repatriate under Soviet control would only return to Japan after the date proposed by Britain. Interestingly, MacArthur volunteered to inform London if the Russian programme were accelerated and all Russian-held Japanese would be repatriated ahead of the British schedule.[72] Privately, however, MacArthur told Gairdner of his opposition to retention, largely on the grounds that the requirement to guard 'prisoners' would be complicated and that they 'would be more trouble than they were worth'. Such were the problems inherent in retention, MacArthur added, that he believed the policy would 'boomerang' upon the British Government.

MacArthur's apparent disinterest was more than sufficient for UKLM who advised the Foreign Office that 'it appears the matter rests entirely between the two governments and that MacArthur has washed his hands of it entirely'.[73] Yet even as draft instructions were sent outlining the British refusal to reimburse JSP and the anticipated 'heavy counter claims' against Japan were being prepared, cracks appeared in the British case. Privately the Foreign Office admitted that UKLM had been given 'insufficient ammunition' to convince MacArthur.[74] As the need to assuage American opposition over retention grew, distinctions between JPW and JSP blurred to the point of insignificance. Above all, Britain wished to be seen to be acting correctly. Consequently arguments over payment became secondary to the much more important need to remain in line with the Geneva Convention:

> The Americans are inclined to criticise us for the delay in repatriating Japanese Surrendered Personnel; allegations have been made against our treatment of Japanese in our hands and from a general standpoint, we are anxious to persuade SCAP that our actions are legally and ethically sound.[75]

Weeks passed with no answer on working pay from SCAP. Before long, the question of completing repatriation of JSP before the end of 1946 became irrelevant. Just four months later, in March 1947, in the wake of the 'British shipping' debacle (examined in Chapter 8), the UKLM representative would meet with a far less sympathetic MacArthur.

EAST VERSUS WEST AT THE FAR EASTERN COMMISSION

While the United States had effectively prevented the USSR and the other Allies from exerting any major influence on the government of Occupied Japan, existing agreements had, however, obliged Washington to seek certain co-operation among the Allies over the fundamental treatment of the country. Negotiations led, eventually, to the creation of the Far Eastern Commission (FEC). As a joint body the FEC offered, in its early incarnation at least, scope for Allied governments to make recommendations on policy towards Japan. Meeting in New York from 26 February 1946 to 28 April 1952, the FEC comprised representatives from, initially, the nine Allied governments represented at the surrender. Much of MacArthur's initial programme for reform had, however, been implemented before the FEC even held its first formal session. Apart from issuing certain instructions over the revised Japanese constitution, the slow deliberations of the Commission, its infrequent meetings, the frequent use of the American veto, as well as SCAP's authority to issue interim 'operational directives' at will meant the FEC was never able to mount a broad challenge to MacArthur's authority.[76] In the first months of its life, however, the Allied member governments took resolutions brought before the FEC very seriously. To Britain's discomfort one such resolution centred on JSP.

In September 1946, as London was considering SEAC's request for JSP retention to the end of 1947, the FEC was examining, at the instigation of the Soviet Union, the 'Statement of Policy on Disarmament and Demobilisation of Japanese Armed Forces and Disposition of Equipment'. The policy targets listed in this statement, part of Washington's formal directive to General MacArthur, were of interest to numerous Asian and Pacific governments, including many not represented at the FEC, as well as the world's press. Paragraph eight of the draft stated that 'all Japanese forces located in Burma, British Malaya, NEI and Siam [Thailand] shall be returned to Japan proper as promptly as transportation facilities will permit'.[77] The proposal also gave additional emphasis to the Potsdam Declaration, which undertook to repatriate Japanese forces promptly.

Britain faced two problems with the draft text to be discussed in the public forum. First, it specifically highlighted Britain's retention of JSP. Second, it potentially undermined Britain's case that shortages of British shipping made delayed repatriation unavoidable. Were this to be presented publicly, any subsequent offer of American or other spare shipping could not easily have been refused. As it stood, the draft allowed Britain no room for manoeuvre other than special pleading with the other Allied Powers, in particular the United States, to permit what was in effect derogation from Potsdam.

Foreign Office preference was to avoid an airing in the FEC of 'issues which would inevitably arise if revision…was proposed'. One of these issues was a suggestion by Moscow in June 1946 that all JSP be declared PW. Were Russia to have returned to this proposal and secured its formal approval, JSP would have been granted numerous additional rights (including pay) as well as having restrictions imposed on their use as labour. Either would have been a most unwelcome prospect for Britain. United States support for, or at least non-opposition to, the Russian proposal appears to have been taken as read in London. (In Europe, American-held SEP had already been declared PW as a result of ICRC pressure. It was logical to assume that American policy for enemy personnel in Asia would not differ.) In August 1946 the United States Joint Chiefs (USJCS) informed Britain of the 'undesirable features' of JSP retention in SEAC, since shipping was being reduced, and not least as it required the continuing operation of reception facilities at American expense (see Chapter 5). While not a direct protest, the USJCS statement meant that Britain had been given formal notice of American disapproval at a time when maintaining American goodwill was a foreign policy priority.

A further discomforting factor for Britain was the openly deteriorating state in SCAP–Russian relations, particularly over delayed repatriation of JSP in the USSR. The fate of 'missing' Japanese surrendered to Soviet forces and shipped to Siberia was becoming a hot domestic political issue in Japan. Apparent Russian willingness to offer improvements in conditions for detained JSP would have reduced domestic pressure, temporarily at least, on SCAP's administration and also the Japanese Government. For Britain, however, such a development would have been quite the reverse. Restrictions on labour and other additional commitments for the guarding, financing and maintenance of PW rather than JSP would have placed immediate and probably unattainable demands upon resources in SEAC. Had the measure passed, the 'free-labour' rationale for retaining the Japanese would have been negated. Loss of the benefits of JSP labour aside, the admission or exposure of failure to meet Geneva Convention standards and the associated risk of international rebuke would have been extremely embarrassing for Britain. There had already been disquiet, for example, over the state of British–run internee camps in Germany.[78]

London was well aware of the 'obstacles to retention' and the 'serious political objections' to Britain's actions. Even within ministerial ranks there were major doubts, and by September 1946 the Foreign Office had already decided that 'the long term employment of Prisoners of War after the conclusion of hostilities' was 'indefensible as a policy.'[79] Conscious of the diplomatic risks involved, Foreign Office officials stressed the need to 'regularise', or in other words secure secret agreement over the prolonged retention with the United States. Earlier assumptions that Britain had to advise other Allied Powers of the derogation from Potsdam were quietly abandoned and references to it deleted in the redrafted conclusions.[80]

With the benefit of hindsight, the question arises as to why Moscow, which held about one million JSP, would unilaterally propose a measure that would have considerably increased its own financial and administrative burden. In all probability, the reason was simply nuisance value in inconveniencing the Western Allies. There was also the potential added benefit of a public relations success with the Japanese public while simultaneously embarrassing Britain and the United States. It is doubtful that any FEC pronouncement, even one sponsored by Moscow, would have had any material effect on the brutal treatment and poor living conditions of

JSP in Siberia. In contrast, for the Western Allies a public resolution would have been difficult to ignore. In the event, however, the glacial procedures of the FEC and SCAP's own 'pre-emptive' interim reports on repatriation progress overtook the Russian proposal and it was not pursued. As the FEC agenda moved on to other topics a relieved Foreign Office continued to negotiate American acceptance of retention. As it did so, SEAC's (SEALF from November 1946) failure to note working hours concentrated minds on how to resolve payment due for work that had not been recorded at all even as JSP labour was being allocated for 1947.

In one sense Britain had been let off the hook at the FEC. Yet no advantage was taken of this unexpected breathing space. Projects continued as planned; with no advice or urging from London to reduce increasing reliance on Japanese labour, War Office policy remained unchanged: it would steadfastly resist repatriation. Neither it nor SEALF had a Plan B.

JSP requirement in SEAC, 1947

(Estimates as at 20 July 1946)

Territory	Services	Civil	Ad/Med/Sick	Total	
From 1 January 1947					
Burma	17,400	15,000	3,700	36,100	
Singapore Colony	13,500	2,000	2,000	17,500	
Malayan Union	8,500	15,200	3,500	26,800	
NEI (Indonesia)	13,500	Nil	Nil	13,500	(To Dutch)
Siam (Thailand)	300	9,000	Nil	9,300	
Total:	52,950	41,200	9,050	103,200	
From 1 July 1947					
Burma	16,800	15,000	3,700	35,500	
Singapore Colony	11,970	1,000	1,650	14,620	
Malayan Union	6,100	14,200	3,700	3,300	
NEI (Indonesia)	13,500	Nil	Nil	13,500	(To Dutch)
Siam (Thailand)	300	Nil	Nil	300	
Total:	48,670	30,200	8,350	87,220	

'Retention of JSP during 1947', 20 July 1946. CAB 119/206.

NOTES TO CHAPTER 6

1. 'Retention of JSP in SEAC during 1947. Annex 1', 27 Aug. 1946. CAB 119/206.
2. *ICRC Report*, 539.
3. HQ ALFSEA to HQ SEAC, 'Repatriation of JSP retained for labour in SEAC', 27 June 1946. WO 203/6118.
4. Mountbatten to MacArthur, 'Repatriation of Japanese from Burma and India', 18 Apr. 1946. WO 203/6339.
5. Woodburn Kirby, *The Surrender of Japan*, 486.
6. Bob Moore, 'Axis Prisoners in Britain during the Second World War: A Comparative Survey', in Moore and Fedorowich, eds, *Prisoners of War and their Captors*, 32. Their repatriation began in December 1945., See *Hansard*, 26 Nov. 1945, Vol. 416, c1045W.
7. PM to Lord Inverchapel (Clarke Kerr), 4 Oct. 1946. CAB 122/1183.
8. 'Admiralty Islands (Manus)', JPS Report (COS), 10 Sept. 1945. CAB 84/75. See also Thorne, *Allies*, 523.
9. Lend-Lease arrangements ended abruptly on 21 August 1945.
10. Takemae, *Allied Occupation of Japan*, 132–3.
11. Ibid, 96.
12. Harry S. Truman, *Memoirs: Year of Decisions, 1945* (New York, 1955), 431–2.
13. Peter Bates, *Japan and the British Commonwealth Occupation Force, 1946-52* (London, 1993), 59.
14. *Hansard*, 22 Oct. 1946, Vol. 427, cc 1490.
15. Dower, *Embracing Defeat*, 363-364.
16. David McCullough, *Truman* (New York, 1992), 600.
17. Harry S. Truman, *Memoirs: Years of Trial and Hope* (New York, 1956), 102.
18. UKLM to FO, 'Retention of Japanese POWs in South Eastern Asia.' 8 Nov. 1946. FO 262/2054.
19. Pyman to Terauchi, 24 April 1946. WO 203/5968.
20. See Chapter 6, n. 43.
21. ALFSEA to HQ JEFSR, 'Visits', 12 June 1946. WO 203/6118.
22. SEAC imposed this condition prior to approving Numata's tour.
23. 'Evacuation of Japanese Chronic sick.' JPS Paper (235), 16 Mar. 1946. WO 203/5965.
24. SCAP to SACSEA, 28 Mar. 1946. WO 203/5967.
25. See Chapter 5, n. 94.
26. ICRC to FO, 'Burma: Japanese Surrendered Personnel and Prisoners of War', 8 Apr. 1947, FO 369/3816B.
27. Later Lt-Gen. Sir H. R. Briggs. (He commanded 'Briggsforce' in North Africa and devised the counter-insurgency Briggs Plan during the Malaya Emergency.)
28. 'JSP Conditions', HQ Burma Command to ALFSEA. 18 May 1946, W0 203/5968.
29. Ibid.
30. HQ Burma Command to HQ ALFSEA, 17 May 1946. WO 203/5968.
31. HQ ALFSEA to HQ Burma Command, 29 May 1946. WO 203/5968.
32. WO to HQ ALFSEA, 'Pay and amenities for JSP', 30 Sept. 1946. FO 371/54306.
33. Personal correspondence with Lt Stuart Guild, ex-RA (Burma and FIC), Sept. 2009.
34. *Hansard*, 13 May 1946, Vol. 422, cc146-7W.

35.   Personal interview with Charles Wicksteed, ex-RA (Burma and FIC), June 2008.

36.   'Extracts from a memorandum...by HQ Japanese Forces, Central Malaya' in 'ICRC Report on JSP in Central Malaya', 13 Mar. 1947. FO 371/3816B.

37.   ICRC to FO, 21 Oct. 1946. FO 371/54306.

38.   'Extracts from a memorandum...[7 Dec 1946] by HQ Japanese Forces, Central Malaya' in 'ICRC Report on JSP in Central Malaya.' 13 Mar. 1947. FO 371/3816B.

39.   WO to ALFSEA, 20 Sept. 1946. WO 208/4780.

40.   WO to ALFSEA, 11 Nov. 1946. FO 371/54306.

41.   War Office to ALFSEA, 20 Sept. 1946. FO 371/54306.

42.   See Chapter 4.

43.   Dominions Office to Australia and New Zealand governments, 'Japanese Reparations: Cost of maintaining Japanese Disarmed Personnel', 15 Apr. 1946. FO 371/5421.

44.   Ibid. For an early British perspective on American concerns over Japan's future see *The Economist* 149, no. 5336 (1 Dec. 1945), 779–80.

45.   Ibid..

46.   Ibid.

47.   Woodburn Kirby, *Surrender of Japan*, 487.

48.   Edwin W. Pauley, *Report on Japanese Reparations to the President of the United States, November 1945 to April 1, 1946*. Dept of State publication 3174 (Far Eastern Series 25), (Washington, DC, 1946).

49.   Takemae, *Allied Occupation of Japan*, 109.

50.   Ibid, 109. Arguments for or against punitive Japanese reparations were topical in contemporary news reporting. *See* Robert E. Ward and Frank Joseph Shulman, *The Allied Occupation of Japan, 1945-1952: An Annotated Bibliography of Western-Language Materials* (Chicago, 1974), 379–91.

51.   Takemae, *Allied Occupation of Japan*, 460.

52.   Tomaru Junko, 'The Post-war Rapprochement of Malaya and Japan, 1945-1961' (PhD dissertation, University of Oxford, 1997), 144.

53.   State Dept Memorandum, 2 May 1946. FO 371/54242.

54.   SACSEA to UKLM, 17 Sept. 1946. FO 371/54306.

55.   Ibid.

56.   Ibid.

57.   Ibid.

58.   Ibid.

59.   FO memo, 'Inducements for JSP stationed in SEAC', 27 Sept. 1946. FO 371/54306.

60.   Ibid.

61.   See n. 65.

62.   Treasury to WO. 10 Sept. 1946. FO 371/54306.

63.   Ibid.

64.   War Office to HQ ALFSEA, 20 Sept. 1946. WO 208/4780.

65.   SEALF to WO. 'To meet working pay for JSP.' 22 Mar. 1947. CAB 122/1183.

66.   'Meeting on JSP pay', 17 June 1947. FO 371/63741.

67.   UKLM to FO, 10 Nov. 1946. WO 208/4780.

68.   Ibid.

69.   FO to WO, 16 Dec. 1946. WO 208/4780.

70. Ibid.

71. Ibid.

72. UKLM to FO, 'Retention of Japanese POWs in South Eastern Asia.' 8 Nov. 1946. FO 262/2054.

73. Ibid.

74. FO to WO, 16 Dec. 1946. WO 208/4780.

75. Ibid.

76. Takemae, *Allied Occupation of Japan*, 99.

77. COS Committee, Draft Report to Defence Committee. 'Retention of JSP in SEAC during 1947. Annex II (11),' 10 Sept. 1946. CAB 122 1182.

78. See Chapter 5, n. 42.

79. PAOC to Cabinet Offices, MOD, COS. 'Political Objections to the Retention of JSP.' 10 Sept. 1947. CAB 122/1182.

80. Ibid.

7

PHANTOM SHIPS

FINAL RETREAT OVER JSP RETENTION

*We can feel free to make plans on the assumption that
no serious obstacles will be placed in our way by the
USG or by any decisions the FEC may take.*

—Foreign Office to Cabinet Offices, 9 December 1946[1]

By Christmas Eve 1946 the cheap repatriation of Japanese Surrendered Personnel (JSP) on the British-preferred timetable seemed settled. Whitehall had concluded that there had been 'no adverse reaction' from the State Department since the Foreign Office had informed it of the intention to retain JSP throughout 1947. Direct American opposition to retention had dissipated following, London believed, the presentation new proposals for pay for labour and material improvement in JSP camp conditions. Although some difficulties had emerged over American preference for payment to JSP to be made by Britain in sterling, London was confident that the expected reparations payment due to Britain from Japan would render the point moot. Also, since the Soviet proposal at the Far Eastern Commission (FEC) to reinstate JSP as PW had lapsed, the international political implications of the retention decision were greatly reduced.[2] British officials understood that SCAP would not raise any further objection provided repatriation was carried out in British-controlled shipping. Quiet relief rather than celebration was the order of the day in London and South East Asia Land Forces (SEALF). This breathing space allowed Treasury and War Office staff to return to the still unresolved issue of working pay for JSP (examined in next chapter), while the War Office considered the implications for construction and other programmes following the eventual departure of the Japanese.

THE QUEST FOR REPLACEMENT LABOUR

Within SEALF the very real prospect of the early loss of JSP labour concentrated military minds. A need for replacement workers was quickly identified and justified. In contrast, colonial civil authorities appeared much more flexible in their labour requirements but remained subservient to military priorities. In London, too, the Colonial Office was similarly concerned over the knock-on effect of a reduced labour force on civil programmes. In particular, it anticipated extended delays in de-requisitioning buildings owing to the diverging civil and military approaches to the question of JSP labour. The Colonial Office found itself in the middle, recording that 'if the Civil Governments have decided that they can make do without the JSP the local Service Authorities, and in particular the Military Authorities, most decidedly have not'.[3]

For the armed services acting as employers the fundamental problem was the drift away of civilian labour at the first opportunity to more lucrative occupations, often in the black market. In November 1946 the British Defence Committee, South-East Asia (BDCSEA) appointed a substantive committee to consider the provision of civil labour in some British territories in Southeast Asia. It was chaired by a representative of the Governor-General of the Malayan Union and comprised representatives of the Special Commissioner, the Governor of Singapore and also the armed services. Much of the Committee's deliberations were concentrated on the effect of the withdrawal of JSP. Burma, however, was excluded from the remit as by February 1947 the new nationalist Government of Burma had informed London that JSP were no longer considered essential for labour.[4]

In Singapore Colony the civil authorities employed 1,310 JSP, mainly in the repair of public utilities such as gas supply, waterworks and electricity generation. Their primary role, however, was identified as clearing anti-malarial drains and main canals, town cleansing and domestic sewage disposal. A key consideration for the Committee was the fact that JSP maintained these vital public health-related services during frequent strikes by civilian government workers. With non-striking JSP labour 'guaranteed', industrial action by public service workers in Singapore was rendered inconvenient rather than catastrophic. There was a similar willingness to use JSP as strike-breakers in Burma.[5] In early 1947 the Singapore Government described

JSP as 'irreplaceable' and foresaw 'disastrous consequences' following their withdrawal.[6] For the civil authorities, therefore, if JSP were not to be replaced by a similarly biddable or tied group their departure heralded a potential shift in labour relations that would have implications colony wide. In this area at least British policy was not consistent. Elsewhere in SEAC/SEALF the anticipated use of JSP as strike-breakers (or worse), for example by the Government of Thailand, was one of the reasons why civil control of JSP was specifically rejected, even when SEAC was urgently seeking a way to reduce its responsibilities towards the Japanese. (In the case of Thailand, however, British concerns were perhaps less motivated by the act of strike-breaking itself than the fact that such action would highlight Britain's abrogation of direct control over JSP.[7])

In the Malayan Union the majority of the 7,615 JSP were employed in food production on plantations and in paddy fields. Here, in contrast with Singapore, the possibility of losing these workers did not generate alarm. Specialists, though, were a rather different matter. Nearly 500 JSP were employed on railways and the civil authorities were loath to lose engineering units, whose bridge-building and repairing and other skills were not duplicated in the local work force.[8] Resignation rather than protest best describes the response of the Malaya Government as it accepted the inevitability of Japanese repatriation. For the Services in Malaya, however, the loss of Japanese labour represented a far more serious threat to ongoing and planned work. Some 8,400 JSP moved stores in depots and worked on garrison construction projects. The blunt assessment of the BDCSEA was that without them all projects would come to a halt. In Singapore, JSP represented almost one-third of the labour employed by the three branches of the Services (16,900 out of 65,000). All three Service branches used JSP labour but to differing degrees. The Royal Navy used 2,400, primarily in the Naval Dockyard for docking, refitting and unloading. Another 2,500 JSP handled stores and maintenance work for the RAF, though it stated that it would not require them after September 1947.

It was, however, the British Army that was the greatest user of JSP in Singapore. In all, some 12,000 worked in port administration, port clearance, movement of stores, and works projects. Without JSP the army anticipated that it would be forced to cut back to essential maintenance only, abandon two-thirds of construction projects and not undertake any new service operations. An immediate consequence was that 6,000 British troops would also be forced to remain in tented accommodation and, as civilian authorities had feared, a large number of properties requisitioned as depots would be held indefinitely. Senior Army officers described the continued use of tents for their men as unacceptable.[9] The Army was particularly sensitive over the question of tented accommodation for troops in peacetime. Following the May 1946 mutiny at Muar (in Malaya) in protest over poor facilities by 258 men of 13 Parachute Battalion (returning from Java), the issue had become something of a cause célèbre. In the House of Commons vociferous criticism of the incident and of the quality of accommodation for SEALF personnel had greatly embarrassed the Government and, of course, the Army.[10]

The BDCSEA sub-committee ventured that the envisioned labour shortage could be solved by a readjustment of the labour force. It identified widespread unfitness (as a result of previous malnutrition) as a temporary but steadily reducing problem. Training facilities were limited and women were underused. Also, no use was being made of 'labour saving machinery'. (The term 'machinery' was relative. The Committee pointed out that since there were few wheelbarrows in Malaya and Singapore—and no factories producing them—materials were transported in small baskets in labour-intensive multiple trips.) Much of the Committee's estimates and forecasts was guesswork, a fact that it readily acknowledged. It identified too many uncertain factors to attempt precision. There was a known but unquantifiable amount of labour preferring more lucrative market gardening (particularly rice production) and black-market operations (producing and distributing consumer goods) to construction work. The Committee felt that this labour would only re-enter the main economy once local prices for food fell sufficiently to make the black market unprofitable. Export-related employment also needed to offer more reward. Tin was the key commodity in Malaya's economy, and would be even more so after shortages of natural rubber during the war had led to the development of cheaper synthetic equivalents outside Southeast Asia. Other uncertain factors as the availability of coal, machinery and electricity all affected the speed at which tin mines could reopen. Paradoxically, if the mines were slow in opening up, more skilled artisans would be available to the British forces. Were the civilian economy to improve then a shortage of skilled workers was inevitable. At the same time, however, the Committee identified the major distorting effect that military projects were having on local labour markets. It estimated that the three Services were employing almost three times the number of local labour compared with 1939. That equated to nearly half of all local labour, despite defections to better-paid civilian jobs. On top of this, the Services were actually looking for more. SEALF anticipated 65,000 civilian labourers but, crucially, only until 1949.[11]

One proposal that found ready support within SEALF was the idea of importing replacement labour for JSP from India or China.[12] While the Command was keen to import more workers, the Committee was sympathetic to the Singapore Government's fears of the consequences of a return to peacetime demand, perhaps as early as 1949, when a large part of the Service work force would be paid off. One major concern was that the imported labour would not be able to be absorbed by local employers and would be left unemployed with predictable social consequences. Conversely,

31. Capt. G. V. Faulkner, MC, addresses JPW at Kokine (Burma), March 1946. (© IWM)

the Committee noted that any move to recruit locally would be at the expense of civil employers and result in wage inflation.

With a requirement for cheap labour identified, the BDCSEA concluded that any imported labour should be permitted to remain in Singapore for a maximum of two years. The problem was far from solved, however, as the availability and acceptability of potential candidates for immigrant labour presented further difficulties. As the Committee was well aware, emigration of labour from India was banned. Javanese ('preferred' by the Malay and Singapore authorities to Chinese) were out of reach because of the Indonesian political situation. Ceylonese artisans were known to be available but were expensive. Chinese labour, the most plentiful, presented particularly awkward problems for the new Malayan Union, particularly over citizenship rights that had aroused serious protest among Malays.[13] Were open emigration allowed to Chinese, more than ample labour would flood into the Union but bringing with it a host of demographic difficulties. This option was quickly discarded as the Committee felt it was certain that the Malayan Union Government would not 'consent to measures which would serve to weighten the racial balance in favour of the already large Chinese community'.[14]

With imported civilian labour effectively ruled out, the solution was thought to lie in uniformed military labour from outside SEALF.[15] The Command warmed to the idea of using a temporary corps of 13,500 men from India. Military authority, it was believed, would guarantee total control over the labour and, equally importantly, its repatriation. Support for this solution gathered pace within SEALF, though not in India. (The Indian Government had previously vetoed the movement of Indian units into SEAC in December 1945 during the Java crisis.) Responses from Ceylon's government towards a military secondment proved favourable. The Colonial Office, however, was greatly concerned lest such a force risked becoming 'a political menace in Malaya'. Such was the Colonial Office's apprehension that it was prepared to oppose the scheme at an early stage even though one possible consequence was the resurrection of even less desirable schemes for the importation of civilian labour from China, India or Indonesia.[16]

Ceylon, however, was preparing for its own independence from Britain and would not permit any force to be raised before its own armed forces had been established. Delays with this option were therefore inevitable. In any case, the Colonial Office raised questions as to how the direct and indirect costs of multi-ship charters and accommodation for 13,500 men (estimated at £250,000) could support a case for 'cheap' Ceylonese labour. Once again, however, the question of shipping availability proved the final decisive factor. An unofficial MOT monthly lift estimate suggested a maximum lift capacity of 2,000 per month. The provision and diversion of extra shipping required, in addition to ongoing and anticipated increased JSP repatriation sailings, proved simply beyond the logistic capacity of SEALF, the War Office and the MOT.[17]

A JAPANESE SOLUTION?

Somewhat bizarrely, even the Japanese attempted to assist in providing alternative labour. General Numata, always keen to explore any avenue that might speed the repatriation of his men, made a parallel proposal in March 1947 that JSP held in Southeast Asia be replaced by a labour force composed of either military personnel or civilians, recruited under contract, in Japan.[18] Numata's offer was almost certainly coincidental but it was welcome none the less. SEALF examined the proposal but rejected the civilian unit as impractical as contracts would not provide the 'degree of control' required by the civil governments or the Services. It was far more enthusiastic about the possibility of employing a Japanese military labour force, although it recognised this would create legal and political difficulties. For SEALF the main drawback to this option was that in May

32. JSP dump artillery pieces off Saishu Island, Japan, in March 1946. (NARA)

1947 MacArthur was expected to announce an ordinance dissolving the Imperial Japanese Army (IJA) and Imperial Japanese Navy (IJN) under the proposed new constitution for Japan. This was entirely consistent with MacArthur's Potsdam remit to demilitarise Japan. Such a development raised two quite separate problems.

First, it would immediately and automatically have deprived Japanese officers of disciplinary powers over their own troops. Similarly British officers would also have lost reciprocal military authority over JSP, who would in fact no longer be 'servicemen' at all, and who would presumably have become a new category, something akin to alien detainees. Since SEALF had simply battened on a limited number of British military and civilian liaison officers to the IJA/IJN commands *in situ*, the entire JSP organisational and supervisory infrastructure in Southeast Asia was technically at risk. Were JSP repatriation to be delayed beyond the announced date of any IJA/ IJN dissolution, the British and regional civil authorities faced potentially enormous 'detainee'-management problems. For the Foreign Office this was yet another budding JSP complication that it could have done without. Bad publicity would have been unavoidable. Once again Britain would have been seen to be delaying the widely expected measures required to achieve the disarmament and demilitarisation of Japan. Since there was unlikely to be any sympathy for the British position from MacArthur or Washington, the War Office resigned itself to seeking a special exemption from the anticipated decree for Japanese forces in British-controlled areas despite the bad publicity this would inevitably bring.[19]

A second problem, this time over potentially re-imported Japanese labour was also political and perhaps even more sensitive. SEALF accepted that were Japan's military forces abolished, any new Japanese labour force would have to be 'enrolled some way into British Forces'. SEALF professed that it was in no position to assess the political and legal difficulties of Japanese enrolment in the British military. In any case, the full nature of the work envisaged would have had to be reported to SCAP, who would no doubt have insisted upon both payment in sterling and supervisory inspections by American representatives. Both of these conditions would have been unpalatable to London. It was also most unlikely that the United States would have permitted any Japanese to work on British military projects, even construction of service accommodation. The US would also have been very aware of the risk of undermining the PW Convention. Such a precedent would have enabled the Soviet Union to claim it was within its rights to put surrendered Japanese in its custody to work on military projects. American concerns aside, a more immediate and difficult issue would have been the reaction in Britain. How the British Government could have attempted to reconcile Japanese enlistment in the British Army with a certainly outraged public is not explained. Perhaps not surprisingly, as the 'difficulties...appeared insurmountable', this proposal also went no further.[20] With no apparent way of replacing JSP labour quickly, the recommendation was to keep to the date of the end of 1947 and use British ships, even though there were serious implications inherent in such a course of action.[21]

WISHFUL THINKING OVER NAVAL REPARATIONS

As Whitehall and the military authorities in SEALF explored the options for replacement labour, British officials also began to make some arrangements for JSP repatriation. MacArthur's objections to the retention had been overcome by assuring him that the Japanese would be returned by the end of 1947 at British expense. Prior to this undertaking the MOT, War Office and SEALF had made careful and repeated calculations of the capacity of British-controlled shipping in Southeast Asia. In fact, assumptions over what might constitute 'available British-controlled shipping' were quite broad. In December 1946 the Chiefs of Staff (COS) noted with satisfaction that the Foreign Office expected that in the future 'we shall presumably be our own judges of the extent to which shipping facilities will permit repatriation voyages'. Indeed, the Foreign Office was growing in confidence: 'The time appears to have come when we can feel free to make plans on the assumption that no serious obstacles will be placed in our way by the USG or by any decisions the FEC may take'.[22] The COS even felt the need to sound a note of caution lest 'more Japanese shipping available than first estimated might "embarrass" [SEALF Commanders]' resulting in 'more capacity to Malaya and Singapore than was needed'.[23] SEALF already had use, courtesy of SCAP in Tokyo, of four Japanese merchant ships reassigned as troop transports. These ships were included in London's calculations as were a large number of ships expected to become available as war reparations.

There was some concern in London over the fate of the surviving ships of the IJN. In December 1945, at the Moscow Conference, the Soviet Foreign Minister Vyacheslav Molotov had proposed their division.[24] Instead, agreement was reached at Moscow that all Japanese capital and larger warships would be scuttled. Britain's preferred position was the scrapping of all IJN vessels but it staked a precautionary claim to a 'full British Empire share'. When it emerged that United States policy favoured equal division among the Four Powers, British officials lobbied US Secretary of State James Byrnes for 'a more equitable division among [those most]...active in the naval war against Japan'. It was also felt in London that some of the Dominions as well as the French and Dutch had legitimate claims on Japanese ships. There proved to be no American support for such a position and, while still at Moscow, Byrnes had stated that he considered the question 'settled'. By July 1946, the Russian attitude over Manchuria, Korea and elsewhere prompted the British to ask Washington whether an equal split was still advisable. The United States, however, remained committed to an equal division among the Four Powers.[25]

In truth, the British Admiralty was far from concerned about the limited operational value of the ships in question. Scant numbers remained seaworthy and almost all suffered from torpedo, bomb or strafing damage. Nevertheless there was expectation in SEALF that several larger former IJN vessels would pass to British control. Destruction of the major surviving ships was not prompt. The cruisers *Kashima* and *Sakawa*, the carriers *Hosho* and

Katsuragi, the support carrier *Kumano Maru*, and the light destroyer *Yukikaze*, were assigned—after makeshift repairs—to extensive JSP repatriation duties around the Pacific, returning many tens of thousands of JSP, PW and Japanese civilians in extremely crowded conditions. (On one voyage in January 1946 *Katsuragi* carried over 5,000 JSP from the Solomon Islands to Japan via New Britain.[26]) As these repatriation voyages wound down, however, MacArthur pre-empted wider demands over remaining IJN spoils. He confirmed that any Japanese warship heavier than destroyer class would be scuttled and, as agreed at Moscow, that destroyers and surface combatant vessels of lesser tonnage would be divided equally, among the Four Powers. Crucially, though, MacArthur also declared that any other IJN vessel 'either wrecked, sunk or... needing more than 60-days [repair] to place in operable condition' was also to be scrapped 'on economic grounds'.[27] This new qualification proved almost all embracing and vastly reduced the number of ships available for division. Since the repair costs to the vessels were to be entirely Japan's, scrappage on the economic grounds was to Japan's advantage. Here again MacArthur was acting unilaterally to implement a policy that directly reduced Japan's reparation expenditure. (Other policies, such as the yen-export ban and the demand that Britain pay JSP for labour in sterling have already been noted.) MacArthur's HQ was determined to keep a tight hold of Japan's purse strings. The precious steel from the scrapped warships went straight to feed Japan's domestic demand, so reducing expensive non-yen ore imports.

In reality, the commitment of the United States to 'equal treatment' to the Four Allied Powers over division of Japanese military assets was restricted to the known and public arena. Advanced Japanese military technology was declared top secret by the US and access restricted to equipment or certain data. (This mainly covered prototype jet-aircraft designs but also included detailed records of biological and temperature 'experiments' on civilians and PW by the notorious Unit 731. Unit 731's scientists were given immunity from prosecution in return for co-operation on American research programmes.[28]) Naval vessels in the top-secret category included the I-400 class of long-range submarines that carried three bomber aircraft in a watertight hangar. The United States Navy intercepted two I-400s, sailing under surrender-compliant 'black flags' in mid-August 1945 after abandoning an attack on the US invasion fleet at Ulthi Atoll. Although perfectly seaworthy, these 122m-long, 12m-wide, 6,000 ton-displacement, state-of-the-art giants were sunk in May and July 1946 shortly after requests were received from Moscow to inspect them.[29]

It was not until February 1947 that just 64 former IJN vessels were offered in lots of 16 to be drawn by representatives of the Four Powers in Tokyo.[30]

(By this time, *Kashima*, *Kumano Maru* and *Hosho* had been scrapped, and *Sakawa* and the badly damaged battleship *Nagato* had been sunk at Bikini Atoll as part of the Operation Crossroads nuclear tests 'Abel' and 'Baker' in July 1946. Britain had also scuttled large but damaged captured vessels such as the cruisers *Takao* and *Myoko* in the Malacca Strait in late 1946.) By definition, therefore, the already 'demilitarised' vessels available to the United States (which intended to scrap its allotment immediately), Britain, China and the USSR were relatively small ships requiring yet further repair or fitting out. They were all unsuitable for use as ocean-going troop transports in Southeast Asia. Even simply taking delivery of these ships presented fresh financial and logistic difficulties for the Royal Navy. SCAP's conditions were strict. Britain was permitted to nominate one port, not further west than Singapore, to receive all the ships in one flotilla. Their Japanese crews were to be shipped home by return and reimbursement of all fuel used by the 16 vessels from Japan to the nominated port was to be made in kind or in gold dollars.[31] Thus the British spoils from the demise of the Imperial Japanese Navy were far from the expected shipping bonus.

AMERICAN IRRITATION OVER DEFINITIONS OF 'CONTROL'

In December 1946 MacArthur dealt the British three blows that had a devastating cumulative effect on SEALF repatriation plans. Unaware of his forthcoming announcement on the scrapping of many IJN vessels, Britain sent a request to GHQ SCAP for four Japanese naval auxiliaries and Japanese crews for use in the repatriation programme. These vessels had been captured in the enlarged SEAC theatre but had returned to Japan, nominally for repair after repatriation voyages. In Tokyo the response from GHQ SCAP was, at best, polite bafflement and then to question the reasoning behind British intentions. Where, MacArthur asked, was the 'British shipping' referred to in previous proposals, so that 'phased release [of JSP] would continue throughout 1947'. Almost as an aside, he also instructed SEALF to return the four merchantmen currently on loan with their Japanese crews in preparation for their own long-delayed demobilisation. With what must have been considerable alarm, Whitehall discovered that the earlier signal to MacArthur giving assurance over repatriation had not read 'British-controlled shipping' but 'British shipping'. Uncomfortably for London, this ambiguous description encompassed not just the continued use of the SCAP-supplied but 'British-controlled' Japanese merchantmen, but also the anticipated capacity from the final division of IJN vessels. Even more calamitous for the British position was that JSP-repatriation planning from SEALF had been based not only on the assumed control of a number of Japanese ships but also, and crucially, that the crews of all these ships would be Japanese. In fact no other 'British shipping' had been allocated to the first months of the repatriation programme whatsoever. Without the SCAP-supplied vessels there was quite simply no lift capacity at all.

In response London apologised to MacArthur for the error and explained the importance of the ships—now any ships—and also the need for Japanese crews. MacArthur, however, promptly rejected the request declaring he no longer had the facilities and that crews for Japanese merchant shipping coming under SEALF control later in the year would not be available.[32] This unexpected but desperately embarrassing reprise of British shipping and manpower shortages threatened to undo months of negotiations with the State Department and MacArthur over JSP. SEALF stressed to the British COS that the provision of services in Southeast Asia was still dire and the overall labour position unchanged. It was also quite clear that SCAP was not going to supply the requested Japanese crews for the Japanese merchant ships. In early 1947 SEALF produced an approximate repatriation schedule based on a 3,000-per-month lift capacity. Even this allowed for no movement before March 1947 after which 1,000 JSP would be shipped per month until September (increasing to 6,000) and from October to December (up to 11,000). A scheduled December departure date carried with it the risk that any delays would result in JSP returning to Japan in January 1948 or even later.

By the end of January 1947 SEALF had lost all confidence in dealing with MacArthur, concluding in a signal to the COS that, 'We feel further approach to SCAP on our level would be fruitless'.[33] American irritation over this development was obvious and unrestrained. MacArthur's vexation was clear. British interpretation of the term 'British shipping', he signalled, 'had caused considerable concern'. Repatriation facilities in Japan had been 'reduced to a minimum predicated on [the fact that the] British would furnish shipping and crews...It will be appreciated that maintenance of repatriation shipping and reception centres in Japan over an indefinite period...is an unwarranted extravagance'. MacArthur then took the initiative, proposing a sweeping solution to assist the British 'within the limit of his reduced capability'. The proviso, however, was that such assistance had to 'result in the early repatriation of Japanese personnel'. His conditions left little room for counter proposals.

In Whitehall the air of gloom generated the desperate hope that a personal request to MacArthur, bypassing SEALF, might work in Britain's favour and so secure the ships and crews. This heavy burden fell on Britain's diplomatic representatives (UKLM) in Tokyo. Previously the UKLM had championed Britain's decision to retain JSP despite SCAP's offer to ship them all home within 1946. MacArthur had given way in November 1946, stating to General

33. The Japanese War Memorial on Mt Cameron in Hong Kong in 1945. (© CW)

Gairdner that he had been charged with the responsibility of returning the Japanese and had allotted shipping for that purpose. Gairdner's assurance that 'British shipping' would be used for those JSP had convinced MacArthur 'that he had discharged his responsibility in the matter and took no further interest'. At the time, London had been gratified by this apparent lack of concern, particularly as MacArthur had downplayed Gairdner's question on whether retention of the Japanese was in fact a clear breach of Potsdam (see Chapter 4). Encouragingly, MacArthur had said the Declaration 'defined no deadline' for repatriation.[34]

Within a week of receiving MacArthur's enquiry, Sir Alvary Gascoigne, the 'political representative' of Great Britain and thus Britain's senior diplomat in Japan, replied on behalf of the British Government. Gascoigne was a former soldier who had known Yoshida Shigeru, the new Japanese prime minister for over 20 years.[35] (He would develop a good relationship with MacArthur and remain in Tokyo until 1951.) Obsequiously Gascoigne explained that 'British-controlled shipping' did indeed include the four Japanese merchant ships and, most importantly, their crews.[36] These crews, he stressed, amounted 'only to about 400 men in all'. Gascoigne must have swallowed hard indeed to admit that Great Britain could not find 400 sailors, merchant or naval, to crew four small vessels. Certainly men were available in Britain but they were far away. Large wartime merchant shipping losses, slow replacement building and Royal Navy demobilisation had left a surfeit of unemployed, experienced seamen. The underlying factor was, once again, cost. British pleas even extended to suggesting that Japanese crews previously earmarked for repatriation 'would react favourably in the knowledge that they were bringing home their countrymen'.[37] Britain and SEALF's problem was two-fold. The first was a reluctance to pay peacetime union rates to jobless British sailors. Linked with this issue was the fact that the Japanese ships were, as the Admiralty admitted, old, 'in pretty poor shape' and 'barely sea-worthy'.[38] Safety concerns over British crews would have required much-reduced passenger-load limits, so greatly increasing the number of return trips, expenditure and overall time necessary to complete repatriation.[39]

The second but far more major problem remained SEALF's ongoing dependence on JSP labour. London stood firm, pressing Gascoigne to negotiate for both the Japanese crews and permission to complete repatriation 'by, but not before, the end of 1947'. The alternative, explained a beseeching Gascoigne to MacArthur, was further delay:

> I am to stress to you, General, that the rehabilitation of British territories…would be very gravely prejudiced indeed if all the JSP were to be withdrawn before the end of the present year. In these circumstances I am therefore to ask you to be so good as to assist the British authorities by furnishing them with Japanese crews to man the four British-controlled Japanese vessels in question (as no alternative crews are available) on the condition that the Japanese Personnel are returned to Japan by the end of 1947. I am further to say that if the British authorities cannot make use of the services of Japanese seamen for these purposes, they will not be able to use the four Japanese ships in question and that this would mean an intolerable strain on the extremely limited amount of British shipping at their disposal.

Thus wrote a senior diplomatic representative of one victorious Great Power to another.[40]

MacArthur was unimpressed. At the beginning of February 1947 he turned the screw. He informed Gascoigne of his 'concerns over the new interpretation placed on the term British shipping by SEALF'. Based on his HQ's 'own interpretation', JSP reception facilities had been reduced with the 'expectation that the British would furnish the necessary ships and crews to conduct the deferred repatriation'. This criticism was sugared by the offer of assistance despite reduced American facilities, 'provided that such assistance would result in the early return of Japanese surrendered personnel in the South East Asia Command'.[41] MacArthur's interpretation of 'early' was before 1 June 1947 for all Japanese including JSP, PW (except those held in connection with war crimes) and any civilians. Massive potential American lift-capability was also revealed almost casually. GHQ SCAP would furnish the necessary shipping once the British had made known their requirements for February, March, April and May 1947. There was a monthly limit of '30,000 spaces'. The British had just to supply fuel. There was also more than a hint of vexation in the offer–cum–instruction. It closed with a curt 'details concerning disposition of Japanese ships recovered in SEAC and now in Japan will be held in abeyance pending receipt of comments on above proposal'.[42]

In London, the MOT had reported that repatriation schedules could not be drawn up without knowing whether the United Kingdom would have use of Japanese ships and crews. In a further unwelcome surprise for the Foreign Office the MOT added that it would be 'impracticable' without 'major repercussions to present military and civil shipping programmes to carry out the proposed repatriation programme solely in British shipping'. Dominating all policy-making was the overriding concern of the Treasury to avoid spending dollars. There was no way around the fact that use of US shipping would incur dollar expenses. British use of the Japanese merchant ships was consequently of immense importance to the War Office and Treasury.[43] The War Office dug in its heels in its guidance to SEALF:

> The question of the retention of JSP until the end of 1947 has already been exhaustively examined and has been approved at the highest level...Based on this implied agreement certain essential work has been put in hand. To advance the date of completion of repatriation at this stage would have serious repercussions in South East Asia on the local civil economy and the Services' accommodation and maintenance.[44]

British officials allowed themselves to feel aggrieved. No doubt growing frustration over policy decisions being repeatedly stymied or vetoed by the United States, or at least perceived that way, played a part. Britain after all was not the only Ally with JSP to repatriate. The Soviet Union held far more and the few, limited reports emerging from Russia suggested they were being kept in appalling conditions.[45] US–Soviet relations were poor and worsening. Russian negotiators had already refused one offer from MacArthur to repatriate 360,000 JSP per month. When in late 1946 a SCAP–Soviet deal was agreed to return 50,000 JSP per month, in a repatriation programme running for two-and-a-half years, unfavourable comparisons were drawn in London with MacArthur's apparent willingness to assist the Soviet Union but not Britain:

> We still consider final withdrawal of JSP before end 1947 unacceptable. [It is] clear SCAP is not going to comply with British request for Japanese crews for Jap ships. If SCAP proposals accepted using Liberty Ships average capacity of 2500 JSP on 1946 terms, namely 300 gold dollars per day, estimated 12 Liberties for three months at total cost to British Treasury of about three and one quarter million dollars. SCAP has now agreed with Russians to repatriate them at 50,000 per month. Russians hold 1.5m JSP so… present agreement with Russians means 2.5 years. From this we conclude that SCAP is prepared to keep repatriation facilities and reception centres in operation for the Russians but not for the British.[46]

It was a touchy subject within London's corridors of power. The Foreign Office sought to maintain American goodwill but the Treasury remained committed to avoiding dollar expenditure, while the War Office, having championed SEALF's case, was unwilling to put it under opposite pressure. Even long-discarded options, such as phased repatriation, were reconsidered in order to make as little use as possible of US shipping. There was no flexibility in the British position. Yet the artless British plan was to work to keep the American offer open until the chance of Japanese crews—'if only as a means of saving dollars'—was definitely lost. Aware of rising frustration and what was at stake, London also felt the need to caution SEALF that it was 'inadvisable to make any reference at this stage to SCAP's reported agreement for the repatriation of the JSP in Russian hands'.[47]

MACARTHUR ADVISES CAUTION

Though extensive assistance with shipping had been secured, the cumulative effects of repeated British diplomatic and logistic failings were not easily discounted. American goodwill was a finite commodity and it threatened to run out. In Tokyo MacArthur gave Gascoigne a private, blunt verbal assessment of British JSP policy. When the transcript was read in London it no doubt caused immense concern, particularly at the Foreign Office. MacArthur was evidently unimpressed by British promises. SEALF's statements had made it 'obvious to him that the British did not mean to keep their pledge of completing repatriation of Japanese Surrendered Personnel from South East Asia by the end of 1947'.[48] Coming from the senior American commander in the Far East, this criticism was certainly unwelcome; coming from a potential American presidential candidate, it bode ill. MacArthur's advice was for Britain to consider the wider picture in Southeast Asia and not SEALF's immediate difficulties:

> From his [MacArthur's] intimate knowledge of this question, and the repercussions which there had already been in the United States and in Japan (…he mentioned the State Dept's most bitter feelings at our retention of these Japanese during 1947, and that he was being continually bombarded by the Japanese PM on the subject) he felt sure that the UK Government would find themselves most awkwardly placed in world opinion if their present pledge was not kept.[49]

As MacArthur saw it, any local benefit derived from the services of 90,000 JSP would be completely outweighed 'by world wide odium which would fall upon us'. In failing to repatriate the Japanese Britain risked an 'intense anti-British campaign in the United States, and much anti-British propaganda in Japan'. There was also the risk that the Russians, who had agreed to repatriate not less than 50,000 JSP a month, would 'beat us to it'.

Gascoigne's opinion was that MacArthur was sincerely concerned over what he termed 'the stain which would blemish the honour of the United Kingdom' should Britain not fulfil its promise to meet the date. This warning put the Foreign Office on notice, for MacArthur's view was almost certainly that of the State Department. Even Gascoigne himself felt it necessary to close his letter with his own cautionary note, vouching for the 'strong feelings which permeate both local American officials, and Japanese, regarding our delay in this repatriation'.[50]

To considerable Foreign Office dismay, MacArthur's suspicions were accurate. Even as Britain was hoping to obtain use of American shipping by any means, in London the Joint Advisory Planning Staff (JAPS) were preparing a draft proposal to the Chiefs of Staff that would effectively require Britain to renege on the 1947 undertaking because of the lack of labour. Evidently from the JAPS/WO/CO viewpoint the undertaking to the Americans was not a primary consideration. The draft proposal read:

> In spite of the Foreign Office's request...it may be necessary to seek the approval of the Defence Committee to slow down the repatriation of JSP during the latter months of 1947 owing to our inability to provide alternative military labour... although we can agree rate of repatriation... [a] firm decision on the date...should not be approved until we have examined the problem of their replacement....[51]

Such a step was anathema to the Foreign Office, which went on the offensive to protect what little favour it had managed to retain with the Americans over the retention issue. To the MOT mandarins' evident surprise the Foreign Office briefed directly against the MOT's position in Cabinet discussions. Official files record the MOT's discomfort, noting it was 'unfortunate that the Foreign Office minister recommended the opposite course'. A more pithy internal memo states that the Foreign Office representative 'killed the proposal with one blow'.[52]

Reports of the death of proposals to delay were premature. In February 1947 the MOT asked the COS to re-examine the question as 'JSP could still not be repatriated during 1947 without disrupting military and civil shipping programmes'. The MOT suggested 'delaying completion of the repatriation of JSP until some time in 1948' and that the extension 'would probably have little effect on the morale of JSP'.[53] For the Foreign Office, the 1948 proposal brought with it potentially catastrophic consequences for Anglo-American relations. It determined to resist, trying to impress upon the Chiefs, the War Office and the Minister for Defence, A. V. Alexander, that agreement with the Americans, even for an end of 1946 date, had been difficult enough and it had only been forthcoming for the end of 1947 on the 'definite...undertaking to use British shipping'. Senior Foreign Office officials made it clear that they were 'extremely reluctant' to have to inform the Americans that Britain no longer felt bound by its earlier assurance that repatriation would be completed within 1947. In addition, they reminded the COS, the MOT, the Burma Office and the Colonial Office of the 'serious deterioration' in the morale of

Japanese in Southeast Asia, and that there was a danger of them becoming a liability rather than an asset, 'both now, in South-East Asia and ultimately as a nucleus of feeling unfriendly to Great Britain'. As far as the Foreign Office was concerned if the choice was to speed up repatriation or to delay it, it strongly preferred the former, and that SEALF should not hope for 1948 but prepare for life without JSP.[54]

On 1 March 1947, to London's enormous relief MacArthur replied, giving SEALF 'complete satisfaction' over vessels—agreeing to supply additional and far larger capacity ships—and, importantly, Japanese crews as needed. Once again a local, British-created problem had, apparently, been solved by sweeping American generosity.[55] Yet differences of opinion between the Foreign Office on one side, and the War Office and the MOT on the other over repatriation as a shipping priority were clear. Almost simultaneously, the two ministries submitted opposing arguments for and against retention. Alfred Barnes, the Minister for Transport, once again argued for a delay into 1948 on the grounds of shortages and other priorities, including the fact that JSP were employed on 'essential defence and rehabilitation work'. In Barnes's opinion, Britain's shipping shortage was so acute that the diversion of vessels for repatriation would not 'justify the sacrifice of other essential work'.[56] It is possible that the Foreign Office would have lost its battle had not General MacArthur added his weight, privately, to the debate via his pithy comments reported by Gascoigne. Unexpectedly, however, the additional revelation of Anglo-American difficulties in a Singapore newspaper article headlined 'Jap Repatriation is TOP SECRET', caught SEALF and London by surprise:

> There has been considerable trouble in reaching agreement over shipping to take JSP away from Malayan shores between SEALF in Singapore and Gen. MacArthur's Headquarters in Japan. The Army in Singapore has indicated that it does not want to ship all the JSP in Singapore and Malaya back to Japan in a short period and have asked the War Office in London for permission to retain the Japs for a few months longer and repatriate them all in small batches completing the job before the end of the year. But General MacArthur has said he can only supply transport for these JSPs…in the early part of the year… There are about 80,000 Japanese still to be repatriated and of these 46,000 are in Malaya.

SEALF HQ acted quickly to persuade the press, who were 'believed to have factual information', to suppress the story. London was informed that it was confident it would not spread beyond Singapore. (The signal forwarding the newspaper the article to London was itself classified 'Top Secret'.)[57] How far this report influenced the COS is a matter of conjecture, but previous press comment had indeed had a disproportionate effect on British JSP policy. Certainly the Government knew it had no monopoly on information concerning JSP and that it faced criticism from the most powerful man in Asia. By early April confirmation from GHQ SCAP of the availability of British-controlled Japanese shipping and additional American-controlled shipping to boost the lift to 15,000 made the end of 1947 a viable date for the completion of repatriation. The COS decided that in light of the UK shipping position the offer from SCAP, while not the most advantageous, left them with 'little choice' in the matter.[58] Britain rolled over, though still sought assurances from SCAP that should any of the Japanese ships break down or sink it would not have to supply replacements.

The reasoning behind MacArthur's 'change of mind' over shipping is instructive. His ascribed anti-British feelings proved to be without foundation. MacArthur's priority, of course, was to carry out his orders from Washington. These required that the Japanese be returned. His initial denial of crews simply reflected commitment to his own existing obligations: the reconstruction of the peacetime economy in Japan and the Pacific. In fact, he had already promised the American Federation of Labor (AFL), representatives of the main American merchant seamen's unions, as well as the Japanese Government not to employ JSP labour on ships working in international waters after June 1946.[59] Understandably, MacArthur was most reluctant to break his word for the sake of four rather insignificant merchant vessels. Once a temporary agreement for repatriation ships from SEALF had been negotiated with the AFL and others, American assistance flowed almost on demand.

NOTES TO CHAPTER 7

1.   WO to COS, 19 Dec. 1946. CAB 122/1183.
2.   Cabinet Offices to COS, 24 Dec. CO 537/2493.
3.   CO memo, 30 Jan 1947. CO 537/2493.
4.   Governor of Burma to Sec. State for Burma, 13 Feb. 1947. CO 537/2493.
5.   John H. McEnery, *Epilogue in Burma: The Military Dimension of British Withdrawal* (Tunbridge Wells:1990), 94.)
6.   British Defence Committee (BDCSEA) Report, 'Employment of JSP'. Jan. 1947. CO 537/2493.
7.   FO to ALFSEA, 29 Jan. 1946. WO 203/2727.
8.   BDCSEA Report, 6.
9.   Ibid.
10.   See *Hansard*, 8 Oct. 1946, Vol. 427, cc 38–39.
11.   BDCSEA Report, 10.
12.   PAOC to COS, 'Retention of JSP in SEA during 1947', 14 Feb. 1947. CAB 122/1183.
13.   Jones, *Conflict and Confrontation in South East Asia*, 3. Major works on this subject include J. de V. Allen, *The Malayan Union* (New Haven, 1967); A. J. Stockwell, *British Policy and Malay Politics during the Malayan Union Experiment, 1942–1948* (Kuala Lumpur, 1979); and Albert Lau, *The Malayan Union Controversy, 1942–1948* (Singapore, 1991).
14.   BDCSEA Report, 10.
15.   SEALF to War Office. CO 537/2493.
16.   File note, 25 Apr. 1947. CO 537/2493.
17.   PAOC, 'Repatriation of JSP in SEA.' 24 Apr. 1947. CO 537/2494.
18.   SEALF to War Office, 4 Mar 1947. CO 537/2493.
19.   SEALF to COS, 31 Jan 1947. WO 203/5969.
20.   SEALF to War Office, 4 Mar 1947. CO 537/2493.
21.   SEACOS 809, 31 Jan. 1947. CAB 122/1183.
22.   See n. 1.
23.   WO to COS (with 9 Dec. FO Memo to Cabinet Offices), 19 Dec. 1946. CAB 122/1183.
24.   FO Memorandum, 'Disposal of the Japanese Fleet', 23 July 1946. CAB 134/596.
25.   Ibid.
26.   For a photograph taken aboard *Katsuragi* at Rabaul, see AWM 099799.
27.   State Dept to Foreign Office, 'Disposal of Japanese Navy', 27 Feb 1947. CAB 122/1183.
28.   Peter Williams and David Wallace, *Unit 731: The Japanese Army's Secret of Secrets* (London: 1989), 207.
29.   Fukui Shizuo, *The Japanese Navy at the End of World War II* (Greenwich, CN., 1947), 35. See also 'Japan's Super Subs', National Geographic Television, 2009.
30.   'Disposal of Japanese Navy', 27 Feb. 1947. CAB 122/1183.
31.   State Dept to Foreign Office, 'Disposal of Japanese Navy', 27 Feb 1947. CAB 122/1183.
32.   SCAP to UKLM, 3 Feb. 1947. FO 262/2054.
33.   SEALF to COS, 25 Jan 1947. CAB 122/1183.
34.   UKLM to FO, 8 Nov. 1946. FO 262/2054.

35.   Peter Lowe, 'Britain and the Recovery of Japan post-1945', in *Britain and Japan in the Twentieth Century*, eds, Towle and Kosuge, 98.
36.   UKLM to SCAP, 8 Feb. 1947. FO 262/2054.
37.   SEALF to SCAP, 17 Jan 1947. CAB 122/1183.
38.   SEALF to SCAP, 17 Jan. 1947. WO 208/3910.
39.   Ibid.
40.   UKLM to GHQ SCAP, 8 Feb. 1947. FO 262/2054.
41.   GHQ SCAP to UKLM, 3 Feb. 1947. FO 262/2054.
42.   SCAP to SEALF, 25 Jan 1947. CAB 122/1183.
43.   PAOC to COS, 14 Feb 1947. CAB 122/1183.
44.   WO to SEALF (COSSEA 604), 24 Feb 1947. CAB 122/1183.
45.   Nimmo, *Behind a Curtain of Silence*, 39–65.
46.   SACSEA to COS (SEACOS 809), 31 Jan 1947. CAB 122/1183.
47.   WO to SEALF, 24 Feb. 1947. CAB 122/1183.
48.   UKLM to FO, 12 Mar. 1947. FO 262/2054.
49.   Ibid.
50.   Ibid.
51.   JPS for COS, 'Retention of JSP in SEA during 1947', 22 Jan. 1947. CO 537/2493.
52.   CO memo. 30 Jan. 1947. CO 537/2493.
53.   PAOC to COS, 24 Feb. 1947. CAB 122/1183.
54.   FO to COS, 6 Mar. 1947. CAB 122/1183.
55.   PAOC to COS, 25 Apr. 1947. CO 537/2493.
56.   MOT to FO, 5 Mar. 1947. CO 537/2493.
57.   Singapore Free Press, 24 Mar. 1947 in War Office to BAS, Washington/UKLM 27 Mar. 1947. CAB 122/1183..)
58.   FO to COS, 7 Apr. 1947. CAB 122/1183.
59.   UKLM to FO, 9 Feb. 1947. CO 537/2493.

8

TAKING THE KING'S SHILLINGS
THE QUESTION OF WORKING PAY FOR JSP

All JSP are now back in Japan, and although so far no awkward questions have been asked about their payment for the work they have done in South East Asia, there is always a possibility that the matter might be raised.

—Foreign Office internal memo, 6 November 1947[1]

Negotiations over shipping for the repatriation of Japanese Surrendered Personnel (JSP), fraught though they had been for Britain's Government and diplomats, had at least been confined to representatives of the American Government and military who had remained relatively discreet. From mid- to late 1947, however, a number of political and financial issues related to the retained Japanese developed almost simultaneously. While not necessarily public, these 'noises off' continued to demand the full attention of the Foreign Office. Among them was a potentially embarrassing proposal concerning JSP from the Soviet Union to the Far Eastern Commission (FEC), which rather alarmingly threatened to result in a British vote against the United States. Retention of JSP even briefly attracted the attention of the Vatican. In addition, differing stances on a suitable working-pay settlement continued to ruffle Anglo-American relations. Proposed JSP pay rates were also questioned by the International Committee of the Red Cross (ICRC), which accused Britain of serious underpayment for JSP when compared with German prisoners of war. All these issues would keep legal, financial and ethical pressure upon Britain until the departure of the last repatriation ship from British territory in Southeast Asia in late October 1947.

FURTHER POST-POTSDAM 'EMBARRASSMENT' AT THE FEC

Even as the Foreign Office congratulated itself on having finally ensured that the end of 1947 deadline for the completion of JSP repatriation would be met, so extricating Britain from its vulnerable position over retention, the JSP issue still threatened further international embarrassment. Other players were also involved. American–Soviet friction over repatriation numbers and schedules for Japanese in Soviet custody was almost a constant source of irritation between the other two Great Powers.[2] Indeed, it is likely that Britain's own retention of JSP severely inhibited the United States' responses to Soviet obfuscation over the issue, or at least forced Washington and SCAP to temper any criticism in official statements or in public meetings of the FEC and Allied Council for Japan (ACJ), and in any announcements in the Japanese press about Soviet-held JSP.

For its part, the Soviet Union was well aware that it was not the sole member of the Allies detaining Japanese. This allowed it a number of opportunities to create Anglo-American discord, or exacerbate it where any was perceived, such as the Soviet proposal to reclassify JSP as PW discussed previously. Another example occurred in the first week of April 1947, again at the FEC. On this occasion the Soviet Union proposed adding an additional paragraph to a standard FEC memorandum to GHQ SCAP. It read simply, 'The final completion of Disarmament and Demobilisation of the Japanese Armed Forces to be carried out in the shortest possible time'. Oddly this broad text was unacceptable to the United States.[3] Interestingly, however, Britain found itself in an uncomfortable position, finding both replacement texts proposed by the Americans 'undesirable'. The US draft texts read:

(i) 'The final completion of Disarmament and Demobilisation of those Japanese Armed Forces not yet returned to Japan should be carried out in the shortest possible time.' Or
(ii) 'It has been the view of all Members of the FEC that the final Disarmament and Demobilisation of all Japanese Armed Forces in existence at the time of the Japanese surrender should be completed at the earliest possible time and the terms of the Potsdam Declaration regarding the return of those forces to Japan should be fulfilled. [The]…purpose of

this document is to formulise a FEC policy with regard to the principles which have in the past governed disarmament and demobilisation of the Japanese Armed Forces and which will continue to apply to the control of military activity in Japan and to such further disarmament and demobilisation as may be required.[4]

From London's perspective both texts exposed Britain to potential criticism. The first version, laying emphasis on the Japanese still outside Japan, was 'embarrassing' to Britain 'in view of the numbers' of JSP still in Southeast Asia. The second version, citing Article 9 of the Potsdam Declaration—that 'Japanese military forces, after being completely disarmed shall be permitted to return to their homes with the opportunity to lead peaceful and productive lives'—was also considered 'embarrassing'.[5] Ironically, London preferred the Soviet version but signalled British representatives (Lord Inverchapel and Sir George Sansom) not to give early open support for this version to avoid upsetting the United States. Indeed, the Foreign Office were perplexed as to why the United States was objecting in the first place, since the Soviet version could, the Foreign Office argued, be construed as referring 'only to the armed forces outside Japan'.[6]

Once again the 'stop-go' procedures at the FEC and ACJ let Britain off the hook. Fortunately for the Foreign Office, this particular motion was not pursued by the Soviet Union. It was just one of many that fell foul of FEC infighting and procedural delays. Thus there was no call for a British vote, which would in any case have gone to the shorter American draft despite its undesirability. There was apparently no question of a public vote against the United States—which would quite possibly have been a post-war first—over an issue as short-term as JSP repatriation.

THE POLITICS OF PAYMENT FOR LABOUR

With repatriation shipping secured for 1947 London again returned to the problem of recording work and calculating pay earned. SEAC's failure to keep records of work performed by JSP had ruined earlier Treasury and War Office plans to issue individual Working Pay Credits (WPC). Since Japanese currency could not be used in British Territory, WPC were once more the payment vehicle of choice, and yet again, despite SCAP's known objections, the intention was to make them redeemable in yen against the Japanese Government. London considered this to be reasonable on the grounds that in the near future Japan would in any case be required to make massive reparations payments to Britain.[7] Working pay due to JSP was estimated at £1,500,000. There was also an intention to claim back from Japan the sum of £1,800,000 paid to the US to cover JSP repatriation in 1946.[8] The co-operation of South-East Asia Land Forces (SEALF) was crucial and the Command was promised wide discretion in adjusting any figures prepared in London.[9] New proposals were submitted for SEALF Area Commands to categorise skilled and unskilled tasks, and then to log working hours of individual JSP to be recorded on WPCs. While there was still determination in London not to make any sterling payment, SCAP's opposition had forced the Treasury to concede the possibility of paying up 'to ensure [the WPC] are honoured if the US Government and SCAP stand their ground'.[10]

For all the enthusiasm in Whitehall over the new scheme, however, no progress could be made until SCAP approved redemption of WPCs in Japan. This proved to be a contentious issue. British representatives in Washington, pressed by London, repeatedly asked for confirmation from the State Department, stressing that payments were not to be made in sterling but in Japanese currency at a rate decided by the Japanese Government. No such confirmation was received. Clearly, the State Department was most reluctant to direct SCAP to order the Japanese Government to honour WPCs. As seen over the question of selection and supply of reparation-quota shipping, SCAP was already acting to reduce Japanese overseas expenditure across the board. This was another very early sign of the divergence of British and American policies over reparations sought from Japan. In the end, Britain's diplomats got nowhere. The best they could offer London was a 'hope' to amend a paper before the FEC that would 'instruct SCAP to issue the necessary order'.[11]

A glaring problem with this revised plan for WPC was that it did not address the issue of the previous 18 months of unrecorded and unpaid JSP labour. The proposed solution was an estimate of the 'total amount of work done by JSP from the time they first commenced a full working programme… until June 1st 1947' (ie, the start of recorded working hours). The 'most equitable and convenient' date chosen as the starting point was 1 June 1946. The UK Treasury's rationale for choosing this date was the assertion that JSP were not in full employment until 'about then'. This date also, conveniently, allowed a 12-month calculation. Somewhat ambitiously, this total was then to be divided proportionally between the approximately 60,000 JSP still in SEALF and the approximately 40,000 already repatriated. Deductions from this total were to include estimates for sick days and rest days for each individual. Another potential drawback was that no records were available to

SEALF of the names, units or addresses of the already repatriated Japanese. As ever, the Treasury was insistent on precise records. Eventually it decided it could calculate the total payment due to this group but it had no way of allocating individual shares. Compromise was the only option, the preferred

34. JSP returning from Sumatra arrive at Otake, Japan in October 1946. (AWM)

method being an FEC policy decision to instruct the Japanese Government to make a lump sum available and then to divide it as equitably as possible between JSP known to have been repatriated from Southeast Asia.

While the June 1946 start date might have come as a surprise to those JSP working for military and civil authorities in Singapore from as early as October 1945 onwards, there was at least recognition in London, even though detailed calculation was impossible, that 'JSP had…worked and some reward has been earned'. (At the same time, a counter argument that they had 'only been reconstructing what they had destroyed' during the war, and consequently deserved no pay was discussed among the War Office, Foreign Office and Treasury, but held to be 'inadmissible'.)[12] Various proposals were submitted to resolve this issue. SEALF suggested that a gratuity be paid to all JSP for the period spent in Southeast Asia irrespective of work done, or any difference between skilled and non-skilled work. To the Treasury the term 'gratuity' was unacceptable as it was 'liable to give the wrong impression of any payment that is made'.

The principle of the one-work category was given further weight when the Japanese HQ intervened and suggested, in the interest of fairness and in light of the lack of records, abandoning distinctions between classes of labour and allocating a flat rate to all.[13] This was quickly accepted as providing the only solution to attempt the calculation of individual work records. Similarly, a single block or lump sum WPC was envisaged for all JSP repatriated prior to 1 June 47.[14] Having justified the formula, the Treasury, perhaps anticipating having to pay out in sterling, outlined its required deductions. Treasury calculations assumed that 10 percent of JSP (approximately 10,000 men) were likely to be unavailable for work either through sickness or injury on any one day. Other deductions or charges were to be calculated for the value of 'amenities' (including clothing, soap, razor blades, toothpowder) and 'holidays' (ie, weekly rest days). The figure of 10 percent seems arbitrary and high. There are no records of strikes or 'work to rule' by JSP. It is not surprising as refusing to work would have required direct insubordination to a Japanese superior, and such confrontation was not in the Japanese military mentality. Consequently there are few directly comparable figures for 'work-shy' Italian or German prisoners in Britain. JSP were not volunteers, as were Italian 'co-operators'. Fewer than 60 percent of Italian prisoners chose to volunteer for labour in Britain when wages were raised from 2 shillings to 7 shillings per week.[15] This probably had much to do with a reasonable level of satisfaction with their basic conditions and the fact that they were under also PW Convention protection. Non-working JSP received a lower-calorific ration. One assumption is that high incidences of sickness or injury among JSP were acceptable to the War Office.

In a final, payment-limiting twist, only JSP working in British territory were to be covered by this scheme. In this way two of the most contentious areas of British use of JSP—French Indo-China and Indonesia—were therefore removed from the pay calculations and, perhaps with an eye to potential future claims, denied legitimacy. (JSP in Java, for example, were used as dock labour unloading British naval vessels, including military transports, from early October 1945 to November 1946 when they were handed over to Dutch control until June 1947.) As SEAC was a joint Allied but British-led Command, the sovereign territory in which particular JSP were put to work would seem to be irrelevant in formulating criteria as to whether payment for 'SEAC work' was due. No payments appear to have been received by JSP for labour from the Netherlands Government.[16] This is consistent with Allied claims addressed in the 1952 peace treaty with Japan (see below).

While there was limited admission by Britain of the use of JSP in a military role, the decision to ignore JSP labour in those volatile territories also meant that there was no official British record that JSP had been retained or utilised for military labour purposes 'near a front line', or placed in known 'dangerous locations' after surrender to British forces, which would have been a clear breach of the 1929 PW Convention. However, there are reports on

35. JSP enter the Ujina Repatriation Centre in June 1946. (AWM)

camp 'activities' and labour by 'Japanese prisoners' by the ICRC which made inspections of the Java camps in early 1946.[17]

PAY CALCULATIONS

While awaiting approval from Washington and Tokyo for the revised WPC scheme, Britain's Treasury and War Office went ahead with preparations for payments. By necessity these calculations included a number of assumptions on JSP numbers at various dates. The Treasury concluded that there were 85,000 JSP in SEALF from 1 June 1946 to 1 April 1947. After April 1947, there were 72,830 minus 15,868 repatriated, leaving approximately 60,000 on 1 June 1947. JSP worked for 48 hours per week for approximately 50 weeks in the year, allowing for a total of 50 non-working days in the year. The rate of pay was three farthings (¾d) per hour. Three pence per week for the whole year was to be deducted for cigarettes, soap, clothing, toothpowder and so on. The Treasury's final calculation was therefore:

Maximum hours worked per year per man	= 2160
	(90% x 2400)
2160 hours @ ¾d per hour	= £6-15s 0d.
Amenities etc. 3d per week for 52 weeks	= £- 13s. 0d.
Maximum earnings of one JSP	= £6- 2s. 0d.
Average strength for year 82,777	
Gross sum… = £6 2s 0d x 82,777	= £504,940.[18]

All that was required to put the plan in motion was General MacArthur's approval of the issue of WPCs. Even though this had not been forthcoming by late June 1947, the Foreign Office was beginning to relax. It took obvious satisfaction in a presentation by the Minister for Defence (A. V. Alexander) to the Defence Committee on the repatriation of JSP which stated the intention to inform the detained Japanese that the repatriation programme 'now in full swing would be continued, and that all JSP in British hands…would be returned to Japan by 31 December 1947'. At the same time the Foreign Office advised the Foreign Secretary, Ernest Bevin, that announcements should be made to all concerned:

> Four-fifths of the JSP who fell into our hands at the end of the Pacific War had been repatriated by the end of 1946. The remaining fifth, about 82,000 have been very worried about their prospects of returning home. This has affected their morale and, consequently, their willingness to work. It is most desirable that, now a definite programme for their repatriation has been settled, they should be informed of it.[19]

Japanese repatriation policy had rarely run smoothly for the Foreign Office. Alas the latter half of 1947 was to prove no different. The planned programme was immediately classified 'secret'. Once again the difficulties were not local to Southeast Asia.

A LETTER FROM THE VATICAN

The first of two international third-party interventions in JSP negotiations occurred in mid-June 1947. Mention has been made of the activities in

Japan of interest groups of JSP next-of-kin. These had been established and organised at local and prefectural levels, even petitioning SCAP and the ACJ for prompt repatriation of men in SEALF (see Chapter 6). Returning JSP were able to provide first-hand 'evidence' to these groups, which no doubt encouraged their campaigning efforts. Inevitably support was sought from men of influence, as was the case when groups of JSP returning from Burma and Malaya petitioned the Catholic Archbishop of Tokyo (and later Cardinal), Doi Peter Tatsuo, to seek papal intervention on behalf of still-detained comrades. Their letter to the Archbishop alleged poor living conditions and many deaths among the 35,000 Japanese still in British hands in Burma. Archbishop Doi made no recorded public comment in Japan but the accusations were sufficiently detailed for him to relay them to Rome. In turn the Vatican passed on its concerns to London.[20]

Awkwardly written in (or translated into) English, the complaint acknowledged that Allied prisoners had worked under Japanese control. While Britain's 'original reason' for retention, the need for 'urgent post-war reconstruction work and food production' was guardedly, if somewhat contentiously, acknowledged, 'just like the Japanese army let the British prisoners and workers of Malay, Siam [Thailand] and Burma [build] the railway', there were complaints of physical and mental pain suffered. It closed with an emotive plea:

> But the real work of these Japanese prisoners of war is the service of British officers, and cheap kitchen work... plate washing, [clearing] waste, ditch draining, lavatory [cleaning], loading and unloading at wharfs, which are not post-war reconstruction. They are like slaves I am sure. Official rationing of food for them is said to be 2,500 calories but real rationing is not so much by far.

Other allegations ranged from lack of toothbrushes and toothpowder, to malnutrition from lack of fresh vegetables and meat. More seriously was the assertion that 1,700 sufferers of malaria and stomach and bowel diseases had died since the end of the war due to acute shortage of rations and medicines. The report claimed 'many bloody incidents' in the camps and that widespread uncertainty had bred despair and led to criminal behaviour and 'moral corruption'. Allegations over unpaid labour in 'works corps' were specific, as was a plea to apply the provisions of international law.[21]

In the subsequent letter to the Foreign Office, the Vatican made no comment on the allegations themselves but simply—and probably more effectively—privately urged the prompt repatriation of the Japanese.[22] Official files do not record if this petition was copied to SCAP or senior American Catholic clergy. It is reasonable to assume SCAP also saw it unless it was sent via the Vatican diplomatic bag. Britain's concern, however, was less with the Vatican and SCAP than with future Anglo-Japanese relations. Certainly the Foreign Office moved quickly to refute *almost* all the charges. In Whitehall the concern was that 'The [allegations are] so far removed from the truth that if the Holy See and the Archbishop of Tokyo are not confronted with an answer, it is highly probable that these mistaken ideas will be believed, and may one day even be produced as evidence against His Majesty's Government and Army'.[23]

An open, public denial was not the preferred course of action, at least as long as the Vatican correspondence remained confidential. Britain had no wish to cause friction with Rome or revisit legal and moral arguments over JSP detention, especially as final repatriation was in sight. There was also a small number of influential Japanese who were embracing the Christian faith amidst widespread and growing pacifist sentiment in the country (one later, formal convert being Prime Minister Yoshida Shigeru).[24] General MacArthur, too, was actively encouraging missionaries to visit Japan and proselytise. Archbishop Doi, therefore, had connections. At one point the possibility that Emperor Hirohito and his family would convert to Christianity and of Japan adopting the faith as the national creed was a realistic and widely discussed possibility. (A prospect heightened when an American Quaker, Elizabeth Gray-Vining was appointed tutor to Crown Prince Akihito in late 1946.) Eventually, however, MacArthur and Hirohito decided against Imperial apostasy but the climate was such that Britain's diplomats had to tread carefully, not least in case of a sudden expansion of papal influence in the Far East.[25]

Britain's response to the allegations in the letter was swift, forthright and detailed.[26] It deserves closer scrutiny as it must be one of the few documents on file presenting a reasoned rather than expressly 'legal' justification for the treatment and retention of Japanese in SEAC/SEALF. Recent wartime comparisons inevitably colour the contemporary argument. The Archbishop was invited to compare and contrast the physical state of JSP at the time of their surrender, when they were 'marched in easy stages' into Burma, and then at the time of their embarkation at Rangoon for repatriation. Reports from ICRC representatives 'continually in attendance' at JSP camps were also available. From these records it would be realised 'how much these men owe to the excellent treatment from the British'. One defence of JSP living conditions was that they 'were the same as for the Indian army units'. This is perhaps a specific comparison with the 1929 PW Convention's requirement that standards for PW be the same as those of 'depot troops' of the detaining power. As for the majority of JSP camps, 'no British or Indian guards were stationed, and barbed wire was not erected, except where it had been erected before the surrender'. The riposte also emphasises the relaxed attitude of the British towards the detainees. 'JSP working parties in general were not sent out with Indian guards, though some special camps housing JSP accused of war crimes were guarded. The camps themselves 'were run entirely by the Japanese Commanders and the only control was enforced by a few British officers, and the Indian guards on stores'. Britain's hands-off approach was also stressed, in that 'policing in the camps was carried out entirely by the Japanese, and the only outside control was a limitation on movement'. Violence in camps was not Britain's concern, as 'discipline was and is enforced by the Japanese officers, warrant officers and NCOs'. Similarly Britain absolved itself of any responsibility for law and order among JSP. Any 'bloody' or 'criminal' incidents were ascribed 'entirely to questions of Japanese control, discipline and methods'.

British officials emphasised that ICRC representatives had 'reported favourably' on camp conditions. This is true but they had also reported unfavourably on a number of camps and hospitals for specific failings.[27] The Foreign Office also felt obliged to describe the Burmese climate for the benefit of His Holiness, explaining that Burma's weather is 'by no means as bad as is described....During the worst month of the monsoon, the sun may not shine for two or three days, but normally one can count on several hours of sunshine daily'.

Internally the Foreign Office accepted that there was 'probably some truth in the allegation that JSP were used as 'batmen' rather than on reconstruction work.[28] For this reason the allegations were copied to the War Office's PW Directorate for comment. In the reply to Rome, there was an admission that 'some JSP may have been called to look after officers', but this was justified on the grounds that the majority of these would have been men who were 'unfit for heavy work'.[29] JSP contributions to port operations were described as 'vital'. The strongest allegation, that of slavery, was brusquely dismissed: 'It is absurd to call the JSP "slaves" when they were free of guards and barbed wire and controlled entirely of their own officers'. This was a suspect defence, however, particularly as in August 1946 the Joint Planning Staff had specifically noted to the Chiefs of Staff the 'strong ethical objections' against retaining JSP as 'slave labour'.[30]

Interestingly, and in contrast to the official response to many ICRC criticisms of JSP working and living conditions, every allegation was addressed, some more convincingly than others. This was probably done with a view to a potential wider, non-legal audience. Claims of inadequate rations and the allegations of poor health were contradicted, the Foreign Office insisted, by ICRC reports. (Though here, too, other ICRC reports had been critical of ration provision in a number of camps.) The Foreign Office insisted that the men 'were returning to Japan in a good state of health and appearance'. As to shortages of daily necessities, such as toothpaste, these were admitted, but justified since 'British and Indian forces also had to do without this type of article'. London was emphatic that 'deaths were not down to the British'. It described JSP at the time of the surrender emerging from the jungle 'emaciated', 'starving' and 'racked with malaria and other diseases and infections'. These men it declared, 'received the best of attention, largely in Japanese hospitals where all facilities were made available under British supervision. Sickness as a result of captivity was very rare.' (The reply does not address accidental deaths or injuries occurring while involved in forced labour.)

Finally, and somewhat predictably, the British response was one based on morality rather than strict legality, pointing out that 'Japan did not ratify the Geneva Convention and her very treatment of Allied prisoners of war proved she had no intention of granting humane treatment in accordance with that Convention'. In contrast, Britain had observed the Convention 'as far as is practicable throughout the war and after the surrender'. The reply closed with perhaps the strongest justification, that of recent and vivid memory: 'It is quite preposterous to compare the ghastly treatment of Allied prisoners of war by the Japanese in the death camps along the Siam railway, with the treatment received by the JSP in the Burma camps. The only point to note is that the same type of Japanese officer controlled both sets of camps'.[31] Presumably the Vatican was temporarily satisfied. It did not pursue the allegations after the return of the last of the JSP from Southeast Asia, and they did not resurface in Japan.[32]

THE INTERNATIONAL COMMITTEE FOR THE RED CROSS CHALLENGES WORKING PAY

Further questioning of British policy over the retention and treatment of Japanese also came in late June 1947, this time from the ICRC, whose delegate in the Far East, C. F. Aeschlimann, had met with General Kinoshita at HQ JEFSR, Kuala Lumpur on 22 May. Mr Aeschlimann had travelled specifically to appraise the circumstances of JSP in Singapore and Malaya, and to inform Kinoshita of the situation facing JSP in southern Vietnam following the confirmation from the French of their repatriation dates. Aeschlimann's particular enquiry, however, concerned the new ruling about pay. Frederick Bieri, Chief Delegate of the ICRC in Geneva, relayed Aeschlimann's report and the conclusions of subsequent deliberations on the pay issue in Geneva to London.[33] With the last JSP repatriation sailings pencilled in, Britain found its new payment policy for JSP faulted on a number of counts.

General Kinoshita himself was evidently highly critical of the WPC scheme in principle and informed Aeschlimann that he would draft a protest. At this point, Kinoshita was aware that SEALF intended to record work performed only after 1 June 1947. This he declared was 'absolutely unjust'. Kinoshita also feared the new scheme would affect discipline, since many JSP would equate earning only from 1 June as inferring a 'postponement of their repatriation'. A further point raised by the General was that once JSP understood their pay was coming from their own Government they would be 'discouraged from putting in long hours'. The reason being that his men did not wish to be a burden on their families in Japan who would be enduring increased hardship as a result.[34] Kinoshita's comments and criticisms, however, almost certainly stem from a brief prepared by General Numata's staff at the JSP Liaison Office at Johor Baru (in Malaya), which was in regular contact with HQ SEALF in neighbouring Singapore for all JSP-related administration. Protocol required the ICRC to seek out Kinoshita at Kuala Lumpur as he was the senior Japanese commander.

Britain's pay proposal was of great interest to the ICRC, which informed the War Office it had investigated to 'see how it compared with the pay of other SEP detained by Great Britain'. For its own study the ICRC compared pay for JSP in Southeast Asia with that for Germans classed as SEP in Italy who received:

a) 4/- [shillings, 1s = 12d] for each week of uninterrupted work, paid into a 'private account card' as from Sept. 1st 1946, to be utilised for canteen purposes.
b) 3/- weekly bonus, paid with retrospective effect from Sept. 1st 1946. This sum may be sent to next of kin.
c) 4/- a week to those who have had a good record since their capture. (About 70%.)

Thus, the ICRC calculated, the majority of German SEP were paid 11 shillings for a 48-hour week. In contrast, rates for Japanese personnel were:

'1½d an hour for skilled workers, ¾d an hour for unskilled workers who were paid in credit slips redeemable in Japan'. Therefore Japanese skilled and unskilled workers received 6 shillings and 3 shillings respectively for a 48-hour week, and did not enjoy the money transfer facilities and canteen advantages of their German opposite numbers in Italy. (Clearly the ICRC had not been informed of the scrapping of the higher rate for skilled labour. General Sir Reginald Denning had previously explained the initial pay scales to the ICRC in Geneva in March 1946.) In conclusion, the ICRC called for 'examination and revision', not only with regard to Japanese pay rates but also with regard to 'the failure to observe the spirit of the Convention and to apply its clauses'. Mr Bieri reminded the War Office it had given the ICRC written assurance over the latter in September 1946. For the ICRC it followed that treatment given to SEP should 'be similar to that given POW, irrespective of race or place of detention'. Citing Article 34 of the PW Convention, the ICRC listed a number of dissimilarities: the first being that German SP were paid from 1 September 1946, the Japanese from 1 June 1947. Article 34, the ICRC stated, required that PW be paid for 'any work they undertake' and that there was 'no leeway in the Article to defer the start' of payment.

A further observation raised the question of whether Britain had simply assumed a lower pay rate because of the typically low wage rates in Asia. The ICRC noted that 'failing an agreement between belligerents', wages based on a 'tariff corresponding to the work executed' implied the rate should be the same as that of local labourers doing the same work. In fact, SEALF, attempting to reduce costs, had imposed a lower-than-market rate on JSP. A third point raised stressed that Article 34 also stipulated that a part of a prisoner's wages be made available to him during captivity. In SEALF, the Committee noted, the Japanese had no available cash and had not been informed how much they would receive for their pay credits after repatriation, and when. In contrast, Britain's treatment of Germans in Italy met these requirements. In conclusion the ICRC described the situation as 'an unsatisfactory state of affairs' and suggested first that JSP pay should be backdated 'from the moment at which work commenced', that Japanese SP wages be raised to the same level as German SEP wages in Italy, and that the Japanese be granted the same monetary facilities: some cash for canteen and local purchases, and a transfer option to next of kin. Perhaps the most awkward criticism of all, however, was the assertion that the decision to make WPC redeemable against the Japanese Government was 'completely out of keeping with the principle underlying Article 34 of the Convention.'[35]

Throughout the working pay negotiation process London's primary objective was the avoidance of a charge on the UK Treasury. Understandably it was on this point that the War Office and Foreign Office focused in preparing a joint reply. Again, the two ministries were not unduly concerned about specific ICRC objections over JSP living and working conditions. In fact, the War Office considered the other points raised by the ICRC as 'trivial' and easily answered.[36] As usual the Foreign Office sought precedent. It found it in the Italian Peace Treaty, Section III, Article 76, in which Italy renounced general and specific individual and PW-related claims:

> 1. Italy waives all claims of any description against the Allied and Associated Powers on behalf of the Italian Government or Italian nationals arising directly out of the war or out of actions taken because of the existence of a state of war in Europe after 1 September 1939, whether or not the Allied or Associated Power was at war with Italy at the time, including the following: …

> 5. The waiver of claims by Italy under paragraph 1 of this article includes any claims arising out of actions taken by any of the Allied and Associated Powers with respect to Italian ships between 1 September 1939 and the coming into force of the present Treaty, as well as any claims and debts arising out of the Conventions on prisoners of war now in force.[37]

Bolstered by this recent and directly comparable legal agreement, London stressed once again that 'as far as circumstances permit' treatment of JSP would be in keeping with the PW Convention. At the same time London confidently rejected the ICRC's contention over responsibility for payment:

> The Convention…is not concerned [with responsibility] for meeting the cost of …payments to prisoners of war…. [P]risoners of war are entitled to a rate of pay (to be fixed by agreements between the belligerents or, pending such agreements, according to standards specified in the Convention) for work other than work in connexion with the administration, internal arrangement and maintenance of camps, but it does not specify that the financial burden involved must fall upon the detaining Power. [W]e are at liberty to press upon the Japanese Government the obligation to waive all claims and debts on its own behalf of Japanese nationals arising against HMG out of Conventions on

prisoners of war now in force, (cf. the Italian Peace Treaty…) and to require that the Japanese Government shall assume responsibility for reimbursing JSP in respect of work for which, if they had been prisoners of war, they would have been entitled to receive pay.

…we feel we have overwhelming support, in equity, for our view that this is an obligation which should be imposed upon the Japanese Government. During the war, the Japanese broke a very great number of clauses of the Prisoner of War Convention and, in particular, the Japanese Government are heavily in debt to us on account of work done for them by British prisoners of war to whom no remuneration was given. Payment given now by the Japanese Government to their own men would do nothing more than offset, to a limited extent, what the Japanese Government already owe to our men.[38]

Here the Foreign Office passed over a no doubt uncomfortable contradiction in its policy, for it had asserted that London was intending to obtain payment from Japan as recompense for British FEPOW labour. For London the most important issue remained the responsibility of meeting the cost of the payments. The United States had already proved lukewarm to the WPC proposal and there may well have been concern that the ICRC would submit a report to the State Department or SCAP. Since the United States also contended that payment obligations rested with Britain this would have bolstered the argument against the position taken by London. Privately War Office officials also doubted whether the ICRC was legally competent to raise the payment matter and were quite happy for the Foreign Office to state that bluntly to Bieri. (This is a curious assumption, as this was precisely the kind of issue a 'Protecting Power' ought to have raised. In the light of the absence of an official Protecting Power, the Foreign Office cannot really have been surprised that the ICRC sought to act in a similar manner.)

There was some modification in the British stance, however. London accepted that work done before June 1947 deserved payment. To this end the War Office informed the Foreign Office that, 'JSP know that is our attitude and considerable efforts are being made to arrive at the right amount'. Underlying the careful use of language was the intention, 'to avoid our saying anything to an outside body which may be taken as a statement of policy by HMG or an interpretation of its policy'.[39]

Months passed and the ICRC, like the Vatican over conditions and labour, did not pursue this issue into 1948. No doubt this was partly a reflection of the ambiguous post-war status of the International Red Cross following the ending of the Swiss Government's role as Protecting Power for Japanese personnel. Britain was, as examined, quite prepared to stonewall and respond by questioning the ICRC's legitimacy to act for JSP at all. A key development was that by the start of November 1947, all JSP had left Southeast Asian waters and so British control. Consequently there was suddenly far less urgency attached to the JSP question altogether. For the ICRC, however, there were other important PW and SEP issues to champion elsewhere, not least in the drafting of revisions to the 1929 Convention on Prisoners of War that would come into existence in 1949, which would have bearing on its future status.[40] From mid-1946 onwards the ICRC faced criticism from the US and Britain on one side, and open hostility from the USSR and its satellites on the other, as it tried to deflect attempts to internationalise its composition and also champion revisions to the Convention at preparatory conferences in Oxford in 1946, Geneva in 1947 and Stockholm in 1948. The most contentious issues being limits to sovereignty over citizens in occupied states and indiscriminate bombing.[41] These serious distractions and, in addition, the start of multinational negotiations towards a peace treaty with Japan effectively rendered the ICRC, from 1948 onward, merely an interested observer of Anglo-Japanese diplomacy.

CHEQUEBOOK DIPLOMACY:
THE PROSPECT OF STERLING PAYMENTS TO JSP

By early November 1947 continuing delay in securing American approval for a WPC proposal for Japanese who had worked in Burma, Malaya and Singapore was causing the Foreign Office some concern. All JSP had left British territories in Southeast Asia at the end of October. Only those JSP detained beyond 1 June 1947 had received WPC. Many others therefore had no individual pay record or certificate of any kind.[42] Meanwhile, although the influential State-War-Navy Coordinating Committee in Washington had apparently passed the WPC proposal, the State Department had not prepared a draft to put before the FEC, and showed little inclination to do so. Consequently the Foreign Office resigned itself to the fact that there was no early prospect of an FEC directive to SCAP to instruct the Japanese Government to accept the certificates. Delay and possible complaints via non-FEC channels increased the risk of the issue attracting unwelcome attention in the British press. The Foreign Office feared it 'might be embarrassing if the question of payment to these JSP were to be raised publicly'. Interestingly, assertion of a *quid pro quo* aspect to Japan's debts owed to Allied PW, as put to the Vatican (above) was dropped in subsequent treaty negotiations with Japan.

In London, the War Office pressed on with the development of a system to allocate all JSP with a certificate. Its solution was to instruct SEALF to compile lists of repatriates, showing the dates of repatriation and the ships involved, and also credits due for the periods both before and after 1 June 1947. These lists were to be kept by UKLM in Tokyo 'until the FEC manage to agree a policy whereby the Japanese Government shall be made responsible for payment to JSP...'. It was accepted that such a convoluted process was not going to be an easy task for the Japanese Government, which 'no doubt would have to make a public announcement...'.[43] In fact it was some weeks before Far East Land Forces (FARELF), which superseded SEALF in August 1947, was able to reply. Once again woeful administration undermined the best efforts of London. The Command admitted that it 'could not obtain this information locally'. No embarkation lists prior to March 1947 could be traced. This was a staggering admission that the names of only 33,000 out of the 85,000 JSP total were known. Helpfully, FARELF suggested that as each repatriation ship 'should have taken five copies of nominal rolls' this information could be compared with lists previously sent to UKLM in late 1946, from which the Japanese Government could compile 'credit cards' for individuals. Lack of information and suitably experienced paymasters, FARELF added, meant that it was unable to undertake any calculation of amounts due. It did, however, propose that the War Office send a special team to Japan for this purpose, or that the task be assigned to the British Commonwealth Occupation Force, which was 'on the spot'. FARELF had effectively washed its hands of the problem.[44]

London was thus placed in a difficult situation. Any negotiation on this issue involving the Japanese Government could only proceed through the good offices of SCAP, which was increasingly less accommodating. In fact the worst-case scenario had already considered and budgeted for, ie, steadfast American opposition resulting in the WPC bill being met by the British Treasury. As a consequence of the lack of paperwork, however, the spectre arose of widely publicised appeals in the Japanese press and on radio co-ordinated by SCAP during 1948 for JSP to come forward to receive overdue pay in cash from Britain. It was a most unwelcome prospect with considerable domestic political ramifications, for news of such announcements would inevitably reach home and generate outrage among former FEPOW and the British public. This danger proved short-lived. Higher policy concerns and State Department procrastination effectively resulted in the working pay issue being swept up amongst the minutiae of reparations calculations and the all-embracing terms of the final Japanese Peace Treaty. Once General MacArthur declared it was time for a peace treaty, complex bargaining and tradeoffs over reparations took place between 1947 and 1948. This was followed by 15 months of negotiations led by John Foster Dulles before the signing of the treaty at San Francisco. In short, reparations policy for Japan underwent dramatic change, putting quite considerable strain on relations with Britain, China and other Western Allies.[45]

As mentioned previously, reparations deliveries by Japan and the accompanying reparations programme were ended in 1949 as a result of unilateral action by MacArthur. This decision met with considerable, widely reported opposition, not least from China and the Philippines. In justifying its position Washington stressed the vital importance of a balanced Japanese economic revival and the fact that American financial support for Japan was not an open-ended commitment. Washington also argued that the Potsdam Declaration provided 'first for economic recovery then for reparations'; and that Japan's recovery was in the best interests of all Asian nations'.[46] Britain was also affected. London (see Chapter 6) had anticipated a limited window of opportunity for reparations and had gambled on seeking a percentage of Japan's exports as the best short- to mid-term deal, the scale of which would dwarf the question of pay for JSP. MacArthur's decision to cease reparations payments far earlier than expected meant the gamble failed.

The Treaty of Peace with Japan, signed (not by the Soviet Union) at San Francisco on 8 September 1951 'settled' all financial issues arising out of the war, despite subsequent attempts to lodge claims against Japan. There have been several well-publicised attempts by former Allied FEPOW to seek compensation from the Japanese state. On each occasion the Japanese courts, in rejecting those claims, have cited the Peace Treaty.[47] In Article 19 of the Treaty, Japan also waived all claims on behalf of its PW and civilians but curiously it omits any reference to JSP:

> (a) Japan waives all claims of Japan and its nationals against the Allied Powers and their nationals arising out of the war or out of actions taken because of the existence of a state of war, and waives all claims arising from the presence, operations or actions of forces or authorities of any of the Allied Powers in Japanese territory prior to the coming into force of the present Treaty.

(b) The foregoing waiver includes any claims arising out of actions taken by any of the Allied Powers with respect to Japanese ships between 1 September 1939 and the coming into force of the present Treaty, as well as any claims and debts arising in respect to Japanese prisoners of war and civilian internees in the hands of the Allied Powers, but does not include Japanese claims specifically recognised in the laws of any Allied Power enacted since 2 September 1945.[48]

In one sense, the JSP working-pay dispute, in fact a relatively small amount of money among hundreds of millions, was lost amidst the detail and the post-war books were 'balanced' without the question being specifically addressed. The same is also true for Britain's assumption that it had the right to put JSP to work at Japan's cost. The revised, 1949, PW Convention prohibits such a situation. Considering the Foreign Office's primary focus on maintaining good relations with the United States, the blurring and fading away of the JSP question was perhaps a satisfactory conclusion. Physical retention of Japanese, if not questions over pay, had at least just avoided extension into 1948. At the end of 1947, however, a peace treaty was still a distant goal. JSP remained a potentially awkward diplomatic problem and one that still had a completely disproportionate capacity to embarrass the British Government. Even the departure of the last JSP repatriation ship from Singapore in late October 1947 was to expose continuing uncertainty and hyper-sensitivity in British policy.

'THE JAPANESE HAVE BEEN MORE FORTUNATE THAN THE GERMANS BECAUSE...'

From late 1946 onwards various reports by FARELF, HQ JEFSR and the ICRC had identified deteriorating morale and discipline among the detained Japanese as a growing problem. Much of this deterioration was put down to the 'uncertainty' of the date of their repatriation.[49] While the British Government was agreeable to the repatriation schedule it was still, however, hesitant to commit to a completion date of 31 December 1947 and stressed that no agreements were to be made specifying that date. No public announcement would be made since London's preference was for the JSP to be informed through military channels that their repatriation would proceed 'at the same monthly rate in the future as in the past'.[50] As long as the capability of Britain to return the men had been in doubt, London had refused to allow FARELF to even hint at a final repatriation date. Once the December 1947 date seemed assured, FARELF again requested permission from the COS to inform the Japanese of the year-end date and, presumably, reduce disciplinary problems following what should have

36. Some of the last British-held JSP to return home at (probably) Ujina Repatriation Centre in late 1947. (AWM)

surely been a major, morale-raising announcement. What seemed a logical, even innocuous course of action to FARELF, however, was considered to have repercussions far from Southeast Asia.

European political considerations were the cause of the London's unease. For here too, Britain faced an embarrassing PW issue. Publicity around the completion of Japanese repatriation from Southeast Asia would, it was now feared, invite unwelcome comparison with the situation of large numbers of German PW still in Britain, many of them labouring in factories and farms. Unsurprisingly the War Office had no wish 'to stimulate demand' for German repatriation.[51] Consequently the JSP programme went ahead quietly and, with what must have seemed to FARELF at least, a contrived sense of caution. Signals on such mundane subjects as shipping schedules and numbers of passengers remained 'Secret'. Frustration arose over this imposed confidentiality, as the steady, almost daily stream of thousands of cheerful Japanese heading into the docks was clearly apparent to locals. The British Defence Committee South East Asia (BDCSEA) pointed this out to the COS in late September 1947, explaining that, as instructed, no publicity was being given but that interest from the press had been aroused. BDCSEA requested permission to provide facts to the press since the last repatriation ship was due to leave Singapore in mid-October and a delay in providing facts might result in 'the publication of speculative reports...[which] might prove more embarrassing as regards the position of German prisoners in the United Kingdom than the publication of the true facts'.[52]

Foreign Secretary Bevin and the Cabinet were not convinced. German PW still in North Africa were in fact under Geneva Convention protection and so due 'prompt' repatriation. Britain was acutely sensitive to potential Russian, and possibly American, criticism at the Four Powers meetings. In the Foreign Office's reply (quoting Bevin) these other concerns took precedence:

> We regard it as most unfortunate that any publicity at all has to be given to the completion of Japanese repatriation but we recognise the story is in any case bound to break before very long either in Japan or Malaya and it will therefore get into the World Press. This is bound to have a serious effect on the morale of German prisoners of war, particularly those in the Middle East whose repatriation has recently been seriously interrupted and it may also have an unfortunate effect in Germany and adversely affect our position in Quadripartite discussion.[53]

Even the prospect of a favourable, if minor, news story—presumably one celebrating the long-desired departure of the Japanese from Malaya and Singapore—counted for little against the bigger priority of avoiding European embarrassment. The Foreign Office dismissed the risk, commenting, 'the worst rumour is what is in fact true, namely that repatriation is complete'.[54] Yet again, there was to be no official announcement. Release of 'factual information' was to be deferred until the 'latest possible date' in order to examine options for 'accelerating the repatriation of German prisoners of war'.[55] Foreign Office unease and weakness over Britain's lack of control over this issue is clear. FARELF Commands were instructed to respond carefully to queries from the press, making it clear 'why the Japanese have been more fortunate than the Germans'. The instruction closed, perhaps with more than a flash of irritation over Britain's now junior status in Asia, 'if indeed there are any reasons other than US policy'.[56] (There was no 'SCAP' in Europe. Equal Four-Power status in Occupied Germany gave Britain an automatic seat and, importantly, an equal vote.) One reason offered for the faster Japanese repatriation in the draft guidelines was that Britain was using 'old and barely sea-worthy Japanese ships'. Fortunately for London, this potential petard was noticed by a calmer mind and reworked to read 'warships unsuitable for use in other than the waters in which they were used'.[57]

There remained, however, the fact that the United States Joint Chiefs (USJCS) had to be informed officially that JSP repatriation was complete. MacArthur's Potsdam obligations and the earlier specific American criticism that the British postponement had 'certain undesirable features' meant the USJCS could hardly be ignored. With some reluctance the Foreign Office concurred but requested 'as little emphasis as possible and not before 18 October when [the] last ship carrying JSP leaves Malaya'.[58] Thus the approved final signal to the USJCS was short but hardly confident:

> 1. It will be recalled in their memorandum…dated 21st November, 1946, the British Chiefs of Staff informed the United States Chiefs of Staff that the question of retention of certain Japanese surrendered personnel in South East Asia during 1947 was still under detailed examination.
>
> 2. It is requested that the United States Chiefs of Staff be informed that the last shipload of Japanese surrendered personnel from South East Asia left Singapore on 18th October, 1947. The only Japanese…now remaining in the area are small numbers connected with war crimes trials.
>
> 3. The Foreign Office are anxious that no publicity should at present be give to the above information.[59]

London had a short but uneasy wait for responses from Washington and GHQ SCAP in Tokyo, where there was little pro-British sympathy. Before long, unwelcome news came that Japanese repatriation had indeed been discussed in the Allied Council for Japan (ACJ). On 29 October the ACJ had been considering the 761,000 JSP remaining under Soviet control. During the meeting William Sebold, the State Department's representative, had referred to the last 2,739 JSP from Southeast Asia as 'water borne en route to Japan'. With some relief UKLM commented that although the Japanese newspapers *Asahi* and *Yomiuri* had subsequently reported that there were no longer any JSP in Southeast Asia, the local English-language press in Tokyo had not made specific reference to the fact.[60] The Foreign Office could not, however, relax. UKLM also gave warning that MacArthur was to make a formal announcement of the completion of JSP repatriation from Southeast Asia as part of an official statement on progress in meeting his Potsdam remit. In London, Foreign Secretary Bevin was immediately concerned, but equally well aware that MacArthur was within his rights to highlight the return of the JSP. He signalled UKLM by return, again seeking Sir Alvary Gascoigne's personal intervention with the General:

> I have been anxious to postpone any announcement for as long as possible... However it is clear that General MacArthur has good reasons...and I cannot ask him to postpone... [but] ask him to word the announcement so as to make it as innocuous as possible... in so far as opinion among German POWs is concerned, e.g. by referring to the type of shipping which was available for the operation.[61]

In the circumstances it was perhaps the best that Bevin could hope for. Yet once again MacArthur came to Britain's aid, choosing to forego a populist, 'pro-consul' image-building opportunity in Japan to smooth distant diplomatic waters. Amenably he informed Gascoigne that he had given Britain 'a clean bill of health' at the ACJ. The sole American concern had been the need to refute a Russian claim that SCAP was obstructing repatriation of JSP in their custody. MacArthur promised that 'nothing more would be said' about repatriation from British areas. With that casual aside Britain's JSP file was effectively closed.[62]

And so the last boatload of the Imperial Japanese invaders of 1941 departed Southeast Asia. An event that ought to have been a moment of considerable symbolic importance and political significance to the British people—and especially to those citizens of her Asian empire who had suffered so cruelly under Japanese occupation—passed without any official public acknowledgement. Yet tens of thousands of Allied soldiers and hundreds of thousands of civilians had died in order to achieve this mass but protracted eviction.

NOTES TO CHAPTER 8

1.   Memo, 6 Nov. 1947. FO 371/63741.
2.   Nimmo, *Behind a Curtain of Silence*, 88–93.
3.   British Embassy, Washington to London, 'Japanese repatriation', 5 Apr. 1947. FO 371/63741.
4.   Ibid.
5.   Memo, 10 Apr. 1947. FO 371/36741.
6.   Memo, 17 Apr. 1947. FO 371/36741.
7.   FO to UK Treasury Delegation, Washington DC. 18 Apr. 1947. FO 371/63741.
8.   Ibid..
9.   Notes on meeting on JSP pay, 17 June 1947. FO 371/63741.
10.   FO to UK Treasury Delegation, Washington, DC., 18 Apr. 1947. FO 371/63741.
11.   Notes on meeting on JSP pay, 17 June 1947. FO 371/63741.
12.   Ibid.
13.   Ibid.
14.   Ibid.
15.   Lucio Sponza, 'Italian Prisoners of War in Great Britain, 1943-46', in Moore and Fedorowich, Prisoners of War and their Captors, 212. See also Bob Moore and Kent Fedorowich, The British Empire and Italian Prisoners of War (Basingstoke, 2002).
16.   Author's correspondence with Oba Sadao, 12 January 2009.
17.   As far as Britain was concerned JSP were 'not PW'. ICRC reports, see FO 371/53796.
18.   Notes on meeting on JSP pay (summary), 17 June 1947. FO 371/63741.
19.   Memo by Secretary of State for Foreign Affairs, 25 June 1947. FO 371/63741.
20.   Vatican to HBM Legation to the Holy See, 'The Condition of the Labour Corps in Burma', 12 June 1947. FO 371/63741.
21.   Ibid.
22.   Ibid.
23.   FO to Holy See (draft), 26 June 1947. FO 371/63471.
24.   Dower, *Embracing Defeat*, 189.
25.   Takemae, *Allied Occupation of Japan*, 379.
26.   FO to Holy See (draft), 26 June 1947. FO 371/63471.
27.   See, for example, ICRC reports in FO 369/3816B.
28.   FO to Holy See (draft), 26 June 1947. FO 371/63471
29.   Aida Yuji for one was critical of his time as a mess servant. See Chapter 6, n. 36.
30.   See Chapter 7, n. 1.
31.   FO to Holy See, 26 June 1947. (Underlining in original.) FO 371/63741
32.   No references to this issue were found by the author in *CJGR*.
33.   ICRC to WO, 27 June 1947. FO 371/63741.
34.   Ibid.
35.   Ibid.
36.   WO to FO, 24 July 1947. FO 371/63741.
37.   Peace Treaty with Italy, 10 Feb. 1947.
38.   FO to ICRC, 5 Aug. 1947. FO 371/63741.
39.   WO to FO, 24 July 1947. FO 371/63741.

40. Convention (III) relative to the Treatment of Prisoners of War. Geneva, 12 August 1949.

41. Geoffrey Best, *War and Law since 1945* (Oxford, 1997), 86.

42. FO to UKLM, Tokyo. 6 Nov. 1947. FO 371/63471.

43. Ibid.

44. FARELF to WO, 'Working Pay for JSP', 28 Dec. 1947. FO 371/63471.

45. Ward and Schulman, *Allied Occupation of Japan, 1945-1952*, 727–97. The literature on the treaty negotiations is extensive. See also Dower, *Embracing Defeat,* and Takemae, *Allied Occupation of Japan, passim.*

46. 'US Repudiates Philippine and Chinese Complaint on Japanese Reparation Removals.' *Dept of State Bulletin* 20 (26 June 1949): 831–3.

47. Specifically, Chapter V, 'Claims and Property', Article 16.

48. Treaty of Peace with Japan, Chapter V, 'Claims and Property', Article 19.

49. COS report on JSP morale, 22 Jan. 1947. CO 537/2493.

50. COS (71) 47, 6 June 1947. CAB 122/1183.

51. WO to SEALF, 9 June 1947. CAB 122/1183.

52. BDCSEA to COS, 25 Sept. 1947. CO 537/2494.

53. Letter from FO (Majoribanks) to COS Secretary, 'Publicity of repatriation of Japanese Prisoners of War', 4 Oct. 1947. CAB 122/1183.

54. COS to FARELF, 11 Oct. 1947. CO 537/2494.

55. Ibid.

56. Ibid.

57. COS minutes, 10 Oct. 1947. CAB 122/1183.

58. WO to JSM, 11 Oct. 1947. CAB 122/1183.

59. BAS Washington to USJCS, 20 Oct. 1947. CAB 122/1183.

60. UKLM to FO, 9 Nov. 1947. FO 371/63741.

61. Secretary of State (Bevin) to UKLM, 7 Nov. 1947. FO 262/2056.

62. UKLM to FO, 10 Nov. 1947. FO 371/63741.

CONCLUSION

'But I've got a ship to catch!'

—General Numata Takazo upon his arrest at

Singapore docks in October 1947 [1]

General Numata left Singapore for Japan, under guard, in early November 1947, in fact just days after his quayside arrest on war crimes charges. He was not destined to be the 'last JSP' to leave Southeast Asia, for with his arrest came a change of status to PW. Numata thus spent a short time in Changi gaol's PW compound as one of several hundred awaiting trial.[2] Since American prosecutors at the International Military Tribunal for the Far East (IMTFE) had laid the charges against the General—the allegations were use of Red Cross vessels to carry troops, arms and fuel in Southeast Asian waters—he was required to answer them in Tokyo. (The charges were later dropped.) Numata went home on a British troopship as a PW travelling under armed escort. Presumably therefore he experienced captivity in Changi, which he had previously visited in February 1946 on his inspection tour, and aboard the SS *Dilwara*, with 1929 PW Convention-established protections. Unfortunately there is no known record as to whether he ever recorded a comparison of the conditions he experienced as a JSP compared with those as a PW.

While it is rather ironic that Numata should return to Japan as a PW, it is certainly apt. He had long disputed the legality of JSP status, slow repatriation and retention. For two years he worked in the best interests of his detained men, never ceasing to phrase his arguments in the language of the PW Convention or to quote the Potsdam Declaration. His quayside finale presents the JSP versus PW issue in a useful vignette. Numata's change of status occurred instantly, on an American whim. Only PW status, ie, by being under full Allied control, allowed the Allies to bring charges against Japanese at the IMTFE.[3] Allied-designated JSP status also offered the advantage of equally quick revocation of that status. Interestingly, the reverse process, changing PW to JSP, would have been in clear breach of the PW Convention.

In 1949 the PW Convention was revised with a view to deny a future victor the power to treat captives as anything other than PW. During the 1939–45 war the sheer scale of the conflict and the vast numbers of individuals involved had placed enormous pressures upon governments and consequently severely tested the 1929 accord dealing with prisoners. There were clear regional variations. In the European Theatre there was a relatively early, calculated and considered assessment of the practicalities and need to control German forces in the event of a capitulation rather than an armistice. In the Far East, in contrast, the implications of the size of the Japanese diaspora was considered only following the abrupt end to the fighting in August 1945. While certain aspects of the European experience did transpose to the Asia-Pacific Theatre, a key difference was that proposals to make Japanese forces 'surrendered personnel' originated with the Japanese Government. For the Allies there was little reason or inclination to reject what was an inherently advantageous proposal that reduced their military, supervisory and financial burdens, despite the lack of precedent or grounding in international law.

Immediate post-war Southeast Asia was in a ferment that took little note of precedent. Peace had come suddenly and unexpectedly. Britain had also been saddled with late, unwelcome—and unrealistic—additional responsibilities in the French and Dutch colonies. In the first days of 'peace', power remained, almost by default, with the Japanese. That British forces were able to land, unopposed, on Java at all was largely the result of continued Japanese resolve. Even once the British had arrived in Indonesia, in pitifully small numbers, dependence on Japanese units remained an undesirable but none the less unavoidable reality. Many of Britain's problems in Indonesia reflect the fact that British interests there were always short term, inherited as they were from the Potsdam discussions, and carried underappreciated risks that subsequently resulted in a military disaster. The defeat of British forces at Surabaya and concerted Indian opposition to use of their troops against 'freedom fighters' convinced Britain to give up any notion of an open-ended military commitment to restore to power the Dutch in Indonesia or, equally, the French in Vietnam even though their restoration was seen as advantageous to British post-war security interests.[4] The intricacies of Indonesian domestic politics never interested London beyond the need for a *Dutch*-Indonesian settlement that would facilitate the early, ie, Potsdam-fulfilling, removal of Japanese troops and thus in turn allow a British withdrawal.[5]

British involvement in Indonesia has been variously described as an 'intermezzo', and even an 'occupation'.[6] Yet SEAC scarcely managed to defend 'three urban enclaves on Sumatra (Medan, Padang and Palembang) and three and a half (Jakarta/Batavia, Semarang and Surabaya, plus the northern half of Bandung) on Java'.[7] Neither term adequately describes a perpetually hazardous, limited deployment in which few of the 48 million Javanese and 10 million Sumatrans ever saw a single British or Indian serviceman. Britain's difficult, contentious and ultimately thankless task in Indonesia was compounded by having 'responsibility without power'.[8] When a demonstration of military power was needed at Surabaya after the slaughter of 49 Indian Brigade—which itself followed an atypical local Japanese capitulation to nationalists—it was displayed at a distance. It was unleashed only for the pre-landing bombardment and bombing of the city. Although 5 Indian Division 'took' Surabaya after a three-week campaign, within two months the city was abandoned. There had never been enthusiasm for British 'boots on the ground' in Java. Only where the Japanese had stood firm, at Jakarta, Bandung and Semarang, did the British build upon and retain a semblance of control.

This raises the question, with the benefit of hindsight, of whether, in their determination to avoid the stigma of becoming PW, the Japanese had in fact missed an opportunity to extract major concessions from the British. In September 1945 Lord Mountbatten threatened the Japanese HQ that failure to obey his orders, ie, widespread deployment to 'maintain law and order', would result in the immediate classification of Japanese troops as PW and detention under guard and 'appropriate disciplinary action taken'.[9] Should generals Itagaki, Numata and Yamamoto and Admiral Shibata have tested British brinkmanship and simply confined their men to barracks, forcing Mountbatten to make what would have been a crucial, irreversible and even fateful decision? In the light of SEAC's shortage of manpower and inability to supervise 750,000 Japanese, a threat of non-cooperation would have placed the Japanese in a position of considerable strength. There were very serious risks inherent in such a gambit. Certainly, without the Japanese, Britain's ability to maintain order throughout the region would have been fundamentally compromised and Southeast Asian history might now read far differently. Japan's surrender opened the way for other, smaller but often important and influential policy and security choices, and even divisions within the Japanese military itself. Japanese Navy officers' encouragement for Indonesian independence and the loss of the Surabaya arsenals to nationalists are just two examples.

Much of SEAC's initial security 'planning' was dependent upon the Japanese military hierarchy playing along. Yet for some time this co-operation could not be taken for granted. One factor that was to SEAC's advantage, in Indonesia especially, had been the manner of the implementation of Japanese occupation policy in Southeast Asia. Indonesia had (for two years) been under a fairly repressive Japanese military administration, and not under the Great East Asia Ministry in Tokyo. Had the Japanese chosen a more populist 'co-prosperity' approach and publicly championed early self-determination, then they would have been under a much-reduced threat from post-war revolutionary violence. Instead the IJA in Java and Sumatra—and the IJN in the islands to the east—had imposed a hard-line Japan- and war-first approach with serious consequences and sacrifices entailed for those under military rule. These ranged from widespread starvation and forced labour to Gestapo-like monitoring and arbitrary arrests. An immediate consequence of those brutal policies was that the Japanese were, if not vilified, then widely disliked. As such they were therefore a very real target for disaffection and even revenge. This threat was clear to local Japanese commanders from Thailand to Bali.

Significantly, in August 1945 Allied 'leniency' towards the Japanese was neither expected nor apparent. Mountbatten had once proposed shooting any Japanese who refused to obey British orders. Clearly his strength of feeling on the issue of security is not in doubt, even if the Chiefs denied him the option of summary execution because it was not, crucially, also American policy and the COS wanted to avoid unfavourable comparisons.[10] There is no question that on occasion deliberate Japanese action had compromised Allied objectives and resulted in great loss of life, as at Surabaya. On the other hand, the efforts of Japanese officers such as Major General Mabuchi, Major Kido (in Java), Major Takahashi and Captain Yamagishi (in Vietnam) redressed the balance.

Questions of a largely answered call of duty aside, there is also another consideration, that of dependency. Quite simply, the Japanese were stranded. Disinterested self-internment far from the arena of nationalist politics—in Indonesia and Vietnam at least—was not viable for them except in the short term. Large Japanese stocks of food, vehicles, fuel, weapons and ammunition became increasingly desirable and valuable commodities. Inevitably, sooner or later other groups would have become strong enough to challenge, camp by isolated camp, for those resources. Many more Japanese would thus have become victims. Drastic law and order measures demanded by the British legitimised Japanese self-protection measures, even lethal force. It was therefore in the overwhelming interest of the JSP rank and file to assist

37. Lt W. A. Weightman (back row, second from left) with Maj . S. Takahara (back row, third from left) in Malaya, December, 1945. (AC)

the British. Crucially to men stuck thousands of miles from their families, co-operation also offered the only realistic chance of return home. Until 15 August that chance had been unimaginable. All Japanese servicemen in JEFSR had written their wills, fully expecting to die and lie forever in a foreign field. The vast majority were grateful for and appreciative of a second chance. Both General Sir Philip Christison and (later Air Chief Marshal) Sir Walter Cheshire considered that Japanese assistance in Indonesia and Vietnam was deserving of military decorations. Their contribution was not acknowledged at the time. Seven decades on, official recognition of this little-known second 'Anglo-Japanese alliance' seems long overdue.

Major political and diplomatic issues also emerged in Southeast Asia from 1945 to the end of 1947. With the effective withdrawal of US forces from SEAC, Britain inevitably faced charges of colonial collusion with other returning European powers. There was certainly an undisguised preference in London for the re-establishment of former neighbours. Indeed, London was uncomfortable over criticism, privately accepted, that it was delaying the departure of British troops in order to assist the French and Dutch. Mounting nationalist opposition and the long-term implications of direct involvement soon reduced direct British support. Sir Maberly Esler Dening OBE, Mountbatten's political advisor in SEAC, admitted that Britain was 'open to the accusation—not without reason—of holding the lists' until the Europeans were in a position to start shooting.[11] Nationalist control of some Japanese in Indonesia further complicated the dilemma for London. (At one point British planners estimating concentration capacity on Rempang and Galang islands doubted whether all JSP in Java would ever come under British authority.[12])

Despite early withdrawal from Indonesia being a professed British goal, leaving any Japanese in Java would have equated to an abandonment of obligations under Potsdam. Foreign Secretary Bevin worried that criticism of slow evacuation put Britain 'in a difficult position' as it was 'almost certain' to be raised at the UN. Conveniently, though, Britain could make the argument to protesting Indonesians that it had undertaken to disarm, concentrate and remove all the Japanese. Thus the nationalist-held JSP in East Java served as a useful front for continued British support of Dutch interests precisely because they remained beyond the reach of SEAC forces. Once all JSP had been evacuated, the Foreign Office anticipated it would become 'more difficult to justify the continued presence of British troops in Java and Sumatra'.[13]

Throughout this period the effect of JSP retention upon Britain's relations with the United States dominated Foreign Office thinking. Frictions existed in many areas of Anglo-American diplomacy in Asia and the Pacific long before the Japanese surrender.[14] Yet post-war political uncertainties resulted in the United States taking a relatively soft line on what might have been contentious and vocal colonial issues. American opinion on the future of colonialism was given short shrift in Paris and the Hague. It was also viewed with some anxiety in London. Certainly US sympathy was in support of political freedoms in Asia but soon it also saw a need for Western unity in debates at the new United Nations. Its own policy goals were therefore contradictory. Importantly, in the summer of 1945 the State-War-Naval Coordinating Committee (SWNCC) advised that the United States should 'not interfere in the British, French and Dutch dependencies in the Far East'. This policy lasted until late 1947, when Indonesia ceased to be peripheral to US interests.[15] In truth, JSP repatriation can be considered as one of many areas where British priorities in Asia ran counter to those of the United States. It was not, though, a strictly colonial issue except for the argument that use of JSP labour reduced Britain's own costs and responsibilities for its colonies. Political pressure from the United States via GHQ SCAP certainly had an impact on British repatriation policy. Once American dissatisfaction over JSP retention became clear, sensitivity over the issue increased. After the British excuse of lack of shipping had been negated by the offer of free American shipping to clear all JSP from SEAC by the end of 1946 this sensitivity increased dramatically.

Yet American dissatisfaction with Britain originated more from exasperation over mundane logistic and financial questions than major foreign policy differences. Unfortunately, the mundane began to impinge on higher-profile international issues, particularly over American relations with the Soviet Union and Occupied Japan. When this happened MacArthur did not hesitate to let his irritation show. In this sense, the persistent, official criticism of JSP retention was a rare and very early example of open American dissatisfaction with British policy in southeast Asia. This criticism, however, although endorsed by Washington and the US Joint Chiefs of Staff (USJCS) was coming primarily from General MacArthur in Tokyo. While MacArthur's distance must have reduced his influence over the State Department somewhat, as a soldier with known presidential ambitions he could not be ignored either in Washington or London.

In considering the extent of MacArthur's direct influence on British administrative changes the chronology of events is key. Curiously it was also in summer 1946 that the fundamental arguments behind established British policy towards German and Italian PW and SEP began to unravel. Since the period of late July to early September 1946 is only a matter of weeks, even allowing for a certain amount of coincidence, the hypothesis that MacArthur's allegations about JSP living and working conditions became the catalyst for a wholesale revision of British policy is certainly plausible. While there was implicit criticism in the initial comments from the USJCS, Britain defended the necessity of JSP retention very firmly. As a corollary, it must be noted that the fallback position of the British COS, which from the start assumed the availability of sufficient British shipping to complete repatriation, proved ultimately to be without foundation. American disapproval of British policy most definitely caused the Foreign Office much unease. Attlee's 'guidance' to Lord Inverchapel in Washington in itself reveals that confidence in the British argument defending retention in the light of Potsdam was far from robust.

American pressure on Britain fluctuated but it was constant. It included criticism of proposed shipping schedules, pique over the lack of consultation on the regional order of JSP repatriation, a direct refusal to clear JSP from Burma, imposing charges for bunkering, issuing short notice of repatriation centre closures and, especially, the sudden announcement of limits to the availability of reduce-priced shipping. London interpreted all these checks and charges as blatantly anti-British. It appears that consideration of any domestic and international pressures on MacArthur—such as the United States' own compliance with Potsdam, in carrying out General Order No. 1 on Japanese demilitarisation, and his agreement with the American maritime unions for example—never arose during Foreign Office deliberations. There was also genuine American concern, expressed directly by MacArthur, that the Soviet Union might beat Britain in the 'repatriation race' and so present Moscow with a propaganda victory. Regular GHQ SCAP bulletins on repatriation, although merely administrative records, all showed SEAC in a poor light.

This mismatch of British paranoia and American realism neatly illustrates the growing chasm between the new civilian primacy championed by Washington and GHQ SCAP, and the old military primacy doggedly maintained by London and SEAC/SEALF. From this arises the impression that by early 1946 Washington had already drawn a line under the Asia-Pacific War, whereas London apparently would not or, more accurately, could not. It is little wonder that the United States, keen to secure the speedy economic revival of the Pacific region, displayed a less-than-sympathetic reaction to what it must have viewed at best as a minor logistic problem. To cap it all, the issue was resolved at a stroke by an unexceptional order by an American Commander to divert a few ships to Singapore.

Britain's Government, distracted with problems closer to home, took a number of rushed steps, perhaps unavoidably, in Southeast Asia after 15 August 1945. Initially, and under the assumption that it was acting in tandem with the United States, it classified the Japanese in SEAC as JSP rather than PW. SEAC, desperately short of men, solved an urgent, regional law and order dilemma by requiring the Japanese to assist with British security policy. Then, again acting unilaterally, SEAC decided to meet a short-term labour shortage by denying JSP repatriation and using them for labour. Before long, as third parties beyond Southeast Asia began to question British actions, doubts began to set in at high levels as to whether Britain was in breach of the PW Convention and Potsdam Agreement. These doubts were widespread and even within the Foreign Office. Derogation from both the PW Convention and Potsdam occurred, at first justified with confidence if not backed by precedent. In London the default Foreign Office line was to stress how closely Britain was following the PW Convention in spirit rather than in the small print. Potsdam proved more difficult, as it did not refer to PW (or JSP) but simply 'Japanese'. Differing opinions among Foreign Office, War Office, MOT and Treasury led to disagreement that detracted from the formulation of an effective, defendable policy for surrendered

38. Two Mitsubishi A6M ('Zeke') naval fighters with RAF markings during evaluation tests in 1946 in Malaya. IJN pilots were supervised by RAF officers. (© IWM)

Japanese. Since those differences stemmed from basic interpretation of Britain's international obligations, finding common ground was in any case never going to be straightforward. Britain's main problem was one of money and resources. It was short of both. In attempting to reduce its expenditure it played fast and loose with American largesse, repatriating JSP at American expense but finding new objections when it was London's turn to foot the bill. Britain's sensitivity over its delinquent position vis-à-vis repatriation delays led it to deceive the United States and attempt to influence the repatriation timetable by using shipping with severely limited capacity to disguise and prolong retention. This ruse resulted in considerable frustration at GHQ SCAP that in turn prompted complaints from the State Department to London.

A number of British slip-ups also contributed to diplomatic and policy embarrassments. In particular, the 'British shipping' fiasco, whereby Japanese vessels, under GHQ SCAP, and with anticipated Japanese crews were incorporated as British in provisional schedules, heralded the end of the internal co-operation established among the War Office/Ministry of Defence (MOD), MOT and the Foreign Office. The question of crews also tested GHQ SCAP's patience. Once the very real possibility emerged that promises made by the Foreign Office during negotiations with MacArthur and the State Department would prove hollow, the FO began to champion earlier rather than later JSP repatriation. In doing so it had to seek ways to argue for the acceptance of a direct cost to the exchequer and inconvenience to the military. Further, it had to overcome the opposition of the MOT and the War Office, both of which saw no great difficulty or moral hazard in putting back the repatriation schedule to Spring 1948 or later. As a result, the Foreign Office was forced, not least for the sake of its reputation with the Americans, to argue strongly against the proposals of its fellow ministries. Further, SEAC's woeful administrative negligence in failing to record the names of JSP under its control and the work they performed had both potentially expensive and humiliating consequences for Britain in Japan and, indeed, at home. No doubt British public opinion would have been outraged by reports of invitations to Japanese to come forward for forced-labour compensation.

Eventually the lack of confidence in British policy culminated in the British Prime Minister authorising his senior diplomatic representative in Tokyo to ask privately for General MacArthur's opinion on the matter. By that time, however, although intra-Government departmental doubts had been kept 'in house', third-party criticisms had not. What had been initially a regional command solution threatened to move outside SEAC/ SEALF. Gradually it became clear that the United States, GHQ SCAP (for the Japanese Government), the ICRC, the Japanese public (via petitions) and the Vatican, all found basic fault with Britain's position. The sheer weight of opposition, even if poorly informed, began to build. Concessions or changes, such as the US decision to class JSP as PW in March 1946, steadily eroded British resolve.

Once the disparity in repatriation rates from SEAC became apparent, British standing in Japan became an increasingly important consideration. Restrained but persistent Japanese Governmental displeasure over retention, conveyed politely via GHQ SCAP, cast a slight but slowly darkening shadow over British deliberations. Dissatisfaction among the Japanese public was more open and strident. There was concern among British diplomatic representatives in Tokyo that future Anglo-Japanese relations, though technically non-existent at the time, once re-established might be marred by bad feeling over the retention issue. Japan's diplomatic isolation had meant that retention of Japanese in SEAC or the denial of pay had never been a direct or formal issue between the British and Japanese Governments but always one between the British Government and—an increasingly pro-Japanese—GHQ SCAP. Essentially the countdown began the moment MacArthur announced that the time was right for a peace treaty with Japan. With such a treaty the highly influential 'go-between' role performed by SCAP on behalf of the Japan's Government would disappear.

Time was against Britain in post-war Southeast Asia. Uncomfortably for SEAC, sudden peace following the atomic bombings of Hiroshima and Nagasaki meant that its supervision of enemy 'prisoners' was judged by suddenly reinstated peace-time standards. In truth, these standards should have posed no major difficulty for a true and confident Great Power. In fact, in late 1945 Britain was neither of these things. Britain's make-do response to its colonial and regional responsibilities resulted in its policies and decisions frequently questioned. This was frustrating enough coming, if quietly, from the United States, a vital and valued ally. Unrestrained criticism from third parties previously rendered ineffective or even irrelevant during total war was irritating and even galling. Britain, effectively broke, militarily and economically exhausted was a little irked by the less-than-total respect shown to it on the post-war diplomatic stage.

Britain's own return to Asia continued to be orchestrated through military channels long after Japan's surrender. In hindsight this is somewhat paradoxical. Numerous examples have been presented of the difficulties met by SEAC/SEALF in adjusting to a peacetime role inherited accidentally, while at the same time funding, resources and personnel available to it were constantly and deliberately reduced by London. Despite all, the Command made do. From the humanitarian viewpoint it did astonishingly well in the circumstances. In fact there was no alternative either in London or Singapore. Britain would not, truly could not, rework its obligations to territories in Southeast Asia as civilian programmes or aid initiatives. Only via war-derived bodies, such as SEAC, the FEC and the ACJ, established by formal but by then outdated treaty, was Britain a Great Power and so the acknowledged equal of the United States. Abandonment of the primacy of military command as the organisational hub for reconstruction in recovered territories would have meant Britain having to demonstrate economic capacity in funding investment in civil projects comparable to that of the United States, which was totally beyond its capability. Yet for a short time the damaging power vacuum left by Japan's sudden defeat also created an atmosphere of uncertainty and expectation of colonial return. This anticipation, in combination with a temporarily distracted but still generous United States, and a residual deference in the region towards the Allies allowed Britain a limited period of grace.

Britain's difficulties over JSP detention are perhaps the first in the sequence of checks to its wide-ranging assumptions over the post-war order in Asia and Europe, over status, over 'Victor's spoils' and, above all, over the extent of British influence. Within months confident justification of detention evolved into bluster, embarrassment and then retreat. In the case of JSP that retreat took place largely out of the public eye. In the years that followed other Asian disengagements would be far more visible. In truth, Britain was preparing to recast its role in Asia long before General Numata boarded his ship home.

NOTES TO CONCLUSION

1.   'Japanese Invasion Chief Goes Home Under Guard.' Reuter, MF 1224, 1126. Oct. 1947. CO 537/2494.

2.   Ibid.

3.   See Chapter 6.

4.   British attempts to mediate in Indonesia are detailed in Tarling, *Britain, Southeast Asia and the Onset of the Cold War* (Cambridge, 1998),87–97.

5.   Roadnight, 'Sleeping with the Enemy', 245–68.

6.   William H. Frederick, 'Between intent and circumstance; Causative factors in the British intermezzo in Java: a local perspective', in *De Leeuw en de Banteng*, P. J. Drooglever and M. J. B. Schouten, eds, (Den Haag, 1996), 25–60; and McMillan, *British Occupation of Indonesia*.

7.   Cribb, 'Political Dimensions of the Currency Question 1945-1947', 113–36.

8.   Buckley, 'Responsibility without Power', in Nish (ed), *Indonesian Experience*, 43.

9.   SEAC HQ, 'Relations with Surrendered Japanese Forces and with Enemy Civilians', 24 Aug. 1945. AIR 40/1850.

10.   COS Committee, 'Treatment of Japanese Forces as Prisoners of War', 9 Sept. 1945. FO 371/46459.

11.   Dening to FO, 11 Oct. 1945, WO 203/5567.

12.   HQ Malaya Command to ALFSEA, 1 Dec. 1945. WO 203/5963.

13.   Request from Bevin for information on JSP evacuation, 29 May 1945; FO reply (Wilson Young), 3 June 1945. FO 371 53796.

14.   Thorne, *Allies of a Kind, passim.*

15.   Robert J.McMahon, *Colonialism and Cold War: The United States and the Struggle for Indonesian Independence, 1945-49.* (New York, 1981), citing SWNCC, 100-101.

BIBLIOGRAPHY

UNPUBLISHED DOCUMENTS

Great Britain

The National Archives, Kew, London
    Air Ministry (AIR): AIR 40.
    Cabinet Office (CAB): CAB 79, CAB 84, CAB 121, CAB 122.
    Colonial Office (CO): CO 260, CO 262.
    Foreign Office (FO): FO 262, FO 369, FO 371.
    War Office (WO): WO 32, WO 172, WO 203, WO 208.
Liddell Hart Centre for Military Archives, King's College, London
    Papers of Wg Cdr T. S. Tull, CBE, DSO, OBE.
        'Mission to Java', unpublished memoir on 'Operation Mastiff'.
RAF Museum Library, Hendon, London
    Papers of Sir Walter G. Cheshire, GBE, KCB.
        'The Gremlin Task Force', report, 1965.

Netherlands

Nationaal Archief, Den Haag
Algemene Secretarie [General Secretariat] (AS)

Nederlands Instituut voor Oorlogsdocumentatie (NIOD), Amsterdam
    Indische Collectie [Indonesia Collection] (IC)
        Papers of David H. K. Soltau
            Unpublished memoir on 'Operation Mastiff'.

PUBLISHED DOCUMENTS

Great Britain

Mountbatten, Earl. *Report to the Combined Chiefs of Staff by the Supreme Allied Commander South-East Asia, 1943-1945.* London: HMSO, 1951.
Post Surrender Tasks Section E of the Report to the Combined Chiefs of Staff by the Supreme Allied Commander South-East Asia, 1943-1945. London: HMSO, 1969.

Parliamentary debates

Hansard, House of Commons Debates, 5th series, vols 411–42. London, 1945–7. [http://hansard.millbanksystems.com]

Japan

Takemae Eiji/竹前栄治 (ed/監修) *Catalogue of Japanese Government Responses to GHQ, Vols 1-24*. Tokyo: MT Shuppan, 1993-94. [GHQへの日本政府 対応文書総集成: 外務省記録 「連合軍司令部 往信綴」1-24巻. 東京: エムティ出版, 1993-94.]

GHQ Supreme Commander Allied Powers: Directives to the Japanese Government, SCAPINS Vols 1-15. Tokyo: MT Shuppan, 1993. [GHQ 指令総集成: SCAPIN 1-15巻 (東京: エムティ出版, 1993.]

United States

GHQ General Staff. *Reports of General MacArthur, Volume I, Supplement. MacArthur in Japan: The Occupation, Military Phase*. Washington, DC: USGPO, 1966.

SECONDARY SOURCES

Aida Yuji. *Prisoner of the British: A Japanese Soldier's Experiences in Burma*. London: Cresset Press, 1966.

Aldrich, Richard J., ed. *The Faraway War*. London: Doubleday, 2005.

Aldrich, Richard J. *Intelligence and the War Against Japan: Britain, America and the Politics of Secret Service*. Cambridge: CUP, 2000.

Allen, Louis. *Burma: The Longest War 1941-45*. London: Phoenix Press, 2000.
The End of the War in Asia. St Albans: Hart Davis MacGibbon, 1976.
Sittang: The Last Battle: The End of the Japanese in Burma, July-August 1 9 4 5. London: MacDonald, 1973.

Anderson, Benedict R. O. G. Java in a Time of Revolution. New York: Cornell University Press, 1972.

Asada Teruhiko. *The Night of a Thousand Suicides*. Translated by Ray Cowan. Sydney: Angus & Robertson, 1970.

Bates, Peter. *Japan and the British Commonwealth Occupation Force, 1946-52*. London: Brassey's, 1993.

Bayly, Christopher and Harper, Tim. *Forgotten Wars: Freedom and Revolution in Southeast Asia*. London: Allen Lane, 2006.

Behr, Edward. *Hirohito: Behind the Myth*. London: Hamish Hamilton, 1989.

Behrens, C. B. A. *Merchant Shipping and the Demands of War*. London: HMSO, 1955.

Best, Geoffrey. *War and Law since 1945*. Oxford: Clarendon Press, 1997.

Bodard, Lucien. *The Quicksand War: Prelude to Vietnam*. London: Faber, 1967.

Buckley, Roger. 'Responsibility without Power: Britain and Indonesia, August 1945-February 1946'. In *Indonesian Experience: The Role of Japan and Britain, 1943-1948*, edited by Ian Nish, 35-52. London: STICERD, 1979.

Cheah Boon Kheng. *Red Star over Malaya: Resistance and Social Conflict during and after the Japanese Occupation, 1941-1946*. Singapore: Singapore University Press, 2003.

Churchill, Winston S. *The Unwritten Alliance: Speeches 1953-1959 by Winston S. Churchill*. Churchill. Edited by Randolph Churchill. London: Cassell, 1961.

Coast, John. *Railroad of Death*. London: Commodore Press, 1946.

Cook, Haruko and Theodore, *Japan at War: An Oral History*. London: Phoenix, 2002.

Cribb, Robert. *Gangsters and Revolutionaries: The Jakarta People's Militia and the Indonesian Revolution, 1945-1949*. Honolulu: University of Hawaii Press, 1991.

Cross, J. P. *First In Last Out: An Unconventional British Officer in Indo-China, 1945-46 and 1972-76*. London: Brassey's, 1992.

Darwin, John. *Britain and Decolonisation: The retreat from Empire in the post-war world*. London: Macmillan, 1988.

De Jong, Louis. *The Collapse of a Colonial Society: The Dutch in Indonesia During the Second World War*. Leiden: KITLV Press, 2002.

Dennis, Peter. 'Netherlands East Indies, 1945-1947: An Unwelcome Commitment'. In *The Imperial War Museum Book of Modern Warfare*, edited by Julian Thompson, 29-49. London: Sidgwick & Jackson, 2003.

Dennis, Peter. *Troubled Days of Peace: Mountbatten and South East Asia Command, 1945-46*. New York: St Martin's Press, 1987.

Donnison, F. S. V. *British Military Administration in the Far East, 1943-1946*. London: HMSO, 1956.

Doulton, A. J. F. *The Fighting Cock: Being the History of the 23rd Indian Division*. Aldershot: Gale & Polden, 1951.

Dower, John W. *Embracing Defeat: Japan in the Wake of World War II*. New York: Norton, 1999.

Dower, John W. *War Without Mercy: Race and Power in the Pacific War*. New York: Pantheon, 1987.

Dunn, Peter M. *The First Vietnam War*. London: Hurst & Co., 1985.

Faulk, Henry. *Group Captives: The Re-education of German Prisoners of War in Britain, 1945-1948*. London: Chatto & Windus, 1977.

Feis, Herbert. *The Atomic Bomb and the End of World War Two*. London: Oxford University Press, 1966.

Fisher, Louis. *The Story of Indonesia*. London: Hamish Hamilton, 1959.

Frank, Richard B. *Downfall: The End of the Imperial Japanese Empire*. London: Penguin, 2001.

Fraser, George MacDonald, *Quartered Safe Out Here: A Recollection of the War in Burma*, London, Harvill, 1992.

Frederick, William H. '*Between intent and circumstance; Causative factors in the British intermezzo in Java: a local perspective*'. In *De Leeuw en de Banteng: Bijdragen aan het congres over de Nederlands-Indonesische betrekkingen 1945-1950.* Edited by P. J. Drooglever and M. J. B. Schouten, 38–52. Den Haag: ING, 1996.

Frederick, William H. *Visions and Heat: The Making of the Indonesian Revolution.* Ohio: Ohio University Press, 1989.

Friend, Theodore. *The Blue-Eyed Enemy: Japan Against the West in Java and Luzon, 1942-1945.* New York: Princeton University Press, 1988.

Fukami, Teiji and Wilbur Cross. *The Lost Men of Anatahan.* New York: Paperback Library, 1969.

Fuller, Richard. *Shokan – Hirohito's Samurai: Leaders of the Japanese Armed Forces, 1926-1945.* London: Arms & Armour Press, 1992.

Fukui, Shizuo. *The Japanese Navy at the End of World War II.* Greenwich, CT: WE, Inc., 1947.

Gardner, R. N. *Sterling-Dollar Diplomacy in Current Perspective.* New York: Columbia University Press, 1980.

Gerbrandy, Pieter, S. *Indonesia.* London: Hutchinson, 1950.

Gibney, Frank, ed. *Senso: The Japanese Remember the Pacific War.* New York: M. E. Sharpe, 1995.

Goto, Ken'ichi. *Tensions of Empire: Japan and Southeast Asia in the Colonial and Postcolonial World.* Edited by Paul H. Kratoska. Singapore: Singapore University Press, 2003.

Hammer, Ellen J. *The Struggle for Indochina 1940-1955: Viet Nam and the French Experience.* Stanford, CA: Stanford University Press, 1966.

Hanifah, Abu. *Tales of a Revolution: A Leader of the Indonesian Revolution Looks Back.* Sydney: Angus & Robertson, 1972.

Harper, Stephen. *Miracle of Deliverance: The Case for the Bombing of Hiroshima and Nagasaki.* London: Sidgwick & Jackson, 1985.

Harries, Meirion and Susie. *Soldiers of the Sun: the Rise and Fall of the Japanese Imperial Army 1868-1945.* London: Heinemann, 1991.

Hata, Ikuhiko. 'From Consideration to Contempt: The Changing Nature of Japanese Military and Popular Perceptions of Prisoners of War through the Ages', in *Prisoners of War and Their Captors in World War II,* edited by Bob Moore and Kent Fedorowich, 253-276. Oxford: Berg, 1996

Hickey, Michael. *The Unforgettable Army: Slim's XIVth Army in Burma.* Tunbridge Wells: Spellmount Ltd, 1992.

Hinds, Allister. *Britain's Sterling Colonial policy and Decolonization, 1939-1958.* Westport, CT: Greenwood Press, 2001.

Hudson, John. *Sunset in the East: Fighting Against the Japanese through the siege of Imphal and alongside them in Java, 1943-1946.* Barnsley: Pen & Sword, 2002.

Ienaga, Saburo. *Japan's Last War: World War Two and the Japanese.* Oxford: Blackwell, 1979.

Indonesian Republic. *Republican Forces Fulfilled Two Tasks of Allied Forces in Indonesia.* Jakarta: Ministry of Information, 1949.

International Committee of the Red Cross, *Report of the International Committee of the Red Cross on its activities during the Second World War, Vol. 1.* Geneva: ICRC, 1948.

Iriye, Akira and Nagai, Yonosuke, eds. *The Origins of the Cold War in Asia*. New York: Columbia University Press, 1977.

Jacobs, Gideon F. *Prelude to the Monsoon: Assignment in Sumatra*. Philadelphia: Philadelphia University Press, 1982.

Jones, Don. *Oba, the Last Samurai*. New York: Jove Books, 1986.

Jones, Matthew. *Conflict and Confrontation in South East Asia, 1961–1965: Britain, the United States, Indonesia and the Creation of Malaysia*. Cambridge: Cambridge University Press, 2001.

Kahin, George. McTurnan. *Nationalism and Revolution in Indonesia*. Ithaca, NY: Cornell University Press, 1952.

Kido Butai Association. *Taishi II*. Kyoto: Semarang kai, 1984.

Keay, John. *Last Post: The End of Empire in the Far East*. London: John Murray, 1997.

Kemp, Peter. *Alms for Oblivion*. London: The Adventurers Club, 1961.

Kratoska, Paul, H., ed. *Asian Labor in the Wartime Japanese Empire: Unknown Histories*. New York: M. E. Sharpe, 2005.
The Thailand-Burma Railway, 1942-1946: Documents and Selected Writings. London: Taylor & Francis, 2005.

Lebra, Joyce C. *Japanese-Trained Armies in Southeast Asia*. Hong Kong: Heinemann (Asia), 1977.

Lewin, Ronald. *Slim: The Standard Bearer*. London: Leo Cooper Ltd, 1976.
The Other Ultra: Codes, Ciphers and the Defeat of Japan. London: Hutchison, 1982.

Lockwood, Rupert. *Black Armada: Australia and the Struggle for Indonesian Independence, 1942-49*. Sydney: Hale & Ironmonger, 1982.

Lucas, James L. *The Last Days of the Reich: The Collapse of Nazi Germany, May 1945*. London: Cassell, 1986.

Marr, David G. *Vietnam 1945: The Quest for Power*. Berkeley, CA: University of California Press, 1995.

McCullough David. *Truman*. New York: Simon & Schuster, 1992.

McEnerey, John H. *Epilogue in Burma: The Military Dimension of British Withdrawal*. Tunbridge Wells: Spellmount, 1990

McMahon, Robert J. *Colonialism and Cold War: The United States and the Struggle for Indonesian Independence, 1945-49*. Ithaca, NY: Cornell University Press, 1981.

McMillan, Richard. *The British Occupation of Indonesia 1945-1946*. London: Routledge, 2006.

Miyamoto Shizuo. 'Army Problems in Java after the Surrender'. In *The Japanese Experience in Indonesia: Selected Memoirs of 1942-45*, edited by Anthony Reid and Akira Oki, 325–40. Ohio: Ohio University Press, 1986.

Moore, Bob and Fedorowich, Kent eds. *Prisoners of War and Their Captors in World War II*. Oxford: Berg, 1996.

Moore, Bob. 'Axis Prisoners in Britain during the Second World War: A Comparative Survey'. In *Prisoners of War and Their Captors in World War II*, edited by Bob Moore and Kent Fedorowich, 19-46. Oxford: Berg, 1996.

Moore, Bob and Fedorowich, Kent. *The British Empire and Italian Prisoners of War.* Basingstoke: Palgrave, 2002.

Mountbatten, Earl. *The Personal Diary of Admiral the Lord Louis Mountbatten, 1943-1946.* Edited by Philip Ziegler. London: William Collins & Sons, 1988.

Mullaly, B. R. *Bugle and Kukri: The Story of 10th Princess Mary's Own Gurkha Rifles.* London: Blackwood, 1957.

National Federation of *Kenpeitai* Veterans Associations. *The Kenpeitai in Java and Sumatra: Selections from The Authentic History of the Kenpeitai.* Translated by B. G. Shimer and Guy Hobbs. Ithaca, NY: Cornell University Press, 1986.

Neville, Peter. *Britain in Vietnam: Prelude to Disaster, 1945-46.* London: Routledge, 2006.

Nguyen The Anh. 'Japanese Food Policies and the 1945 Great Famine in Indochina'. In *Food Supplies and the Japanese Occupation in Southeast Asia*, edited by Paul Kratoska, 208-226. New York: St Martin's Press, 1998.

Nimmo, William F. *Behind a Curtain of Silence: Japanese in Soviet Custody, 1945-1956.* Westport, CT: Greenwood Press, 1988.

Nish, Ian, ed. *Indonesian Experience: The Role of Japan and Britain, 1943-1948.* London: STICERD, 1979.

Anglo-Japanese Alienation 1919-1952: Papers of the Anglo-Japanese Conference on the History of the Second World War. Cambridge: Cambridge University Press, 1982.

Noble, Ronnie. *Shoot First!* London: Pan, 1957.

Oba Sadao. 'My Recollections of Indonesia, 1944-1947'. In *Indonesian Experience: The Role of Japan and Britain, 1943-1948*, edited by Ian Nish, 3-34. London: STICERD, 1979.

Ooka Shohei. *Taken Captive: A Japanese POW's Story*, translated and edited by Wayne P. Lammers. New York: John Wiley & Sons, 1996.

Overmans, Rüdiger. 'German Historiography, the War Losses and the Prisoners of War', in *Eisenhower and the German POWs: Facts Against Falsehood*, edited by Stephen Ambrose and Günter Bischof, 127–69. Baton Rouge: Louisiana University Press, 1992.

Pacific War Research Society. *Japan's Longest Day.* London: Souvenir Press, 1968.

Raben, Remco, ed. *Representing the Japanese Occupation of Indonesia: Personal Testimonies and Public Images in Indonesia, Japan, and the Netherlands.* Zwolle: Waanders Publishing, 1999.

Reid, Anthony and Oki, Akira, eds. *The Japanese Experience in Indonesia: Selected Memoirs of 1942-45.* Ohio: Ohio University Press, 1986.

Richard L-G. Deverall. *Stalin's Prize: Japanese Prisoners-of-War.* Baltimore, Uptown Press, 1951.

Rijpma, Stance. 'The Blade's Edge'. In *Representing the Japanese Occupation of Indonesia: Personal Testimonies and Public Images in Indonesia, Japan, and the Netherlands*, edited by Remco Raben, 139-140. Zwolle: Waanders Publishing, 1999.

Rosie, George. *The British in Vietnam: How the twenty-five year war began.* London: Panther, 1970.

Roskill, S. W. *The War at Sea, Vol. III, Pt. 1.* London: HMSO, 1960.

Sano, Peter Iwao. *One Thousand Days in Siberia: The Odyssey of a Japanese-American POW.* Lincoln, NE: University of Nebraska Press, 1997.

Sareen, T. R. *Japanese Prisoners of War in India, 1942-46: Bushido and Barbed Wire.* Folkstone: Global Oriental, 2006.

Sato Shigeru. *War, Nationalism and Peasants: Java under the Japanese Occupation, 1942-1945.* New York: M. E. Sharpe, 1994.

Sayers, R. S. *Financial Policy, 1939-45.* London: HMSO, 1956.

Sfikas, Thanasis D. *The British Labour Government and the Greek Civil War, 1945-49: The Imperialism of Non-Intervention.* Keele: Keele University Press/Ryburn, 1994.

Shibata Yaichiro. 'Surabaya after the Surrender'. In *The Japanese Experience in Indonesia: Selected Memoirs of 1942-45,* edited by Anthony Reid and Akira Oki, *341-374.* Ohio: Ohio University Press, 1986.

Shikimachi Genatro. 'In Singapore', in *Senso,* ed. Frank Gibney, 226–7.

Sjahrir, Soetan. *Out of Exile.* New York: John Day & Co., 1948.

Sleeman, Colin, ed. *Trial of Gozawa Sadaichi and Nine Others.* London: William Hodge, 1948.

Slim, W. J. *Defeat into Victory.* London: Pan, 1998.

Smail, John R. W. *Bandung in the Early Revolution: A Study in the Social History of the Indonesian Revolution.* New York: Cornell University Press, 1964.

Smith, Arthur L. *Churchill's German Army: Wartime Strategy and Cold War Politics, 1943-1947.* Beverly Hills, CA: Sage, 1977.

Smith, Kevin. *Conflict over Convoys: Anglo-American logistics diplomacy in the Second World War.* Cambridge: Cambridge University Press, 1996.

Smith, Timothy O. *Britain and the Origins of the Vietnam War: UK Policy in Indo-China, 1943-50.* London: Palgrave Macmillan, 2007.

Sponza, Lucio. 'Italian Prisoners of War in Great Britain, 1943-46', In *Prisoners of War and Their Captors in World War II,* edited by Bob Moore and Kent Fedorowich, 205–26. Oxford: Berg, 1996.

Stockwell A. J. *British Policy and Malay Politics during the Malayan Union Experiment, 1942–1948.* Kuala Lumpur: Royal Asiatic Society, 1979.

Strauss, Ulrich. *The Anguish of Surrender: Japanese POWs of World War II.* Seattle: University of Washington Press, 2003.

Sullivan, Matthew B. *Thresholds of Peace: Four Hundred Thousand German Prisoners and the People of Britain, 1944-1948.* London: Hamish Hamilton, 1979.

Takemae, Eiji. *The Allied Occupation of Japan and Its Legacy.* London: Continuum, 2002.

Takezawa, Shoji. *What About the Emperor's lunch?* in *Senso,* ed. Frank Gibney, 254–5. New York: M. E. Sharpe, 1995.

Tamayama, Kazuo. *Railwaymen in the War: Tales by Japanese Railway Soldiers in Burma and Thailand, 1941-47.* Basingstoke: Palgrave Macmillan, 2005.

Tanaka, Hiromi. 'Japanese forces in post-surrender Rabaul'. In *From a Hostile Shore: Australia and Japan at War in New Guinea,* edited by Steven Bullard and Tamura Keiko, 138-52. Canberra: Australian War Memorial, 2004.

Tanaka, Sayu. 'The Kwantung Army's Final Broadcast'. In *Senso: The Japanese Remember the Pacific War*, edited by Frank Gibney, 237–8. New York: M. E. Sharpe, 1995.

Tanida, Isamu. 'The Army's been a good life'. In *Japan at War: An Oral History*, edited by Haruko Cook and Theodore Cook, 416–9. London: Phoenix, 2002.

Tarling, Nicholas. *The Fall of Imperial Britain in South-East Asia*. Singapore: Singapore University Press, 1993.

Tasaki, Hanama. *Long the Imperial Way*. London: Gollancz, 1951.

Taylor, Alastair. *Indonesian Independence and the United Nations*. London: Steven's & Sons, 1960.

Thorne, Christopher. *Allies of a Kind: The United States, Britain and the War Against Japan, 1941-45*. London: Hamish Hamilton, 1978.

Thorne, Christopher. *The Issue of War: States, Societies and the Far Eastern Conflict of 1941–1945*. London: Hamish Hamilton, 1985.

Toland, John. *The Rising Sun: The Decline and Fall of the Japanese Empire, 1936-1945*. New York:

Bantam Books, 1971.

Towle, Philip and Nobuko Margaret Kosuge, eds, *Britain and Japan in the Twentieth Century: One Hundred Years of Trade and Prejudice*. London: Tauris, 2007.

Truman, Harry S. *Memoirs: Year of Decisions, 1945*. New York: Konecky & Konecky, 1955.

Truman, Harry S. *Memoirs: Years of Trial and Hope*. New York: Doubleday, 1956.

Ugaki Matome. *Fading Victory: The Diary of Admiral Matome Ugaki*. Pittsburgh: University of Pittsburgh, 1991.

Van der Post, Laurence. *The Admiral's Baby*. London: John Murray, 1996.

Villa, Brian L. 'The Diplomatic and Political Context of the POW Camps Tragedy', in *Eisenhower and the German POWs: Facts Against Falsehood*, edited by Stephen Ambrose and Günter Bischof, 52-77. Baton Rouge: Louisiana University Press, 1992.

Ward, Robert E. and Shulman. Frank Joseph, *The Allied Occupation of Japan, 1945-1952: An Annotated Bibliography of Western-Language Materials*. Chicago: American Library Association, 1974.

Wehl, David. *The Birth of Indonesia*. London: Allen & Unwin, 1948.

Weste, John. 'Shipping and Shipbuilding'. In *Britain and Japan in the Twentieth Century: One Hundred Years of Trade and Prejudice*, edited by Philip Towle and Nobuko Margaret Kosuge, 107–18. London: Tauris, 2007.

Wild, Colin and Peter Carey, eds. *Born in Fire: The Indonesian Struggle for Independence, an Anthology*. Ohio: Ohio University Press, 1988.

Williams, Peter and Wallace, David. *Unit 731: The Japanese Army's Secret of Secrets*. London: Hodder & Stoughton, 1989.

Willmot, H. P. *The Second World War in the Far East*. London: Cassell, 2002.

Wilmot, Chester. *The Struggle for Europe*. London: Wm Collins, 1952.

Woodburn Kirby, Stanley. *The History of the Second World War: The War against Japan, Vol. V. The Surrender of Japan*. London: HMSO, 1969.

Yamaguchi, Hideo. 'The reason I don't sing the national anthem'. In *Senso: The*

Japanese Remember the Pacific War, edited by Frank Gibney, 273–4. New York: M. E. Sharpe, 1995.

Yamamoto, Tomomi. *Four Years in Hell*. Tokyo: Asia, 1952.

JOURNAL ARTICLES

Bootsma, N. 'The Discovery of Indonesia: Western (non-Dutch) Historiography on the Decolonisation of Indonesia'. *Bijdragen tot de Taal-, Land- en Volkenkunde (BKI)* 151-1 (1995), 1-22.

Connor, Stephen. 'Side-Stepping Geneva: Japanese Troops under British Control, 1945-47'. *Journal of Contemporary History* 45, no. 2 (April 2010), 389–405.

Cribb, Robert. 'Political Dimensions of the Currency Question 1945-1947'. *Indonesia* 31 (1982), 113–36.

Fujita, Kazuya. 'Japanese Military Currency (1937-1945): Quantities Printed and Issued'. International Bank Note Society Journal, 42, no. 3 (2003), 1–24.

Goto Ken'ichi. 'Caught in the Middle: Japanese Attitudes toward Indonesian Independence in 1945'. *Journal of Southeast Asian Studies* 27 (1996), 39–48.

Han Bing Siong. 'Captain Huyer and the massive Japanese arms transfer in East Java in Oct. 1945'. *BKI* 159: 2/3 (2003), 291–351.

Han Bing Siong. 'The Indonesian Need of Arms after the Proclamation of Independence'. *BKI* 157-4 (2001), 799–831.

Han Bing Siong. 'The Secret of Major Kido: The Battle of Semarang, 15-19 Oct. 1945'. *BKI* 152-3 (1996), 382–428.

Kinoshita, Hanji. 'Echoes of Militarism in Japan'. *Pacific Affairs* 26, no. 3 (Sept. 1953), 244–51.

Newsinger, John. 'A forgotten war: British intervention in Indonesia 1945-46'. *Race & Class* 30, no. 4 (1989), 51–66.

Parrott, John. 'Who Killed Mallaby?' *Indonesia 20* (1975), 87–111.

Remmelink, W. G. J. 'The Emergence of the New Situation: The Japanese Army on Java after the Surrender'. *Kabar Sebarang* 4 (1978), 57–74.

Roadnight, Andrew. 'Sleeping with the Enemy: Britain, Japanese Troops and the Netherlands East Indies, 1945-46'. *History* 87, no. 286 (2002), 245–68.

Springhall, John. 'Kicking out the Vietminh': How Britain Allowed France to Reoccupy South Indo-China, 1945-46'. *Journal of Contemporary History* 40, no. 1 (2005), 115–30.

Tarling, Nicholas. 'Rice and Reconciliation: The Anglo-Thai Peace Negotiations of 1945'. *Siam Society Journal* 66, no. 2 (1978), 59–112.

Tomlinson, B. R. 'Indo-British Relations in the Post-Colonial Era: The Sterling Balances Negotiations, 1947-1949'. *Journal of Imperial and Commonwealth History, Vol. XIII*, no. 3 (May 1985), 142–61.

THESES

McMillan, Richard, O. S. 'The British Occupation of Indonesia: 1945-46'. PhD thesis, University of London, 2002.

Parrot, J. G. A. 'The Role of the 49th Indian Infantry Brigade in Surabaya, 25 Oct.-10 Nov. 1945', MA thesis, Monash University, 1977.

Squire, Clifford, W. S. 'Britain and the Transfer of Power in Indonesia, 1945-46'. PhD thesis, University of London, 1979.

Tomaru, Junko, 'The Post-war Rapprochement of Malaya and Japan, 1945-1961'. PhD thesis, University of Oxford, 1997.

PRESS, PERIODICALS, TELEVISION AND ONLINE ARCHIVES

La Bern, Arthur, 'I was in Surabaya when the shooting began!' *The War Illustrated*, No. 221, 7 December 1945, 505.

The Economist 149 (1 Dec. 45), no. 5336: 779–80.

Fraser, L. V. 'The Gremlin Task Force: Japanese Aircrews and Aircraft Flying for the RAF in French Indo-China'. *Flight,* 6 December, 1945, 612.

'Japan's Super Subs', National Geographic Television, 2009.

Spencer, H. B. (ex-RN), 'Dutch landings and re-occupation of Bali and Lombok'. Memoir, 29 July 2005 http://www.bbc.co.uk/history/ww2/peopleswar/stories/51/a4607651.

US Department of State. 'US Repudiates Philippine and Chinese Complaint on Japanese Reparation Removals'. *Dept of State Bulletin* 20, 26 June 1949.

PERSONAL INTERVIEWS

Aoki Masafumi, 16 IJA *kenpeitai* (NEI), 3 November 2005.

Lt Stuart Guild, 27 Field Rgt, Royal Artillery (Burma)/114 Field Rgt, RA (FIC), September 2014.

Philip Kaiserman, RAF Servicing Commando Unit 3209 (FIC), 3 October 2005.

Oba Sadao, 27 Ind. Mixed Bde, 16 IJA (NEI), 20 October 2005.

John Pike, CBE, PNBS, Intelligence Corps (Burma and NEI), 10 July 2006.

Charles Ritchie, 178 Field Rgt, Royal Artillery (Burma and NEI), March 2006.

Takado Eichi, Kido *Butai*, 16 IJA (NEI), October 2005.

Charles Wicksteed, 114 Field Rgt Royal Artillery (Burma and FIC), June 2008.

SIGNIFICANT CORRESPONDENCE

(See also 'Burma Star Association' in Acknowledgements)

Lt Stuart Guild (see 'Personal Interviews'), various Sept 2007 to June 2015.

Maj Philip Malins MBE MC, 19 May, 19 September 2006.

Oba Sadao (see 'Interviews'), 20 October, 2 November 2005; July, November 2008; January 2009.

Takado Eichi (see 'Interviews'), January and May 2006.

ARCHIVE PHOTOGRAPHS AND FILM

Numerous photographs of JSP are held by the Imperial War Museum, London; Institute for War, Holocaust and Genocide Studies (NIOD), Amsterdam; and the Australian War Memorial, Canberra.

A number of films featuring footage of JSP in various locations in Southeast Asia are also held by the IWM (for example, JSP on Rempang are shown in JFU 425). Other JSP film footage is held by the AWM and is viewable online, including some of the Japanese bayonet fencing shown in photograph No. 22, AWM ref F07408).

INDEX

Lightning Source UK Ltd.
Milton Keynes UK
UKHW020615060519

342177UK00007B/1720/P